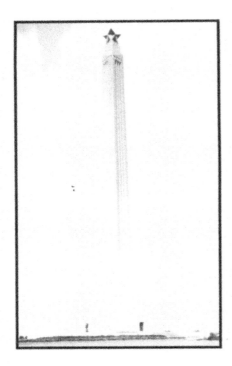  

GENL. SAM HOUSTON

Left to right, top: San Jacinto Monument; General Sam Houston; Erastus "Deaf" Smith; The Alamo; David Crockett.
Center: Battle of San Jacinto; Interior of the Alamo; Another view of the interior of the Alamo.
Bottom: The Alamo; Interior view of the Alamo; Dawn at the Alamo.

INTERIOR ALAMO
SAN ANTONIO, TEXAS.

DAUGHTERS OF THE REPUBLIC OF TEXAS

PATRIOT ANCESTOR ALBUM

TURNER PUBLISHING COMPANY
Paducah, Kentucky

TURNER PUBLISHING COMPANY
Publisher's of America's History
412 Broadway, P.O. Box 3101
Paducah, KY 42002-3101
270-443-0121

Library of Congress Control No. 95-60750
ISBN: 1-56311-641-3
Limited Edition. Printed in the U.S.A.
Additional books available from
Turner Publishing Company.

Top center: The Alamo
Bottom left: Stephen F. Austin (Father of Texas)
Bottom center: The Cradle
Ovals, top: Mrs. Hally Bryan Perry and bottom,
Miss Betty Ballinger — Co-founders of the
Daughters of the Republic of Texas.

The Library
Galveston
D

the W. P. Ballinger home "THE OAKS" in
in 1891, was born the thought of the
of the Republic of Texas.

TABLE OF CONTENTS

3

Daughters of the Republic of Texas, Inc.

"Texas, One and Indivisible"

Custodians:
The Alamo, San Antonio
The French Legation Museum, Austin

Owners:
The Cradle, Galveston
Republic of Texas Museum, Austin
DRT Research Library, San Antonio

Helen Burleson Kelso, President General 1999-2001, 10555 Le Mans Dr., Dallas, TX 75238-3667. Phone 214-348-0668

How we love our Texas history! Our members are devoted to perpetuating the memory and spirit of the men and women who achieved and maintained the independence of Texas.

We promote historical research into the earliest records of Texas, especially those relating to the Revolution of 1835 and the 1836 - 1846 Republic of Texas period which ended February 19, 1846. It was on that date that the Annexation Agreement of the Republic of Texas with the United States of America was consummated. We foster the preservation of documents and relics of that period, and encourage the publication of records of individual service of patriots of the Republic and other source material for the history of Texas.

A hearty welcome to Turner Publishing Company's Volume II of DRT family histories written by some of our members about their ancestors! These stories demonstrate the incredible variety of our pioneer families, their multi-ethnic origins from all parts of the world, their paths to Spanish and Mexican Texas and the Republic of Texas - and some of their trials and tribulations.

Read, enjoy, and learn more about early Texans!

With warm wishes to you from

Helen Burleson Kelso
President General 1999-2001

(270) 443-0121   P.O. Box 3101
(270) 443-0335 Fax   Paducah, KY 42002-3101

In 1995 The Daughters of the Republic of Texas allowed Turner Publishing Company to publish the first volume of the *Patriot Ancestor Album*. The result was overwhelming with members submitting hundreds of photographs and information pertaining to their ancestors. Ancestors who ventured west to settle an uneasy land. From exploration by the Spaniards to war with the Mexican government and its declaration of independence in 1836, the Republic of Texas has a vivid past.

It is with great pleasure I present to The Daughters of the Republic of Texas a second volume dedicated to them and their ancestors. The hundreds of biographies and photographs contained herein are a great example of the proud heritage this prestigious group displays. It is members like you who help preserve the legacy for our future generations. As a publisher, I understand the desire to help record history no matter how painstaking the preparations might be. My sincere thanks to each of you who have taken the time to do such a chore.

I would like to extend a special thank you to Mrs. Helen Kelso and the staff of The Daughters of the Republic of Texas Library for their continued help in seeing this project to the end. Without your continued support, love for history and your family, this book could not exist.

Turner Publishing Company is proud to present this *Daughters of the Republic of Texas Patriot Ancestor Album*, Volume Two. May God bless each of you in your continuing efforts to preserve the history of Texas.

Dave Turner
President

STATEMENT OF PURPOSE

The Daughters of the Republic of Texas, by virtue of the authority delegated by the State of Texas, is the custodian of the Alamo, San Antonio, Texas, Shrine of Texas Freedom, and the French Legation, Austin, Texas, Embassy in the days of the Texas Republic. These ancient structures, requiring continuing renovations, are maintained as museums solely by gifts and efforts of the Daughters, who are dedicated to the perpetuation of the memory and spirit of those who achieved the independence of Texas. The DRT encourages and provides for historical research, and maintains its DRT Library at the Alamo, well-known as a source of early Texas history. The DRT fosters the publication of historical documents and records, and preserves relics of early Texas in the Republic of Texas Museum in Austin, Texas.

DRT Headquarters and Museum
510 East Anderson Lane
Austin, TX 78752-1218

Phone (512) 339-1997
Fax (512) 339-1998
E-mail: drt@onr.com

OBJECTIVES

* To perpetuate the memory and spirit of the men and women who achieved and maintained the independence of Texas.

* To encourage historical research into the earliest records of Texas, especially those relating to the Revolution of 1835 and the events which followed; to foster the preservation of documents and relics; to encourage the publication of records of the individual service of the soldiers and patriots of the Republic, and other source material for the history of Texas.

* To promote the celebration of Texas Honor Days: Lamar Day, January 26; Texas Statehood Day, February 19; Texas Independence and Flag Day, March 2; Alamo Heroes Day, March 6; Goliad Heroes Day, March 27; San Jacinto Day, April 21; Texian Navy Day, the third Saturday of September; Gonzales Day, October 2; Stephen F. Austin's Birthday, November 3, and Founders Day, November 6.

* To memorialize all historic spots by erecting markers thereon; and to cherish and preserve the Unity of Texas as achieved and established by the fathers and mothers of the Texas Revolution.

THE FOUNDING OF THE DAUGHTERS OF THE REPUBLIC OF TEXAS

Hally Bryan Perry

In the summer of 1891, Hally Bryan (Perry) and Betty Ballinger spent much of their time reading the volumes of Yoakum's History of Texas. Mr. Ballinger, Betty's father, had converted his small law office into a library containing books that told the story of the struggles for Texas independence. These stories fascinated Hally and Betty, who were first cousins.

After the death of Mrs. Bryan, when Hally was only four years old, the two girls grew up together in the Ballinger's home in Galveston. Betty's grandfather had fought at the Battle of San Jacinto and Hally was a descendant of Moses Austin. They decided to do something to keep alive the ideals of the pioneer Texans and to preserve for future generations the heritage of people and events that led to the formation of the Republic of Texas.

Colonel Guy M. Bryan, a member of the Texas Veterans Association (veterans of the Texas Revolution of 1835/6), took his daughter and niece-in-law to Houston to meet with other women whose families had served the Republic of Texas. On November 6, 1891, when the group organized. Mrs. Anson Jones, widow of the last President of the Republic of Texas, was chosen the first President of "The Daughters of the Lone Star Republic." On April 21, 1892, in Lampasas, the organization changed its name to "The Daughters of the Republic of Texas.

The small library building in Galveston is preserved and known today as "The Cradle." Each year on November 6, the Daughters of the Republic of Texas celebrate Founders Day, honoring Hally Bryan Perry and Betty Ballinger.

Betty Ballinger

OUR ASSOCIATION

The Daughters of the Lone Star Republic was organized by cousins Betty Ballinger and Hally Bryan. They conceived the idea in 1891 of perpetuating forever the memory of the Texas pioneer families and soldiers of the Republic of Texas by forming an association of their descendants. This organization would soon come to be known as the Daughters of the Republic of Texas.

ELIGIBILITY FOR MEMBERSHIP

Any woman having attained her sixteenth birthday is eligible for membership, provided she is personally acceptable to the Association and is a lineal descendant of a man or woman who rendered loyal service for Texas prior to the consummation of the Annexation Agreement of the Republic of Texas with the United States of America, February 19, 1846.

The applicant must furnish legal proof of her lineal descent from a man or woman who served in any of the following capacities;

* As a colonist with Austin's Old Three Hundred, or any colonies authorized under the Spanish or Mexican governments before the Texas Revolution, or those authorized by the Congress of the Republic of Texas.

* As an officer or private in the service of the Colonies or of the Republic of Texas.

* As a loyal citizen, male or female, regardless of age who established residence in Texas prior to February 19, 1846.

* As a recipient of a Land Grant authorized by the Provisional Government of the Republic of Texas. These grants include "Toby Script"; 1st, 2nd, 3rd and 4th class Headrights; Preemption Grants; Landscripts; Colony Contracts; Bounty Certificates and Donation Certificates.

Please contact the Business Office for information concerning membership dues and fees, a list of DRT related items for sale to members, a list of chapters in your area or other details.

CHILDREN OF THE REPUBLIC OF TEXAS

Mrs. J. M. Olivarri conceived the idea of organizing the CRT in 1934. Thirty-four children formed the first chapter that was sponsored by the DRT Alamo Mission Chapter in San Antonio.

The CRT is a junior organization of the DRT with membership consisting of boys and girls ages birth to 21 years.

Emphasis is placed on the study of Texas History, and attempts to interest members in the preservation of documents and relics, and encourages members to cherish their heritage.

THE CRADLE

This building was originally the law office of William Pitt Ballinger, father of co-founder Betty Ballinger. Now known as the Cradle, it is cherished by the Daughters as the place where Miss Ballinger and her first cousin Hally Bryan Perry formulated the idea for their new organization. The Cradle has recently been restored to reflect the original furnishings of the late 1800s.

Location: 2903 Ave. O 1/2, Galveston
Hours: By Appointment
Admission: None-Donations accepted
Address: P.O. Box 3537, Galveston, TX 77552

THE ALAMO

Travis, Bowie, Crockett, Bonham—names forever connected with the heroic cause of liberty. These dedicated men and 185 others fought more than 4000 Mexican troops led by Santa Anna during a thirteen day siege.

The defeat of the Alamo was the rallying point in the Texas Revolution. "Remember the Alamo!" was the cry as Texans fought for freedom from tyranny and for a government separate from that of Mexico.

Erected in 1754, the Alamo was used as a chapel for the Mission San Antonio de Valero. Occupied and abandoned many times over the years, it was in disrepair by the early 1900s. Miss Clara Driscoll purchased property north of the Chapel in 1903 when the Daughters learned the site was to be sold for a hotel. The State reimbursed her in 1905 and turned the Alamo over to the care of the Daughters.

Location: Corner of Houston and Alamo Streets, San Antonio.
Hours: 9:00 a.m. to 5:30 p.m. Mon.-Sat.
10:00 a.m. to 5:30 p.m. Sun.
Closed December 24-25 and for special occasions.
Admission: None-Donations accepted.
Address: P.O. Box 2599, San Antonio, TX 78299
Telephone: 210/225-1391

The Alamo church viewed from west, 1996
Photograph by Robert Maxham
DRT Library, VN96.53C

FRENCH LEGATION

Construction of the French Legation was begun in 1840 and completed in the Spring of 1841. The Legation was built by Comte Alphonse Dubois de Saligny, charge d'affaires of His Majesty Louis Philippe, King of France, to the Republic of Texas.

The house was purchased in 1948 by the State of Texas from the Robertson family in whose possession the Legation had been for 100 years. The historic house was put into the custody of the Daughters of the Republic of Texas by the State in 1949. The Daughters have restored and maintained the Legation for the public to whom it was opened as a museum on April 5, 1956.

Location: 802 San Marcos St., Austin
Hours: 1 p.m. to 5 p.m.
Closed Mondays
Admission: $2.00 adults, $.50 children
Address: 802 San Marcos St., Austin, TX 78702
Telephone: 512/472-8180

The French Legation
DRT Library, CN00.004

DRT LIBRARY

The Texas History Research Library is part of the Alamo complex and has been developed and is supported and maintained by the DRT for the use of all researchers.

The need to encourage the study of Texas history and to preserve its documents was of sufficient importance to the founders of the DRT to be stipulated specifically in their charter, in 1893.

The library contains materials pertaining to the history of Texas-in particular, the period of the Texas Republic-and associated fields. Books, documents, maps, photographs, periodicals, early newspapers, clippings, and family papers are among the materials in the library's files and closed stacks. A catalog is available for the use of researchers to aid in locating information, and library staff provide assistance in retrieving materials for use. Duplication services and photographic reproduction services are available.

Location: Alamo Complex, San Antonio
Hours: 9 a.m. to 5 p.m., Monday-Saturday
Admission charge: None
Address: P.O. Box 1401
San Antonio, TX 78295-1401
Telephone: 210/225-1071
Fax: 210/212-8514
E-mail: drtl@drtl.org

DRT Library, 1995
Photograph by Jim Zintgraff

DRT HEADQUARTERS AND MUSEUM

The Republic of Texas Museum was housed, in 1903, in one room of the State Capitol building. The collection of Republic-era artifacts grew rapidly through the dedicated efforts of the DRT and more space was required.

The Texas General Land Office moved in 1916 from the old Land Office building on the Capitol grounds and a portion of the structure was turned over to the Daughters of the Republic of Texas for use as a museum.

The DRT museum occupied the second floor of the building until 1989, when restoration of the deteriorating structure began. Four years later, during the 100th year of the DRT, the Daughters purchased a building of their own to house the museum and the organization's headquarters.

The Business Office, located in the west portion of the building, handles the sale of many DRT-related items, including stationery, the Annual publication, the Manual of Procedure, and all books published by the DRT.

The office also maintains the membership records of the association and houses all of the applications and related documents dating from 1891 to the present. The office staff can do limited searches on ancestors registered with the DRT for a small fee plus copying costs.

Location: IH 35 and US 183, Austin
Office Hours: 8 a.m. to 5 p.m., Monday-Friday
Museum Hours: 10 a.m. to 4 p.m., Monday-Friday, September-May
10 a.m. to 4 p.m., Monday-Friday, June-August
Admission: $2 Adults, $1 DRT Members, $1.50 Seniors, $.50 Students
Address: 510 E. Anderson Lane
Austin, TX 78752
Telephone: 512/339-1997
E-mail: drt@onr.com

DRT Headquarters and Museum.

DAUGHTERS OF THE REPUBLIC OF TEXAS
CHAPTER, DISTRICTS, MEMBERS

Total Members at Large   331

District I
Alpine - HALLY BRYAN PERRY	27
Canutillo - DAVID G. BURNET	41
El Paso - PASO DEL NORTE	34
Fort Stockton - TUNAS CREEK	10
Midland - AARON ESTES	51
Monahans - THOMAS WILLIAM WARD	17
San Angelo - FORT CONCHO,	67

Total Chapters: 7
Total Members: 247

District II
Arlington - CHARLES CALVIN McCOY	31
Brownwood - WELCOME W. CHANDLER	37
Duncanville - CEDAR MOUNTAINS	27
Euless - ISAAC LOW	11
Fort Worth - FRANCES COOKE VAN ZANDT	124
Granbury - CONANCHE PEAK	35
Grand Prairie - CROSS TIMBERS	22
Mineral Wells - GEORGE WEBB SLAUGHTER	33
Stephenville - BOSQUE RIVER	29
Wichita Falls - REBECCA JANE FISHER	30

Total Chapters: 10
Total Members: 379

District III
Dallas - CHARLES S. TAYLOR	62
Dallas - JAMES BUTLER BONHAM	240
Dallas - MARY ANN LAWHON	68
Denton - PETERS COLONY	24
Irving - PETER JAMES BAILEY	25
Mesquite - HIRAM BENNETT	66
Mount Pleasant - ANSON JONES	13
Paris - GEORGE WASHINGTON STELL	42
Plano - COLLIN McKINNEY	51
Sherman - SOLOMON BOSTICK	34
Sulphur Springs - NATHAN FOSTER ROGERS	13
Texarkana - JAMES BOWIE	22

Total Chapters: 12
Total Members: 662

District IV
Center - WILLIAM CARROLL CRAWFORD	70
Chireno, - HALFWAY INN	16
Crockett - DAVID CROCKETT	53
Hemphill - JAMES FREDERICK GOMER	88
Jasper - JOHN BEVIL	43
Livingston - JOHN FLOYD GILBERT	29
Longview - JOHN TILLEY EDWARDS	53
Lutkin - MARY HALL MANTOOTH	82
Nacogdoches - STONE FORT	124
Palestine - FORT HOUSTON	37
San Augustine - EZEKIEL CULLEN	129
Tyler - CHARLES G. DAVENPORT	57

Total Chapters: 12
Total Members: 781

District V
Belton - SAM HOUSTON	39
Bryan - ROBERT HENRY	95
Burnet - JANE WELLS WOODS	47
Corsicana - JOSE ANTONIO NAVARRO	38
Franklin - MARY O'NEAL McCUISTION	28
Lampasas - ORAN MILO ROBERTS	58
Marquez - FORT BOGGY	29
Navasota - ZUBER HADLEY	31
San Saba - SAN SABA RIVER	13
Temple - BEN MILAM	63
Waco - STERLING C. ROBERTSON	117

Total Chapters: 11
Total Members: 558

District VI
Brenham - DR. RICHARD FOX BRENHAM	29
Coldsprings - WILLIAM COCHRAN	29
Columbus - DILUE ROSE HARRIS	29
Friendswood - BLUEBONNET BRANCH	53
Houston - MISS IMA HOGG	95
Houston - SAN JACINTO	313
Houston - TEXAS STAR	68
Huntsville - PRESIDENT HOUSTON	42
Kingwood - SETH HURIN BATES	24
Montgomery - JUDGE NATHANIEL H. DAVIS	36

| Oakhurst - CO-LON-NEH (THE RAVEN) | 13 |
| Spring-Tomball - NEW KENTUCKY | 48 |

Total Chapters: 12
Total Members: **779**

District VII

Beeville - RIO MEDIO	28
Brownsville - FORT BROWN	31
Corpus Christi - CLARA DRISCOLL	117
Edna - TEXANA	29
Rockport - STENSON-SIMPSON	41
San Antonio - ALAMO COURIERS	90
San Antonio - ALAMO HEROES	87
San Antonio - ALAMO MISSION	476
Uvalde - CADDEL-SMITH	92
Victoria - JAMES W. FANNIN	58

Total Chapters: 10
Total Members: 1,059

District VIII

Austin - REUBEN HORNSBY	40
Austin - STEPHEN F. AUSTIN	32
Austin - TEXIAN	35
Austin - WILLIAM BARRET TRAVIS	159
Bastrop - BARON DE BASTROP	19
Fredericksburg - DR. WILHELM KEIDEL	31
Gonzales - GONZALES	55
Kerrville - JOSHUA D. BROWN	71
La Grange - MONUMENT HILL	33
Llano - LLANO	29
Luling - CORNELIUS SMITH	52
New Braunfels - FERDINAND LINDHEIMER	147

Round Rock - MARTIN WELLS	44
San Marcos - MOON McGEHEE	27
Seguin - ABISHAI MERCER DICKSON	35
Smiley - ELIZABETH ZUMWALT KENT	20

Total Chapters: 16
Total Members: 829

District IX

Angleton - FORT VELASCO	19
Baytown - SOLOMON BARROW	83
Beaumont - TEJAS	57
Freeport - CRADLE OF TEXAS	153
Galveston - SIDNEY SHERMAN	64
Liberty - FRANKLIN HARDIN	81
Pasadena - JAMES W. BROWN	72
Port Arthur - BRIT BAILEY	29
Sugar Land - FORT SETTLEMENT	53
Winnie-Stowell - JAMES TAYLOR WHITE	29

Total Chapters: 10
Total Members: 640

District X

Amarillo - PALO DURO	69
Lubbock - GENERAL JAMES SMITH	76
Odessa - PRESIDENTS OF TEXAS	50

Total Chapters: 3
Total Members: **195**

TOTAL DRT CHAPTERS 103
TOTAL DRT MEMBERS 6,460

DAUGHTERS OF THE REPUBLIC OF TEXAS
PAST PRESIDENTS GENERAL

*Mrs. Anson Jones	1891-1908
*Mrs. Rebecca Jane Fisher	1908-1927
*Mrs. Clara Driscoll	1927-1931
*Mrs. 0. M. Farnsworth	1931-1935
*Mrs. Carrie Franklin Kemp (Acting President)	1935-1937
*Mrs. Madge W. Hearne	1937-1939
*Mrs. Frederick Schenkenberg	1939-1941
*Mrs. Ben F. Edwards	1941-1943
*Mrs. Walter Prescott Webb	1943-1945
*Mrs. Paul Lobit	1945-1947
Mrs. Henry R. Maresh (Thelma Burnett Maresh)	1947-1949
*Mrs. Henry R. Wofford, Sr.	1949-1951
*Mrs. H. C. Vandervoort	1951-1953
* Ms. Edna Hinde	1953-1955
*Mrs. Barclay Megarity	1955-1957
*Mrs. Joe N. Sanderson	1957-1959
*Mrs. H. Raymond Hagan	1959-1961
*Mrs. Murray Ezell	1961-1963
*Miss Sarah Milita Hill	1963-1965
*Mrs. Robert F. Hallock	1965-1967
*Mrs. William Lawrence Scarborough	1967-1969
*Miss Naomi-Ray Morey	1969-1971
Mrs. M. M. O'Dowd	1971-1973
*Mrs. George Plunkett Red	1973-1975
Mrs. Hugh B. Lowery	1975-1977
Mrs. Eugene M. Addison	1977-1979
*Mrs. George F. Hollis	1979-1981
Mrs. B. F. McKinney	1981-1983
Mrs. Rex L. Arnold	1983-1985
Mrs. Grady D. Rash	1985-1987
Mrs. Henry L. Averitte	1987-1989
Mrs. Donald Oscar Naylor	1989-1991
Mrs. Betty Fagan Burr	1991-1993
Mrs. Donal Ray Barnes	1993-1995
Mrs. Charlie Peter Briggs, 111	1995-1997
Mrs. Tookie Dempsey Walthall	1997-1999

*Deceased

DAUGHTERS OF THE
REPUBLIC OF TEXAS
PATRIOT ANCESTORS

BENJAMIN FRANKLIN ADAMS was born in 1820 in South Carolina. He came to Texas in 1835. He received a Travis Bounty for service in the Army of Texas and a First Class Headright Certificate for his early citizenship. He married Brazilia Holt, daughter of John Holt and Elizabeth Ruff Cannon in Shelby County, TX about 1840. In 1841 he served in a Minute Man unit of the Texas Rangers in Robertson County. He was a freemason in Shelby County being initiated in 1848. He served the Confederacy early in the Civil War. Benjamin Franklin and Brazilia had the following children all born in Shelby County: Mary Elizabeth, abt. 1841; John Franklin, 1842; Thomas C., 1845; Sarah Adora, 1848; Jesse C., 1847-8; Calhoun, 1850; William M., 1854; Preston, 1857; and Benjamin Franklin Jr., 1859. Benjamin Franklin Adams Sr. died between 1860 and 1870. Brazilia died in 1906 in Shelby County, TX.

William M. Adams, listed above, married Nancy Jane Benson, daughter of Sampson and Mary Benson, Aug. 8, 1877 in Tarrant County, TX. They had these children: Minna M., 1879, Mary Ellie, 1881; James Savage, 1884; Ira Thomas, 1885-6; Rufus Bryley, 1889; George, 1891; Ara Benson, 1892; Addie Pardo, 1894; Charles Tarpy, 1898; William Henry, 1901, and Dora Beatrice, 1903. William died in Shelby County in 1924. Nancy Jane died in Shelby County in 1941.

Benjamin Franklin and Brazilia, William M. and Nancy Jane, and several of their siblings and children are buried in the Adams Cemetery in Shelby County, TX.

Addie Pardo Adams, listed above, married Estelle Everett Brummett, daughter of James Robert Brummett and Ada Helen Davidson, Nov. 4, 1923 in Childress County, TX. They had one daughter, Patricia Anne, born 1931 in Childress County, who married Charles Albert Ross Jr., Aug. 20, 1950 in Lubbock County, TX. They had one daughter, Cynthia Anne, born 1955 at Walker AFB in Roswell, NM, who married William Edmon Hardy, Aug. 16, 1975 in Lubbock County, TX. Cynthia Anne and William had two sons, Christopher Ross, born 1981 in Deaf Smith County, TX, and Timothy Patrick, born 1985 Randall County, TX.

Patricia Anne Ross Hardy
DRT Certificate number 21791 for Benjamin Franklin Adams
DRT Certificate number 21792S for Brazilia Holt

Cynthia Anne Ross Hardy
DRT Certificate number 21793 for Benjamin Franklin Adams
DRT Certificate number 21794S for Brazilia Holt

CONRAD AND DOROTHEA WITTE AHRENS,
Conrad Ahrens born Feb. 16, 1808, Ohberg, Hanover, Germany. Dorothea Witte born March 17, 1814, Germany. They sailed from Bremen, Hanover, Germany September 1845 on Brig Margaretha ship, arrived in Galveston, TX Dec. 1, 1845. From Galveston they went by ox carts and walking to New Braunfels, TX and onto Fredericksburg, TX.

Their children are: Christain born 1833, died 1845; Heinrich born 1834, married Dorothea Brathering; Conrad C. Jr. born 1836, married Karolina Nebig; Christain H, born 1842, married Hulda Roeder; William, born 1848, married Katherina Durst; Dorette Sophie Augusta, born 1851, married Peter Schuch; and Charles Friedrich (Carl) born 1853, married Martha Frantzen.

Dec. 15, 1847, Conrad Ahrens was a signor of a petition creating Gillespie County.

1855 they homesteaded land in the Cherry Springs Com-munity, Gillespie County. Conrad and his sons hauled freight with teams of horses and mules to Llano, Kerrville, and Austin, TX.

Conrad Ahrens died April 26, 1884 and Dorothea Witte Ahrens died March 17, 1890. They were buried on their land in the William Ahrens Cemetery.
Marian Ahrens Armstrong, (GGGD)

JEPTHA PATTERSON AINSWORTH (HAINSWORTH)
was born April 8, 1816 in the Mississippi Territory. He married Louisa Mary Collins, daughter of Lucy Hendrick and Jacob Collins, on April 21, 1838 in Madison County, MS. Louisa was born April 8, 1815 in Georgia. They arrived in Liberty, TX on Oct. 24, 1838 and were granted 640 acres of land. Making the trip with them from Mississippi were his brother Asberry Sebastian Hainsworth, James P. Collins and George M. Reese. James Collins was married to Eliza, sister to Jeptha and A.S.; Jeptha, A.S. and George Reese married the "Collins" sisters. Shortly after arriving in Texas both Jeptha and A.S. dropped the "H" from the front of Ainsworth.

Jeptha and Louisa had seven children and they were: John M. born 1839 Liberty, TX; Louisa born Sept. 4, 1844, married Hugh Word; Ann E. born 1847 Liberty, TX, married James Taylor; James Monroe born 1850 Polk County, TX, married Elizabeth Humphries; Lucy born 1853 Polk County, TX, married Norman Woods; Elizabeth (twin to Lucy), married Leonidas Fleming; Franklin Collins born May 17, 1856 in DeWitt County, TX, who married Anna Belle Hardie.

Like many early Texans Jeptha was a rancher, he also was a circuit riding preacher. He died in 1882 and West Texas, perhaps Wilson or McCulloch County, Louisa died Sept. 9, 1900 and is buried in Voca Cemetery.
Katy Hale Kruse, (GGD), 20084

GENERAL GEORGE G. ALFORD, June 17, 1793–April 1, 1847-
New York native, George G. Alford, an officer in the War of 1812, came to Texas from Missouri in 1836. During the Texas Revolution he served as Sam Houston's Quarter Master General. Captured by Mexican Forces after the war while on a supply trip for the Republic of Texas, he was released through intervention by the U.S. President, Andrew Jackson. Alford later owned a Houston County Plantation and served as Justice of the Peace and County Judge.

General Alford is buried in Greenwood Cemetery in Crockett, TX, Houston County, where a Daughter's of the Republic historical marker has been placed.

General Alford was my great-great-grandfather on the maternal side of my family.
Mary Katherine Fain Beatty
Ida Margaret Fain Hall

NEEDHAM JUDGE ALFORD, son of Jacob and Elizabeth Bryant Alford, was born on July 12, 1789 in North Carolina. He married Martha Waddell on Feb. 18, 1815 in Franklin County, MS. Martha Waddell was born in South Carolina on May 15, 1798. They had 10 children: (1) Samantha born Feb. 5, 1818; (2) Thomas Seaborn born Feb. 1, 1821; (3) Elizabeth Bryant born Sept. 16, 1823; (4) Needham Bryant born July 30, 1825; (5) Richard born about 1827; (6) Jesse Powell born Dec. 30, 1828 (7) William Theodore born Feb. 20, 1832; (8) Jacob Lauhon born

Dec. 27, 1834; (9) Noel Waddell born Dec. 15, 1838; (10) John Waddell born Nov. 14, 1842.

Needham Alford and wife, Martha Waddell

In 1832 Needham Judge Alford, a Methodist preacher, and Sumner Bacon, a Presbyterian, held a few days of meetings in Sabine County near the present site of the town of Milam, TX. This opened the movement for preachers to come into this area. While there, Needham Alford challenged an antagonist who threatened to horsewhip any preacher who spoke, saying, "Well, I'm about as able as any man on this ground to take a whipping." As a consequence, he became known in Louisiana as the "Bulldog Preacher". Masonic records show that Needham Alford was initiated into Jackson Lodge, No. 35, Milam, TX in 1848 and in 1863 joined the Springfield Lodge No. 74, in Limestone County.

Needham Judge Alford died Sept. 19, 1869 and his wife Martha Waddell, died Nov. 7, 1876. Both are buried in Limestone County, TX in unmarked graves.

Needham Judge Alford's son, Noel Waddell, my great-grandfather, married Elizabeth Smith, born Feb. 4, 1840 in Robertson County, TX. She was the daughter of John D. Smith and Elizabeth Nelson. John Smith and his father, Sion Smith, received land grants and served in various capacities of the Republic of Texas. Noel and Elizabeth Alford are buried in the same site as Needham Alford.

Elizabeth T. Mohle # 18478
Frances T. Cree # 19464
Alamo Mission Chapter, DRT

HUGH ALLEN, born May 21, 1801, South Carolina, parents Hezekiah and Martha Allen; married Caroline Matilda Frasier, 1820, Warren County, TN. Children: Margaret, Mahala, Martha, Caroline M., James Madison, Hugh Jr., Elizabeth, Daniel Parker, Sarah Jane and Rebecca Sterling Allen.

The Allen family walked to Texas, arriving June 11, 1837; Land Grant Certificate #190; first settled Blossom Prairie, Red River County, TX. The family relocated in 1846, settled on land in upper grant of Mainzer Verein, Cibolo Creek, Bexar County; built first home in the area and planted first corn crop. Their home was always open and often used as an overnight stop for wayfarers. In 1858 the family lived in McCulloch County, 18 miles north of Fort Mason. See related story under Caroline Matilda Frazier.

Hugh Allen, farmer, rancher, Methodist, served in 30th Brigade, Bexar County, Van Dorn Mounted Rifles, Commanding Officer Captain W.A. Haile. He died in 1866 at Red Rock in Bastrop County, and is reportedly buried at High Grove Cemetery, though his grave has never been located.
Bonnie Allen Chambless, (GGGD), 21294

JAMES MADISON "MATT" ALLEN, born July 15, 1832, Smithville, DeKalb County, TN; parents Hugh Allen and Caroline Matilda Frazier; married Sarah Marcell McKinney, Dec. 9, 1852, Menger Hotel, San Antonio, Bexar County. Matt, age four years, walked to Texas with his parents, five sisters and one brother, a

journey of 10 months. Sarah M. McKinney was the daughter of Benjamin F. McKinney (Kentucky) and Mary Ann Smith (Arkansas). Children of Matt and Sarah: Rosabura, Henry, Samuel, Lillie, Daniel, Hugh, Belle, Benjamin, twins Richard and Radney, Dee, Marcelle and Mittie Neoma. Matt, Sarah and their first two children moved to Burnet County in September 1855. 11 other children were born in Burnet County from 1858 to 1879 where they later married and raised families.

Matt Allen-child and citizen of The Republic of Texas, farmer-rancher, lifetime member of Baptist Church, served with the Frontier Rangers (1862-63), transferred to the Confederate Army (1863-65), died June 9, 1904, Pioneer, Eastland County, buried Cross Plains Cemetery, Callahan County,-a gentle, kind and spiritual man, a man of courage and pride, and an inspiration to those whose lives he touched and to those descendants who cherish the memories and stories of a pioneer settler and his family.
Bonnie Allen Chambless, (GGD), 22258S

PHILIP JEFFERSON ALLEN, son of Valentine and Frances Collins Allen, was born Feb. 27, 1805, in the old 96th District of South Carolina. This family moved to Bedford County, TN shortly after his birth. His father operated freight shipping wagons across the Carolinas and Tennessee. In 1831, Philip Jefferson Allen met and married Jane Walker, while farming the family's land in Madison County, AL. Philip and Jane Allen migrated to Benjamin J. Milam's Spanish land grant, "El Mina", in May of 1835. While in the land grant, Philip soon became involved in the fight for Texas independence by shipping arms to the Texas armies. He also served at the Alamo.

The Allen family was started with the birth of their first son, James Valentine Allen while in Bastrop and the land grant. Other children in the family, born after the family's move to northern Hays County were: Martha, Sara E., William Martin, Philip Hansborough Bell, John Thomas and Andrew Jackson. The P.J. Allen family was well known for its community, county and state work, and that area became known as "Allen's Prairie." P.J. and Philip H.B. Allen were some of the County's first commissioners. William Martin Allen was one of the oldest living Texas Confederate Veterans. William M. and P.H.B. Allen were also some of the oldest living Chisholm Traildrivers in the state. George M. Allen, grandson of P.J. Allen, was Sheriff of Hays County, a Texas Ranger and the first Liquor Control Commissioner of Texas. Philip Jefferson Allen was honored with a DRT DEFENDER OF THE REPUBLIC OF TEXAS MARKER, Dec. 5, 1999, at his grave at Allen Cemetery, Buda, TX.
Gayle Grantham, GGGD
Linda Barron, GGGGD

BENJAMIN W. ANDERSON SR. was born January 1751 in South Carolina. He was the son of Joshua Anderson and the grandson of Abraham Anderson.

Some time after the revolution (1776-1781) several of the Anderson families left Newberry County, SC and settled in Georgia. Benjamin was granted a headright of 800 acres of land in Greene County, GA in 1793 as a resident of that county. The first eight children Benjamin's first wife, Polly Currington, were born in that county between the years 1790 and 1806. The ninth child died in infancy. Polly died after this time and before 1813. Benjamin married his second wife, Margaret Jane Williams in 1813.

Their first two children, Caroline and John W., were born in Georgia. The remaining 14 children were born in Alabama.

Benjamin, at age 75, started out with a colony for Texas, composed almost entirely of his married sons and daughters, their children, his single children and his slaves. They arrived in Nacogdoches, TX on Christmas Day, 1834. This date was carved on the trunk of a large oak tree to mark this occasion.

Mrs. W.D. Peevey, granddaughter of Benjamin, told about their early life in a newspaper article printed in the Nacogdoches, TX newspaper. Her parents died when she was very young and she was raised by Benjamin and Jane Anderson. His farm was five miles from where the present town Chireno, TX is situated. There were no schools nearby, so Benjamin had a small log school house built, employed a teacher and paid his salary.

When Texas Independence was declared, John W. Benjamin's son was a soldier in the Battle of San Jacinto. Benjamin contributed by helping finance and outfit the militia. He appeared before the Board of Land Commissioners of San Augustine County on Feb. 1, 1838, and proved that he arrived in Texas before March 2, 1836 as a married man and was entitled to one league and one labor of land. This land was located in Hopkins and Wood Counties. He participated in one way or another in two major battles, the American Revolution in 1775-76 and the Texas Revolution in 1835-36.

It is a matter of record that five of his sons, 13 grandsons and five sons–in-law went from Texas and fought under the Stars and Bars of the Confederacy in the War Between the States.

To the last of his life, Benjamin Anderson was an alert and vigorous man. At the age of 96, he dared to enter a horse race. His horse fell and Benjamin's leg was broken. He said he'd always been too impulsive and enthusiastic. However, he recovered and closed the chapter of his life at a ripe old age, having lived wisely and well, to the honor and reverence of a large line of descendants in many parts of Texas.

Benjamin died Sept. 14, 1853 in Nacogdoches County He is buried at the Black Jack Cemetery, but the grave is lost.

A long, vigorous, interesting and fruitful life was that of Benjamin W. Anderson Sr.

Diann Ham Anderson, DRT 020061
Betty Jean Ham Tiller, DAR 636520

BENJAMIN ANDERSON was born April 7, 1805 in Tennessee. He married Prudence Kemp, who was born in Georgia on May 7, 1809. They lived in the Territory of Arkansas where their first two sons were born. Their next six sons were born in Purdy, McNairy County, TN. Their daughter and youngest son were born in Hunt County, TX. Their children were: Nathaniel Kemp, born March 1828, married first, Ann Margaret Culver and second, Ella Runnels Peters, was a merchant, County Assessor, and Collector, and Civil War Captain: Joseph L. born around 1832 who married Sally; William, born around 1834, married Jemima Farmer; Elijah M., born around 1836, married Elizabeth Jane McCombs; Benjamin F. born around 1838 married Lydia Jane Franklin; Edward T. born around 1840, married Mary A. Babb; James F. born Nov. 20, 1842, married Ruth A. Maxwell and was proprietor of a small hotel in Greenville; John W. born around 1845; Mary J. born Dec. 10, 1847; Louis M. born 1852, married Bell Barnett.

Ben and his family left Tennessee to join the Mercer Colony in Texas. They arrived in 1845 before Hunt County was founded

in 1846 and Greenville in 1847. He qualified for the land grant. Before Greenville was founded, Ben opened his first store about six miles east of Greenville. In 1847 he purchased a lot in Greenville and opened one of the first two stores there in 1848. Benjamin Anderson died Jan. 14, 1874 and his wife died April 14, 1879. Both are buried in East Mount Cemetery in Greenville, TX.

Dorothy Anderson Hagen, (GGGD), 21962S

JOHN W. ANDERSON was born Jan. 27, 1860, and Georgia. He was the son of Benjamin W. Anderson and Margaret Jane Williams. At age 75, Benjamin Anderson started out with a colony for Texas, composed almost entirely of his married sons and daughters, their children, his single children and his slaves. John W. was among this group. They arrived in Nacogdoches, TX on Christmas Day, 1834. After arriving, the bark from the large oak tree was removed and the date of the arrival of the Anderson colony was carved on the trunk of the tree.

John W. Anderson is our Texas patriot, a soldier who participated in both the Battle of San Jacinto and the Siege of Bexar (San Antonio). He served in the battle of San Jacinto by guarding the baggage at Harrisburg and by waiting on the sick. He was one of 20 men who was assigned to this duty by Sam Houston. He appeared before the Board of Land Commissioner of San Augustine County and proved that he arrived in the Republic prior to March 2, 1836, as a single man and was entitled to one-third league (1476 acres) of land. He also received two land grants, one for 640 acres and one for 1280 acres, for his service in the Battle of San Jacinto. He also received a special Bounty Warrant for service at the Siege of Bexar in 1835. It is said that he sold the warrant in Waller County.

The great painting depicting the surrender of Santa Ana to General Sam Houston, who is wounded and lying propped up under a large oak tree on the battlefield, includes pictures of men that served in the battle. John W. is one of these men. The artist used pictures borrowed from relatives to support his work.

John W. Anderson married Elizabeth Briley on Dec. 30, 1840. They had 12 children, Andrew Jackson Anderson, was their firstborn. He was born Jan. 16, 1842 in Nacogdoches County, TX.

Elizabeth Briley Anderson died in 1891. John W. died June 25, 1898 at the age of 82. Both are buried at Cold Springs Cemetery, Garrison, TX.

Diann Ham Anderson DRT 020061
Betty Jean Ham Tiller DAR 636520

NATHANIEL KEMP ANDERSON, son of Benjamin and Prudence (Kemp) Anderson, was born in March 1828 in Saint Francis County, Territory of Arkansas. From an early age he lived with his parents in Purdy, McNairy County, TN.

In 1845 Nathan traveled with his family to Texas as a member of the Mercer Colony. He qualified for a land grant of 320 acres. In addition to farming, he was at various times, Greenville City Marshall, a teacher, acting Justice of the Peace, merchant, Assessor and Collector of Hunt County, and a Captain of the Confederate Company A, 32 Cav., 15 Reg't Texas Cavalry.

Nathan first married Ann Margaret Culver on March 20, 1851 in Greenville, TX. Their five children were: James Harvey, born April 10, 1853 first, married Mary Wilmoth Peters and second, Lou Rucker, was a bookkeeper and Deputy County Clerk;

John H., born 1855, married Mary Emma Robertson and was a dry goods clerk and Deputy Sheriff; Nancy J., born 1857; Martha E., born 1860; Nat, born 1862. Nathan married second, Ella Runnels Peters on June 5, 1870 in Greenville, TX. Their five children were: Benjamin Estes, born in 1872, married Nell and was a laundry manager; Thomas Cooper, born August 26, 1876, who married Bertie Houston Gaskin and was a cleaner and dyer, school policemen, and salesman; Robert Sayles, born February 1883; Bess born Jan. 12, 1884, married Knox Charles (K.C.) Jones; Julian Pauncifote born March 1890, married Bertha Fay Stripling and was head of the Tulsa office of the T.P. & W. Railroad.

Nathan died Dec. 22, 1903 in Greenville. Ella, his wife, died Aug. 6, 1936 in Houston, TX and is buried in Forest Park Cemetery.

Dorothy Anderson Hagan, (GGD), 21963S

MIRANDA WOODRUFF ARDOIN

MIRANDA WOODRUFF ARDOIN was the daughter of Sara Pevehouse Smith. Sara was a widow with five children and found it difficult to make a living. Attracted by notices offering free fertile land in the Texas Brazos Valley, Sara sold her farm in Arkansas. She packed her belongings and her children, including her older daughter, Mary, joined a wagon train, and headed for the Texas Territory in 1833. After many difficulties, the group of weary travelers reached the farmlands near Brazoria at the end of January 1834.

Miranda Woodruff Ardoin

Not far from Sara's new farm was the farm of John Woodruff. He had come to the Texas Territory in 1831 with Stephen F. Austin's Second Colony. He admired the widow's spunk in doing a man's work on the farm while capable young Mary ran the home. On Oct. 18, 1835, they made a bond to be married.

On March 11, 1836, they were in the Runaway Scrape. Four more children were born to Sara and John. My great-grandmother, Miranda, was their second child and was born April 27, 1839. After Sara's death when she was six years old, Mary and her husband Anson Jones took Miranda and her siblings into their home to live.

When Miranda was 18 years old, she married Serand Ardoin on July 2, 1857. They lived in Old Gonzales until Serand returned from serving in the Confederate Army for four years. He served with Hood's Fourth Brigade and laid down his arms and was paroled at the final surrender of Lee's Army at Appomottox. Ten children were born to Miranda and Serand.

Her sister, Mary Smith McCrory Jones was the first president of the Daughters of the Republic of Texas. Miranda Woodruff Ardoin was admitted into the Daughters of the Republic of Texas on Feb. 23, 1901. Her number is 298.

Miranda died Feb. 1, 1925, and is buried in Evergreen Cemetery in El Paso. On Dec. 16, 1985, a dedication service was held in El Paso, where two plaques were placed on her grave stating that she was a Citizen of the Republic of Texas and that she was a Daughter of the Republic of Texas.

Nadine Dees Hicks Hays, (GD), 13053

JAMES HARVEY ARMSTRONG

JAMES HARVEY ARMSTRONG, son of John and Anna Armstrong, was born in Middle Tennessee on Oct. 25, 1820. James was married three times, first to Julianne Clark in 1842 in Tennessee. They had three children, James, Julianna and William. He married Elizabeth Winfrey on Aug. 29, 1850 as his second wife. To this union were born Elizabeth and Matilda. Thirdly, James married Martha Rebecca Coppedge on July 10, 1855 in Upshur County, TX. This couple had 12 children who were Junius, Charles, Samuel, Ella, Safronia, Mary, Newton, John, Lela, Joseph, Lula, and Jesse.

James Harvey Armstrong

James came to Texas at age 19 and received a Conditional Land Certificate in 1839. He sold this certificate in 1843. In 1844, he received a Headright for 640 acres of land in Texas. He sold this Headright in 1846, returning to Arkansas. In 1854, deciding he loved the Lone Star State, he returned and bought 500 acres in Upshur County where he spent the remainder of his life except for fighting with Company F, 14th Texas Infantry in the Civil War.

James died in 1889 and Martha in 1903. They are buried in the Murray League Cemetery near Ore City, TX.

James Harvey Armstrong was my great-great-grandfather.
Joan Cervenka Cobb, DRT # 20590

CAPTAIN HAYDEN S. ARNOLD

CAPTAIN HAYDEN S. ARNOLD (ca. 1805-1839), army officer in the Texas Revolution and Legislature in the Republic of Texas, was born in Tennessee, the son of Levi and Ruth Arnold. Leaving his wife and children safe in Franklin County, TN, he journeyed to Texas arriving in December 1835. At Nacogdoches on Jan. 14, 1836 he took the oath of allegiance to the Provisional Government of Texas and enrolled for six months service in the volunteer auxiliary Corps.

On March 6, 1836, Arnold was elected Captain of the Nacogdoches Volunteers, which became the First Company of Colonel Sidney Sherman's Second Regiment Texas Volunteers. Captain Arnold led the Nacogdoches troops at the Battle of San Jacinto, where his company was first in the charge on the Mexican Army. His new London Yager rifle was shot from his hands and broken through at the breech. The company was discharged on June 6, 1836 at La Bahia by General Thomas J. Rusk.

Captain Arnold was elected to represent Nacogdoches in the House of Representatives of the first Congress of the Republic of Texas. He served from Oct. 3, 1836 to June 13, 1837. In 1836 president Sam Houston appointed him to serve as Secretary of a Commission to treaty with the Indians. He later served as District Clerk pro-tem of the Nacogdoches District until at least Dec. 20, 1838.

Captain Arnold died on July 3, 1839, at his home in Naacogdoches. He was survived by his widow Selina and three children, James R., Sophronia K., Hayden S. Arnold Jr. Selina was appointed executrix of his estate. She died in Nacogdoches on Aug. 30, 1840 and was buried next to Captain Arnold in Oak Grove Cemetery, Nacogdoches, TX. In 1936 the State of Texas erected a monument at Captain Arnold's grave.

James R. Arnold (1823-1900) married Sarah Muckelroy.
Sophronia K. Arnold (182?-1849) married George W. Long.
Hayden S. Arnold Jr. (1837-185?) died unmarried.
Mary Ann King Butler, (GGGGD), #21900

MARY KATHERINE NEELY ATWOOD was born Jan. 16, 1811 at Maury County, TN to Charles Rufus Neely and Louisa Polk. Mary Catherine's grandfather, Ezekiel Polk, was the grandfather of the 11th President of the United States James K. Polk. Her father fought in the Creek War and after the war moved his family to Alabama near Tuscumbia where he farmed. He died in 1820. Mary Catherine returned with her mother to Maury County and in 1822 they came to Hardeman County, TN. June 10, 1829 Mary Catherine married William Woods Atwood in Bolivar, TN. They came to Texas in January 1839 and located in 1840 on Gilleland Creek in Travis County. Children of the Atwoods were Louisa, William Woods Jr., Mary Josephine, Adella Belle, Rufus Neely, Jane Brown, Octavia Polk, and Charles Joseph. Mary Catherine gave herself to the work of training her children and creating for her family a home in a wild frontier land. A great grandson wrote that as a small boy he remembered her as a quiet, gentle, little old lady and delighted in listening to her stories of frontier life. She died Aug. 19, 1896 and was buried in Oakwood Cemetery, Austin.
Billie Palm Bryant, GGGD, 21191S

WILLIAM WOODS ATWOOD, born Jan. 4, 1804 in Maine. He was a merchant in Bolivar, Hardiman County, TN, when on June 10, 1829; he married Mary Catherine Neely, daughter of Charles Louisa Polk Neely. She was born Jan. 16, 1811 in Maury County, TN. The Atwoods had eight children but only four lived to maturity. Louisa and William Woods Jr. died in Bolivar and were buried in the Polk Cemetery. In 1839 Mr. and Mrs. Atwood and daughters, Mary Josephine and Adele Belle, moved to Matagorda County, TX. In 1840 they moved to Travis County on Gilleland Creek. Four children were born in Texas: Rufus Neely, Jane Brown, Octavia Polk and Charles Joseph. Jane and Charles died in childhood. Rufus Neely died as a Confederate prisoner at Camp Douglas, IL, March 7, 1863. His body was later returned to Austin and interred in Oakwood Cemetery, April 13, 1867. Mary Josephine married James H. Durst, Jan. 11, 1854 in Austin. Adella Belle married August B. Palm June 26, 1861 in Austin. Octavia Polk married Thomas Chalmars Bittle Jan. 25, 1866. The Atwoods were well known for their good citizenship and hospitality. Mr. Atwood served as a Commissioner of Travis County 1846-1848. He died Jan. 2, 1871 and was buried in Oakwood Cemetery, Austin.
Billie Palm Bryant, (GGGD), 20744

JAMES BRITON BAILEY, born in 1779, grandson of Kenneth Bailey of the 'Baillies' of Dundain, Scotland and a direct descendant of King Robert the Bruce of Scotland. Bailey came to the Spanish territory of Tejas in 1818 with his wife and children. His Spanish land grant was recognized by Stephen F. Austin on July 7, 1824. Bailey became a member of Austin's "old 300" colonists, as his homestead and cotton plantation were established prior to Austin's arrival in "Tejas." Bailey was a Lieutenant in the militia and later promoted to Captain by Governor Viesca. Bailey fought for Texas independence in the battles of Jones' Creek and Belasco, but died of cholera in 1833, prior to

Drawing of Brit Bailey

San Jacinto. Until his death, Bailey continued to add to his acreage, which extended from Houston southward toward the coast. Legend says that Bailey was buried, standing up facing west, as specified in his will, with his rifle and whiskey jug by his side. My great-great-great-grandmother, Nancy, refused to put the judge in the casket, so according to "legend", Brit's ghost comes back, with his lantern, to look for the jug, which is demonstrated by a ghostly light emanating periodically on "Bailey's Prairie" in West Columbia, TX. The Whitcomb family, descendants of Bailey, continue to own property on Clear Creek, still pristine with original live oaks, is part of the original land grant. This portion of Bally's land was "settled" by Bally's granddaughter, Mary Thomas Thompson and her husband James, who are buried in the family cemetery on our property in Friendswood, TX. The property also adjoins Webster, TX, and is near NASA, south of Houston.

JOHN ALBERT AND ELIZABETH KOKERNOT BARBER John Albert Barber, the third child of Samuel and Elizabeth Barrow Barber, was born on July 27, 1818, in Louisiana and moved to Texas with his family at the age of 11 years. John and Elizabeth Kokernot were married in 1846 and lived in Liberty County until about 1849, when they moved to the Big Hill area of Gonzales County.

Caroline and D.L. Kokernot

Elizabeth was born on Dec. 4, 1831, in New Orleans, the first child of Capt. David Kokernot and Caroline Dittmar Kokernot. The Kokernots made their home in Texas when Elizabeth was four months old.

In about 1853, the Barbers left Gonzales for Refugio and Aransas counties, settling, finally, near Rockport, where they raised their children: Amos Hamilton, who became a prominent South Texas minister; Addison L.; George Albert; David W.; Amanda (Ives); Eliza (Williams); Bettie (Ives); Clara (Williams); John Edward; and Martha (Ives).

Elizabeth Kokernot Barber

The Barbers owned large holdings of land in Bee and Refugio counties and John was active in various positions of leadership until his death at the early age of 51 on Dec. 19, 1869. Elizabeth died on Nov. 15, 1905, and both are buried in Rockport Cemetery.
Rachel Virginia Kelley Kreutzer, (GGGD), 13965S, 14574S

ELIZABETH BARNHILL, Elizabeth Hungerford Smith was the daughter of James Norman Smith and Sarah Jenkins. Elizabeth was born Aug. 9, 1814 in Maury County, TN and was named for her maternal grandmother, Elizabeth Hungerford daughter Barton Hungerford and Jane Warren of Charles County, MD. Both of Elizabeth Hungerford Smith's grandfathers-James Turner Smith of Maryland/North Carolina/Tennessee and Philip Jenkins of Maryland/Virginia/Tennessee were Patriots of the American Revolution. In 1832, Elizabeth Hungerford Smith married William Calhoun of Tipton County, TN. Widowed in 1841, she moved to Texas with her four children: Samuel Daniel, William T.M., John Richard, and

Elizabeth Hungerford Smith Calhoun Barnhill

Lizzie. Elizabeth, arrived in Texas the spring of 1842, escorted by her brother-in-law, Francis Stanton Latham, Editor, Memphis Eagle Newspaper. She was also accompanied, by a cadre of Tennessee volunteers calling themselves "The Texian Wolf Hunters". The arrival is described in F.S. Latham's writings "Travels in the Republic of Texas-1842," edited and published by Gerald Pierce through Encino Press, Austin, TX in 1971. Elizabeth joined her father's family settling near Cuero by 1845. She supported her children by teaching school in Clinton. In 1848, Elizabeth Hungerford Smith Calhoun married John D. Barnhill and had three daughters: Martha, Sallie, and Lydia. Elizabeth Barnhill died in Dewitt County, TX in February 1864. Additional information on Elizabeth Barnhill may be found in Bennie Lou Hook Altom's essay, "Elizabeth Barnhill and the Texian Wolf Hunters," based on Pierce and Latham's books, and winner of the 1997 Daughters of the Republic of Texas Mamie Wynne Cox historical essay award. The essay is available at the DRT Library in Austin, TX, Maury County, TN Library, Dallas Public Library and the Library of Congress.

Bennie Lou Hook Altom, (GGGD), 20043-S

WILLIAM NICHOLAS BARKER (1810-1865) was the son Britton Barker and Celia Watts. Both parents were dead by the time he was 12. He was then raised by his maternal grandparents, Thomas and Mary Watts. He married Alitia Humble in Monroe, Ouachita County, LA on Dec. 6, 1832.

He and his wife were in Texas prior to 1836, settling in Liberty County, later Walker County. He took part in the battle of San Jacinto. He was the grandfather of the noted Texas Historian, Eugene C. Barker.

The children of William and Alitia were: William Nicholas (born about 1833), James William (1836-1926), Henry (1839-1917), Thomas (1842-1902), John (1846-1928), Mary Jane (1847–1926), Joseph (1850–1888); Cicero (1853–1926); Charles (1854–1873); Amanda (1856), Altha (1859). The five older boys were Confederate Soldiers.

Bonnie Gene Balke Kuykendall, (GGGD) of William Barker

URIAH BASS JR. was the fourth child born to Andrew Bass Jr., the Younger), who was born in Dobbs County, NC, ca. 1775, and his wife Christian. Uriah was born 1784-8 and Wayne County,

NC. This line of Bass family was large. They were wealthy—they were given "classical" educations. They were found in Dobbs, Johnson, Duplin, Craven, Wayne, and Bertie Counties from 1692 through 1790, and in Alabama and Texas in the early 1830's.

They were wealthy, large landowners, with many slaves, with plantations extending from Goldsboro to Mt. Olive (N&S) and 15-20 miles both E&W of that line (Hwy U.S. 117). Uriah and Ruth's extensive plantation was SW of Goldboro, along the Neuse River, Mill Creek, Beaver Dam Creek, Crooked Marsh, and Falling Creek lying within Wayne County. Uriah married Ruth (A.) Pipkin ca. 1807 – 8 in Wayne County. They had three children in Wayne County (one of them was Nancy Bass, my GGGD who married Henry W. (Bud) Cave, and were in South Carolina by 1815 where their next three children were born, and were in Marengo County, AL ca. 1825, where their last child was born. From Marengo County they moved on into Texas. They were prominent, well–to–do, land-owning family, and they owned many slaves. They recognized the challenge Texas gave with her Alamo heroes, her free land, and her struggles to keep what she had won.

Their children were: Susannah Bass married Ebenezer (Edwin) Newton, Nancy Bass married Henry W. (Bud) Cave Bass, Richard Bass married Mary Green, Mariah Bass married Elias Rush, Elizabeth Bass married John P. McGraw, Bass—unm 1840.

Our Uriah was in Texas in the early 1830's. He was in Liberty County, Caldwell County, Bastrop County, and Milam County. He worked with his cousin William Bass who was deeded 1/2 a league of land March 9, 1838 from Jonathan Burleson, as colonist for Austin and Williamson. He was in Liberty County, November 1839. Uriah is listed on Oct. 2, 1839, as "returning to the U.S. to try to sell land". He served as emissary on several trips "back" to the U.S. to encourage other settlers and colonist to come to Texas. He served the Republic as a colonist, settler, loyal patriot, citizen, and emissary. He died on one of his trips "back"—in Marengo County, AL in 1841-43. He left his mark along the trail—for all eternity—on this great land—and we who follow, can do well to carry on where he left off. Please, God, that we do as well.

Ethel Jewel Morgan Burch, (GGGGD of Uriah Bass), DRT Member #20013S
Uriah Bass, Jr. #20013S

SETH BATSON SR. was born May 7, 1794 in Burke County, GA. He married Mary Fowler in Jones County, GA, on Feb. 20, 1811. She was born June 24, 1796, in North Carolina. They came to Texas in late 1840 and settled in Liberty County, where he farmed and raised livestock. They paid taxes in this county in 1842 on land, livestock and slaves. The little town of Batson, TX, is located today on some of this land and named for this family.

Seth Batson served in the War of 1812 while living in the Mississippi Territory. His widow, Mary Fowler Batson, later received bounty land for this service. There were several of his brothers, also lived in the Mississippi Territory and came to Texas when they came. Some of these brothers fought for the independence of Texas. Some of the Batson family moved on to Madison County.

Seth Batson Sr. died in Liberty County at his home on Aug.

25, 1844. His wife Mary Fowler Batson, continued to live and work her lands with the help of some grown sons, a daughter and devoted slaves. She paid taxes at this location in 1846. In 1847, she and her children moved to Grimes County and built a home at "Look Out Mountain," this was at the settlement of Rogers Prairie, known now as Normangee. She had the first post office of this community in her home.

Grimes County was at this time Indian Territory. There were a lot of homes burned and families killed during this period. The first Batsons in the Colonies were shown on the 1718 census in Virginia as landowners on the "Island of Accowmacke," this was Thomas Batson from England. He was a great-grandfather to Seth Batson.

From this point, the Batson families moved to North Carolina, South Carolina, Georgia, Mississippi, and Louisiana, into Texas. Each place they settled for several years, buying land, building homes and were involved in settlement activities. At each place, there were children born, marriages into other families, deaths of family members and as they moved on to the next state, there were those who were settled and preferred to stay in that state.

The Batson families helped establish Baptist churches at several locations. The men were also involved in promoting and helping establish Masonic lodges in various settlements.

Thomas Batson was around 30 years of age during the years of the Revolutionary War. The Archives of History as proof of his service during 1780, from the District of Wilmington and Onslow Counties in North Carolina.
Robbie Bowen Bennett, 017640

ISAAC BATTERSON, son of Stephen Batterson (Revolutionary War veteran) and Sarah Wardwell was born June 10, 1791, in Fairfield, CT. He married Amelia Nash (born Feb. 4, 1795, New York, daughter of Jonathan Nash and Ann Raymond) Sept. 30, 1813 in Connecticut.

Eight children: William, born and died April 1815; Harriet, born Dec. 20, 1816, died January 1817; Mary, born Dec. 20, 1816, married Williams Sawyer; Amelia, born Nov. 19, 1818; Catherine, born April 8, 1823, married James Nelson Montgomery; Julia Ann, born Dec. 25, 1825, died Oct. 27, 1836; William H. born March 25, 1828, died June 11, 1828; William Barrett Travis, born March 13, 1836, married Mary J. Page.

Memorial plaque for Isaac Batterson.

In 1833 Isaac and his family emigrated to Texas where he founded the settlement known as Clinton named after his home in New York. Later it was renamed Galena Park as there was already a town in Texas by the name of Clinton. He was the first Justice of the Peace in Harrisburg County, and helped the Allen brothers survey the town site of the proposed city of Houston. He was also a friend of Sam Houston and it was the floor of his cabin that Sam Houston used to make rafts to ferry his troops across rain-swollen Buffalo Bayou to fight the Battle of San Jacinto.

Isaac died Feb. 19, 1838, Harris County, Republic of Texas,

and his grave has been lost to industry. Amelia died July 6, 1861 and is buried in Galveston. *Submitted by Anita Stoerner Crona.*
Catherine Batterson, (D), (DRT #83, Wife of Patriot), married James Nelson Montgomery
Ellen Amelia Montgomery, (GD), (DRT #51, Real Daughter), married James William Golledge Jr.
Rose Ellen Golledge, (GGD), married William Edwin Ellis
George Whitfield Ellis, (GGGS), married Clara Willie Muske
Natalie Ellis, (GGGGD), married Oswald Richard Stoerner
Anita Joan Stoerner, (GGGGGD), (DRT #19530), married Otto Gregory Crona, Jr.

JEAN BENJAMIN BAVOUX emigrated to the Republic of Texas in the month of October 1941 and received a Land Grant, Class Fourth, in Denton County. In 1842 his wife Mary Catherine joined him. She was accompanied by their two children, Ambrosine and Jean Baptiste. He died in 1847.

Jean Baptiste Bavoux was in Waller's Regiment, Texas Cavalry, CSA. He was a member of the United Confederate Veterans and the Woodmen of the World. He was also a charter member of the Society Francaise de Biefaisance, (French Benevolent Society of Galveston) in 1860. He died in 1916.
Frances B. Terwilliger, (GGGD), 01234
Frances B. Terwilliger, (GGD), 01234

THOMAS BEATTY was born 1798, in South Carolina. He married Mary Jane McHenry in 1822, both their parents were Irish immigrants. They had 11 children born in Georgia, Mississippi, Louisiana and Texas. They were Caroline H., born 1824, married John R. Bevil; Sisly, born 1827, married Andres Isaacs; Charles Romberg, born 1829, married Nancy Blewitt; Hulda, born 1833 married Warren Hall Bevil; Mary, born 1835, married William Booth; George, born 1837, died 1863; Martha Jane, born 1839, married Abner Carter; Thomas Boston, born 1839, married Mary Louis Barclay; Eliza, born 1843, married Perry Isaacs; John, born 1845, died 1863; James F., born 1847, married Virginia Nelson.

Thomas Beatty served as Chief Justice in Jasper County for a while but was a millwright and farmer by trade. He died in Tyler County in 1862.

"Hulda" Margaret Mahuldah Melvinia Elizabeth, named after her grandmothers, born in Georgia Dec. 7, 1831 died in Tyler County, Nov. 11, 1908. On April 8, 1852 she married Warren Hall Bevil, son of John R. and Frances Boynton Bevil, born Aug. 10, 1826, Jasper County, TX, died Jan. 23, 1865. They are buried in the Harts Mills Cemetery. Their children were: Frances Jane, born Feb. 19, 1853, died Feb. 18, 1894 married Dennis Hampton Hart, son of Richard Jefferson Hart and Epsy Ann Bazer, Oct. 10, 1892; John Randolph, born Nov. 28, 1854, married Martha Adeline Hart; Thomas Beatty, born Sept. 12, 1856, married Phoebe Barclay; Charles Warren, born 1859 married Mattie Phillips; George M., born Dec. 2, 1861, married Appless A. Bullock; Andrew Hall, born Nov. 30, 1864, married Alice R. George.
Ginne Liles, (GGGGGD), 20402
Eugenia Letbetter, (GGGGD), 21971

JOHN BEEMAN, son of James Beeman and wife Nancy Moore, was born Oct. 20, 1799 at Murfreesboro, NC. He married Emily Manly Hunnicutt on June 19, 1823 in Green County,

IL. Their children were: Elizabeth, Margaret, William H., Samuel H., Isaac H., Clarissa, Nancy, all born in Illinois, and John Scott born at Bowie, TX.

They arrived in Texas Dec. 6, 1840 settling first in Dalby Springs in Bowie County. John then went to Indian patrol at Bird's Fort then to Tarrant County finally settling in Dallas County April 4, 1842 on the Lagow Headright, east side of White Rock Creek (today is mesquite).

John was a farmer, millright, trader, buying and selling, lending out his own money. He was known as the first banker of the settlement of Dallas. He was well educated, religious, a man of his word, considered the "Patriarch" of the settlement.

He served the Republic as a Texas Ranger and Captain A.W. Webb's Co. in 1841. He was chosen to represent his district and attended the first Legislation.

He died March 12, 1856. Both he and Emily are buried in the Beeman Family Cemetery, Dallas, TX.
Eulene Maxwell Wilkerson, (GGGD), 20941

JAMES CARREL BELL

JAMES CARREL BELL, son of Silas Bell and Lucretia Walker Bell, was born on March 1, 1820, in Kentucky, and was in Texas before he was 15. He came to live with his mother, who was here with her parents, James Walker Sr., and Catherine Miller Walker, in Stephen F. Austin's first colony, Old Three Hundred. James was too young, at 15, to be in the Army, but was allowed to join a company of fillibusters under General Burleson, going into Bejar on Dec. 5, 1835.

Selah Bell Miller and her son Deno.

Our family story came from the writings of two James' children, John Miller Bell and Margaret Frances Bell, edited by a grandson, Boyce Harrell, father of Laverne Harrell Clark.

James' stepfather, William S. Brooks, taught him the art of pottery making, and he became a furniture and wagon manufacturer.

He was married to Eliza Baker on June 23, 1844 in one of the early marriages of Fayette County.

In 1852, his family accompanied him to Tennessee to bring a wagon train of settlers to Texas. The train left Tennessee on Aug. 20, 1852, and arrived at old Warrenton on Oct. 12, 1852.

He received hundreds of acres from his mother, which were added to his land grant for his army service for Texas independence. He served in the Civil War, shown on his monument erected by the state of Texas on his grave and Muldoon Cemetery. James died Aug. 4, 1880. Eliza died Oct. 26, 1906 and is buried by his side.

James and Eliza had 15 children all born in Fayette County, and the stone house in which they lived could possibly have been built by her father, Daniel Baker, a stone mason. One of the daughters was Selah Bell, who was married to August Charles Miller on Dec. 24, 1884. They were my grandparents.
Irma Geraldine Brannan Miller, DRT 20951

JOSIAH H. BELL

JOSIAH H. BELL, born Aug. 22, 1791 in Chester Dist., SC; son of John and Elizabeth Hughes Bell. After an apprenticeship in Nashville with his uncles, tailors and hatters by trade, he sought his fortune with his friend Moses Austin. They mined, traded with Indians and sold merchandise and bargained with the French and Spanish governments, which served them well as later pioneers in Texas. Bell married Mary Evaline McKenzie on Dec. 1, 1818, in Christian County, KY. The newlyweds settled in Natchitoches, LA, where they lived until Moses Austin convinced Bell to join him in founding a colony in Texas.

James H. Bell, Associate Justice 1858-1864.

Bell and his family crossed the Sabine April 22, 1821, thus preceding Stephen F. Austin into Texas. The Bell family became one of the first of the "Old Three Hundred" families settling Austin's first colony. Bell became Stephen F. Austin's trusted adviser, and was left in charge of the colony while Austin was in Mexico City to secure his land grants. Austin wrote of him as a man "having particular merit over the rest as having a fine and well-established reputation for probity, calmness and intelligence, judgment and virtue."

Josiah settled for a short time near Washington, then descended down the Brazos "about five miles below La Bahia Road" at a spot which became known as "Bell's Landing" (now Columbia). For a short time in 1836, it seems to have been used as the capital, with President Houston occupying a small house in the Bell yard. Bell and his lovely wife provided accommodations for President Houston and other distinguished public men and foreign dignitaries, until Bell's death on May 17, 1838.

Three children lived to perpetuate Josiah's family in Texas: Elizabeth Lucinda, Thadeus C. and James Hall Bell. The undersigned is a descendant of James Hall Bell (born Jan. 21, 1825), a distinguished lawyer who served on the Texas Supreme Court for a 1858-1864. He was married to Catherine Elizabeth Townsend on Dec. 1, 1847 in Houston. He died in Austin, TX on March 13, 1892, survived by his wife and six children. His son, Barclay Townsend (born Oct. 30, 1852 in Columbia), married Lillian Grafton Alsworth (born March 2, 1855 in Columbia) on May 5, 1874. Barclay and Lillian traveled by covered wagon to settle in the Panhandle of Texas. In later years, they lived in the home of their daughter, Emily Townsend Bell and E.S. Ireland in Hereford, TX, where Barclay died July 29, 1930, and Lillian died at the age of 98 on May 17, 1953. The Bells and the Irelands are buried in Hereford Cemetery.
Elizabeth Ireland Holt, (DRT #19764)

WILLIAM BENNETT

WILLIAM BENNETT was born c. 1788 in Wilkes County, GA (s/o Reuben Bennett and Elizabeth Peachly Tarpley). He married on Jan. 7, 1808 in Georgia to Nancy Roan (born 1788 Georgia-died aft. 1860 Texas) d/o James Roan and Mary Jarrott. William and Nancy had four children: Mary Peteet, James R.

Bennett Reuben W. Bennett and Elizabeth Bennett. William Bennett and family lived in Georgia for a while and then moved to Sumpter County, AL. He served as Justice of Peace for a short time in Alabama. Then William moved his family to Texas before 1835. They came first to Sabine area and later moved to Montgomery County, TX. (now Grimes County, TX) The oath that Wm. signed to enter Mexico (now Texas) stated he came in 1830. William fought for the Republic of Texas from Oct. 1, 1836 to Aug. 29, 1837 and was discharged April 29, 1838 due to illness. He died before 1841 in Texas. The Republic of Texas gave the heirs of William Bennett a land grant (#320) for his service to the Republic.

Margaret Elizabeth Bennett Powell, granddaughter of William Bennett.

William's name has been seen as William M. and William R. in some records. The land grant says heirs of William Bennett.

Ruth Ann Clift Bowen, third great granddaughter of William Bennett.

Ruth Ann Clift Bowen, (GGGGD), DRT #19204

HARRIET CAROLINE CLARK BERRY born Dec. 22, 1808 in Lincoln County, TN, Harriet Caroline Clark married General John G. Berry on Dec. 2, 1824 in Lincoln County, TN. Caroline was the daughter of blacksmith Barnhill Clark and wife Rachel who lived in the vicinity of Mulberry, TN.

Barnes and Rachel Clark migrated to Texas in 1826. The Berry family came in early 1837 to San Augustine, TX where they made their home.

Caroline and John G. Berry had eight children: William C., America Jane, Ann Eliza, Elisha W., Caroline, John G. Jr., Kenneth L. and Benjamin Rush Wallace.

Caroline died in San Augustine, TX, Aug. 6, 1854 after a protracted illness. Her obituary in the *Redlander* reads, "The sickness of Sister Berry was protracted and painful in the extreme, yet she bore it with that Christian fortitude which sayeth, "God doeth all things well," and while we mourn her death we rejoice to believe that our loss is her eternal gain..... The writer became acquainted with the deceased in the year 1837 or 1838 and from an uninterrupted friendship with the family since, I say of truth, that a better neighbor, a purer heart, a more kind and affectionate mother or devoted wife never lived."
DeLayne Fay Wojtkiewicz Maxwell, (GGGGD), 21996-S

GENERAL JOHN G. BERRY, born Oct. 5, 1800 in Anson County, NC, General John G. Berry married Harriet Caroline Clark on Dec. 2, 1824 in Lincoln County, TN. Emigrating from Lynchburg, the Berrys arrived in San Augustine early 1837.

Sometime in 1839, General Berry, who came to Texas with

a considerable purse. Estimated by some at $20,000.00, contracted to build a lavish hotel on the northeast corner of Columbia and Harrison Streets. A detailed description of Berry Hotel, perhaps San Augustine's grandest hotel, is provided in *Two Centuries in East Texas.*

A San Augustine pioneer for 34 years, Berry was a "General" in the Cherokee War and in the Regulator/Moderator War. He fought in the Mexican War, marching over a thousand miles. His public services included Customs Collector, County Treasurer and Wesleyan College Trustee. He was a merchant and the owner of Berry Hotel. He was a railroad entrepreneur and a riverboat captain of his 900-bale steamboat "Big Ben" which plied the Sabine River. His will included over 17,000 acres of land before the division among his eight children.

"Rip" Ford, who knew him personally, summed it up best- "General Berry ... and others... were efficient laborers in every work the public good demanded."
DeLayne Fay Wojtkiewicz Maxwell, (GGGGD), 21584
Nancy Wray Crocker Wojtkiewicz, (GGGD), 21994
Lori Frances Lodestro Allen, (GGGGD), 21995

ISAAC BEST, the son of Stephen and Sarah Humphrey Best, was born about 1774 in Pennsylvania. April 9, 1794 he married Mary Margaret Wilkens in Garrard County, KY. In 1808, they moved to Missouri settling in Montgomery County on "Best Bottom".

Their children were: John (born 1794), Issac Jr. (1796), Humphrey (1797), Sarah (Sally 1800), Phoebe (1802), Mary (Polly 1804), Margaret (Peggy 1807), Ebenezer W. (1808), Stephen (1810). Best had a mill near his blockhouse fort. When Stephen F. Austin's wagon caravan, known as Austin's Old 300, left Missouri in 1822, Isaac, wife, and five children were in the colony. The colonists settled on bottom land of Brazos River. Aug. 19, 1824, Isaac Best received a Spanish land grant of one sitio. That 1826 census classifying them as a farmer, stock raiser with the household including his wife, three sons, two daughters, and four slaves. At the demise of Isaac Best, he left intestate some 8,000 acres, estimated at $14,000 and a number of slaves. A creek in Waller County was named for him, Best Creek. Best departed Feb. 8, 1837, and his wife in February of 1852. The 14 years Best lived in Texas he left his mark of identity as he did in Missouri.
Odelle Hamilton, (GGGGD), 16926
Marjorie Sheffield Chamberlin, (GGGGGD) 21589
Linda Hall Cain, (GGGGGGD), 21592
Terry Hall Ferguson, (GGGGGGD), 21232
Jerry Fay Hall, (GGGGGGD), 22109

JOHN RANDOLPH "JACK" BEVIL, son of John Randolph Bevil and Leodice Burton, was born Aug. 24, 1784 in Mecklenburg, VA. He married Frances Boynton on Sept. 3, 1806 in Warren County, GA. Francis, daughter of Amos Boynton and Sarah Snow, was born Oct. 26, 1878 in New York. She was a descendant of Stephen Hopkins of the "Mayflower". John and Frances finally settled in Jasper County, TX in the early 1820's. Their eight children were: John Jehu, born 1807, married Ann Jane Taylor; Alfred Munroe, born 1812, married Adelia Gilcrest; Frances born about 1814; John Randolph, born 1820, married Caroline Beatty; Riley W., born 1820; Stewart Boynton, born 1824, married Sarah Ann Spurlock; Warren Hall, born Aug. 10,

1826, married Margaret Mahulda Melvinia Elizabeth "Hulda" Beatty; Joseph Francisca, born 1832.

John Bevil was Alcalde of the Municipality of Bevil in 1834, represented the Municipality at the 1835 Consultation, served in the Texas Revolution and was Chief Justice of Jasper County He died Nov. 10, 1862 and is buried in the Harts Mill Cemetery in Tyler County, TX.

Warren Hall Bevil and Hulda Beatty, born Dec. 7, 1831, daughter of Thomas Beatty and Mary Jane McHenry, were married April 8, 1852, in Jasper County, TX. Their six children were: Frances Jane, born Feb. 19, 1853 died Feb. 18, 1894, married Dennis Hampton Hart, son of Richard Jefferson Hart and Epsy Ann Bazer, Oct. 10, 1892; John Randolph, on Nov. 28, 1854, married Martha Adeline Hart; Thomas Beatty, born Sept. 12, 1856, married Phoebe Barclay; Charles Warren, born 1859, married Mattie Phillips; George M., born Dec. 2, 1861, married Appless A. Bullock; Andrew Hall, born Nov. 30, 1864, married Alice R. George.

Ginne' Liles, (GGGGGD), 20402
Eugenia Letbetter, (GGGGD), 21971

MAJOR JONATHAN BIRD was born in 1783 in Tennessee, probably Giles County and died in 1850 and Titus County, TX. While living in Bowie County, TX, Bird received a brevet appointment of Major from General Edward H. Tarrant to found a fort and settlement on the West fork of the Trinity River. The appointment was made on Aug. 7, 1841. He raised a company of 40 soldiers and outfitted them, bought provisions and left Bowie County in October of 1841. There is a complete list of the provisions.

He was married to Miss Browder in Tennessee. They had, at least two daughters: Malinda, who married William Truelove; and Rachel, born 1818 in Alabama, died Aug. 10, 1863, in Hood County, TX, married circa 1839 in Marion County, AL, William Franklin Ernest born Aug. 7, 1813 Giles County, TN, died 1878 in Hood County, TX.

When Sam Houston gave settlement rights to the Peters Colony, instead of Major Bird, he abandoned the fort, dismissed his troops, and returned home. He petitioned the State of Texas for the $653.50 he had spent on the expedition, which was quite a large sum in 1841! Sam Houston vetoed payment. Jonathan worked four years to get his money repaid. Congress finally passed an Act for the Relief of Jonathan Bird on Jan. 8, 1845 giving him taxes from Bowie County. He gave Power of Attorney to a lawyer, Joseph D. Lilley. Jonathan died in Robinson County in 1850 before collection of all of his money.

Children of Rachel and William Ernest were:
Mary Bird, Nov. 17, 1839, married 1. John C. Gibbs; 2. William Patterson
Josiah-probably died young
Lycurgus Blackburn, Aug. 31, 1845, Marion County, AL, died Oct. 31, 1936 in Mason County, married 1. Elizabeth Patterson; and 2. Sarah Olive Baxter Newsom in 1874. Civil War veteran,
Frederick W., 1846. Married 1. Mary Etta Swinney, 2. Sarah Cline
George Lemuel, 1850, married Sally Elizabeth Creech
Thomas H.
Coleman, 1852

Richard M., 1856
John David (Dave), 1858, married Florence Chalk
William Ahab, Aug. 10, 1863, married Rachel Joanna Bush on Aug. 1, 1882, Mason County, TX.
Children by second wife were: Charles born 1869
Peter-never married. Died on a ranch in New Mexico.
Caroline Latham Ingram, (GGGGD), DRT #11172

GEORGE W. BLAIR, the third child of James Blair was born 1824 in Illinois. He is listed on the 1840 Gonzales County Poll Tax. George first married Palena Ann Hocker. He married his second wife, Mary Jane Elkins. She was from Turkey Cove, VA. George is listed on the 1860 Red River County Census as a laborer. All of their eight children were born in Texas.

Valerus Gordon Hector and Sarah Jane Blair Hector.

His first wife, Palena died 1849. She was the daughter of Henry C. Hocker and Mary Mitchell. George died May 16, 1852, Red River County, TX, when his daughter, Sarah Jane Hocker was four years old. Mary Jane died not long after. Georgia's first wife was the oldest sister of Sarah Jane Hocker who married Astyanax Troy Hector. Astyanax and Sarah had a son, Valerus Gordon who married Sarah Jane Blair, the daughter of George W. Blair and Mary Jane Elkins. Valerus was George's nephew by marriage as well as his son–in–law. After George died, Mary Jane and her children lived with her father–in–law, James Blair. One day she came in from the fields complaining of a headache and laid down across the bed. A few hours later, she was dead. Mary Elizabeth, the youngest child continued to live with James. The older three children went to live with Mary Jane's sister, Cynthia Elkins Smith in Williamson County, TX.
Gerald Dean Hector Lilly, (GGGGD), 17208

JAMES BLAIR arrived in Red River County, TX on Dec. 25, 1837. He is listed in the 1840 census of the Republic of Texas. He is also listed on the 1840 Red River County and the 1840 Austin County Poll Tax. He was given a conditional certificate (619) for 640 acres Jan. 2, 1840. On Sept. 7, 1841, it was changed to an unconditional certificate.

James was born in St. Clair, IL, in 1800 to George Blair, who migrated to land grant for 640 acres in Red River County. His daughter, Polly Stone, Illinois in 1794 with his father. It is recorded in the history of the St. Clair County that George donated property to the city and named the town of Belleville, IL.

James married Martha Bonham in 1820. They had six children: Polly, Eliza, George W., Emaline, John D. and William J. After Martha's death in 1831, James married Nancy Brantley. There were six children born of this marriage also James Monroe, Elizabeth, Sarah Jane, Samuel R., Elias Barton, Francis Marion.

James served in the Black Hawk War under Captain Tate

and mustered out in 1832. In 1841, he received a died in 1850 leaving four small children. James traveled back to Illinois to get the children and brought them to Texas and raised them on the farm.

Gerald Dean Hector Lilly, (GGGGGD), 17208

CARL BLOOMBERG, born in 1798 in Kulm Prussia. Under the auspices of the Mainzer Verein for the immigration to Texas, his wife Catherine Ruff and eight children left Germany Aug. 19, 1845 on the ship Neptune. Carl was highly educated. Owner and headmaster of a boy's Academy. Adventuresome Carl believed a bright future existed in Texas. They landed in Indianola, Lavaca County, Dec. 22, 1845. The family settled first in Fredericksburg, where Count Meusaback's Colony was already established. Carl was pressed into service as teacher and minister. Because of the constant threat of Indians, they returned to New Braunfels and bought land in Schumannsville. For several years, Carl tried farming. Later he ran a freighting company. He said that he had to pass through an Indian village when he went between Schumannsville and New Braunfels. He died in 1856 of yellow fever. His son Ernst (1836-1902) married Margarethe Zipp (1839-1928) in 1858. Ernst farmed on the family farm. One of their 11 children was Pauline (1870-1957) who married Gustav Koehler, a farmer (1871-1923) in 1892. One of their six children was Elsie (1905-1994), manager of a gift shop, who married Gilbert Nagel (1901-1983) in 1926. They had two girls named Pauline and Kathryn. Kathryn married Nathan Kiser, an engineer, in 1957. They had three children.

Kathryn Nagel Kiser, (GGGD), 08602

WILLIAM BLUNDELL, born ca. 1795 in Virginia to Miles Henry Blundell. He and his wife, Elizabeth, moved to Kentucky, then, to Texas in the early 1830's the family was first to patent land in the area. Blundell Creek runs through their land and Indian mounds are beside the creek.

John B. Blundell

He served in Captain William Becknell's Company in Burton's Cavalry for Republic of Texas Summer 1836-1838. Was honorably discharged. He was a farmer and furnished corn to Texas' Army.

1840 census lists his property: Poll one; Land 784; three slaves; and one metal clock.

1860 he had one slave, one tract land in Hunt County and one track in Lavaca County.

When, an old man, he was granted Veteran Donation 471 for 1280 acres in Travis County. Also, $250.00 annual pension for 1836 and $75.00 for 1838.

Children:, John B., born Nov. 14, 1826 and married Caroline M. Campbell Aug. 5, 1852. He died July 10, 1894 and is buried in Brogdon Cemetery in Pottsboro District, Grayson County.

I only know two other children's names: Louisa and William, Jr.

Have not found record of death of William, probably in 1881 or 1882.

Ruby Lou Beach Moore, (GGGD), #13184

FRANCES ANN (TANDY) BOALES (ca. 1809-1892) was born in Louisa County, VA to Ralph and Matilda (McGehee) Tandy. Her father's maternal lines include the Mills, Clopton and Booth families of colonial Virginia and England. The Tandy family moved to Christian County, KY in 1816, where in 1826 Frances Ann married Calvin Boales (1800-1853), son of James and Elizabeth (Bradshaw) Boales. Frances Ann and Calvin had three children in Kentucky: Dabney McGehee (1827-1917), James Addison (1829-1910), and Elisabeth (ca. 1833-ca. 1855).

James Edward Boales

By 1834, the family had immigrated to the State of Coahuila and Texas, which was already engaged in hostilities with Mexico. In December 1835, they were sworn as colonists in Robertson's Colony. Calvin served as Captain of a company of Mounted Rangers during the 1836 Revolution, and Frances Ann and her family participated in the "runaway scrape". The Republic established, she and Calvin settled on his headright labor near Old Nashville on the banks of the Brazos River (present Milam County) and had four more children: Ellen (ca. 1837-1867), Austin Henry (1841-1899), Margaret Ann (1847-1911) and Richard Brazile (1850-1940). Calvin continued service in Captain George B. Erath's ranging company against Indian depredations on the frontier in 1839, leaving Frances Ann as head of the household for many months.

After Calvin's untimely death in 1853, she moved with her family to Bee and San Patricio counties; in the 1880's to Bandera and Edwards counties. She died in Leakey, TX in 1892. A Citizen of the Republic of Texas Memorial Marker was placed on her headstone in 1987 by her descendants.

Caroline Boales Bass, (GGGD), 13302
Leona Boales Bass Marcellus, (GGD), 14275
Avis Boales Wheeler Armstrong, (GGD), 14298

BENJAMIN BOWLES came with a group of families from Missouri to Texas in 1827. Wife Betsy/Elizabeth was daughter of Daniel and Lucinda Smith Jeffries and niece of Henry Smith, first American Governor of Texas, 1835. (The Smiths' parents/Betsy Bowles' grandparents were Magdalen Woods and Rev. James Smith, Separatist Baptist Evangelist). Benjamin Bowles, who had applied for land near the San Jacinto River, acquired land in Milam/Bell County, Bastrop and Brazoria. He operated a brick factory business in Brazoria (Bowles-Bowen, a son–in–law). Other surnames of daughters included: Gillette, Maxey, Fessenden; Sample. After Benjamin's untimely death, Jesse P. Bowles, eldest son, was among minors who settled with their mother in Houston (cited

Memorial of Henry Smith

among First Baptist Church founding members: "Mrs. Bowles of Kentucky"-state of coming together of families- Bowles, Jefferies, Smith; Woods- before some moved to Missouri).

Memorial of Henry Smith

Youngest son of Benjamin and Betsy, Henry S. Bowles, namesake of his great uncle, was born the year of the families' move to Texas, 1827, and married, in 1849, Martha White, daughter of Abel and Nancy Denman White (Patriot Album I). Named heir was son Benjamin Burleson Bowles. Among surnames of daughters were: Young/ Hittson, Duer, Stautzenberger/Roberts, Marshall; Whatley. Henry Bowles died in Hempstead, 1876, year of birth of grandson Benjamin Bowles Whatley, born to Julia S. Bowles and Martin Franklin Whatley and married, in 1909, to Johnnie Ruth Shapard. Surnames of their daughters were: Kemp, Lucky, Allman, Fritz. Son is John Franklin Whatley. Oral history tradition seeks documentation for connection of these families to Indian ancestry primarily through Chief John Bowles, killed in East Texas battle, 1839.

Governor Henry Smith, with Sam Houston and Chief Bowles, had secured a treaty (dropped by successors) granting the lands they were planting in grains and vegetables to peaceful tribes. Smith used a large button from his coat imprinted with a circled five-point star is the first official Texas seal. His magnificent bronze statue, financed in 1936 by DRT, may be seen today overlooking highway 36 east of Brazoria Elementary School. Carved in two granite columns are facts detailing significant contributions to the republic of Texas. Site of the Smith farm home in Brazoria also has a 1936 Centennial Marker now face down by an uprooting tree on private ranch property inaccessible to the public. Although Governor Smith-who married successfully three Gillette sisters, losing two to early deaths-had nine children, his descendants also have various surnames beginning with (Harriet Smith) Fulton. The documented importance of their patriot ancestor has made it easier for cousins to connect branches to family trees.
Julia Ruth Whatley Kemp, (GGGD) of Benjamin Bowles and Abel H. White), #19422

SUSAN BRADY, born to Ezekial A. and Mary Castleberry Brady in Alabama on Sept. 8, 1842. Ezekial A. Brady was born in 1812 in Georgia. He first married Caroline Morris on Dec. 31, 1835 in Upson County, GA. He then was married to Mary Castleberry, born in Georgia and 1824, on Feb. 25, 1840 in Upson County. A son, James was born to Ezekial A. and Mary before they left Georgia.

Upson County was created in 1824 from land ceded to Georgia by the Creek Indians at the Treaty of Indian Springs in 1821. This area extended from the

Susan Brady

Ocmulgee River to the Flint River through middle Georgia. There was a large influx of settlers into the area before Upson County was created from Monroe County, a portion of Pike County and a small section of Crawford County in 1824. The first census of Upson County in 1830 showed a population of 7013.

According to records, Ezekial was a blacksmith. Apparently, the family was ready to head west toward the Republic of Texas. Their second child, Susan, was born in Alabama. Since Susan was born in 1842 and the arrival date in the Republic of Texas was soon after, the family traveled across the southern states during a period of three years.

The family arrived in the Republic in time to receive a preemption grant of 320 acres of land dated Jan. 22, 1845. The grant was located on Big Cypress Creek, a tributary of Red River, in what was known as Red River County. The area was later in what is now Titus/Franklin Counties.

The 1850 Census Record of Titus County shows a daughter, Rachel, as a three year old. Other census records of 1860-1870 show other children: Twins Kissiah and Ezekial; Joseph; Richard; Demarris; John and Theodicia.

Hopkins County Court Texas Records show that E.A. and Mary Brady sold a portion of their land to Wm. Pickett in February 1875 for a sum of $100.00. Wm. Pickett had married Susan in 1866.

Then, Hopkins County Texas Court Records show that Susan, Kissiah, E.A. Jr.; Demarris; and John as heirs of E.A. and Mary Brady all joined in the sale of the additional land dated Sept. 4, 1889.

Susan Brady Pickett died Feb. 3, 1904 and is buried in the Sherley Cemetery, Hopkins County, TX. The Peter James Bailey Chapter of the Daughters of the Republic marked her grave with a Citizen of the Republic of Texas Marker on April 28, 1996. Susan is my maternal grandmother.
Ouineola Pickett Carpenter, #18881

CADER BUXTON BRENT arrived in the Republic of Texas in 1838. When he reached Texas from Henry County, TN, he received a third-class land grant #385 for 640 acres on Dec. 27, 1839, in Houston County. Members of the Brent family still own much of this land today.

Cader Buxton was born Nov. 26, 1818, in Halifax County, NC, to James and Sarah Simmons Brent. Sarah and James first moved their family to Tennessee and then headed to Texas in 1838 with five of their eight children. Three daughters married and remained in Henry County, TN.

In 1838, Cader Buxton Brent married Rebecca Cottrell Speer, born Feb. 14, 1825, to Levi and Sarah Dixon Speer of Surrey County, NC. The Brents farmed and ranched in the Holly Community, where they reared and educated their eight children.

Both Cader Buxton and his brother Peter E. served in the Mexican War. Cader Buxton was a Fourth Corporal and Peter E. was a private in Samuel Highsmith's Company from May 1848 until December 1848.

Also, Cader Buxton and his son James Augusta and Peter E. served the confederacy during the Civil War. Cader Buxton served in the reserve Cavalry Company of the 11th Brigade, Trinity County. (Trinity County was formed in 1850 from part of Houston County.) Peter E., who served in the 13th Calvary, County B, was killed in the war. James Augusta, who served in the 20th Infantry Company I, has a Civil War marker in the Holly Cemetery.

Cader Buxton Brent died Jan. 31, 1908, and was buried in the Holly Cemetery. His wife, Rebecca Cottrell, died Aug. 12, 1893, and was buried there also.
Claire Jean Click Clapp, (GGD), 14783

BETHANY BREWER, daughter of Henry and Susannah Mitchell Brewer was born March 8, 1808, in Georgia. She was married to William Taylor Brewer. They moved to Texas at the time her parents Henry and Susannah Mitchell Brewer relocated around Nacogdoches. Bethany and William T. had 1O children. They were: Preston William, born Aug. 7, 1831, married Mary Baugh; Henry Dexter, born Dec. 21, 1834, married Josephine; Cecila Ann, born 1836, married J.L. Winkle; Julia Ann, born Feb. 20, 1839, died Jan. 8, 1858; Kinion Kendrick, born March 24, 1840, married Elizabeth Carter (died in child birth), married Victoria Adeline Bivens; Susie A., born Jan. 4, 1842, died Dec. 15, 1850; Matilda S., born Nov. 12, 1843, married Robert Scott (died in the Civil War), married John Gail Smith; William Burton, born Feb. 18, 1845; Clarissa Letitia, born May 29, 1846, married Henry Bivens; Nancy, born Dec. 29, 1848, married W.G. (Whig) Bivens.

They received a land grant in Kaufman County and moved with the family in June 1840 where they farmed and ranched until their deaths.

Bethany and William T. are buried in the Brewer Cemetery in Prairieville, Kaufman County, TX.
Arlene Spann Garey, (GGGD), 22550
Jacqueline Garey, (GGGGD), 22551

HENRY BREWER was born on Oct. 24, 1776 in North Carolina. He married Susannah Mitchell on Aug. 31, 1800, in Greene County, GA. They had 11 children: Tempie, Aug. 12, 1802, married William Parker; George, Sept. 30, 1804, married Elena Brewer; Sarah, July 3, 1806, married Greenberry Brewer; Henry Mitchell, June 3, 1807, married Elizabeth Scarborough; Bethany, March 8, 1808, married William Taylor Brewer; Nancy, 1810, married Abram Scarborough; William Christian, Dec. 15, 1812, married Amanda Taylor; Mary, April 23, 1814, married Thomas Dorsey Brooks; James, 1816, married Harriett Brewer; Clarissa, November 1817, married Alexander McKinza; John, Jan. 23, 1819, married Nancy Taylor.

His big dream took him to the area of Nacogdoches, TX. He received his Mexican Land Grant Oct. 22, 1834, where he settled with his family on Brewer Mountain. Henry and son, John, fought in the Battle of Nacogdoches. Henry Mitchell Brewer and sons–in-law, Thomas Brooks and Alexander McKinza fought in the Battle of San Jacinto. Henry was an adventurous, hard working man with strong family values as that trait is apparent in his descendents.

Henry and Susannah are buried in the Brewer Cemetery in Nacogdoches County, TX.
Arlene Spann Garey, (GGGGD), 22550
Jacqueline Garey, (GGGGGD), 22551

KINION KENDRICK BREWER, son of Bethany and William T. Brewer was born March 24, 1840 in Nacogdoches County, TX. He married Elizabeth Carter, Nov. 4, 1867. They had a daughter Mary Louise. Elizabeth died in childbirth. He married Victoria Adeline Bivens Sept. 4, 1870. They had 10 children. They were: Julia Ann born Jan. 18, 1872, married Meno

Hunt; Robert Lee born Dec. 17, 1873, died Aug. 7, 1874; William Elbert born Aug. 28, 1875, married Emma Mitchell; Lillie Belle born Nov. 19, 1877, married Hiram Hilburn; Samuel Ross born Aug. 28, 1880, bachelor; Fannie Mac born Jan. 19, 1883, married William J. Blaylock; Charles Preston born Aug. 1, 1885, married Nora Myrtle Jones; Christopher Columbus born March 28, 1888, married Rosa Blaylock; Walter Riley

Kinion Kendrick Brewer and wife, Victoria Adeline Bivens

born June 24, 1891, bachelor; Bessie Mae born April 1, 1895, married Addison Nix.

Kinion entered the Civil War as a sergeant. He fought in battles at Shiloh, Murfreesboro, Chickamaugua and the siege of Vicksburg. He also served as a frontier scout.

Kinion Kendrick and Adeline Victoria are buried in Sidney, Comanche County, TX.
Arlene Spann Garey, (GGD), 22550
Jacqueline Garey, (GGGD), 22551

SAMUEL C. BRICE owned land in Shelby County, TX by 1839. He was born in Spartanburg, SC in 1781. He married Elizabeth Price in Wilkinson County, MS on March 10, 1814. They had 10 children: John Coulter born Dec. 11, 1814, married Hettie Frame, son born ca. 1817; daughter born ca. 1819; daughter born ca. 1821; Nancy born 1824, married Sherman Grosvenor; Rosannah born 1826, married William Webb; Samuel C. Jr. born 1828, married Mary Jane Thompson; Sarah G. born 1831; Eliza born 1836; Margaret J. born 1838, married Guilford West.
Patsy Cummings McKelvy, (GGGD of Samuel Brice), DAR #21279

WILLIAM B. BRIDGES is listed with "Austin's Old 300", served in the volunteer Army of Texas under Captain John Alley in 1835, was Post Master for the Lyon's Post Office, was Justice of Peace in Fayette County. He was a hat maker. A merchant advertised on Feb. 12, 1831 in the "Mexican Citizen", a San Felipe newspaper; "wool hats made by William B. Bridges, warranted rain proof".

Bridges came to Texas in the early 1820's; his land grant is dated July 21, 1824. It is believed that his first wife and children had died in Mississippi before he came to Texas. He married in 1824 to Mrs. Cynthia Ross. They had three daughters: Mary, Elizabeth, and Martha.

DeWitt Clinton Lyons

Cynthia Bridges died in December 1831. Bridges then married Eliza Ann Lyons Tribble.

Eliza Lyons Tribble Bridges was the daughter of James and Martha Lyons. James and Martha Lyons had nine children: Seymour Clinton, John, Harriet, Eliza, George, Clarissa, DeWitt Clinton, Julia, and Warren. Seymour Lyons married William B. Bridges' daughter Mary. DeWitt Lyons married Bridges' daughter Elizabeth.

On Oct 15, 1837, James Lyons and son Warren were doing chores on their farm near Schulenberg, Fayette County. A band of Comanche Indians attacked them killing James. Warren was taken captive and raised as a Comanche. In 1848, he returned home. Martha Lyons died Aug. 20, 1873. William B. Bridges died in 1853.

Shirley Cottle Reed, (GGGGD), DRT #16842

GEORGE WASHINGTON BROOKS

GEORGE WASHINGTON BROOKS was born May 21, 1808, Virginia. On April 19, 1831, he married Eliza Ann Clayton in Jefferson County, MS. They applied to Austin's colony, May 1831. His headright certificate is dated Feb. 22, 1838.

By 1832, Brooks was serving in the Army of the Republic of Texas, at the Battle of Velasco. As Brooks was leaving on a recruiting trip back east, his friend William Travis criticized his unshaven appearance. When Brooks replied that he had no razor, Travis loaned him his own. Fate decreed that the razor would never be returned to its rightful owner, and the razor remained in the Brooks family for three generations. Tradition held that each young man had his first shave with it.

The family eventually settled in DeWitt County, and numbered 12 children before the death of Eliza Ann around 1860. In 1864, Brooks married a Civil War widow, Rachel Ann Jane Rhode Roach, of Lavaca County and fathered three more children. He raised horses and mules for the Confederacy and burned a trunkfull of Confederate money after the War. One of his sons, Old Texas Brooks, married the sister of Rachel Roach, Margaret Elizabeth Rhode, in 1875. Their eight children included three sons who grew to adulthood: Texas Telefus, Sam Houston, and my grandfather, Henry Clayton. In 1965, the heirs of Sam Houston Brooks donated Travis' razor to the Alamo, where it can be seen today.

George Washington Brooks died Feb. 1, 1887 and is buried at Harwood, Gonzales County.

Jan Baertl, (GGGD), 18688

JOSHUA D. BROWN

JOSHUA D. BROWN, 1816–1877, born in Madison County, Kentucky and died Feb. 16, 1876 in Kerr County, Kerrville, TX. He followed his parents to Sabine County prior to Oct. 1, 1837. Edward Brown and Jenny Cambell moved in 1831. Joshua received final unconditional certificate for 640 acres, July 1844, # 90.

Attesting to his service record he swore that he participated in The Texas Revolution, Mounted Volunteers, Captain Adam Zumwalt's command, in the Wall Campaign in 1842, fought against the Mexican Army at Salado Creek in Bexar County Sept. 11, 1842 at the

Joshua D. Brown

Dawson Massacre, was in the Summerville Campaign, known as the Mier Expedition 1842, Captain Isaac Mitchell's command of the regiment of Colonel James R. Cook; crossed the Rio Grande into Mexico at Laredo and returned; served in the Cherokee Expedition, General Ruskin's command 1839; and was in Colonel Ben McColloah's Spy Command. Brown's declaration was to obtain a Texas Veteran's pension.

While in Green DeWitt's Colony at Gonzales he became a good friend of Major James Kerr. He moved to Currys Crossing, now in Kendall County and learned the trade of shingle making from cypress trees. He moved up the Guadalupe River and started his shingle-making business. Other men gathered and the settlement was called "Brownsburg". The site chosen in 1846 is now the 900 block of Water Street. The postal authorities requested the name "Brownsburg" be changed. Brown selected Kerrsville to honor his friend Captain James Kerr. In 1866 the "s" was dropped, and "Kerrville" it remains.

Joshua married Eleanor Smith July 20, 1846 in Gonzales County. Mary Louisa was born in 1847. Eleanor died in 1848. Joshua married Sara Jane Goss May 20, 1849, in Gonzales County. Sara was born May 8, 1833 in Randolf County, NC. They had four boys and three girls.

In 1855 Joshua signed a petition to form a new county out of part of Bexar County. In 1856 he purchased 640 acres owned by Benjamin Cage. At the first session of Kerr County Commissioners Court he proposed the county site on four acres in Survey 116. On Oct. 18, 1856 the deed was accepted for Kerr County. He purchased 2,000 acres, which part now is the site of Veteran's Administration Medical Center.

Joshua's life was interrupted with the Civil War and he enlisted March 4, 1862, in the company of Mounted Volunteers, Texas Frontier Regiment, under the command of Colonel James M. Morris. His enlistment period was up on Feb. 7, 1863.

Joshua and Sara Jane are buried in the Brown-Goss Cemetery in Kerr County, Kerrville, TX. The cemetery received a Texas Historical Marker on April 17, 1946.

Eleanor Ann Brown born 1851-Peter O.A. Rees
John William Brown born 1854-Francis Henley
Mary E.L.A. Brown born 1847-
James Stevens Brown born 1859-Martha Ann Witt
Nicholas J. Brown born 1861-Elizabeth Fenley
Virginia A. Brown born 1868-Charles Barlemann
Alonzo Potter Brown born 1870-Grace Ida Stulting

Mary Louise Auld Saunders Lehman, (GGD), DRT 20830

MRS. MARGARET "JACKSON" BROWN

MRS. MARGARET "JACKSON" BROWN's parents are Thomas Jackson and Louise Cottle, and they came to Texas in 1829, joined DeWitt's Colony and received a grant of a league and a labour of land on May 5, 1831 in Gonzales County, TX. Thomas Jackson is of Irish descent, while the Cottles ancestors were in Plymouth, MA in 1620. Thomas Jackson and Louise's brother George Washington Cottle died at the Alamo, March 6, 1836. The Jackson's known children are Lee, Margaret and George. Lee was killed by Comanche Indians in the Battle of Bandera Pass while serving with Colonel Jack Hayes Ranger Company in 1843.

Margaret Jackson married James S. Brown June 16, 1844 in Gonzales, TX, divorced March 1857 in Kerr County, TX. 14 months later James married Rachel Turner and moved to Karnes County, TX.

After the divorce, Margaret promptly moved to Bandera County, TX. Where, she bought and sold parcels of Ranch land where she raised horses, mules, goats, sheep and hogs to support herself and the children. Their lives were threatened many times by Indians. One night during a full moon Margaret heard a commotion in the horse corral, shot into the darkness and heard an Indian howl in pain as he fled. Her children loved to tell that story to their families.

Margaret homesteaded land in 1889 on the East Frio River, then in Bandera County, TX receiving her certificate after she was 70 years old. She died there in 1892.

The chimney is still standing on the ranch where she homesteaded. It is made of handcut limestone, native to the area. *Margaret Evans*

JOHN W. AND KIZIAH BRUMMETT

JOHN W. AND KIZIAH BRUMMETT were early Texas settlers. John W., a farmer, was born in Kentucky on July 28, 1815. He married Kiziah Jones, born in Kentucky in 1815, on April 11, 1846 in Fannin County, TX. Kiziah, entitled to 640 acres of land by virtue of a Mercer Colony Certificate, was a widow with five children when she and John married. Her children: Mary Jane Jones born in Missouri in 1834, married Alvin S. Hovey from Vermont on March 23, 1860; Rebecca Jones born in Missouri in 1836, married David Yarbrough on Nov. 11, 1860; Samuel D.C. Jones born in Missouri in 1838; John Jones born in Missouri in 1841; and Sarah

William Pierson Brummett, son of John and Kiziah

E. Jones born in Texas in 1843, married (1) John Taylor, Jan. 20, 1863, (2) George Sadler, Dec. 1, 1870.

John and Kiziah's children: William Pierson Brummett, America Brummett, and Josephine Brummett. William Pierson Brummett was born June 1847. He married Tennessee Sadler, who was born July 12, 1851. They were married Jan. 2, 1868 in Atascosa County, TX at the home of W.D. Sadler. Tennessee was the daughter of William D. and Elizabeth Clark Sadler who

L to R: Sarah E. Jones/Brummett Taylor Sadler and Kiziah Jones Brummett

came to Texas from Jackson County, TN after 1850. One of the children of William and Tennessee was Elizabeth Kiziah, born July 23, 1869 in Frio County, TX. Elizabeth was married on Dec. 29, 1883 to Allen H. Shoemake, born Sept. 6, 1863 in Frio County, TX. America Brummett, born Nov. 3, 1849 in Texas, died Oct. 11, 1932 in Frio County, TX. She married (1) William Bishop, Jan. 24, 1867, (2) Wade Hampton, (3) Theodore Pharlow. Josephine Brummett, born March 2, 1855 in Texas, married Nathaniel Tomas Mangum Dec. 24, 1868.

John W. Brummett, who received a headright in Delta County, TX, died on May 13, 1881 and was buried in the Brummett Cemetery, Frio County, TX. The cemetery, which has a Texas Historical Marker was deeded to Frio County Sept. 21, 1889 by Kizzie Brummett and her son William P. Brummett.
Audrey Ruth Shoemake Roby Mercer, (GGGD), 20119-S
Jo Nell Shoemake Robertson, (GGGD), 14504
Margaret K. Shoemake Jenschke, (GGGD), 14354

JAMES BUCHANAN

JAMES BUCHANAN was born circa 1811 in Alabama. He came to Texas in 1834 with his wife Mary (who was born circa 1814) and their first child, William. They were with Stephen F. Austin's Fifth Colony. They received a league of land in Burleson County, TX from the Mexican Government on Oct. 19, 1835.

James Buchanan, a private in the Texas Army, fought and died a hero at the Alamo March 6, 1836 and is buried there. His wife Mary was pregnant at the time of her husband's death. 44 days later, she gave birth to their second son, James Houston on April 19, 1936 in San Felipe, TX.

Oliver Peter Buchanan, grandson of James Buchanan

James Houston married Ellen Jones, who was born circa 1840 in Alabama. They had six children: James Curtis, Aaron C. Pharaoh, Oliver Peter, Estelle, and Roxie. My grandfather, the fourth child, Oliver Peter Buchanan was born Sept. 13, 1872 in Dimebox, TX. His picture is shown above.

Oliver Peter married Alice Clements Bonneville on June 2, 1902. They had six children: Gladys Marie, Ollie, Oliver Peter, George Oliver, James Houston, and Alice Marguerite (my mother). Oliver Peter and Alice Clements were early settlers of Midland County when it was the frontier of Texas. The first producing oil well in Midland County was drilled on their extensive ranch in 1944. On Dec. 14, 1928, Oliver Peter died in Marlin, TX. His wife died June 8, 1970 and they are buried in Midland, TX.

Alice Marguerite was born Feb. 18, 1914. She was married on March 28, 1931 to Durward Elder, who was born on May 4, 1912. I was their only child, Blanche Joan Elder, born on Nov. 22, 1931. Alice later had four more children prior to her death on Sept. 30, 1983. She is buried in Midland, TX.
Blanche J. Elder Sullivan, (GGGD), 21603
Jo Anne Sullivan Moore, (GGGGD), 21716

DANIEL M. BUIE

DANIEL M. BUIE was born May 16, 1808, in North Carolina to Malcolm Buie. The earlier Buies were leaders in the Philadelphus Church in Robeson County, NC. They were devoted and active members in the Presbyterian Church and required their ministers to preach in their native Gaelic.

After Daniel's grandfather died in about 1823, Daniel's father, Malcom, migrated to Henry County, TN. Daniel Buie, who had settled in Henry County with his father pushed further westward and became the first Buie on Texas soil.

Daniel received his Texas land grant, number 1432, the Feb. 1, 1838. He settled in Nacogdoches County, which later became Henderson County. His land was on the line of present day Van Zandt and Kaufman Counties. The area schools were named after him, and he was very active in the early development of the community. He farmed this area until his death on Aug. 15, 1876.

In about 1832, Daniel married Frances Caudle. He and Frances had eight children, and several of their children were born in Texas. Their children were: Mary C., born about 1834; William R., born about 1835; John Alford, born 1838 married Amanda Harrison; Susan E., born 1841 married Rev. Stanley;

Robert Daniel, born 1843; Margaret Ellen, born 1845 married James A. Bivins; Alford E., born May 11, 1849 married Elizabeth Denson; and James M., born May 10, 1858 married Emma Lides. Daniel and Frances Buie are buried, along with many of their children, in the Cedarvale Cemetery, which once was named Heidle-Buie, in Kaufman County, TX. Daniel's tomb has the earliest date of birth in the cemetery.

Margaret E., listed above, married James A. Bivins in 1865. He was the son of James G.W. and Naomi Bivins, and he was born in 1839 in Tennessee. Their children were: Henry Daniel, born Feb. 2, 1866 married Minnie Gordon; William M., born Feb. 18, 1867 married Ella Stuart; Sarah Jane, born Dec. 11, 1869 married Charles Jackson; John, born 1872; Richard Elmer, born March 11, 1873 married Gustie Ophelia Crisp; Thomas A., born Feb. 18, 1875; Mary born 1879 married Vinson Ashworth; and Samuel, born March 30, 1888. James A. Bivins and Margaret Buie Bivins are buried in Cedarvale Cemetery near her parents, Daniel and Frances Buie.

Roxanne Burchfiel, (GGGGD)

JAMES M. BULLOCK

JAMES M. BULLOCK was born in 1820 in North Carolina. He came to Texas in 1843. He married Amelia P. Fuller ca. 1849 in Upshur County. Amelia was the daughter of Benjamin F. Fuller and "Polly" Castleberry who came to Texas in 1834 first settling in San Augustine County. James and Amelia had 12 children: Martha Bullock born ca. 1853; James H. Bullock born ca. 1854, Benjamin F. Bullock born February 1855, married Susan Henderson; Thomas W. Bullock born February 1858; Joseph Bullock born ca. 1859; Amanda B. Bullock born 1859, married Albert "Boone" Forqueran 1875 Caldwell County; Susan Adaline Bullock born Feb. 20, 1861, married Newton Blackmore 1885 Caldwell County; Stephen T. Bullock born 1863; Richard J. Bullock born 1865; Melissa "Lizzie" Bullock born 1867, married Horace Scales Ridout 1883 Caldwell County; Samuel Bullock born 1872; and Oliver born 1873. James died in 1883 in Caldwell County and is buried in the Wells Cemetery. Amelia died in 1905 and is buried in the Preece Cemetery in Travis County. James M. Bullock was a Private, 29th Brigade of the Texas Cavalry, Confederate States Army. His 1863 Springfield rifle is still in family hands.

Shirley Blackmore Smith, (GGGD), #17475
Peggy Blackmore Tombs, (GGGD), #17476
Camille Blackmore Garey, (GGGD), # 17477

CHARLES BARNETT BURKHAM

CHARLES BARNETT BURKHAM, second son of James (E.) Burkham and grandson of Charles Burkham, was born July 28, 1833, in the Burkham Settlement along the Red River in Northeast Texas. He married (1) Elizabeth Jane in 1854. A first son, James, was born to this marriage. It appears Elizabeth died during the time Charles Barnett was serving with his brothers in the Texas Calvary, 23rd Regiment, Company "F", as a beef herder. His second wife was Nancy Partain, a widowed seamstress with at least three young children. Several children were

Charles Barnett Burkham

born to the couple prior to her death in the late 1870's in Hopkins County.

Charles Barnett married an orphaned girl, Martha Frances "Fannie" "Red" Morris, born March 26, 1862, in Travis County, Texas, in Stout's Creek Church in Hopkins County on Aug. 10, 1879. To this marriage were born 14 children: Kimp, born Feb. 13, 1881, married (1) Elvina "Vennie" Newkirk, Jan. 19, 1903; Carrie, born Feb. 7,

Samuel Marvin Burkham and wife, Fearl Ester McCullough

1883, married Lee Easley, July 3, 1898; Charles "Chock", married ___; Martha Frances "Fannie", born Jan. 18, 1885, married (1) __ Burkhead, Dec. 16, 1900, (2) __Murphy, died ca. 1983; Jennie, born Nov. 18, 1887, died Jan. 27, 1892; Samuel Marvin, born Jan. 11, 1890, married Fearl Ester McCullough, Mt. Vernon, Franklin County, Nov. 26, 1911, died May 3, 1946, Carlsbad, NM, buried Lookout Cemetery, out of Malaga, NM. His twin, Susannah, married W.T. Miller, died July 26, 1908, no issue; James "Jim", born Jan. 12, 1892, served in WWI, never married; Jeff, born Dec. 30, 1893, married Clara Winters, died Carlsbad, NM; Tommy, born Jan. 21, 1895, died June 9, 1912, no issue; Stonewall Jackson "Boss", born Jan. 26, 1898, married Addie Frances circa 1961, died Jan. 24, 1980, no issue; Ora, born Feb. 12, 1904, married James Buchanan, died circa 1997; Nollie, born Sept. 22, 1906, married Cy Hart, died in the New Boston, Texarkana area.

The seven children of Samuel Marvin and wife, Fearl Ester McCullough are: Dessie, born in Hagansport, TX, Franklin County, July 3, 1913, married James Fearney Wheat Dec. 29, 1930, who was born Jan. 30, 1908, Holdenville, OK, and died Dallas, TX, Sept. 6, 1972; Bertha, married Hoy Hancock; Dortha, married (1) Ray Pruitt, (2) James Simmons; Velma Angie, married Chris Skinner; Tommie, married Oscar Weisz; Woodrow Boss, married Ruby __; and Albert Cidney, married Katy __. Sons, grandsons, and great-grandsons continue the farming tradition in West Texas and New Mexico.

Charles Barnett was a stock raiser and farmer. Family stories say he had a turning mill, gristmill, and other early industries. He was a member of the Masonic Order. Sons, grandsons, and great-grandsons continue the farming tradition in East and West Texas and New Mexico.

Martha Frances, as one of the last surviving widows of the Confederacy in Texas applied for her husband's pension in 1936. A $10,000 check from Standard Oil, endorsed, but never cashed, was found among her papers, along with tax receipts and other papers showing her attempts to hold on to the land following her husband's death in 1914. She died in Sulphur Bluff, TX, in 1960, with hundreds of descendants attending the funeral. Charles and Martha Frances are buried in Wims Cemetery near Hagansport, Franklin County, TX.

Eunice Wheat Futrell, (GGD), No. 13284S
Mary Katharine Futrell Jovicich, (GGGD), No. 13288S

CHARLES (E.) BURKHAM

CHARLES (E.) BURKHAM was born circa 1779 in Virginia. Charles and his wife, Nancy Ann Abbet, born in Indiana, list their arrival in Northeast Texas as July 4, 1816 (Wavell Registro, 1833). They married in Madison County, KY, Sept. 30,

1804. Children born before their caravan arrived in the area were: James (E.), circa 1805, Clay County, KY; Susannah, Feb. 29, 1808, in Indiana; and Cynthianna, circa 1810. Children born in Texas were; Ahijah, circa 1820; Phillip who died as a young boy; and Benjamin Franklin, circa 1825. James married Matilda, circa 1830, and died June 1880; Susannah, married first to James Barker, widowed, then married neighbor Hudson Posey Benningfield. She died in Atascosa County, TX, in 1880; and Cynthianna who married Thomas Holloway, lived in Louisiana, probably widowed, and returned to Hopkins County with her children to be near her brother, James, in Hopkins County by 1854. Ahijah married Louisa Jane Birdwell, Feb. 8, 1849, and died Oct. 2, 1854, probably in Bowie County. Benjamin Franklin married Lucinda-The Burkhams were farmers and stock raisers.

It was not until 1819 that the United States and Spain settled a boundary dispute created during the Louisiana Purchase of 1803. The U.S. relinquished its claim to the south side of the Red River. Grants given by Spain and then Mexico were uncertain and in confusion for early settlers. Walter Pool and Charles Burkham were the first in the area, soon followed by Claiborne Wright in September of 1816. All were anxious to have clear title to the rich Red River lands.

By March 1820, the family was permanently located in the Burkham Settlement at the mouth of Mill Creek in present Bowie County. *Brown's Indian Wars and Pioneers of Texas*, tell of early encounters with the Indians. In 1827, Captain Burkham, Nathaniel Robbins, and newcomer, Dr. Lewis B. Dayton, were given permission by the Mexican government to raise an army to go against the fierce Comanche and Pawnee. Burkham made a plea on June 12, 1827, to residents near Pecan Point, both north and south of the Red River, urging them to join and fight. The majority wanted to wait for help from the United States soldiers at Fort Towson, so an "army" was never raised.

Burkham served as sheriff, coroner, and a commissioner to form a passable road to Sevier Township and to permanently locate a Seat of Justice for the county on Oct. 23, 1832. Several meetings of the court had been held in the Burkham home.

Charles Burkham purchased additional land through an agent in Nacogdoches in 1834. He and Ben Milam, who had improved six acres of land while living in the Burkham Settlement, went before Mexican officials in an attempt to clarify land titles.

In 1836, Charles and 16 year old Ahijah joined Thomas Robbin's Company of mounted riflemen from Red River County and rode to join the Texas army. His eldest son, James, was with William Becknell's Company (Becknell had lived in the Burkham Settlement for a time).

In the Clarksville Cemetery, a blackjack oak may still stand, known as Page's Limb. In the winter of 1837, Charles Burkham, riding his well-marked mule, and a neighbor went to look for a run-away slave. Legend tells of their stopping at the house of a man named Page. Page, thinking their heavy saddlebags contained gold, murdered both men. Days later, neighbors, looking for the men, came upon Page's son–in–law riding Burkham's mule. A confession was forced. Page was arrested and brought to Clarksville where citizen's court voted to hang him.

In February 1838, a Republic of Texas Board of Commissioner granted posthumously to Charles Burkham his first-class land grant. Early maps show other grants to Charles and his sons, Ahijah, James, and Benjamin Franklin.

James Burkham was administrator of his father's estate. An appraisal and sale was held of household belongings, cattle, horses and equipment. James advertised in the Natchitoches paper for Cynthianna and her husband to come for the settlement. Susannah and Hudson Posey Benningfield were nearby. Ahijah and Benjamin Franklin's interests, were, represented by long-time friend, James E. Hopkins.

Nancy Ann Burkham died of a stroke in 1845. Legend tells of gold she had buried after Charles' death, but she could not speak to tell her children where to find it. Following the settlement of the estate, James and Benjamin Franklin moved to the newly formed Hopkins County. That same year, Hudson Posey, Ahijah, and Benjamin Franklin marched south to join the Curtis Call in the Mexican War. Later, Susannah and Hudson Posey Benningfield and their children settled in Atascosa County.

Some accounts of early events in Northeast Texas list James (E.) Burkham, as the first Burkham to Texas. Captain Charles Burkham arrived in the area in 1816 under Spanish rule. He swore his allegiance to Mexico and no doubt said he was a Catholic. He served as a spy for the United States, and a bill to pay him for his services was before the United States Congress in 1834. He knew men such as Milam, Houston, and Crockett, and played a part in forming the Republic.

The Burkham settlement is noted on early maps of Texas. A Burkham School and Burkham Creek were named for him but no longer exist. He rode, along with his sons, to fight for Texas at San Jacinto, arriving one day subsequent to the battle. More may be read about Burkham and this area in Rex Strickland's *Chronicles of Oklahoma*. The name Charles has been passed through the Burkham line to the present time. It is a rich Texas heritage.

Dessie Burkham Wheat, (GGGD), No. 15277
Eunice Wheat Futrell, (GGGGD), No. 13282
Mary Futrell Jovicich, (GGGGGD), No. 13287

JAMES (E.) BURKHAM, born in Clay County, KY, in the late summer of 1805, came to Northeast Texas by wagon with his parents, Charles and Nancy Ann (Abbot) Burkham. The Burkham's list their arrival in the area as July 4, 1816. (Wavell Registro, 1833). By March 1820, the family lived in the Burkham Settlement at the mouth of Mill Creek in present Bowie County.

The area was rich in game and hunting for the most part was easy; however, bear hunts could become harrowing. One account tells of a bear fight in the water. Burkham's life-long friend, Henry Stout, lost his knife trying to stab the bear underwater. Burkham, paddled the skiff wildly to prevent it being turned over by the bear and Stout struggling underwater. Stout finally killed the bear with the help of Captain Charles Burkham's bear dogs (Red River Recollections, 1986.)

Great granddaughters of James Burkham, daughters of Samuel Marvin Burkham are Dessie Burkham Wheat, Dortha Burkham Pruitt Simmons, and Bertha Burkham Hancock.

As his father's eldest son, James was Charles' assistant in the business of fighting marauding tribes such as the Comanche and Osage, keeping good relations with the nearby Caddo Indians, serving to keep good and passable roads repaired, cutting timbers for more farming land, riding circuit to obtain jurors for the court, and maintaining peace in the Burkham Settlement.

In the Texas War of Independence, James rode with Captain William Becknell's Company of men from Red River County to join Houston's army. They arrived one day subsequent to the Battle of San Jacinto. For his service to the Republic, he received a first-class grant in Red River County, a bounty grant of 320 acres in Lamar County, and land in the future Hopkins County, along with a pension of 250 dollars. James and Henry Stout witnessed the pension request in 1875.

James Burkham married Matilda__, born circa 1812 in Tennessee. The following children were born in Red River County; Elliott (B.), born circa 1832; Charles Barnett, born July 28, 1833, died, Jan. 23, 1914; William T., born circa 1838; Thursy Ann "Teresa", born circa 1841; and Thomas Jefferson, born circa 1844. The above sons all served in Company "F" of the 23rd Regiment of the Texas Confederate Calvary, along with James' younger brother, Benjamin Franklin (Joining at Sulphur Bluff, Hopkins County). Children born in Hopkins County were: Mary C., born circa 1852; James, born circa 1853; and John, born circa 1858.

James and Matilda moved to Hopkins County near the present community of Sulphur Bluff about 1846. James joined the newly formed Old Tarrant Lodge, No. 91, of the Masonic Order. He probably had been a member along with his father of a lodge in Red River County. Their son, Charles Barnett, was a successful stockman and lived nearby.

Matilda Burkham preceded her husband in death, circa 1875. James died June 4, 1880, according to the census record, almost 64 years following his arrival in the beautiful Red River Valley of Northeast Texas.
Eunice Wheat Futrell, (GGGD), No. 13285S
Mary Katharine Futrell Jovicich, (GGGGD), No. 13290S

REBECCA BURLESON, Aaron Burleson born 1790 Kentucky and Rebecca Rutledge born 1795 Kentucky, married in 1810 Madison County, AL and had 10 children.

After serving in the American Revolution, Aaron was on his was to meet his good friend, Daniel Boone. He was killed by Indians while, crossing the Clinch River in Hardeman County, TN. After the death of Aaron, Rebecca married John Baker. No children were born of this marriage. John died prior to the arrival of a wagon train in Texas. Rebecca resumed using the Burleson name after the death of her husband. Rebecca stated, in February 1838, before Bastrop Texas Land Board that she was the head of household and had immigrated to Texas in 1835. She received a league and a labor, which she located in Milam district. On 1847, she sold this land to John R. Burleson. The descendants of Aaron and Rebecca number in the thousands, and they include numerous distinguished families who made valuable contributions to the early history of Texas.
Gerald Dean Hector Lilly, (GGGGGD), 17208

JAMES BURLESON, son of Aaron Burleson II and Volley Hogan Burleson, was born on May 4, 1758 in North Carolina. He married Elizabeth Shipman on Dec. 25, 1791. Elizabeth was born in 1775. James Burleson served the Republic of Texas as soldier and received a land grant. His residence during the Republic of Texas was San Augustine, TX and Mina, Bastrop County, TX. The Burleson name is of Scandinavian origin, settling in

Wales in 1617. Four brothers came to the United States, two settling in the North and two in the South. Burlesons were the first in the U.S. to make thread on a large scale and one of the first to pack meat. James Burleson was a relative of Dr. Rufus Burleson, founder of Baylor University, and a relative of General Edward Burleson, famous Indian fighter who came to Texas with James Bowie. He served in the Creek War, was Commissary for Andrew Jackson, and fought in the battle of New Orleans in 1815. He migrated from North Carolina to Tennessee, then to Alabama, on to Missouri, then back to Tennessee before 1827, when he moved to Texas. James Burleson died on Jan. 3, 1836. He was my great-great-grandfather.
Patricia Phillips Pate

JOHN BURLESON "Hopping" John Burleson, born Oct. 19, 1795, Rutherford County, NC to Joseph Sr. and Nancy Gage Burleson. A knee injury gave his walk a slight hop thus the name. Some of the places where his family lived were Jackson County, TN, Madrid, MO area and Madison County, AL. There he met and married Mary Margaret (Peggy) Pride born ca. 1796 on Feb. 14, 1814.

Eight children were born to them, confirmed by 1830 census Marion County, AL: Nancy, Dec. 25, 1814; Polly Dec. 8, 1817; Joseph Pride June 3, 1819; Abigial July 15, 1822; James Nov. 28, 1824; Elizabeth March 24, 1827; Johnathan April 26, 1829; and Aaron March 11, 1833 (born after census date). The family excluding Molly moved to Texas in 1837, verified by the Supreme Court of Texas case 28TX383. They are also on the tax record of Bastrop County 1840.

Peggy died March 17, 1847, Gonzales County TX. John married Mrs. Sarah Katherine McInnes Nov. 17, 1848. They had one child: Mary Ann Washington born March 13, 1850. John died at Lampasas April 13, 1878.

One may rightfully be proud of our Burleson ancestry for their bravery and unselfish contributions to Texas.
Jim Ellen Wells Adams, (GGGD), DRT 018534
*Burleson Family Bulletin Vol. X No. 3 P.1386. Permission granted by Editor Helen Burleson Kelso.

JOSEPH BURLESON JR. was born March 4, 1808, in Washington County, TN. He married Allie Murray Seaton Nov. 1, 1827, in Hardeman County, TN. He came to Texas in 1834 along with his father, Joseph Burleson Sr. They were in Stephen F. Austin's "Register Of Families" and received a land grant and settled and farmed four miles northwest of Smithville, Bastrop County, TX, on the Colorado River. His father's Bible is in the Alamo Museum. His mother, Nancy Gage, died Jan. 19, 1815, before he came to Texas.

Joseph and Allie are listed in the 1850 Bastrop County Census with the following children: George W., Joseph, Sarah J., Marion W., Susan M., James M., John F., and Murray. Marion W. was erroneously listed as a male. While residing near Smithville the Indians were very troublesome. He was in the Texas army, but after the fall of the Alamo he returned home to move his family to a safer place ("the runaway scrape"). Like many other settlers, he had no wagon and only one horse, but with the help of a neighbor, he made a wagon to which he hitched a yoke of young, wild steers, and was able to keep pace with the other settlers as they fled the Mexican army. His wife and two children rode the horse, and all arrived in safety at the Sabine River, where they remained until after the battle of San Jacinto. He returned to his home on the Colorado River late in the summer and planted a crop of corn and was able to help feed the community. Although he was not in the regular Texas army, he was a member of a company of minutemen, which took part in many skirmishes with the Indians and Mexicans. In 1846 he moved to Buckner's Creek, Bastrop County, where he engaged in farming and stock raising. Around 1870 he married Sarah E. Ansley and moved to Burnet County. He lived until 1891 at 83 years of age and is buried in Strickling Cemetery there. His first wife Allie died July 16, 1882, and is buried in the Burleson Family Cemetery near Smithville.

Elizabeth Graham Marsh Christian, (GGGD), 0226815
Diana Kent Marsh Fontana, (GGGD), 0226825

JOSEPH PRIDE BURLESON, born June 3, 1819, Marion County, AL to "Hopping" John Burleson, Oct. 19, 1795 Rutherford County, NC and Mary Margaret Pride Burleson ca. 1796, Alabama. Seven children (Molly stayed in Alabama) moved with their parents to Texas in 1833 and lived near Bastrop.

On April 26, 1849, Joseph Pride married Martha Jane Mauldin in Caldwell County, TX, daughter of William Poe and Sarah Jane Bryan Mauldin. While living there their first three children died in infancy and one nearly six years old. They moved to Lampasas County where four children were born: John Washington, Sarah Louisa Jane, Mary Elizabeth and Nancy Mariah. They moved to San Saba where Martha Louella and James Beverly (my grandfather) were born. They lived a short time on the South Conch River, Tom Green County, but encountered Indian "troubles". A favorite ole grey mare was stolen several times but after a few days would always find her way home. The family returned to San Saba and then started their trek westward, Goldthwaite, Brownwood, Garden City and to Dawson County at a place called Chicago. Their son, John, was trying to establish Chicago as the new county seat but failed. The town became Lamesa.

Joseph Pride died March 21, 1911 and was buried in the Lamesa Cemetery. Martha Jane died Sept. 18, 1917 and was buried beside him. Several of their children and grandchildren are buried there.

Jim Ellen Wells Adams, (GGD), DRT #018534
Information: an unpublished paper by Lynn Mauldin, (GGS), William Wesley Mauldin

MARTHA JANE MAULDIN BURLESON, born Dec. 29, 1830, Haywood County, TN to William Poe Mauldin and Sarah Jane Bryan Mauldin, was the second child of nine. She was 16 when her mother died (1847) in Caldwell County, TX.

Martha Jane's parents were educated people and had lived an affluent life at the plantation home of Susan's parents, Stephen and Rachael Bryan. Rachael came from a family of well–to–do Marylanders.

Martha Jane was 11 years old when her family (relatives both of her mother and father) moved to Texas. Some settled in Selby County but William Poe family settled in Washington County in the year 1841. Later the family moved near Lockhart. William Poe held several appointed offices in local and county offices. From her father, Martha Jane learned many remedies to help the sick.

Martha Jane married Joseph Pride Burleson April 26, 1849 in Caldwell County, TX. Their first three children died before

age six. Six children were born in Lampasas: John Washington June 6, 1857, Sarah Louisa Jane, Nov. 20, 1861, Mary Elizabeth Jan. 20, 1861, Nancy Mariah July 29, 1863. Martha Louella Jan. 17, 1867 and James Beverly April 5, 1869 (my grandfather) were born in San Saba.

As did their parents, the Joseph Pride family moved many times finally settling in Lamesa, Dawson County in 1903. Both were members of the Baptist Church. Joseph Pride died 1911 and Martha Jane died Sept. 18, 1917, both are buried in the Lamesa Cemetery.

Jim Ellen Wells Adams, (GGD), DRT #018534
Information: Unpublished paper by Lynn Mauldin, (GGS) William Wesley Mauldin.

MARY IVY BURLESON, a maternal great-great-grandmother, known by many as Little Granny, was born Oct. 20, 1841 at Rapides Parish, LA. Her parent's William and Louisa (Barton) Hay had seven children. The family moved to Texas in 1844 when Mary was three and her sister Caroline born the same year. Her first marriage, July 22, 1857 to Daniel Williams, they had three children, two died young. Then, Daniel Williams was killed by Indians in 1865. A story handed down, about Mary outside of her home making soap as they did those days, when she realizes an Indian was near, continued to stir mixture of lye in pot, when the Indian came up from behind she threw the lye on him. She married Jacob Burleson on July 16, 1868. They were parents of nine children, two of them died young. At the age of 91 on July 19, 1932, Mary died and was buried beside her husband Jacob Burleson, at Texas State Cemetery in Austin, TX.

Mary Burleson

Mr. & Mrs. Don Bigbee

SARAH ANN BURLESON, born May 22, 1817 in Lawrence County, AL, was the daughter of Aaron Burleson and Rebecca Rutledge. Sarah married Lorenzo D. Baker July 15, 1834 Hardeman County, TN. Their children are, Cynthia Jane born 1837, Mississippi, John C. born 1842 Texas, Spearman H. born 1846, Texas, Amanda H. born 1848, Texas, Malinda Elizabeth born 1851, James born 1855, Johnson born 1859, and Dixie born 1860. Lorenzo's father was John Baker who was married second to Rebecca Burleson. Lorenzo was born of the first marriage. His mother's name is unknown.

Sarah Ann Burleson Baker died Aug. 31, 1878 and is buried in the Brite Cemetery, Atascosa County, TX. Lorenzo D. (L.D. and Sallie) Sarah are listed on the 1850 Rusk County, TX census and the 1846 Grimes County, TX Poll Tax List.

Gerald Dean Hector Lilly, (GGGGD), 17208

LYDIA CAMPBELL, born 1787 in Stokes County, NC, to William and Lydia Campbell. About 1808, William moved his family to Madison County, AL, where Lydia married George Hunt, son of John Hunt; namesake for Huntsville. The Hunts moved into Lincoln County, TN where John Campbell, Manerva, William J, Sarah A., George W., Alexander D., and David M. were born. The last two children Elizabeth A. and Palmyra E. were born in Alabama.

The oldest son, John Campbell Hunt was in Texas by 1835 or earlier. After participating in the victory at San Jacinto, he persuaded his parents to migrate to Texas in 1837. There George and all the older boys filed for land. Sadly George Hunt developed a fever and died in Washington County in 1838.

Lydia and the younger children settled first in Bastrop County, then later in Fayette County. John Campbell Hunt is buried in the Oliver Hill Cemetery near Smithville, with brothers George W., Alexander D., and David M. Lydia was still shown as a farmer on the 1860 Census when she was 73. She died in 1875 survived by only two of her children, Manerva, the eldest daughter and Palmyra the youngest daughter.
Doris Maxwell Dell, (GGGGD), 13819

HARRY CAMPBELL

HARRY CAMPBELL, son of Jesse and Sarah Jones Campbell, was born Feb. 15, 1805 Washington, Orange County, VT. Married Sarah Jane, daughter of Moses Darling ca. 1829. He moved to New York where he acquired much property. The family lived in Elmont, Queens (now Nassau) County where my great-grandmother Caroline was born March 9, 1836.

Caroline Campbell Blundell

He moved to Jay County, IN. There he heard of great opportunities further west. They headed to Texas with merchandise for opening a store. Along White's Creek they decided was ideal for the family. Fall 1845 they settled in what became known as "Crossroads", the main avenue of traffic to Cedar Springs (Dallas) and on to Austin. He later named the town "Elmont", remembering New York.

He built the first house and opened first business in the area: mercantile and tavern. The family, with a few others, established a Baptist Church: New Home Baptist, later named Elmont Baptist. That church celebrated her 125th anniversary June 1994.

Children: Sarah Jane, William, John, Caroline, Mary, and George.

Sarah Jane died July 31, 1887 and Harry Aug. 12, 1887. Both are buried in Wiley Cemetery near Collinsville.
Ruby Lou Beach Moore, (GGGD), 14717S

JOHN CARMEAN AND SARAH T. BRISBANE

JOHN CARMEAN AND SARAH T. BRISBANE, John Carmean, son of Blades and Catherine Lear Carmean, was born March 1, 1811, Franklinton County, OH. John came to Texas by of way of Illinois in 1833.

He either met Sarah Brisbane on the way, shortly before, or immediately after arriving, since they were married April 10, 1834, by Judge, "three legged Willie" Williamson. They settled first, in Mina (now Bastrop), then moved to Washington County, and had five boys: William, Charles, James, John and Isaac Newton. The town of Carmine is named in John's honor, as he donated land for the railroad depot.

During the Texas Revolution John participated by hauling supplies. On the census as a farmer, John was actually a cattleman. He raised cattle in Washington, Austin and Lee counties, except for a few years when James and Charles took the cattle to Commanche County. When, James was killed by Indians in '62, Charles, who was reportedly in the Texas Rangers, took the cattle back to Washington County.

It is on record that John Carmean signed up "for the duration" in the Texas CSA during the Civil War.

Sarah died in January 1863, and is buried in Burton, TX, with six other Carmeans. She was born in Kentucky to William and Hannah Harrison Brisbane Dec. 3, 1814, the fifth of six children.

She was said to be a cousin of William Henry Harrison, President of the United States. Sarah came to Texas with her father, and two sisters, Mary and Emily, in 1833 or early 1834.

John Carmean moved in with his son, when Charles married Laura Bell in 1876. In 1889, to collect on a loan, the family moved to a ranch in Erath County. In 1896 they built a house in nearby Hico, where John lived until his death in 1897. John Carmean is buried in Oakdale Cemetery, Hico, TX.
Caroline Elizabeth Carmean Forsythe, (GGD), 18190

ROBERT CARR

ROBERT CARR, my paternal great-great-grandfather, was born Dec. 14, 1799, in Bordentown. NJ. He was reared by a maiden sister, Nancy Carr. He was bound out to learn a trade: brick mason. He ran away when 13 years old.

In Pickens County, AL, about 1828, he married Susan (Sookie) Roberts, widow of Tipton Grady, who had two children: Daniel (born 1822) and Mary Ann (born 1826). Susan Roberts was born Oct. 7. 1801, in Russell County, VA. Her parents were Daniel Roberts and Elizabeth Kyser.

Robert and wife, Susan Roberts Carr

Robert Carr and family arrived in Texas in 1837, where they joined Sookie's brother, John Isaac Roberts, at Gonzales. Their children: James Alexander (born 1829), Robert Jefferson (1830), Sarah Ann (1833), John Isaac (1836), Nancy Caroline (1837, Noxubee County, MS), James (1840) and Martha (1840).

February 1838, Robert received a land grant of 640 acres (Deed Book A, page 140) in Gonzales County. His land was 40 miles from the town of Gonzales. He served as minister of the gospel and Justice of the Peace. Robert Carr appointed constable, Gonzales County, Republic of Texas, Nov. 19, 1838, signed, Sam Houston, President.

He died April 22, 1879, and was buried in City Cemetery #1, San Antonio, TX.
Jackie Colleen Carr Paschal

JESSE H. (HUNTER) CARTWRIGHT

JESSE H. (HUNTER) CARTWRIGHT was born about 1787 in Nashville, TN and married Nancy Gray. They came to Texas in July 1825 from Woodville, MS to settle in Stephen F. Austin's colony. Austin's Register of Families says that Jesse was 38 and Nancy 26 in 1825. The 1826 census indicated one son, one daughter, two servants and eight slaves. His title to a league and a labor of land in Fort Bend and Lavaca Counties was granted March 31, 1828.

In 1836 he represented Harrisburg County, in the first Congress. Apparently he divorced Nancy and remarried in 1843. Nancy died in 1847 in Fort Bend County and Jesse died in 1848 in Guadalupe County, His probate records indicate two James C. and Jonas G., petitioned to administer his probate. The records also indicate two minor children, Annarilla (Anne Audlia) born 1832 and Norvel, and a widow, Elizabeth. Annie married Josiah Ogden in 1852 and settled in Freestone County. She died in 1858. Josiah and Anne had twin sons who died shortly after birth, and three daughters, Mary C. Ogden Harper, Martha E. Ogden Quarles and Rebecca Ogden Ogden.

Dorothy Neil Harper, (GGGD)

JESSE HUNTER CARTWRIGHT, born in 1787 in Nashville, TN and thought to be a descendant of Thomas Cartwright. He married, Nancy Gray ca. 1819 in Woodville, MS. Nancy was born about 1799. He and Nancy came to Texas in 1825 as one of Stephen F. Austin's Old Three Hundred. He is listed as having one son, one daughter, two servants, and eight slaves. He received a land grant of one league and a labor in Ft. Bend County. In 1830, he built a home on Oyster Creek. He held various public official posts, became a realtor and was a Representative in the first Texas Congress.

In 1841, he moved to Guadalupe County. His children were Minerva, born 1820, Josias G, born 1824; James C., born 1827; Anne Audlia, born 1832; Norvel, born 1834, and Claudia (?). Minerva married Churchill Fulcher Jr., Anne married Josiah Ogden and Claudia married Nicholas McNutt. Supposedly he and Nancy divorced. Nancy died in 1847 in Ft. Bend County and Jesse died in 1848 in Guadalupe County. His probate record names his widow, Elizabeth and two minor children, Anne and Norvel.

Dorothy Nell Harper McDermott, (GGGGD)

SUSAN AVAMINTA CHESSHER, daughter of James Chessher and Thriza Morgan, was born in 1835 near Jasper, TX. Her family moved about 1840 to Jefferson County. Her father deeded her 200 acres before she was married. She wed William Goodwyn, son of William Goodwyn Sr. of Shelby County, TX in 1852. Her father deeded her land and buildings in Hardin County when their first child was born, Eglintine G. (born 1857, died 1940, then came Selistine (born 1859, died 1915 and William A. (1861-1940).

William was in the warehouse business on the banks of Pine Island Bayou and then helped build a road from Beaumont, TX to Town Bluff in Tyler County. He enlisted in the Civil War in Woodville in 1862 and was in Co. "F" Vol. Inf. first Reg. He died Feb. 3, 1863 in Charity Hospital at Gordonville, VA because of sickness.

Susanna married S.L. Ward in 1867. They had one child, Estelle born 1870. Susanna became very sick and her father and mother had died leaving no one to care for the children. The children were sent to Shelby County to their Goodwyn kinfolk where they lived, married, and died there.

Alice Othodell Smith, (GGGD)

THOMAS E. CHESHER, born in South Carolina about 1816. He received title to 320 acres of Montgomery County, TX land, Dec. 15, 1839. Thomas applied for a lost title then transferred possession to Jacob De Cordova, Sept. 23, 1847. He married widow Susan Dawson Sept. 23, 1948. The 1850 census lists Thomas, age 34, Susan, 29, George W., 1, Anne E. Dawson, 10, and John M. Dawson, 8. The 1860 census list them in Madison County.

Thomas joined the Confederate Army in 1863. On a march to Sabine Pass, he contracted pneumonia, died in battle, and was buried in a mass grave. The 1870 Brazos County census lists the family as Susan, age 50, George, 21, Joe, 18, William, 16, Susan, 13, and Alvin 11. By 1880, after the death of his wife Rencie Lee, George moved to Wise County and married Mary Virginia Elliott.

My grandfather, Lemuel Luther, was born March 19, 1884, near Bellevue, TX. He married Amma Mae Langfitt, Nov. 13, 1904, at Post Oak Indian Mission, Oklahoma Territory. Amma was born July 14, 1886 in Goldthwaite Mills, TX and died Jan. 22, 1986, age 99, in Iowa Park, TX. Lemuel died Jan. 12, 1969 in Iowa Park, age 84.

Karen Sue Bradberry, 017465, Wichita County

REDMON CHOATE, born on June 8, 1799 in Tennessee. The Choate family had their beginning in America with the arrival of the ship Cecelius at Annapolis, MD on April 15, 1676, carrying Christopher Choate I. The next two generations remained in the Baltimore area. Redmon's father, Squire, moved on to Tennessee where Redmon was born. Redmon met and married Sarah McKenzie in McNairy County, TN on July 14, 1825. The exact date of his arrival in Texas has not been determined, but it was before Texas gained her independence

Redmon and Sarah Choate

from Mexico. His first land acquisition was in 1835. During the Republic he received a total of 2614 acres in Shelby County. One of these tracts was on the Sabine River where he and his family lived until the Regulator-Moderator War. He then moved his family to another grant in the Mt. Herman community. Here he raised his family. The old log home is still standing today. He and Sarah had 13 children. Redmon died on Feb. 13, 1861 and is buried on his land in the Choate Cemetery.

Sarah Ann Choate, born June 26, 1846, died Feb. 13, 1931, married Thomas Casrel McKenzie in 1865. They had seven children. They spent all of their life on their farm in Shelby County, TX. Both are buried in the Choate Cemetery.

Mary Francis McKenzie, born July 16, 1875, died Jan. 4, 1945, married Joseph Edward Ellington on Dec. 22, 1894. They owned a general mercantile store in the little town of Grigsby, between Center and Nacogdoches. They had three daughters, Maud, Clifford, and Tommie. Both are buried in the Mt. Herman Cemetery.

Maud, born Oct. 15, 1895, died March 3, 1977, married Condy Buford January on July 10, 1919. They operated a county store in the community of Pine Ridge some seven miles from Center. Their children were: Doyle (born 1920, died 1922), Wanda (born 1922), and Reba (born 1932). Maud and Condy are buried in Oaklawn Cemetery in Center.

Wanda married Henry Grady Ramsey, and had two sons, Donald and Mark.

Reba married Donald Revere James, and had one daughter, Terrilynn.

Wanda January Ramsey, (GGGD), 17512
Reba January James, (GGGD), 17513

WILLIAM AND ELIZABETH CHRISTIAN arrived in Nacogdoches, TX March 14, 1840. According to their land grant, William died June 1840. The family lived in Henderson County, near Rusk. They had (at least) four children:

George Anderson, born 1812, died 1901, married Nancy Evans who had been captured by Indians;

Isabella Moffitt, born 1813, married Chaney Couch who was killed by Indians;

Piera, born ca. 1815, married Joseph Campbell;

Elizabeth "Eliza," born 1822, married William Liles/Lyles.

George stayed in East Texas, and is buried in Old Union Cemetery. Eliza and William Liles moved to Hopkins County and were in Manor, TX by 1874. The Campbells came to San Saba County one year after the Christian, Couch, and Latham families. Piera is buried at Bend, TX.

According to records, Elizabeth Christian married a second time to Wiliiam Brewer on May 14, 1848. He died in 1867 and is buried in Old Union Cemetery. After his death, she moved to San Saba County and died in the spring of 1868 and is buried in the Lathum Cemetery. It is thought that William Christian is buried in Old Union Cemetery.

Caroline Latham Ingram, (GGGGGD), 11172, (supplement numbers 12070 and 12071)

SUSANNAH GRAVES CLAMPITT, an early Texas colonist, arrived with Steven F. Austin's second colony in early 1825. She married Nathan Arnett Clampitt in Davidson County, TN, Sept. 5, 1803. Nathan died Feb. 24, 1823, in East Feliciana Parish, LA. Recent research indicates Susannah descended from Captain Thomas Graves, an Englishman, who settled in Virginia in 1608.

After Nathan's death, Susannah and her children (with exception of Mary Ann Clampitt) Ezekiel, Nathan Arnett Jr., Francis Graves, and Elizabeth, went to Texas. The Mexican Government granted Susannah one league of land in present Washington County, TX, just south of where Yegua Creek joins Brazos River.

Bible records and land deeds show Susannah Graves Clampitt married Moses Cummins about 1835-1840. Susannah died in Washington County, TX. Aug. 3, 1868 and is buried in an unmarked grave.

Nathan Arnett and Susannah (Graves) Clampitt had the following children:

(I) Ezekiel Clampitt, (born June 14, 1805) married Catherine Arnold in Louisiana. Ezekiel, his wife and one child traveled with Susannah Graves Clampitt to Texas in 1825. He was granted one league of land by the Mexican Government, which adjoined his mother's grant. Their children were: James M., Benjamin Franklin and Richard G.

(II) Mary Ann Clampitt (born Nov. 2, 1807 in Tennessee, died Nov. 7, 1899 in Alabama) married July 1, 1824, Benjamin Eddins (born Feb. 21, 1794 in South Carolina, died July 2, 1853 in Alabama) in East Feliciana Parish, LA, with the consent of Susannah Clampitt. Benjamin and Mary Ann returned to Madison County, AL where Benjamin's father, a Baptist Minister, Rev. William Eddins, and his grandfather Benjamin Eddins, both South Carolina Revolutionary War soldiers from Old Ninety-Six District, SC, and of Huguenot ancestry, were of the earliest settlers in Madison County, AL. Benjamin and Mary Ann had six children:

(1) Francis W. Eddins married Sarah Ann Hargraves. They had two children, William and John.

(2) Susannah Elizabeth Eddins, (born 1831 in Tennessee, died 1888 in Alabama) married Feb. 9, 1852, John Bolling Eldridge (a descendant of Pocahontas). They had three children: Robert, Margaret Tabitha Diemer and Simen Adaline.

Margaret (Maggie) Tabitha Diemer Eldridge (born June 22, 1856 in Tennessee, died 1915 in Tennessee) married Sept. 17, 1873, William Joseph Hill (a Confederate Soldier, born April 11, 1838, died July 23, 1917). They had five children: Kate Eldridge, Walter Vance, Maggie Sue, Oscar Julian and William Earnest. Walter Vance Hill (born July 6, 1881 in Tennessee, died Feb. 22, 1959 in Arkansas) married Aug. 2, 1903 Nellie Hall and had five children: William Henry, Robert E., Eddie Margaret, Dessie Maud, and Nellie Ethel. Eddie Margaret Hill (born April 12, 1909 in Tennessee, died Sept. 19, 1993 in Texas) married June 8, 1927, Lacie Edward Tucker (born Jan. 22, 1906 in Alabama, died June 29, 1990 in Texas) and had Margie Faye and Elner Leatrice.

Simen Adaline Eldridge (born April 1, 1859 in Tennessee, died Sept. 22, 1926 in Texas) married A.J. McClain in Madison County, AL and moved to Stephens County, TX. They had seven children: Flora Ennis, Lura B., Edna May, Faustina, A.E., Porter M., and Charles A.

(3) Anna Rebecca Eddins married David B. Smith. They had eight children: William, Mary, Richard, Ann, John, Susie, Byers and Biji.

(4) Benjamin Graves Eddins (born Oct. 23, 1836, died Oct. 31, 1914) married Dec. 5, 1859, Sarah Ann Bayless (born Feb. 12, 1843, died Dec. 26, 1886). They had nine children: Mary Elizabeth, Benjamin Bartley, Thomas Terah, Jacob Vance, William Richard, Alta Lena, Lewis Aymette, Sallie Pearl and Minnie Myrtle. He married second Nancy Tucker and had one child: Eula Magdalene.

(i) Thomas Terah Eddins (born Jan. 24, 1867, died March 13, 1935) married Feb. 2, 1890, Mary Alice Griffis (born April 26, 1871, died March 13, 1948). They had three children: James Oscar, Lillie Mae and Rosa Etta. Rosa Etta Eddins (born Oct. 23, 1894, died March 24, 1963) married Jan. 27, 1915, Mina Bridgeforth Holt (born April 27, 1894 – died Dec. 7, 1978). They had three children: Cecil Audine, Mary Catherine and Margaret Louise. Cecil Audine Holt (born May 21, 1917, died Dec. 15, 1983) married May 2, 1937, Grace Virginia Loveless (born Sept. 5, 1917) and had Terry Loveless Holt.

(5) Mary Adline Eddins married John B. Bayless. They had seven children: Alice, Betty, Addie, William, Clara, John and Walter.

(6) Richard Walker Eddins married Josephine Finley. They had 11 children: Alva Hugh, Abram Francis, Robert Elkanah, William Pressley, Mary Elizabeth, Emma Josephine, Anna Laura, Benjamin Carrol, Walton Finley, James Clampitt and Thomas Henry.

(III) James Clampitt born Feb. 15, 1812

(IV) Elizabeth Clampitt born May 4, 1814, married June 14, 1827, Elliott McNeil Millican. They had eight children: Mary, Lucinda Jane, John Earl, Elliott Jr., Robert, William H., Jasper N. and Susannah Elizabeth.

(V) Nathan Arnett Clampitt Jr. (born April 13, 1817, died Sept. 27, 1872), married April 21, 1842, Mary Ann Dallas (born Jan. 28, 1827, died June 6, 1881). They had 12 children: George Washington, Seaborn Grover, Lewis Wells, William Francis, James Robert, Ora, Ida, Thomas, Elizabeth, Nathan Arnett III, Ora Ann, and Nathan Walter.

(VI) Francis Graves Clampitt (born Oct. 23, 1820, died ca. 1849), married Sept. 8, 1841, Mary Elizabeth Harris. They had three children: Helen F., Susan E. and Francis Graves Jr.

Researched, compiled and submitted by Terry L. Holt, a descendant of Benjamin Graves Eddins and Margie Tucker Stewart, a descendant of Susannah Elizabeth (Eddins) Eldridge.
Mary Bettye Clampitt Aston, (GGGD), 11880
Margie Faye Tucker Stewart, (GGGGGD), 22164
Elner Leatrice Tucker Pettiet, (GGGGGD), 22174

JOSEPH ALVEY CLAYTON, born in Marshall County, TN in 1817. He moved to Texas in 1835. He fought in the battle of San Jacinto as a private in the artillery under Lieutenant Colonel James C. Neill all under the command of General Sam Houston. He saw action at the battle of Chapultepec during the Mexican War. Joseph also did much scouting in the early Indian Service, besides working with surveying parties during the formative period of statehood in Texas.

Joseph returned to Tennessee in 1847, where he and Amanda Poole were married. Together they returned to Texas and settled in the vicinity of Washington on the Brazos. They moved to Chatfield, Navarro County in 1852.

Early in 1861 Joseph Clayton traveled to Austin as a delegate representing Navarro and Hill counties at the Secession Convention. He voted with other Texans to secede from the Union. After hostilities began he served as the captain of a reserve company in the 19th Infantry Brigade, Texas Militia.

After the war he returned to Chatfield where he continued to farm. In 1873 Joseph was injured in a farm accident. Amanda, ill at the time, died on July 29. Joseph died two days later on July 31. They are buried in the Chatfield Cemetery. They had eight children. The second child Mary E. (Mollie) was my grandmother.
Roberta Bachman Braun, (GGD), 20731

BLOUNT CLEMENTS, arriving in Red River County, TX in 1841 from Tennessee with his family, Blount Clements (born 1821, North Carolina) was a property-seeking nomad involved in ranching and farming interests. The first records revealing Blount Clements in Texas are found in the Land Office Records where he was awarded a headright land grant of 320 acres in Fannin County (Myers Grant) as a single man. On the rolls as a Texas Ranger serving two terms (alongside his brother William Clements).

His enlistment with Colonel Ben McCulloch's Co. gave him an opportunity to be a traveler, citizen, protector, and landholder. He moved throughout Central Texas at the time Texas was recovering from her wounds of independence-seeking, new statehood formation, Civil War involvement, Reconstruction and Indian containment. He lived with his family, consisting of Charlotte George Clements (born 1821, Georgia), Martha A. (1851), Mary E. (1853), Drucilla Charlotte (1855, married Gideon Porter Watson), Addie (1856), Delilah (1859), Andrew "Buddie" (1861), Lucinda (1863), Georgetta (1865), Ellen "Allie" (1866), Jeannette "Jennie" (1868), John Blunt (1871), and William (1877)

in Travis County (1846), Coryell and Burnet counties (1856-59), Comanche County (1860-64), Lampasas County (1865) and Williamson County (between Census years).

Remaining behind in the capacity Texas Ranger to defend the families and citizens of Texas during the Civil War, he voted, paid taxes, conducted business and served the State in its toughest years of formation. His death in 1885, unrecorded in newspapers of the era, preceded his Texas immigrant father's (John C. Clements), who died in 1887 at the age of 100. Blount Clement's widow moved to Oklahoma in late 1900 after selling her homestead in Travis County, but as of this writing, 10 generations of descendants remain in Texas.
Donna Beth Lee Shaw, 021249

JOHN C. CLEMENTS came to Texas April 1841. He received a fourth Class Grant #5 in Red River County Aug. 2, 1841. His son, William, born in North Carolina 1825/6 was my great-great-grandfather.

His son, George Washington, my great-grandfather, was born Travis County, TX June 10, 1853. He married Annie Laura Stokes Feb. 27, 1887, Lometa, Lampasas County, TX. They had four children.

Their son, Elbert Irwin, was born March 25, 1888 Lampasas, TX. He married Clara Berry Feb. 1, 1906, Lampasas, TX. Their daughter, Theresa Bernice, born Dec. 31, 1906. She married Worth Walton Hannan June 23, 1926, Lampasas, TX.

Their daughter, Carolyn Clairice, born Sept. 3, 1930 Pecos, Reeves County, TX. She married Carroll David Parman, Lampasas, TX Aug. 18, 1950.

They had one son, David Walton, born Aug. 11, 1952, San Marcos, TX and one daughter, Andra Jane, born Sept. 30, 1953, San Marcos, TX
Carolyn H. Parman, 15129

JOHN C. CLEMENTS, came to Texas at the age of 53, bringing a rich heritage of farmers, merchants and landowners. With his wife, Martha, and seven children, he arrived in the spring of 1841. The Republic of Texas represented a challenge for people arriving from many states including North Carolina. Many had to sell their homeland and live with friends and families in other states while they waited for their land grants. It took individuals with strong determination and patience to withstand the test. One such man was John Calvin Clements.

John C. Clements

His land grant of 640 acres was located in Clarksville, Red River County, in the northeastern corner of the state. This county was one of the entrances of the immigrants coming to Texas. People arriving would go to Red River and get their assigned land. It is not known if this was one of the reasons that John soon traveled to Central Texas. What is known, through the research of his family and ancestors, is the love and respect he developed for the Republic of Texas.

Anne McCullock and his father, William Clements, married in Dinwiddle County, VA on Jan. 26, 1786. John was born the following year. William Clements was a prominent landowner and a Blacksmith in the counties of Edgecombe, Martin and Pitt.

John's first wife is unknown. She died between the years of 1826 and 1829. Cynthia Utley became his second wife in 1830. North Carolina Marriages, 1741-1868 states, "Calvin Clements married Synthia Utley on April 6, 1830." In Tennessee Cousins by Worth S. Ray, p-751, "John C. Clements married Cynthia Utley of Wake County, NC". His third wife was Martha. Her last name is unknown.

Ancestors: George Clements was John Calvin Clements' great-grandfather. His will states "sons, Benjamin and George B., daughter, Elizabeth Clements, wife, Susana. He leaves his wife land on Rocquist Pocosin adjoining Richard Swain (George B.'s father-in-law)." Will dated Feb. 22, 1729, Bertie County. Abstract of Wills North Carolina 1690-1760. Susana's maiden name is believed to be Bell.

George B. Clements, John's grandfather, was born apx. 1727, State Census of North Carolina 1784-1787. In an Oct. 27, 1746 deed, George B. Clements sold land belonging to his father, May Court, 1748. It was at this time that John's great-grandfather died. The deed, p.135, states he purchased it from John Herring.

On Aug. 10, 1747, George B. Clements bought 172 acres on South Branch of Rocquis from Richard Swain. Colonial Bertie County, NC Deed Books A-H 1720-1757, Book G, p-47. George married Richard's daughter, Patience Swain. George and Patience are John's grandparents.

Patience Swain Clements was the daughter of Richard and Ann Charlton Swain. Ann was the daughter of William Charlton. "The Swains of Nantucket" by Robert H. Swain. The first two names of their five sons were William and Charlton. William was John's father.

In the Deeds of Bertie County NC, 1757-1772, the dec'd Richard Swain of Bertie County, "bequeathed to his wife Ann Swain now dec'd the use of several slaves and certain household 'stuff'." This is dated Feb. 8, 1762. Mentions: William Swain, Patience Clements, George Clements, Susanna and Thomas Spencer. Wit: Alexander Ray. July Court, 1762.

George B. Clements and Patience had five sons and three daughters. The daughters were not mentioned in the will. Deed Book D, p. 244. They are as follows: Isaac, under 21, William, Charlton, George Jr., Hardy, Challon, Susannah and Margaret. His will reveals wife, Elizabeth. It is not known when Patience died. Elizabeth gets the land and plantation that he now lives "until my son" Isaac, comes to the age of 21 years and then she will have the lower half of said land to be divided with Isaac." To son William, 100 acres of land in Pitt County. Challon's name appears on one deed of William buying land. Charlton, Challon and George's names are witness, Pitt County. October Term 1796. Book N p. 394-395. It is known from other deeds that Charlton's wife was Allison. George Jr. married his cousin, Sarah Swain.

George B. died 1797/98 in Bertie County, NC. Elizabeth Clements sold "unto the said John Rhodes my right and dower Land where on I now live." Witnessed by James Ward, it reveals the passing of John's grandfather. Book S, p-5 Bertie County, NC. Although George B. owned land in Bertie and his will was found there, on the 1790 Census of NC, he was in Pitt County.

In *Colonial Soldiers of the South*, 1732-1774, by M.J. Clark, George Clemmons, is listed as a private under a list of men of the Martin County Militia "after 1774 indicating that he served

in the Revolution War. The deed was listed under the North Carolina Militia.

Little is known about George's second wife, Elizabeth. In a 1799 Bertie County will of her brother, John Pierce, it states her parents were William and Cloanah Pierce. Wills Book E, Bertie County, P-61-62.

In 1783, Pitt County Deeds p. 88, Book unknown, William Clements, John's father, is buying 100 acres on North side of Tarr River and South side of Flat Swamp. It is witnessed by Peter Jolly and David Gurganus, dated Oct. 30, 1783. Three years later, William married.

William married in the same county as his two sisters, Margaret and Susannah. Margaret married Thomas Hanks, Dec. 23, 1784. Susannah married Jeremiah Browder on Jan. 28, 1790. William married Anne McCullock on Jan. 26, 1786. These were in the county of Dinwiddie, VA. Virginia Marriages in Rev. John Cameron's Register and Bath Parish Register, published by Virginia Genealogical Society.

Two of John's brothers and one sister have been found. They remained in North Carolina. William H. lived in Martin County on 100 acres, North side of Flatt Swamp. Oct. 18, 1822. This land was bought from his father and signed by Edmond and Charlotte Andrews. Book G. p. 254, Martin County Deeds. It is not known where the third brother, George R., lived in North Carolina. George R. helped William H. out financially with the Blacksmith shops, after the death of their father. William died in 1846 / 47. Estate Deed of William Clements, Book O p. 379-383, Martin County, NC.

In 1827, John was living in Pitt County, close to his sister, Charlotte Andrews and her husband, Edmond. Her father gave them 325 acres in Pitt County. The deed was signed by John's older brother, William Jr. and Mary Clements.

William was appointed commissioner along with four others: John Ingles, John Seigh, John G.S. Schinck and Robert Whyte. They were assigned in November 1792 to regulate the Town of Salisbury, Windsor, Tarboro and Warrington. Edgecombe County Book 8 p. 88-89, witnessed by Thomas Blount and James Renn.

When William finished his term as commissioner, he sold to Humphrey Hardy a certain acre or two lots of land in Windsor, Bertie County. "King and Queen Streets and adjoining the Court House Lot...," Bertie County Deed Book T, P-74-75, dated March 21, 1804.

John C. was probably living on his father's land at the beginning of his marriage to his first wife. Shortly after the birth of his first child, Mary Margaret, he bought 100 acres in Pitt County. This was next to William Crawford, Luke Ward, and William Clements' line. The deed, was witnessed by Edmond Andrews Jr. and John Rollings. It was sold by John Brittain. This deed is dated Sept. 9, 1815. Book T of Deeds, Pitt County, p. 220-221.

On Dec. 9, 1839, Mary E. Clements was born, completing his family of three sons and five daughters. Two years from his arrival, John lost his wife, Cinthia. Goodspeed's History of Tennessee, published in 1887.

Other children born to John and Cynthia were Isabelle, born 1831, Cinderella born 1832. Children with his first wife were, Mary Margaret "Polly" born 1814, Atkinson born apx. 1817, Drucilla born 1820, Blount born 1821, and William born 1826. Travis County, TX 1850 Census Record. (Atkinson, Dallas County District Court No. 14, Index to Civil Minutes, Case No. 383, 1846-1875. Date of judgement Aug. 11, 1859, Book B. p. 590.

Atkinson died a little more than a decade after arriving in Texas and receiving his land grant of 320 acres.

The last recorded location of John, before entering Texas, was in Johnson County, AR. He and Atkinson were on the Tax List in 1839, "Johnson County Patent Book, Roll 33, 1838-1860".

Descendants: William Clements, John's third son, was born in Pitt County, NC in 1826. He lived in Tennessee for a short time before arriving in Texas at the age of 15. 10 years later he married his first wife, Martha George, on June 12, 1851. "Travis County, TX. Marriage Records 1840-1882". To this marriage, seven children were born: James Atkinson, born March 29, 1852, died April 6, 1928, George Washington, born June 10, 1853, died March 13, 1926, Sarah J., born 1854, John born 1856, Martha born 1858, Delila born 1860 and Andrew born 1865. Martha died on May 21, 1865.

William married Martha's sister, Deliah George, on June 25, 1866. Martha and Deliah were daughters of Frederick and Martha Alsabrook George, Jones County, GA. William and Deliah had three children. Andrew was born 1865. Aaron Elias was born in 1867. Rollings Alsabrook was born in 1871, Travis County Census Record, 1870 and 1880.

James Atkinson Clements was born in Travis County, TX. He married the youngest child of Isaac and Harriet Cavendar Jackson, Amanda Susan Jackson. The Jackson family was from Georgia. They were married on Dec. 18, 1873 in Travis County. Eight children were born to this marriage. They were as follows: William Isaac born Dec. 27, 1874, Horace Atkinson born June 26, 1877, Henry Lonzo born Sept. 1, 1879, Joel Irving born Aug. 20, 1882, Martha Alzada born Dec. 26, 1885, Adelia Belle born June 8, 1888, Julia Alice born Dec. 21, 1891, and James Orian born Jan. 26, 1894, Family Bible Records.

Joel Irving married Julia Estelle Smith on Aug. 6, 1913, in Colemen County, TX. Three children were to this union. Julia Maurine born April 6, 1915. She died the same day, having lived for only two hours. Joel Frank born May 23, 1919. Frank married his first wife, Gertrude Melvin, on Easter 1947. He married Jeanne Howard on Aug. 8, 1954. They had three adopted children, Keith born 1957, Karen born 1960, and Susan born 1963. Joel's second son, James Henry was born on Dec. 15, 1921.

James Henry married Nettie Lee Gray on May 30, 1942, in Austin, TX. He was on leave from active duty during World War II. Captain Clements was a pilot in the 44th Bomb Group, 506 Bomb Squadron. He retired from the Air Force Reserve, in 1982, as a Lieutenant Colonel. Nettie is the daughter of David Elmer and Mattie Compton Gray of Caldwell County, TX. James and Nettie have two daughters: Marsha Louise born Oct. 9, 1943 and Julia "Judy" Maurine born Dec. 2, 1948.

Marsha Louise was born in Austin, TX. She married Larry V. Schaefer and has four children. They are as follows: Jeffery, Lisa, Amy and Jimmy. Their youngest son was adopted.

Judy was born in Dallas, TX. She married her first husband, Gary Glenn Gough, on Aug. 12, 1967. He was the father of her two children, Kellie Rae and Joel Brian. She married her second husband, William Tarrant Garrett III, "Bill", on March 19, 1976. Bill adopted their children.

Kellie Rae Garrett was born on Nov. 28, 1970. She married Bill Heckert, a soldier during the Gulf War. They have one daughter, Katherine "Katie" Monika. She was born on Dec. 3, 1994 in Columbus, GA. Kellie's brother is Joel Brian, born Feb. 6, 1973.

They were born in Dallas, TX and are presently living in the area.

Judy is proud to share the knowledge of her third great-grandfather, John Calvin Clements, with others. There are many stories telling the hardships of coming to Texas.

John Calvin Clements' ancestors have not been written about, until now. Like many of the Texas pioneers, John C. was proud to be a citizen when Texas became a state.
Julia Clements Garrett.

JAMES P. COLLINS AND ELIZA G. AINSWORTH COLLINS, James P. Collins was born about 1816 in Wayne County, MS. His parents were Christopher C. Collins and Rachel Hendrick Collins. James P. married Eliza G. Ainsworth about 1837. They arrived in Texas Oct. 24, 1838. He served the Republic of Texas as a citizen and soldier and received a land grant of 640 acres on the west bank of the Trinity River in Liberty County in 1839. This area became a part of Polk County when it was created in 1846 and is presently in San Jacinto County, which was established from Polk County in 1870.

James P. was elected Justice of the Peace in Polk County in 1846. In 1851 the family moved to De Witt County where he served as sheriff from 1852 to 1854. He later served as J.P. in De Witt County. In about 1861, the family moved to Leesburg, now Leesville, in Gonzales County. Collins was elected J.P. in Gonzales County in 1869. He died Dec. 23, 1879 probably in Goliad County while visiting his daughter, Carrie E. Collins Porter. His place of burial is unknown. Eliza G. Ainsworth was born in Mississippi Territory, now Washington County, AL, Feb. 11, 1809, died June 3, 1863 and is buried in Antioch Cemetery, Gonzales County.

Children of James P. and Eliza were:

1) Eli Li Kershaw Hendrick Collins, born Oct. 31, 1839, Liberty County, Republic of Texas, died Nov. 18, 1915, Garza County, TX, married first Mrs. Anastasia (Annie) Brown Tennelle Asher, 1859, married second Elizabeth Brooks, Nov. 8, 1885, De Witt County, TX,

2) Asbury Sebastian Collins, born February 1840, Liberty County, Republic of Texas, died Aug. 21, 1908, Goldthwaite, Mills County, TX, married Allene S.?;

3) William Greenberry Collins, born 1843. Liberty County, Republic of Texas, died Sept. 4, 1908, Sweetwater, Nolan County, TX, married first unknown, married second Emily Josephine Ables;

4) John Franklin Collins, born Dec. 11, 1845, Liberty County, Republic of Texas, died June 28, 1918, Louise, Wharton County, TX, married first Mary Ellen Asher, April 15, 1869, Bastrop County, TX, married second, Marietta Burriss, Oct. 30, 1879, Goliad County, TX;

5) Carrie Eliza Collins, born Aug. 3, 1849, Polk County, TX, died March 28, 1914, San Antonio, TX, married William S. Porter, Dec. 17, 1874, Gonzales County, TX. The sons all served in the Confederate Army during the Civil War.

James P. married second Mrs. Mary H. Talley Campbell in Gonzales County on Oct. 1, 1863. Their children were (1) Dugall Collins, born circa 1864, Gonzales County; (2) Lanny D. Collins, born circa 1867, Gonzales County; (3) Lucinda D. (Lou) Collins, born circa 1867 (probably a twin of Lanny), married John M. McCamy; (4) Clement Eugene Collins, born Aug. 28, 1870, Gonzales County, died Dec. 8, 1939, Frio County, TX, married Nancy (Nannie) Theressa Wright, Aug. 13, 1891, Gonzales

County; (5) Amza Mae Collins, born circa 1876, married Willie McGuffin, July 11, 1891, Guadalupe County, TX.

James P. and Eliza G. Ainsworth Collins were my great-great-grandparents.
Mildred Jo Porter Soward.

WILLIAM COLLOM, born in 1794 in North Carolina. He and his brother, Charles, served with the East Tennessee Militia in the War of 1812, serving Jan. 5, 1814 to Aug. 1, 1814.

In the early 1820's, William and his brothers, two sisters, the father George (the mother deceased) and young George, (a son by a deceased wife) left Tennessee to settle in the new Territory of Arkansas. They traveled by keelboat down the Mississippi and Red River to Hempstead County, AR where they took up land.

Martha (Patsy) McKinney, fourth child of Daniel and Margaret McClure McKinney, born Nov. 12, 1801 Lincoln County, KY near Crab Orchard; died 1887 at her home near Val Alstyne, TX; married Bill Collom. The marriage rites were performed at her family home in Hempstead County, AR by her uncle, Collin McKinney.

In 1830 the Colloms moved to the Wavell Red River Colony in Texas, belonging to the new Republic of Mexico, to take advantage of the liberal land grants available to new colonists.

William Collom served as Commissioner for Miller County, AR Territory. He and 24 other settlers raised money to defray traveling expenses for Colonel Ben Milam to go to Mexico to present the colonists' petition to the governor of Coahuila and Texas to send a Land Commissioner with authority to confer land titles.

Miller County, AR records and court procedures 1834-38 reveal legal transactions, service in juries, court procedures involving Colloms and McKinneys.

Patsy and William McCollom had five children. William died sometime in the fall of 1835 and was probably buried at his plantation in Red River County.

On April 20, 1836, Patsy and other Red River Colonists pledged a donation of $35.00 and a rifle to help outfit a company of men preparing to join General Sam Houston's army.

Patsy later married a Mr. James McBride. She died in 1887 and is buried in the Van Alstyne Cemetery.
Margaret Cannon Boyce Brown (Mrs. Spencer), (GGGGD), 4556
Margaret Brown Lewis (Mrs. J. Keet III), (GGGGGD), 16099
Maria Stanton Boyce Brown, (GGGGGD), 16100
Anne Stuart Boyce Folkes (Mrs. Lee), (GGGGGD), 18950

SAMPSON CONNELL SR., son of Giles and Elizabeth Gibbs Connell, was born about 1787 near Spartanburg, SC. He married Milly Cook, daughter of David and Milly Cook about 1810 in Tennessee. They had 10 children: Edward born about 1812 died young; Elizabeth born about 1814 married Jacob Mitchusson; William O. born Nov. 10, 1816 married Loumisa Wills; David Cook born Sept. 18, 1819 married Sarah Jane Clark; George Tinsley born about 1820 never married; Sampson Jr. born Dec. 5, 1822 married Missouri Elizabeth Hudspeth; Giles born about 1823 died young; James Gibbs born December 1824 married Minerva Black; Archibald born about 1826, died young; Mary Ann born June 26, 1827 married James Wilson Wills.

Sampson was in the War of 1812 and also fought in the Battle of New Orleans.

Sampson and Milly with their seven children came to Texas

in 1834, settling first at Mina where Milly died in August 1834. He is quoted as saying that during the runaway scrape, he moved his family on a pair of old trucks that went crunchy, crunchy. He was a wagon master for the Texan Army and was listed in the Garrison of Bexar when Colonel J.C. Neil left the Alamo in February 1836. Family tradition says he delivered the last load of supplies into the Alamo. He was at Gonzales when news was received about the fall of the Alamo and the slaughter of Fannin and his men at Goliad.

He participated in the Battle of San Jacinto on April 21, 1836 and was in the First Regiment of Texas Volunteers under Colonel Edward Burleson and in Company C under Captain Jesse Billingsley. By 1838, he and his family were living in Washington County. Sampson received a land grant and one labor as a colonist and head of a family and a 640 acre donation for serving in the Battle of San Jacinto and many other donations of land for payments for his army service. He died July 27, 1845 near Brenham and family tradition says he is buried in Old Independence Cemetery in an unmarked grave.
Billie Connell Jordan, (GGGD), 12466
Lillian Magill Gholson, (GGGD), 13578
Halsey Davis Gee, (GGGD), 19693
Sally Gee Grieder (GGGGD), 19694
Mary Gee Carruth, (GGGGD), 19695

CHANEY AND ISABELLA MOFFETT CHRISTIAN COUCH, arrived in Nacogdoches, TX March 14, 1840 along with her parents, William and Elizabeth Christian. They lived near Rusk in Henderson County, TX, until moving to what is now San Saba County, TX in the early 1850's to find a drier climate for their youngest daughter Margaret Ann. Moving to San Saba County with them were their eldest daughter Elizabeth Caroline and her husband John "Jack" Latham. They first settled on a tributary of Wallace Creek, named Latham Creek after Jack Latham and moved to southwestern San Saba County about 1855. They are listed as founders of San Saba County. They had two daughters Elizabeth Caroline born Jan. 8, 1832 and Margaret Ann born Oct. 24, 1842. Elizabeth Caroline married Jack Latham Dec. 17, 1850 and Margaret Ann married William Lawrence Hayes in 1864 in San Saba County.

Chaney born Aug. 5, 1813 South Carolina, was killed by Indians on the family ranch in San Saba on Oct. 7, 1864. Isabella born circa 1812-13 Kentucky died September 1887, on her ranch where she raised cattle and horses. Her home still stands, as does a building used as a school and church named Couch's Chapel. Both are buried in the "Lathum Cemetery" which boasts an historical marker and the four graves there represent three generations of the family. Their descendents still live in the community and Isabella's home is still inhabited by her great-grand-daughter.
Caroline Latham Ingram, (GGGGD), 1172 (Supplement numbers 12068 and 12069)

CORNELIUS COX, son of Christopher and Hannah Johnson Cox, was born around 1800 in Kentucky. He married Katherine "Katy" Jackson on April 1, 1824 in Monroe County, IN and had moved to Dallas County, TX by 1845, when he first appears on the tax rolls. He owned a farm near the community of Scyene. Katherine "Katy" Jackson Cox was born around 1801 in Kentucky. Cornelius Cox died in Dallas in 1857, his wife "Katy" predeceased him; they were buried in the Old Elam Cemetery, near their home, it has since been destroyed.

Mary Ann "Mollie" Tucker and George Henry Cox circa 1868

Cornelius and Katy had nine children who made the trip to Texas with them and one (Margaret) who was born in Dallas County. They were: Andrew Jackson who married Arrenna Ratliff; Hannah who married George Markham; Joseph who married Narcissa Elam, Martha A. Emmitt, and Armanda J. Wilson; Harvey who married Emily Jane Elam and Rebecca Phipps; Elizabeth who married Richard Bruton, Christopher Columbus who married Drucilla Elam and Margarette Jane Brown; George Henry who married Mary Ann Tucker; Jacob W. who married Huldah Jane Moore; Cornelius Jackson who married Huldah Ann Kemp; and Margaret who married William Murphy Kemp.

George Henry Cox, pictured and listed above, was born in Brown County, IN, in December 1838. He was a member of the sixth Texas Cavalry CSA and married Mary Ann "Mollie" Tucker in Madison County, MS on Dec. 24, 1868. Their children were: John Henry who married Mary M. Redwine; Mary Catherine (deceased 1883); William M.T. who married Fannie Lindsey; Joseph Constantine (deceased 1883); David Sylvester who married Rosa Ann Cloud; Rosa Ann Cox (deceased 1881); and Viola Virginia married Wash Hickson. George Henry farmed in Comanche County and later owned a meat market in McCaulley. His wife died Aug. 20, 1894 in Comanche County and is buried at Stag Creek Cemetery. George Henry Cox died in December 1909 and is buried in the McCaulley Cemetery in Fisher County.

V. Katherine Cox Sullivan, (GGGD), 21859
Barbara Mae Cox, (GGGD), 22126

WILLIAM CRABTREE, born ca. 1791, died 1846, married Mary Lee, had 11 children. May 8, 1836, mustered in under Captain Wheelock's Company, of Texas Rangers under command of Brigadier General Felix Houston. Issued Land Grant, June 1838 Certificate #817. His son, William Carroll Crabtree, (1818-1889) married three times, 1st Mary Ann Estes, 2nd. Eugenia James Valeria Wray and 3rd Mrs. Paralee (Boyd) Jenkins. William was a blacksmith and had nine children. A tall man, dark hair with one blue eye and one brown.

Daughter, Eliza Cassenda "Belle" Crabtree, (1869-1959) married Thomas Newton Orrell Aug. 26, 1887, had four children. "Belle" had reddish brown hair, blue eyes and a small frame.

Daughter, Eula Mae Orrell, (1890-1970), married Walter Harvey McAdams July 10, 1909 Navarro County, TX. Two children: Katie Belle & Linda Frances. Known for her sense of humor.

Daughter, Katie Belle McAdams married Arthur Washington Smith Nov. 3, 1932 Navarro County, TX. She was Assistant Librarian for the Clayton Library Houston, TX, and Family Historian.

Daughter, Norma Sue Smith married George Edwin Overturf Jr. in Houston, TX. Member of DRT Ft. Worth Chapter.
Mrs. Sue Overturf

WILLIAM CARROLL CRAWFORD was the son of Nancy Carroll and Archibald Crawford born in Fayetteville, NC, Sept. 13, 1804. During his infancy his parents moved to Georgia. They died when he was seven years of age. He found a home with a Christian family and resided there until age 18. Upon reaching 18 he was hired as an apprentice in a tailoring establishment. He continued in this trade for seven years. During this time he began studies to prepare for the ministry. He accepted Christ and joined the Methodist church. In 1830 he was licensed to preach. He joined the Alabama Methodist Conference and was a circuit rider for four years.

William Carroll Crawford

In 1834 William Carroll Crawford married Rhoda J. Watkins, a daughter of the Hon. Lewis Watkins, a prominent early settler of Tennessee. During their married life William and Rhoda had 13 children. Their name's in order of birth as follows: Julia A., Mary E.; Charles W.; Sarah J.; William C.; Texana; Luis F.; Martha W.; Louis A.; Rhoda E.; and Alice C.

Due to ill health brought on by traveling the circuits of Alabama, William and Rhoda joined her family on their journey to Texas. They arrived Jan. 5, 1836 and settled in Shelby County.

William Carroll Crawford was one of the two men elected from Shelby County to attend the conference at Washington on the Brazos. Sidney O. Penington was the other delegate elected.

They both signed the Texas Declaration of Independence. William Carroll Crawford also played a role in the writing of the Constitution of Texas.

In closing a quote from William Carroll Crawford gives a clear picture of the man and patriot, "When I came here in 1836 and saw the country then as she lay sleeping like an infant in her smiling beauty and undeveloped loveliness, ignorant of the possibilities which nature had in store for her favorite child, I could not then see with the eyes of a prophet, and the great future in store for Texas did not reveal itself to me at that time. I settled in Shelby Country, which then was bounded on the west by the Rio Grande. For more than 53 years I have lived and labored among the people; and every year has added to my wonder and admiration of their progress and development. And today, having lived 83 years, and through experience and age become a prophet, I can look forth over her wonderful prospects and see a future so proud in possibilities, so rich in resources, and development that I pause in awe at the magnitude of the state which I have helped to create."

William Carroll Crawford died Sept. 3, 1895, and was buried in the Cow Creek Cemetery near Dublin, TX. His body was moved to the state cemetery in Austin in 1936.

SOPHIE CAMPE CRENWELGE was born in Platendorf, Hanover, Germany 1839. Sailing from Bremen, Germany on the Everhadt ship with her parents, Christain and Sophie Klause

George Wilhelm Crenwelge Family; L to R: (Back) Dora Crenwelge Kolmeier, Sophie Crenwelge Holtzer, Adolph Crenwelge and William Crenwelge. (Front) Lena Crenwelge Ahrens, Mary Crenwelge Suber, Sophie Campe Crenwelge and George Wilhelm Crenwelge.

Kampe, arriving in Galveston, TX Dec. 18, 1845. Her mother and two siblings died at sea and her father with the remaining siblings died enroute at Victoria, TX.

An orphan she was taken to Mainzer-Adels orphanage in New Braunsfels, Texas. Later adopted by George Holecomb family of Sisterdale, TX. The Holcomb family moved to Comfort, TX.

At age 12 (1852) Sophie Campe went to Fredericksburg, TX to work at the Nimitz Hotel until her marriage to George Wilhelm Crenwelge. Their children are: William born 1862 married Olivia Wendel; Adolph born 1864 married Sarah Wendel; Heinrich born 1866 died 1866; Marie Christina born 1868 married W.L. Suber; Dorothea born 1874 married Otto Kolmeier; Lena born 1870 married Peter Ahrens; and Sophie born 1876 married H.A. Holzer.

They operated a wheelwright business in Fredericksburg and had land in Cherry Springs Community.

She was an honored guest at the 75th Jubilee of Comfort, TX, 1929. She died Jan. 8, 1930 and George Wilhelm Crenwelge died July 7, 1923. Both are buried in the City Cemetery in Fredericksburg, TX.
Marian Ahrens Armstrong, (GGD of Sophie Campe)

ANCESTORS OF DAVID CROCKETT:

ANCESTORS OF DAVID CROCKETT: Gabriel Gustave de Crocketagne of Norman descent, born 1618, in Southern France. His son, Antoine de Saussure de Crocketagne, born 1643, Bordeaux, France. Antoine at age 21, an excellent horseman, and very handsome, made an appearance before King Louis XIV. The King granted Antoine a commission in his Household Troops. He met and married 1669, Louise de Saix, resigned his commission, and became an agent to Maurys Wine & Salt Monopoly. Their first child: Gabriel Gustave de Crocketagne 11, born 1672, France.

The King issued the "Edict

David Finley Flowers

of Nantes" late 1672, ordering all Huguenots to leave France within 20 days. Antoine, Louise, and infant son fled to Bantry, Ireland. Eager to lose French identity, they changed their name to "Crockett."

*The Crocketts are related to Marquis De Lafayette, his mother was a De Saix.

David Crockett

Joseph Louis Crockett (son of Antoine and Louise) was born 1676, Ireland, married Sarah Stewart of Donegale, Ireland. They emigrated to America 1716.

John Crockett, born 1754, married Rebecakah Hawkins, 1779, Rogersville, TN. Their son, David ("Davy") Crockett was born Aug. 17, 1786, died March 6, 1836 in Texas at the Alamo, "Davy" married Margaret "Polly" Finley Aug. 14, 1806, their daughter, Margaret Finley Crockett married Wiley Flowers. Their son, David Finley Flowers, born August 1844 in Texas, died October 1924. He was "Davy and Polly's" grandson. His son, Thomas Finley Flowers, born Feb. 11, 1881, died Dec. 5, 1939, married Ida Love Carter Feb. 14, 1905. He was my father.
Margie Rea Flowers Erwin, 004506
James Butler Bonham Chapter DRT, (03/56)

JOHN HENRY CUMMIN(G)S

JOHN HENRY CUMMIN(G)S received his first land grant in what was soon to become the Republic of Texas from the Mexican government on July 29, 1834. He received his second land grant on Jan. 5, 1835.

These were in the area of what was to become Walker, Montgomery and Nacogdoches Counties. In his application for land he states that he comes with his family, consisting of wife and seven children, from the United States of the North. Two of these children were from his wife Elizabeth's first marriage to Charles Roque/Rock.

Probably John Henry died in 1836-37 because Elizabeth was married to John Bethea and had a daughter born in 1838. John Henry's will was probated on Aug. 31, 1841 in Montgomery and Walker Counties. It is interesting to note that after his bills were paid, the children's half of his estate was worth so little that the courts wouldn't divide it among them. This was a league of land bordering on what is now Lake Livingston!!

John Bethea died in 1874 and Elizabeth in 1875, both in Walker County, TX.
Patsy Cummings McKelvy, (GGGD) of John Henry Cummings, 21279

SAMUEL CUNNINGHAM

SAMUEL CUNNINGHAM was born in Tennessee in about 1786. He moved to Alabama when some of the Indian land along the Alabama-Mississippi border was "opened up" for settlement. His son, Frank Cunningham, was born in Mississippi in about 1837. Samuel, his wife Eleanor, and their children moved to Texas sometime between 1837 and 1843. Samuel and Eleanor's next child, Armenti, was born in the Republic of Texas in 1843.

Samuel bought 917 acres of the John D. Clements Land Grant on Oct. 1, 1845, in Gonzales County, Republic of Texas. Samuel had two farms between his place and Valentine Hoch's place, near the present location of Hochheim, TX. Samuel's land was on both sides of the Guadalupe River. There were several Cunningham families that lived in this area, but their family relationships have not been established at this time. James A. Cunningham was appointed administrator of the deceased Samuel Cunningham's estate in December 1873.

There were several Kelso and Boothe families living near the Cunninghams in Gonzales County, later DeWitt County, TX. There were many marriages between the Cunningham, Kelso, and Boothe families; Susan Cunningham and Alfred Kelso Jr. were married two months before the Civil War ended. They had their first child during the Reconstruction Period after the war. He was born on March 10, 1869, and Alfred and Susan named him Robert E. Lee Kelso. When Robert E. Lee Kelso was a young teenager, he got a job driving a mule team and wagon to haul large granite blocks that were used in the construction of the Capitol Building in Austin, TX.

The Kelso families had a history of twins being born in the family. One Kelso family had 22 children, which included five sets of twins. Robert E. Lee Kelso and his wife Amanda Simpson had eight children and the last two, Frank Pierce and Alfred Leon, were twins. They were born on July 6, 1909, and their birth certificate was handwritten and listed their names as, "Tom & Jerry". The birth certificate was not corrected until 1974 when Frank Pierce Kelso needed a copy for his retirement papers. Frank Pierce Kelso married Helen Lounieta Ragan on Jan. 15, 1940, and they had one child, Bobbie Denise Kelso. Bobbie Denise married Joe Hugh Hutchins on Jan. 12, 1963, and they had one child, a son, Christopher Kyle Hutchins.

Bobbie D. (Kelso) Hutchins, (GGGD), 21649

JOHN WARREN CURTIS, born Dec. 25, 1819 in Tennessee. He was the son of Benjamin Browning Curtis by his first wife, whose name has been lost, but whom one of the sons of John W. Curtis thought must have been Margaret Genety (the name he gave his second daughter by Mary Ann Collom), the first, their oldest child, having been named Martha for his wife's mother, Martha (Patsy) McKinney.

When John Warren Curtis was 9 years old, his father married again. The second wife was Elizabeth Short, and she and Benjamin were married Jan. 4, 1829 in Jackson County, TN. In 1833, Benjamin with his wife Elizabeth, John Warren Curtis, and two small brothers started for Texas. However, when they got to Van Buren, AR, "the yellow fever was raging and they would not let them cross the river." Benjamin and his family stayed in Arkansas settling in Washington County.

In 1843 John Warren Curtis was in Texas where he married Mary Ann Collom that year, becoming a resident of the Republic. In his application for a headright Certificate in Peters' Colony, Curtis states that he "came to the Colony as a family man prior to July 1, 1833, and settled on the East Fork of the Trinity in Old Fannin County." The following land documents in the General Land Office deal principally with the disposal of the 640 acres of "Unlocated land" granted him as a Colonist. Fannin third Class Certificate No. 3046 for 102 acres was patented in Collin County. Fannin third Class Certificate 1127 for 250 acres was patented in Collin County. Nacogdoches third Class Certificate No. 3589 for 2380 acres was patented in Dallas County.

In 1849 John W. Curtis went to California in the "gold rush" bringing home a "stake" and leaving behind in California some property in the care of a "cousin." In 1852, he acquired land from the government in what is now Parker County, TX (Parker County

was formed in 1855 from Bosque and Navarro Counties with 22 males, and with Weatherford, the county seat. Don Carl Curtis, son of John W. Curtis by his second wife Mary Amos (born May 7, 1840, died Jan. 2, 1917) said in 1925 that his father was closely associated with all the early history of Parker County. A generous man, he gave land for a cemetery, which is now known as the Curtis Cemetery. His first wife, who died Feb. 14, 1857, is buried there, as is he himself, Mary Amos (second wife) and many of his descendants. During the Civil War, when all the young men were fighting for the South and the defense of the frontier settlements were left to the old to protect the families from Comanches. John W. Curtis became a Lieutenant of the Frontier Patrol. He died July 27, 1892.

Margaret Cannon Boyce Brown (Mrs. Spencer), (GGGD), 4556
Margaret Brown Lewis (Mrs. J. Keet III), (GGGGD), 16099
Maria Stanton Boyce Brown, (GGGGD), 16100
Anne Stuart Boyce Folkes (Mrs. Lee), (GGGGD), 18950

EBINEZER DAKAN, son of Jacob and __, was born on March 23, 1823 in Ohio County, VA. He and his father, Jacob, were farmers and came to Red River County, TX in October 1840. Jacob, being a married man, was given a conditional land grant in Panola County, TX, as well as an unconditional land grant in Lamar County, TX. He also received two preemption land grants in Franklin County, TX. By 1846, he was living in the Red River County, TX area. Jacob Dakan died intestate and his will was

L to R: Barry and Bertha Dakan, circa 1904

probated Oct. 2, 1848. Ebinezer Dakan was a single male of 17 on arriving in Texas in 1840, and received a conditional land grant in Panola County, TX, as well as an unconditional land grant in Harrison County, TX, where he was living by 1846.

On Feb. 18, 1847, Ebinezer Dakan married Sarah Ann Love, born July 1, 1829, from Arkansas, in Mason Springs, Harrison County, TX. Born to them were four children.

They were: Elizabeth, born in

L to R: Ebinezer Dakan, Judge George Washington Dakan, Celia Bryan Dakan, Willie Edwin Dakan and Bertha Dakan (holding cat) and on steps Hosea Cornelius Dakan and Clinton Basil Dakan. Taken at their home in Stamford, TX circa 1899.

1849; Mary Jane, nicknamed "Dutch", born 1850, married William Brown, who was a diary man; George Washington, born Dec. 31, 1851, married Celia Bryan, and was an attorney and judge; and Andrew J., born 1856. By 1859, Ebinezer and Sarah moved to Erath County, TX, settling on Green's Creek, near Alex-ander, TX. On Oct. 22, 1859, Sarah Dakan died of Billious Fever (Typhoid Fever). In 1860, Ebinezer married Nancy Jane Arendell, daughter of Thomas and Polly (Williams) Arendell. Ebinezer and his family continued farming as well as raising horses.

The Dakan horse brand was a horizonal D, with a line drawn through the middle, and was placed on the right shoulder of their horses. From 1863-1864, he was an Erath County Commissioner for Precinct #2, as well as county commissioner for Confederate Indigent Families of Texas. In 1863, he served in Company A, Rangers for Frontier Protection, and in 1864, served in Major George B. Erath's Company, second Frontier District. On March 9, 1864, Ebinezer Dakan died.

George Washington Dakan, listed above, at age 18, sometimes assisted in driving Indians from the Texas frontier during the early 1870's, under the direction of their neighbor and friend, Colonel James Buckner "Buck" Barry of Walnut Springs, Bosque County, TX. Colonel Barry, a Texas Ranger (1845-1867), was also a frontiersman, Indian-fighter, rancher, stockman, and Texas legislator. It was he who introduced George Dakan to his niece, and future wife, Celia Bryan.

Celia was the daughter of James Robert Bryan of Onslow County, NC and Deborah (Parsons) Bryan, of Tipicanoe County, IN. She was one of six siblings and was born with her twin sister Mary, on March 31, 1855, in East Texas near Athens, Henderson County, TX. G.W. and Celia were married on Nov. 24, 1874, in Iredell, Bosque County, TX. Their children were Maude E., born Jan. 9, 1876, died April 29, 1880, and Stella M.R., born May 30, 1878, died May 7, 1880. Both are buried at Howard Cemetery in Desdemona, Eastland County, TX; Willie Edwin, born April 21, 1881, married Mae Hague, and worked for the Texas Central Railroad; Ebinezer, born Aug. 30, 1883, was a physician, graduated from Baylor Medical School in Dallas, Dallas County, TX, and practiced medicine in Oklahoma Indian Territory; Alletha, born Feb. 2, 1886, died of Typhoid Fever on Sept. 25, 1899; Clinton Basil, born June 24, 1888, was a rancher and served in WWI; Hosea Cornelius, born Nov. 7, 1890, married Mae Eagle, was a journalist for the San Antonio Light newspaper, and an attorney; Bertha, born Oct. 11, 1893, married Bedford Forest Galloway, of Mesquite, Dallas County, TX, was a registered nurse who was a 1917 graduate of the Baylor School of Nursing in Dallas, Dallas County, TX; and Rastus Barry, born March 17, 1901, who was a mechanic.

George Dakan was one of several men responsible for the development of Desdemona, Eastland County, TX, as well as county judge, Justice of the Peace, land agent and a life member of the Baptist Church for both towns of Desdemona and Eastland, Eastland County, TX. G.W. was a County Attorney and Judge, and was a member of the law firm Hammon, Davenport and Wells in Eastland, Eastland County, TX. He was active in local and state Democratic politics. Judge Dakan built a two-story brick building across from the Eastland County Courthouse at 113 1/2 South Lamar that was known as the Dakan Building because of his name bricked in letters at the top of the structure. In Stamford, Jones County, TX, he organized the Stamford lodge and became its first worshipful master, serving in that capacity 14 years. Celia Bryan died on Dec. 6, 1901 in Stamford, Jones County, TX, and was brought to the Eastland Cemetery in Eastland, Eastland County, TX, to be buried.

Judge Dakan married Mary A. Vaughn on Dec. 25, 1902. They had a son, Henry Eugene, born Oct. 8, 1908, died Oct. 13, 1910. George Washington Dakan died in his summer home in Christoval, Tom Green County, TX, of acute indigestion, on June 3, 1929. His body was brought by train to Eastland, Eastland County, TX to be buried under the auspius of the Eastland Masonic Lodge at Eastland Cemetery.
Deborah Parsons Franklin
Jeannette Galloway Franklin

REV. WILLIAM DAUGHTERY, The following article depicting the life of Rev. William Daugherty was printed in the *Methodist Protestant*, the official publication of the Methodist Protestant Church of Texas in 1881. The article has been edited by Ouida Daugherty Smith descendant of Rev. Daugherty and a member of the Daughters of the Republic of Texas.

William Daugherty was born in Kentucky on Aug. 22, 1797. At the age of 10, he moved with his parents to eastern Tennessee and lived there until maturity. In his 22 year, he married Sallie Cecil. Four sons were born in Tennessee: Harrison, Nathaniel, James, and John. In 1830, he moved to Arkansas where he lived for 14 years. In Arkansas, he and Sallie had five more children: Samuel, Nancy, George, Joseph, and William. On Jan. 12, 1842, the wife of his youth died. On Feb. 28, 1843, Mr. Daugherty married his second wife, Matilda Pagitt.

Mr. Daugherty moved his family to the Republic of Texas in January 1845, stopping for seven months in Kaufman County before moving on to settle in Cherokee County where the Indians had only recently been removed from the territory. The first vote he cast in Texas was for a delegate to the Annexation Convention.

Being a man of deep faith and feeling the need for a religious presence in this otherwise wild and unruly area of the Republic, Mr. Daugherty entered into a religious social compact with other men of different denominations in the vicinity with the understanding that when strong enough, each would have the privilege of withdrawing and joining a church of his choice. Mr. Daugherty and his family joined with 50 others in forming the first Methodist Protestant Church in this part of the Republic. At the first quarterly meeting of the church, Mr. Daugherty was licensed to preach. Rev. Daugherty was assigned to the Cherokee Circuit under his beloved friend and pastor, Rev. L.L. Dillard. Having laid aside his earlier study of the law, he devoted himself exclusively to the ministry.

In the early spring of 1859, Rev. Daugherty was asked to become a missionary to regions beyond the Colorado River 300 miles from home. When he entered upon this work, there was only one organized Methodist Protestant congregation west of the Colorado River. Rev. Daugherty ignored worldly honors and emoluments considering himself the servant of the Master and His church.

Rev. Daugherty preached as far south and west as San Antonio often traveling as far as 800 miles on horseback from the seat of the conference in Rusk. Within 12 months, he was so successful in building up the church that a petition was sent and granted to establish a separate conference. When this Western Conference was organized, Rev. Daugherty was selected as its first president. Having labored faithfully for five years in this western territory traversing the whole country, escaping the dangers of hostile Indians, and seeing the church established, he felt his mission was accomplished. In 1865, he returned home to Cherokee County where he continued to preach and serve the Lord until his death on Sept. 13, 1887.
Ouida Daugherty Smith

EDWARD BOIT DAVIS, son of William Patrick and Louisa Davis, was born on Nov. 12, 1804 in Mecklenburg County, VA. Although orphaned at an early age he became a successful merchant and married Martha Royster of Washington D.C. on March 5, 1825. Four children were born: Edward, Eugenia, Alexander, and Mary. The marriage was ended by mutual consent with a friendly good-bye.

Edward migrated to Mississippi where he became a planter, land speculator and surveyor, moving to Texas about 1836. He acquired land in Grimes and Montgomery Counties. He served the Republic of Texas in what was known as the Tidwell Campaign. In 1840 he joined Colonel Francis A.B. Wheeler, Commander of the Militia of Montgomery County, in an expedition to expel hostile Indians becoming a colonel.

On Oct. 10, 1844 he married Mary Ellen Lawrence who was the daughter of Texas pioneer Martin Byrd Lawrence and Mariah Hart David, a first cousin of Jefferson Davis. To this union were born 12 children: Emaline Allen, Ann Maria, Leanah, William P., Adeline, Harriet Maxey, Lee Algernon, Lula Edward, Edward Boit Jr. and three boys who died in infancy. The couple farmed in Montgomery County, later moving to Grimes County where Edward was in business as a merchant in Courtney, Anderson and Iola. He died on June 19, 1874 at Anderson Prairie, four miles south of Iola.

Joyce J. Smither, (GGD), #8097

JAMES FOSTER DAVIS, born Feb. 15, 1822, in North Carolina. His family had moved on into Georgia by 1838. James was their fourth child. The family lived in Jones County, Stewart County, and Webster County before James came to Texas.

James Davis was a tall man, six feet tall, with blue eyes, light hair, and a fair complexion. He was a handsome man, tall, blonde, young, adventurous. Texas beckoned. He fell under her spell and responded to the call of colonization in Texas, a land of heroes, tradition and hope. He was ready to establish new life in Texas. James F. Davis came to Texas the first time with Shackleford as a surveyor's helper. James was in Texas by 1840. He served the republic as a colonizer with Shackleford, a settler, patriot, and citizen in Milam and Washington Counties. A certificate to apply for land was issued, to him by the Board of Land Certificates in and for the County of Washington. He returned to Georgia to encourage other family members to return with him to Texas, and to marry the girl he left behind when he first came to Texas. He married Sara Jane Little when he reached Georgia. They were in Stewart County. Conditions in Georgia kept him from returning immediately to Texas. The slavery issue was growing. The war began. James F. Davis enlisted and served the South's cause.

By 1868 James came back to Texas. He had his wife Sarah Jane (Little) and their seven children with him. Some of their children were Margaret Jane Davis (who married Thomas Preston Morgan, Bastrop County), Cullen F. Davis (who married Mrs. Nancy Standifer Dilly, Travis County), Thomas (Tom) Henry Davis (who married Minerva Pope, Bastrop County), Mary Davis, Frances E. (Fannie) Davis (who married Joel Anderson Morgan, III, Bastrop County), and Harriet (Hattie) Davis (who married Adam C. (Ad) Denson, Bastrop county). They were in Burleson County, then moved to Bastrop County around Pea Ridge and Smithville. Later, they moved on into Milam County to Milano, with the Thomas Preston Morgans. James Foster Davis died at Milano, April 6, 1884. They are buried in the Smyrna Cemetery near Milano. He has a CSA marker at his grave.

We walk the trails they made. We carry their genes in our bodies. Our "rootage" from this Old One grows deep in this sandy Texas soil.

Ethel Jewel Morgan Burch, (GGGD) of James Foster Davis, 19574

MARY DAVIS was born in San Augustine County, TX, on Nov. 10, 1837. She was the daughter of Edward B. and Eliza A. Brown Davis. Her father moved to San Augustine, along with his father, Warren Davis, and his brother, Elias K. Davis, during the 1820s, from Kentucky. They were among the first settlers to arrive in the immediate San Augustine area. Warren Davis received a land grant there and is one of the few Revolutionary soldiers buried in Texas.

Mary Davis married William Harrell, son of William and Elizabeth Haygood Harrell, on Dec. 11, 1856, in San Augustine. They farmed for a livelihood and had three children. Her husband enlisted in the Confederate Army at San Augustine and was a member of the 25th Texas Cavalry. He was captured by Union forces at Arkansas Post, AR, and died a prisoner of war at Camp Butler near Springfield, IL, in March 1863. She died April 1, 1863, at San Augustine and is buried in the Davis Family Cemetery. Many of their descendants continue to reside at San Augustine.

Rosine Mary Sanders Rawson, (GGD), 14015S

JOHN WESLEY DEVILBISS was a Texas Methodist Circuit Rider from 1842 to 1885. He preached the first protestant sermon in San Antonio at the County Clerk's Office on Commerce Street in 1844. He lived long enough to attend a church meeting at Travis Park Methodist Church.

He was born in Frederick County, MD in 1818 to parents Priscilla and Alexander DeVilbiss. At 13, young Wesley worked in a saddle shop as an apprentice to his employer. At 15,

Rev. John Wesley DeVilbiss and second wife, Martha Lucinda Kerr

he was converted at a camp meeting. Later he attended Methodist Colleges in Augusta, KY and Ohio.

The Bishop in Ohio invited volunteers for Texas. Wesley and five other preachers to be responded.

He crossed the Sabine River into Texas in 1842. His first assignment was Egypt on the Colorado River. Later, he was assigned to Gonzales where Indians roamed.

In 1845, he married Judge Menefee's daughter, Tabitha, in San Antonio. They built an elm log cabin in Seguin. Their daughter lived a few hours. The mother lived two months.

In 1848, Reverend DeVilbiss married Martha Lucinda Kerr in San Antonio. They had seven children.

As an agent of the American Bible Society, DeVilbiss helped establish the publication Texas Christian Advocate and Southwestern University in Georgetown.

Reverend DeVilbiss died repairing a fireplace on Jan. 31,

1885. He was buried in Oak Island United Methodist Church Cemetery.

Ruby DeVilbiss Laxson Tetsch, (GGD), 17758

WILLIAM "BUCK" DICKERSON came to Texas from Leon County, FL in 1839. He settled with his wife, Lucinda Creely, in San Augustine County. William and Lucinda were married in Leon County, FL Feb. 8, 1834. William's parents are unknown but the 1825 Florida State Census lists only one Dickerson family in Leon County. The head of this household was John Dickerson. He had four males living in his household of the correct age to be William and his brothers. It may never be verified but this John Dickerson could be William's father. John is a very common name but it is worthy of note that the name John has been passed down through the Dickerson families.

A family legend related by the daughter of Pearl Henley, granddaughter of William "Buck" Dickerson, says that William killed a man in Florida and hewed out a log to escape from the area. He went to Texas having a brother, James, living in San Augustine County. He later sent for his family to join him there. Also, legend says that Lucinda Creely Dickerson was of Indian origin, perhaps Seminole. William "Buck" was fair skinned, blue eyed and blonde, Lucinda was brunette. Many of the Dickerson descendants are blue eyed brunettes and many of the descendants still live in or around San Augustine County.

William and Lucinda had three children in Leon County, FL. They were: Cynthia Ellen, born April 11, 1835; Thomas Jordan born 1838, married Martha Ann Head in Newton County, TX Aug. 27, 1857 and James Leonard born Dec. 24, 1839. After James' birth, Lucinda joined William in Texas. They had five more children in San Augustine County. They were: William Leroy "Lee" born 1841; John Marshall born Oct. 17, 1843; Edmond Elisha born Nov. 13, 1845; Levi I. born 1847 and Benjamine Franklin born Feb. 19, 1852.

Lucinda died about 1894 and William died about 1897 and both are buried in Dickerson Cemetery in San Augustine County, TX.

Cynthia Ellen married James S. Pursinger Hardy on Nov. 1, 1855 in San Augustine County and died Oct. 22, 1916. James Leonard "Len" married Mary Catherine Hatton on Aug. 10, 1858 in San Augustine County died Oct. 28, 1903. William Leroy "Lee" married Lushia "Lucy" Day Barnes on Aug. 25, 1860 died about 1865. John Marshall "Marsh" married Nancy Vosha and Mary Elizabeth "Nannie" Chappel Sept. 10, 1925. Edmond Elisha "Lish" married Arminta "Tee" Matilda Lewis and Lula "Lou" Rogers. Levi I. died before the 1860 San Augustine Federal Census, family legend says that he was killed in a wagon accident. Benjamine Franklin "Frank" married Mary Rebecca Lewis died Aug. 16, 1923.

WILLIS DONAHO, born in South Carolina on March 22, 1804. It is not known when he left South Carolina, but he lived for a time in Mississippi before he arrived in Texas in 1832 as a widower with two children. He lived along the Texas-Louisiana border near Bon Weir and ran a ferry across the Sabine River for several years and there he met and married Hannah Alexander.

Hannah, a widow with two children, arrived in Texas in 1832. Willis and Hannah were married in 1836 in Louisiana, as there was no one where they were living in Texas who could marry them. They had four children, one of whom was Matilda Angeline

Donaho who married John Seaton Knutson in Walker County, Nov. 4, 1852. Matilda and John had William Calvin, my grandfather on Dec. 15, 1854. There are many affidavits in the Texas General Land Office, which prove that both Willis and Hannah received land grants in Texas in 1836.

Willis Donoho, (GGGD), 19686
Helen Knutson Parker, Alamo Mission Chapter DRT 19686

DANIEL DOWNER, born Sept. 12, 1822, in Thakeham, Sussex County, England, was the ninth child born to William Downer and Ann Wells. Daniel came to Matagorda County, TX, and received a grant of 320 acres in 1839. He married Anne Duffy on Sept. 26, 1846, in Matagorda County.

Anne was born June 24, 1819, in Germany to Peter Duffy and Ann Grisar. They had two daughters, Mary and Annie, and one son who died at birth. Daniel was a farmer and rancher. He died Aug. 22, 1877, and is buried in an unmarked grave on his land. Anne died on Nov. 18, 1907 and is buried in Palacios, Matagorda County, TX.

Annie Downer, born Dec. 18, 1852, married Friedrich Cornelius June 24, 1875, in Jackson County, TX. Friedrich was born Dec. 2, 1850 in Germany. They had nine children before she died on April 2, 1894. He died April 30, 1946. They are buried in the Cornelius Cemetery in Matagorda County.

My grandmother, Dora Cornelius, firstborn, was born April 1, 1876, in Matagorda County. She married George Andrew Duffy, born to August Duffy and Epsy Green Murry on May 6, 1873, in Matagorda County. They married April 7, 1897, in Matagorda County. They had Annie, Leo, my father, and Louie. Dora died March 17, 1952, and George died June 7, 1958. They are buried in El Campo, Wharton County, TX.

Bobbie Duffy Dykes, (GGGD), 016651

JOHN DRODDY, son of William Droddy and Ruth Ellison, was born in Virginia about 1790. He married Sarah Hays and was in Texas by 1838 in the Bevil Municipality. He received a Headright Certificate (# 226) for one Labor of land in Newton County. John was a Methodist preacher and years later moved to Milam County, TX.

He and Sarah Hays had four known children. They were: Addney Samuel born about 1820; William Alexander, my husband's ancestor, born May 16, 1823 in Missouri who married Dicey Watson in Newton County, TX July 12, 1849, Isabella, born about 1824 who married John Frazier and Mary Jane, born about 1825 who married Micheal Nugent.

William Alexander fought in the Mexican War and kept a diary, which is preserved at Stephen F. Austin Library in Nacogdoches, TX. He was also a corporal in the Confederate States Army.

John Droddy married Mrs. Sarah Furnash in Burleson County after the death of Sarah Hays. He died Jan. 7, 1845 and is buried near Caldwell, TX according to his Old Testament which has texts marked that he used to preach his sermons on. The bible was published in 1829 and in my possession.

JOSEPH R. DUNMAN, born to John and Jane Gilchrist Dunman on March 10, 1795 at St. Martin's Parish, LA. In early 1812, Joseph served as a private in Colonel Alexander de Clouset's Regiment of Louisiana Militia. In 1824, Joseph and his wife, Nancy "Ann" Greer moved into the Atascosito District with their five children and cleared and established farms. Legal possession was blocked due to rescinding of Colonization Law of 1823. Stephen F. Austin advised appeal to Mexican Authorities. Madero granted a league of land in Liberty County on April 1831. By Certificate #217 Dunman received 1/3 league in Galveston; and by Certificate #222, he was given a labor in Harris County.

The latter part of February 1836, Dunman served as courier delivering to Liberty and Anahuac Travis' immortal plea for reinforcements to the Alamo. "From the 15th May to 13th October 1836" He was "engaged in driving and fencing beeves for the use of Fort Galveston" according to State Archives. Joseph died April 3, 1959 in Harris County, leaving everything to his wife with son Joseph W. executor of the will.

Dunman's Prairie at Houston was named for this family.
Williene Smith Story, (GGGGD), 3427

HILLIARD DURDIN, born in 1798 in Georgia. John Durdin, Hilliard's father, moved his family to Spanish West Florida circa 1807. John was issued a passport through the Creek Indian Nation by the Governor of Georgia on Oct. 8, 1807.

Hilliard married Sarah Richardson about 1820, and had at least two children before moving to Simpson County, MS. He remained there until December 1839, when he emigrated to Texas. Hilliard received a conditional land certificate May 3, 1841, and his unconditional certificate Nov. 25, 1844. The land which he claimed was located in Jasper County.

Hilliard moved to Tyler County before 1850, where he established a large farm, and at the time of his death in 1863, he was cultivating several hundred acres of land.

Hilliard's and Sarah's children were: Edith (Eda) (born 1822, died ca. 1881), married Joseph R. Laird; Nancy (born 1824, died 1911), my ancestor, married William Seamans; Martha A, (born 1827, died 1886), married William A. Parsons; John Jeptha (born 1829, died 1897), married Martha Ann Frances Goode; William James (born ca. 1831, died 1864), married America V. Durham; Canzada (born 1833, died 1914), married Anderson M. Gibson; Lucinda (born ca. 1835, died ca. 1878), married Isaac W. Peters; General L. (born 1837, died 1877), married Mattie Fulgham; Elizabeth (born 1839, died 1898), married James T. Morgan; Sarah (born ca. 1842, died ?), married (1) W.M. Fulgham, (2) E.J. Parsons.

After Sarah's death circa 1853, Hilliard married Elizabeth P. Durham, widow of Levi Durham, circa 1854. Hilliard and Elizabeth had no children from their marriage.

Hilliard was a charter member of the Antioch Primitive Baptist Church, which was organized in 1841 in Buna, TX. He was a charter member and first church clerk of the Philadelphia Primitive Baptist Church, which was organized in the early 1850's near Woodville, TX.

Hilliard died June 29, 1863, and is buried in Pilgrim Rest Cemetery, Tyler County, TX. In 1996, his descendants erected a large monument to his memory at the cemetery.
Ann Crews Laird, (GGGGD), 8061

MARY ELIZABETH EAKER NEW, the daughter of William Armstrong Eaker and Elizabeth Wilford Eaker. She was born Feb. 4, 1838 Mayfield, Graves County. KY. Her Father received a Land Grant in San Augustine County, TX in 1839. She had family in Kentucky and would go to Kentucky to visit them from time to time. On Nov. 13, 1855 she married William Harris New in Graves County, KY.

William is the son of James Bert and Frances Spencer New. William and Mary made their Home in Llano County, TX. They had nine children: James (born 1857), Nancy (born 1859), Amos Frank (born 1861), Thomas (1862), Felix (1866), Edward (1867), Joe (1873), William (1875), and John (1877). The New children grew up in Field Creek.

In 1890 William and Mary along with several of their married children moved to Fort Griffin, TX. After the Fort was closed the family moved to Comanche, OK and Mary Elizabeth Eaker New died Dec. 03, 1914 and is buried beside her husband of 52 years in Comanche Cemetery, Stephens County, OK.
Christine Elizabeth Clark Holland Varnell, (GGGD), 21746
Ardis Marie Clark Holland Christensen, (GGGD), 021749
Verna May Foreman Clark Holland, (GGD), 021743

WILLIAM ARMSTRONG EAKER, son of Michael and Polly Armstrong Eaker was born Sept. 04, 1813 in Christian County, KY. About 1832 he married Elizabeth Wilford. In 1839 he came to Texas and received a Land Grant in San Augustine County, TX.

William and Elizabeth had six children. Felix G. (born 1833), Nancy (born 1834), Mary Elizabeth (born 1838), Amos (born 1841), John (born 1844), and Michael (born 1845). The family moved to Llano County by 186o. Three of Williams' son's fought in the Civil War for Texas. He was a farmer and raised racehorses also.

His first wife Elizabeth died about 1863 and in 1866 he married the widow Sarah Ann Scarbrough Smith. They had four children: William (born 1868), Sallie (born 1869), Yancy Young (born 1870) and Ida (born 1873). He is the grandfather of the famous World War II General, Ira Eaker. He lived out the remainder of his life in Fieldcreek, Llano County TX. He died March 13, 1884. He is buried in a field on what is now the Panther Creek Ranch, Fieldcreek, Llano County. TX.
Jenny Joann Varnell, (GGGGGD), 22562
Christine Elizabeth Clark Holland Varnell, (GGGGD), 21744
Ardis Marie Clark Holland Christensen, (GGGGD), 021747
Verna May Foreman Clark Holland, (GGGD), 021741

ROBERT MOSBY EASTLAND, during the 17th century members of the Eastland family immigrated to America; Robert Mosby Eastland who eventually lived in Texas descended from that family who had settled in Kentucky and then Tennessee. In 1833 the first Eastland to settle in La Grange, TX, was William Mosby Eastland. Eastland County was created Feb. 1, 1858, and was named in William's honor.

Robert Mosby Eastland had been born Jan. 29, 1810, in Sparta, TN, son of Thomas Butler Eastland of Woodford County, KY, and his wife Nancy Mosby Eastland. The White County, TN Oldest Marriage Book (page 20) states that he married Elizabeth (Eliza) Brazeale on Sept. 12, 1843, by the Rev. Jesse Cole.

Maria Lewis Johnson Root, GGD of Robert Mosby Eastland

Two years later they settled in La Grange, TX, where they reared two daughters, Josephine and Fannie. Both daughters later married important Burnet men.

Robert Mosby Eastland taught at Rutersville College, an important institution in Rutersville seven miles from La Grange. Chartered by the Congress of the Republic of Texas, in 1840, the coeducational college provided an opportunity for young people to acquire the education which early Texas families valued. He received a Republic of Texas Land Grant, fourth Class, in 1841 and, possibly, another grant in 1842.

Elizabeth (Eliza) Margrave Brazeale, born Nov. 15, 1824, in Kingston, Roane County, TN, was still a young woman when widowed by the death of Robert Mosby Eastland. She married Warren J. Hill ca 1858 and, widowed again, married Emanuel Sampson on April 16, 1868. Eastland died c 1851; Eliza died many years later in 1904 For further information about Elizabeth Margrave Brazeale Sampson/Hill/Eastland's life refer to Burnet County History by Darrell Debo, two volumes published in 1979.

For information about Robert Mosby Eastland refer to the Daughters Of The Republic Of Texas Patriot Ancestor Album, Vol. I, published by the Turner Publishing Company, Paducah, KY, page 86. Rutersville College and the town of Rutersville, TX are discussed at length in The New Handbook Of Texas, edited by Ron Tyler, published by the Texas State Historical Association, in 1996, page 733. Watterson Folk Of Bastrop County, TX, by D. L. Vest and An Early History Of Fayette County by L.R. Weyand and Houston Wade are excellent sources.

Robert Mosby Eastland's life, particularly his work at Rutersville College, bring great pride to his descendants.
Elizabeth Lewis Root Jones, (GGGD), 19450

LEWIS ENDT AND MARY ANN MILES, Lewis Endt

was born in Baden, Germany about 1800-02. His port and exact date of entry is unknown. His naturalization papers and obituary would indicate that he came about 1817 still under the age of 18. No other documentation has surfaced to about his movements in the 10 years following his arrival into this country until January 1827, when he married Jane Holliman in Woodville, Wilkinson County, MS. The following year he married Mary Ann Miles on April 17, 1828. Mary Ann was born May 19, 1813 in Tennessee or Kentucky, possibly the daughter of Moses Miles. The 1830 Federal Census places Lewis in Wilkinson County, MS as of June 1830. Immediately afterwards they left for Texas, where on June 15, 1830 Lewis signed a Character Certificate in Austin, TX on behalf of himself and "my wife, Mary age 15 of Mississippi."

How long and where Lewis and Mary lived in Texas is not known, nor is it known whether or not they went to Texas in a group with others. The political climate of the time may have contributed to their moving back to Mississippi sometime around 1836-37, when their first child James Ballance Endt was born in Yazoo, MS. on April 9, 1837, and the Choctaw lands were opened to settlement. By the time the 1840 federal census of Mississippi was taken, they were living in Yazoo County. Land records show him witnessing land conveyances with Martin Anding and James Ballance, earlier friends from Wilkinson County. An interesting note: Lewis and Mary Ann named some of their children Anding, Ballance, Cage after their friends, Martin Anding, James Ballance, and Henry Cage. There does not appear to be a blood or family relationship.

The 1850 census placed the family in Harrison County, MS.

By 1860, the family was living at Bayou Manchac, in Ascension Parish, LA. He listed himself as a cotton planter, had considerable property and slaves in Ascension and Livingston Parishes. Here, he and Mary Ann raised their children James Ballance, who married Kate Suter in New Orleans in 1860; Josephine, born abt. 1840 who never married; Lavinia, born abt. 1842, who married Thomas Suter (a brother of Kate) in New Orleans, Sept. 12, 1864; Lucia Cage, born Nov. 25, 1845, who married William P. Denham in Baton Rouge; Anna Elizabeth, born abt. 1852, who married William Biberon in Baton Rouge; Celeste Anding, born May 1, 1848, who married William Hiram Stevens in Baton Rouge on Oct. 4, 1871; Marshall, of whom nothing is known, but presumably died young; Lewis Jr., who died at age 16 in New Orleans; and Nellie May, who married J.W. Pearce in Baton Rouge.

Lewis died at Bayou Manchac on Jan. 30, 1872. His burial place is unknown. His wife and children sold the property in 1881 and moved to Baton Rouge, joining the Methodist Church there. Of his children, James a veteran of the Civil War went to Texas and lived in Galveston and Beaumont. He died in Beaumont in 1921 and was buried in San Antonio. Lucy and William Denham lived for a while in Ranger, TX, and are buried in Magnolia Cemetery in Baton Rouge, LA. Mary Ann moved to New Orleans where she lived with her daughter Nellie Pearce until Mary Ann's death March 15, 1899.

JOSEPH EVANS, son of Joseph Evans Sr. and Elizabeth Earnest, was born in 1809, in Wayne County, KY. He married Mrs. Alice Thompson Dickson Nov. 28, 1828 in Morgan County, AL. Alice, the daughter of James and Violet Thompson, was born in 1806 in South Carolina. They moved to Jackson County, TX in 1839.

Their nine children were; Martha Jane, born 1829, married Robert H. Andrews; John T. born 1831, died 1850, Celia E., born 1833, died 1850; Joseph H. born 1835, died 1864; Felix Earnest, born 1840, died 1906; Clark Owen, born 1843, married Martha M. Ewing; James born about 1841, died 1843; Alice Susan, born Jan. 8, 1845; Julia Atheldria, born 1848, married Edgar Powell Moore. Joseph Evans married Mrs. Nancy Blanton, June 1, 1853, Gonzales County, TX and had two more sons, Andrew J. born 1855, married Mary Frances Bauers; and Robert D. born 1862.

Joseph received a Headright Certificate for 640 acres in 1839; he was a farmer and cattleman. In 1842, he served in the Jackson County Rangers. Joseph died Jan. 27, 1874, near Waelder, Gonzales County, TX.

Alice Susan Evans, named above, first married Francis Jallett Holliman, Dec, 26, 1866, and had one daughter, Mary Elizabeth, born Dec. 7, 1867, died April 21, 1954, married John Alexander Johnson, July 23, 1885. Francis Jallett 'Doc' Holliman, born 1842, was the son of Barden L. Holliman and Nancy ONeal. Susan married Madison Matthew Mullins, Oct. 12, 1872, and had five children; Nora Earnest born March 23, 1874, married Boyd Preston Peeler; Annie Doak, born 1877, married Frank Johnson; Mattie Gertrude, born Aug. 3, 1880, died May 25, 1968, Josie, born 1883, married Adtkinson; Robert Monroe, born Dec. 1, 1887, married Myrtle Peeler.
Ginne' Liles, (GGGGD), 20402
Eugenia Letbetter, (GGGD), 21971

DANIEL FARRIS, born ca. 1800 and his wife, Keziah, was born ca. 1810, both in South Carolina. They arrived in Texas in

January 1835. As listed in The First Census of Texas, 1829-1836, in Sabine District: Daniel, age 32, and his wife, Keziah, age 30. At that time they had seven children, two were born in Mississippi: James born 1830 and Jameson, born in 1832. Five were born in Texas: Jackson, in 1835; Sarah Jane, born in 1837; Lucinda, born 1839; Louisa, born 1841; and Thomas, born in 1844. The fourth child, Sarah Jane, married Jesse Bean Ratliff on Jan. 19, 1854 in Caldwell County. Sarah Jane died on Sept. 13, 1917 in Llano County and was buried in Six Mile Cemetery. It is unknown when or where Daniel or Keziah died.

Frances Maurine Perkins Godwin, (GGGGD), 20871-S

SARAH JANE FARRIS, daughter of Daniel and Keziah Farris, was born July 27, 1837 in Texas. Sarah Jane married Jesse Bean Ratliff in Caldwell County on Jan. 19, 1854. Their children: James, born Feb. 15, 1855, died July 12, 1918; Samuel Houston, born July 7, 1857, died Dec. 17, 1930; Baldwin Harrison, born Oct. 8, 1859, died Feb. 24, 1937; Sarah Keziah, born Aug. 24, 1861, died Nov. 4, 1867; Thomas Jesse, born March 27, 1863, died Dec. 25, 1944; Laura Jane, born Oct. 10, 1866, died Mar. 28, 1921; Sarah Rebecca, born April 27, 1868, died Feb. 20, 1933; William Henry, born July 2, 1871, died Jan. 21, 1930; Louise Matilda, born Jan. 9, 1873, died Nov 15, 1876; Netty May, born March 27, 1877, died April 1, 1954; Reuben Jacob, born Oct. 17, 1879, died Jan. 10, 1932; Nancy Jane, born April 29, 1884; died Nov. 2, 1961; Deedy, born Dec. 29, 1885, died April 6, 1887; and Eva, born Jan. 16, 1893, died Feb. 27, 1893. Jesse died May 31, 1902, and Sarah Jane died Sept. 13, 1917. They are buried in Six Mile Cemetery, Llano County. Samuel, the second son, married Arrenia White, daughter of Abel White and Elizabeth Craton Jones. Later they moved to Llano County where Samuel was a rancher, and they had eight daughters. Arrenia died Nov. 6, 1930; Samuel died Dec. 18, 1930 and buried in the Flat Rock Cemetery in Llano County.

Frances Maurine Perkins Godwin, (GGD), 20872-S

ELI FENN came to Texas in 1832 in search of his father—in-law, David Fitzgerald, whom the family had not heard from in 10 years. Fitzgerald had recently died when Eli arrived.

In January 1822, David Fitzgerald had arrived in Texas with his son John Fitzgerald, Joseph Frazier, and two slaves at the mouth of the Brazos River in a 40-foot boat. Fitzgerald and passen-

1896 Hillcoat Ranch in Brackettville, TX. (Back) Tom Hickey, Lottie Fenn, Rebecca Fenn, Mollie Fenn, Lizzie Williams (Front) J.J. Fenn, Jr., Mary Fenn McKeever, Sally Fenn, and Belle Fenn.

gers from the Lively proceeded up the river to present day Richmond. Fitzgerald received a land grant as one of the Old 300. David Fitzgerald was born in Georgia about 1765. David's daughter, Sarah Catherine Fitzgerald, born on a Georgia plantation Aug. 22, 1797, married on Jan. 24, 1817, Eli Fenn, born in Hancock County, GA on Jan. 7, 1794. Their children were Jesse Thadeus Fenn born in Mississippi about 1817 and John Rutherford Fenn, born Oct. 18, 1824 in Lawrence County, MS. Eli arrived in Texas in 1832, in 1837 was a signer of a petition for Fort Bend, TX to become a county, and later served on the first Fort Bend County Grand Jury. Eli died in 1840, and Sarah died in 1860.

An interesting experience of young John Fenn's in 1836 was his capture by Santa Anna's forces as they crossed Fort Bend County. He escaped the next day and joined his family on the Runaway Scrape.

Jesse Thadeus Fenn married Irene Trotter and died in Fort Bend County in 1874 leaving a large family. John Rutherford Fenn married Rebecca Matilda Williams, daughter of Daniel Williams and Ann Fitzrandolph Ayers on April 13, 1852 in Fort Bend County, TX. Rebecca was born in 1835 at Woodville, MS; her family came to Texas in 1845 and settled on Oyster Creek in Fort Bend County.

John and Rebecca's children: Francis Marion Otis Fenn married Lottie Benson they had one son Rutherford Benson Fenn. Mary married James McKeever; they had no children. Belle married Horace Clarke; they had no children; and Joseph Johnson Fenn, born in 1868 in Fort Bend County, married Mollie Walker on June 20, 1888; Mollie was born at Walker's Station, TX, on Oct. 14, 1873 and died on Sept. 18, 1963. Their children were: John McKeever, born about 1889, never married, died Dec. 30, 1974; Joseph Johnson Jr., born Aug. 7, 1891; and Sally Ayers, born Aug. 31, 1894, died in Kinney County, TX at the age of 4.

Joseph Johnson Fenn Jr. married Laura Dietz at Lake Charles, LA, March 7, 1931 and died Sept. 26, 1971 in Houston, TX. Laura was born in Hye, TX on March 1, 1902 and died Oct. 29, 1991 in Houston, TX. Their three children: Mary Elizabeth Fenn, born Feb. 15, 1932; Joseph Johnson Fenn III, born July 22, 1933; and William Preston Fenn, born Oct. 6, 1940. Mary Elizabeth married Charles Morgan Stamey on Sept. 2, 1965. Charles' children: Sherry, Charles Jr., Mark, and Melinda. Joseph married Mona Mary Moyle on Sept. 12, 1959. Their children: John, William, Susan, Rebecca, Joanne, and Laura. William Preston married Dorothy Jean Haisler on Aug. 13, 1960 their daughter: Leslie Veronica Fenn.

Mary Elizabeth Fenn Stamey, (GGGD), 015295

MARY SUSAN SIMONS FISHER, born Jan. 1, 1843, at Texana, TX. On Dec. 4, 1861, Mary Susan married Reverend Orceneth Asbury Fisher. She was the daughter of Captain Thomas Simons and Susan Thomas Simons, who arrived in Texas in 1835. Reverend Fisher was the son of Dr. Orceneth Fisher and Elizabeth Watts. Dr. Orceneth Fisher came to Texas in 1839 in order to report to the Methodist Church on conditions in Texas. He returned to Illinois and published a book, *Sketches of Texas* in 1840. The following year he and Bishop Morris led a group of five wagons to Texas.

O.A. Fisher was in that group of pioneers. Children and their spouses: Fannie and Harper Simpson, Sterling and Susan Harper, Judith and Albert Harper, Annalee and Sidney Fly, Travis and Ola Boyce, Jesse and Kate Wentworth, William and Mattie Taylor, Elizabeth and Murray Wentworth, Ella and Rollie Harper, Thomas and Lula Barrow, and Carrie and Gordon Laughter.

A son, a grandson, and three great-grandsons became Methodist ministers.

Mary Susan Simons Fisher died June 17, 1912.

Carrie Laughter, (Real Daughter), 6511
Anna Lee Ratliff, (GD), 6512
Mary Frels, (GD), 8213
Mary Katherine Crenshaw, (GGD), 20918
Suzanne Brantley, (GGD), 8581
Carol Strarup, (GGD), 8047

Mary Susan Simons Fisher

GREENLEAF FISK, The Father Of Brownwood, TX", was born May 19, 1807, in Albany, NY. He died Jan. 26, 1888 in Brownwood, TX; is buried in Greenleaf Cemetery of Brownwood, TX. He attended Lanes Theological Seminary in Ohio and Hanover College, Indiana, where he studied law. His military service was with Mina Volunteers, Battle of San Jacinto.

Greenleaf began earning his own living at the age of 12, working on a dairy farm in New Jersey. He moved to Texas in 1834. Where he met and married Mary A. Manlove, the daughter of Bartholomew Manlove. She was a young lady of sterling qualities.

Greenleaf Fisk

Greenleaf joined the Mina Volunteers under Captain Jessie Billingsly and served in the Battle of San Jacinto. After the war he returned to Bastrop to find his wife and her family who had fled because of Mexican threats. After sometime, he found her and his first-born son, William A. Fisk. The family returned to Bastrop. Greenleaf held many public offices including member of the Senate, County Judge, Mayor and Chief Justice.

Mary A. bore him seven children before her death: William A., James B., Ann Elizabeth, Josiah, Margaret Jane, Sarah Ann and Mary Elmira.

Greenleaf later married Mary Hawkins, who bore him eight children: Greenleaf Jr., Cicero, Emma, Hosea, Naomi, Mattie, Phoebe and Milton.

In 1860 he moved the family to Brownwood, TX. Portions of which he had surveyed in 1846. When drought left the main settlement without water and a problem with an alternate town site, Greenleaf donated 60 acres of land and an additional 100 acres for county use. He was known thereafter as "The Father of Brownwood".

WILLIAM B. FLATT was born in Gasconade County, MO, in 1821. When his father James died in 1826, his mother Margaret listed their children: Delia Hooper, Mary Flatt, John Flatt, William Flatt, James Flatt, and Albin Flatt, living in Gasconade County, MO. William's father James (born 1788-89 in Madison County, KY) and William's mother Margaret Peggy West (born 1790-91 in Barren County, KY) married Sept. 17, 1801.

William's grandfather John Flatt (born 1759 on the Delaware River) had married Patience Logston, volunteered to fight in the Revolutionary War, and been associated with the Mammoth Cave, known as Flatt's Cave at one time in Kentucky. William came to Texas in 1839 where he married Lucinda Burton, daughter of Benjamin Burton (Bruton), Red River County, about 1844.

Lucinda (born 1823, Washington, County, IL) and William's children were Delila Ann, Alvin, Arthur, Leasel, Anne M., William McK., and Minnia A. Flatt. Alvin married Margaret A.E. Fuller, Jan. 11, 1866. Their daughter Dora Emma (born Aug. 11, 1875) married Marion Lewis Chapman, Feb. 22, 1891.

William Flatt died 1865, and Lucinda died 1875, both in Van Zandt County, TX.

Gelene Duncan Simpson, (GGGD), 19930

JUAN NEPOMUCENO FLORES, born in San Antonio de Bexar Nov. 7, 1811, died Dec. 2, 1878, served in Colonel Juan N. Seguin Company as corporal, Jan. 1, 1835 to Oct. 11, 1836. As first Lieutenant, Oct. 14, 1836 to Oct. 14, 1837. Participated in Storming of Bexar December 1835, and the Battle of San Jacinto April 21, 1836. He continued in the Texas Volunteers for two years after. Service Record No. 4223. He was issued a Headright Certificate for a League and a Labor of land May 11, 1838 by the Bexar County Board. May 15, 1838 was issued a donation certificate No. 82100' for 640 acres of land for having participated in the Battle of San Jacinto.

Later he received a Bounty Certificate No. 3487 for 1280 acres of land for having served in the Texas Army from January 1835 to Feb. 25, 1837.

Flores was the son of Antonio Flores de Abrego and his wife Maria Antonia Rodriquez, a descendant of the Canary Islanders who arrived in San Antonio March 9, 1731 to establish the First Civil Government in what is now Texas.

Juan Nepomuceno Flores and his wife, Maragarita Josepha Valdes had three children, Antonio Serapio Flores, Juan Nepomuceno and Mariano. The latter two died childless.

Antonio Serapio married Ursula Xeminez. They had 11 children.

One of their sons Carlos Alberto Flores married Lucinda Tarin. Their two children are, Aurelia Flores Deuvall and John Charles Flores.

Aurelia Flores Deuvall, daughter of Carlos A. Flores, 10108 FM 1303

JAMES FORSYTH was born in Logan County, KY ca. 1805. He immigrated to Texas in 1820, crossing the Sabine River at Logansport and settling in what later became Shelby County and there he married Dorcus Latham, daughter of King Latham, who came to Texas among the pioneers of the Republic of Texas.

James Forsyth was one of three children. His brother John, who died in Harris County, TX and a sister, Mrs. Margaret McFadden, wife of Samuel McFadden and she died near old Pulaski.

James and Dorcus Latham Forsyth owned and operated a small farm at Beckville and he located there after he had been forced to leave Shelby County in 1842, because of his refusal to take sides in the Regulator-Moderator War, moving first to Houston County, and then to Panola County. James Forsyth died ca. 1867 at Beckville, Panola County, TX.

James and Dorcus had the following children: John, William, Margaret, James P., Amanda, Samuel, Caroline and Nelson.

Amanda Jane Forsyth married James Henry Womack Nov. 15, 1865 and their son; William Lark Womack who was my Grandfather married Lillie Nae Bishop. Their son, Bob Clyde Womack, my father married Stella M. Townsend.

Wanema Womack Bullard, (GGGD of James Forsyth), DRT #20808

LUDEWIG CARL FERDINAND FRANCKE was born in Guestrow, Mecklenburg, on June 28, 1818, at 11:30 p.m., the son of Reverend Peter Heinrich Francke and his second wife, Helena Elizabeth Henriette Augustine von Kamptz.

He studied piano and violin for some time in Berlin, but on realizing that he was not gifted enough to become a musician of first rank, he decided to study law. After securing his degree at the University of Jena he practiced law in Mecklenburg. He apparently soon became dissatisfied with the existing autocratic restrictions of German officialdom immigrated to the Republic of Texas in 1845. Francke's motive for leaving Germany is not known, whether it was his distaste for law, or a love of adventure, or the unhappy political conditions in Europe at that time.

On Oct. 25, 1847, Louis Francke joined the Texas Ranger Force and took part in campaigns against the Indians and in the Mexican War, serving for about two years. According to family tradition, he traveled to Mexico City during this period as a member of a troop guarding a shipment of silver. This may have been the silver paid Mexico by the United States Government in the purchase of Texas and the Southwest. He also spent some time in California during the Gold Rush there.

On Nov. 10, 1853, he received his naturalization papers. On this document his name is spelled Lewis Franke, and this spelling of the family name has been customary since.

He married Bernhardine Helene Friederike Dorothea Romberg in 1853. She was the eldest child of Fredericke Bauch Romberg and Johannes Christlieb Nathaniel Romberg, a poet and farmer living on the San Bernard River near Cat Spring. After the Rombergs moved to the Black Jack Springs community in Fayette County the Frankes soon followed them and purchased a farm there. During these first years of their married life they also lived at Independence, where he taught music and languages at old Baylor College. They soon found, however, that their limited financial means made it impossible for them to associate on terms of equality with the wealthy planter families of the vicinity. So they left Independence, returning to their farm near Black Jack Springs. There, Louis Franke farmed during the rest of his life, although he also practiced law on the side. Their home at first was a small log cabin, but later additional rooms were built to accommodate their growing family.

In 1859, after a severe illness, his physician advised a sea voyage to restore his health. His trip to Europe also seems partly to have been prompted by religious motives. He had evidently become a skeptic during his younger days; his wife's family also were atheistic in belief. Neither he nor his wife had any affiliation with a church at this time. After the birth of their older children, husband and wife began to feel the need of some definite religious faith. While in Europe, therefore, he made a study of the doctrine and organization of the different denominations. Conversation with his old pastor in Germany convinced him that he was still really a Lutheran and should return to the church of his fathers. On his return to America, he and his wife became members of the Lutheran Church.

LOUIS AND BERNHARDINE FRANKE had become acquainted with Conrad Schueddemagen and his wife Wilheimine Bauer Schueddemagen of Round Top, TX. Their admiration for Mrs. Schueddemagen led to a fast friendship, resulting many years later in four intermarriages of the two families.

Louis Franke, sketch by Francke Steinhauser, Rome, Italy 1859.

The Civil War period of 1860-1865 brought many material hardships. Like his father-in-law and his wife's brothers, as well as other German Americans of that time, he probably was not in sympathy with the cause of slavery.

At the close of the Reconstruction Period, during Governor Davis' administration, Louis Franke was elected representative from Fayette County (in 1872), and as such was a member of the first Democratic legislature following tile ousting of the "carpet baggers." This legislature is known in Texas history as "The Great Liberator." He was chairman of the Immigration Committee.

At the end of the session, on Feb. 19, 1873, at 7:30 in the evening, as he was descending the steps of the Old Capitol at Austin (at the foot of the hill on which the present Capitol stands), after having drawn his legislative pay of $260 in anticipation of leaving for home the next day, he was fatally injured and robbed by some unknown assailants. He received two head wounds and in falling down the steps he broke his thighbone. When he was found later, lying unconscious on the steps of he building, he was carried to the home of a friend where he died at 4:30 the next morning. His body was taken home to Black Jack Springs for burial by a guard of honor. His grave is in the family burying ground on the farm. The murderers were never found, and so far as is known robbery was their only motive.

His widow, who was not yet forty at the time of his death, refused a government pension which friends offered to secure for her, and resolutely took charge of the operation of the farm and the rearing of their eight children. With the help of her sons she increased the farm holdings to more than seven hundred acres. She not only prospered financially but also succeeded in making honest, upright men and women of all her sons and daughters.
Helen Franke, GD of Louis Franke.
Gertrude Franke, GD of Louis Franke and Metche Franke, GGD of Louis Franke, both Daughters of the Republic of Texas)

HARMON FRAZER, son of William Frazier and Dicy Dover of Scotland, was born circa 1788 in South Carolina. Mr. Frazier served as first sergeant in Captain Peter Searcy's company, first Regiment Tennessee Militians in the War of 1812. He married Martha "Pasty" Wallace June 27, 1816.

Mr. Frazier moved his family to Texas by January of 1835 and was given a Mexican Title to one league, located in present Tyler County, TX. Like many settlers he left the area with the Run-a-way scrap of 1836 and settled in Sabine County were he surveyed and laid out Sabinetown. He also served as county clerk along with his son William B. Frazier, who was District clerk. With the Texas War of Independence he served in their army.

Harmon and Pasty had 10 children before her death circa 1839.

William Bascomb, born July 25, 1817; married Oct. 29, 1857 to Mary E. Brown, Alexander L., born Feb. 19, 1819. Caroline Elizabeth, born March 5, 1821 and on Sept. 8, 1838 she married Robert Holmes Bloomfield from England. After his death in about 1844, she married James Clark. Caroline died circa 1900; Martha Agnes was born on Feb. 10, 1823 and married Alfred Leroy Kavanaugh on July 15, 1845. Martha died Feb. 8, 1901; Mary Louisa was born June 30, 1825; George M., born Jan. 5, 1828, married Jan. 4, 1858 to Mary Edgar and second to Billy Lambert. George died Aug. 27, 1908 and is buried in Alpine, Brewster County, TX; Tennessee Jane was born March 8, 1830, she married Jeremiah Spiller on Feb. 13, 1848; On Sept. 13, 1832 Tom Jefferson was born; A child who died at birth was born in October of 1835 not long after this family arrived in Texas from Tennessee; The last child born of this marriage was Edmund P. on Jan. 21, 1837, died March 13, 1846.

By 1844 Mr. Frazer returned to Tyler County and there he married Mrs. Nancy "Durdin" Pool, widow of William Pool. His land was located on part of the fenced in village of the Indians where he had a trading post. He also was a Methodist preacher and performed the ceremony of his step-daughter, Mary E. Pool. Mr. Frazier was a Mason and continued to survey many tracts of land. He served in the Civil War with the Mt. Hope Home Guard and was a charter member of Bethany Church.

This second marriage also produced 10 more children. The first was twins, James Durden, and Cinthillia Milvina, born Aug. 3, 1844. Charles Wesley born Oct. 16, 1846 and died June 16, 1860; Robert L., born May 24, 1849 was also a twin to a brother who died at birth; on March 8, 1851 John Harmon was born and he died May 10, 1936. He also was a twin to Mary Priscilla; Nancy Texana was born Feb. 4, 1856 in Polk County and Sept. 21, 1871 she married Hilliard Durdin Laird. Nancy died Jan. 28, 1940, George E. born Sept. 28, 1859, died March of 1860; last came Sam Braxton on Dec. 26, 1861. Sam died June 17, 1884.

Mr. Frazer left a paper trail that showed he was not only a dreamer, but a doer. With his wisdom he began dividing all his property before his death on Dec. 7, 1874. Nancy lived until Aug. 27, 1875.

Margaret Linda Hale, (GGGGD), 17226

CAROLINE MATILDA FRAZIER, born 1802, Virginia; parents Joseph and (?) Frazier; married Hugh Allen, 1820, Warren County TN. See Hugh Allen for info on children. Family left Tennessee in 1836, walked to Texas, arrived 1837, first settled Red River County on Land Grant # 190.

Family relocated in 1846 to Cibolo Creek in Bexar County, March 1858 found the family living on the San Saba River at Fort Belknap Crossing, 18 miles North of Ft. Mason in McCulloch County in a log and field-stone home built by Hugh Allen and son–in–law Wm. R. Turner. The home was designed and built over a spring-fed creek thus creating running water for the home. That portion of the old historical home is still in use and is presently known as Wau–Ban–See, an Indian name meaning "Mirror Water". The area surrounded by mountains was a favorite camping spot for the Indians. Fearing that family, livestock and property were in grave danger from marauding Indians, Hugh Allen wrote Gov. Runnells a letter on Nov. 21, 1858

pleading for protection. Soon after that, a white man was scalped in the area, the property was sold and the family moved back to Bexar County.

In old age, Caroline and Hugh moved to Burnet County and lived with their son, Daniel Parker Allen, on the Colorado River. Caroline was baptized in the Strickling Baptist Church in 1866 and died on Dec. 6, 1867. She is buried in the old Burnet Cemetery. Caroline was a devoted wife, mother and pioneer settler who left simple tracks in history, tracks that her descendents still honor today.

Bonnie Allen Chambless, (GGGD), 22257S

AMBROSE COWPERTHWAITE FULTON, born July 7, 1811 in Sadsbury, Chester County, PA, the son of Joseph and Esther Cowperthwaite Fulton. About 1828 he went to sea. He heard Davy Crockett speak in Benton, MS in 1831 and maintained that Crockett's words gave him the courage to make his own way in the world. That year he settled in New Orleans.

Ambrose C. Fulton

On Oct. 11, 1835, he called a meeting for the friends of Texas to meet at Banks Arcade where several speakers, including Fulton, addressed the assembly. Resolutions were presented and volunteers signed up to enter in the aid of Texas.

On October 17 the ship Columbus left New Orleans with 380 volunteers (Captain Robert C. Morris second Company of New Orleans Greys), and Fulton numbered among them. After arriving in Texas, he was wounded at the Siege of Bexar. Fulton witnessed the capitulation of General Cos, and, like many others, believed that no further action would be taken to subdue Texas. He returned to New Orleans and did not participate in the actions of 1836.

On Aug. 7, 1839 in Philadelphia, he married his first cousin, Mary Cowperthwaite, daughter of Ambrose and Deborah Lehman Cowperthwaite. Their children were: Syrella Lehman, (1841-1848), never married; Le Claire, (born 1843, died 1928), never married; George Clarence, (born 1845, died 1846), never married; Harry Clifford, (born 1847, died 1911), married Ella Sickels in 1876; Mary Josephine, (born 1849, died 1850), never married; Theodore, (born 1851, died 1914), never married; Adele, (born 1854, died 1881), never married; Fanny, (born 1855, died 1943), married Zadok Ingram Nutt, DDS in 1882; Mary Cowperthwaite, (born 1857, died 1942), married Robert Alexander Holliday, DDS, in 1884.

In 1842, Fulton, moved to Davenport, IA. A commercial building contractor, he also served as a Scott County Commissioner. In 1854, he was elected to the Iowa State Senate.

In 1884, 73-year-old Fulton returned to "the Lone Star's Lexington", Mission Conception. He puzzled as to where the veterans of that conflict might be. "I have searched, advertised, but not a sign of one is to be found." He also visited "Santa Anna's Waterloo" at San Jacinto before returning to Davenport.

Ambrose Cowperthwaite Fulton died Oct. 16, 1903 at Davenport, IA. His wife preceded him in death on June 11, 1897.

LOUCINDA HUNTER GAINES was born 1821 in Elbert County, GA to John Gaines and Elizabeth Rucker Herndon. John Gaines was the grandson of Heironeum Gaines and Margaret Talliafero of Albemarle County, VA. John Gaines migrated with his family to Talledega County, AL, where Loucinda married William Hunt the grandson of John Hunt-namesake for Huntsville, AL.

In 1837, she joined her Hunt in-laws for the migration to Washington County, TX; later Loucinda and William Hunt made their home on the Colorado River in Fayette County. Their children, all born in Texas, were: John Dillard, Elizabeth A., Sarah P. Martha Ann, Alexander David, Lydia Evelyn, Mary F., Alice L. and Willie Lou. William died in 1864 and widow Loucinda operated their farm and reared their large family during the difficult time after the Civil War.

Loucinda died 1886 and is buried with her husband and other family members in the Old City Cemetery, La Grange, Fayette County, TX.

Frances Nuckols Cook, (GGD), 13733

JOHN GALLION was born about 1805 in Ohio. He married Sarah Rhoads, born 1805/1806 and they were married about 1826. John came to Texas with his family and widowed mother Eleanor Gallion, wife of Elijah Gallion. It is said that on June 30, 1838, Eleanor Gallion went to the San Augustine Courthouse to apply for a headright land grant. She received one league and one labor. Her land grant was lost until 1898 when her granddaughter, M.F. Rogers, found it and claimed it. John and his family settled in present day Trinity County. John and Sarah had five children: Sena Roberta born 1826/1827, married Thomas Trevathan about 1844 or 45 in Trinity County; Lucy C. born 1832, married W.W. Spencer; Pheoby/Pheeby born 1833, married A.G. (Allen Greer) Rogers; Dollhean born 1835, married Isaac Dawson and Eliza N. born 1836 married A. Chandler.

John Gallion received 25 leagues from the Mexican government in 1835 located in DeZavala Colony in what is now Sabine County, TX. He lived there until 1853 or 1855 when he purchased two land grants in 1855. One from Mr. Conklin it was for 320 acres and another 320 acres from Thomas L. Trevathan one of his sons–in–law. These tracts constituting 640 acres were located in Trinity County, TX near the little community of Trevat, named for the Trevathan family that settled there. He and Sarah developed the land into a cattle ranch and a farm and lived out their lives there. It is not certain where they are buried, but it is believed in the Trevat Cemetery.

The Third Legislature State of Texas Chapter CLX appointed John Gallion in February 1850. He was to serve together with Jesse James, Benjamin B. Ellis, Solomon Adams, James Marsh, Henry Ward, and Duke M. Hornsby as commissioners to locate a site for the county seat of the newly established county of Trinity. Today the county seat is Groveton, TX. John Gallion served one term as County Commissioner.

Lanelle Hodges Killebrew, 21280
Sheila Kaye Killebrew, 21935

JAMES GENTRY came to Texas prior to 1839 and received Land Grant Number 299. Born in 1792 to James and Mary Gentry of Albemarle, VA, he married Peachy Langford in 1823. Their daughter, Elizabeth Catherine, was born in Virginia in 1827. James and Peachy farmed in Williamson and Gonzales Counties. Their other children were Charles, Polly, James, Ellen and Caroline. In 1851, when James' father died at age 94 in Albemarle, the younger James Gentry, age 59 by then, and his daughter, Catherine, rode horseback back to Virginia to help settle the estate. Peachy died in 1871 and James in 1875 in Gonzales. Location of their graves unknown.

In 1857, Catherine married James Mahan. Their children were: Jeannette Catherine, Josephine Scott and Alice Todd. James Mahan died in 1869, leaving three daughters, all, under age 11, for Catherine to raise. Jeannette Catherine was the designated "boy", riding fence and burning prickly pear for the cows. Catherine Mahan died in 1898, and is buried at Lytton Springs. Location of James Mahan's grave is unknown.

In 1878, Jeannette Catherine married Martin V. Browder, and they farmed extensively. Their children were: Belle Matilda, his daughter from a previous marriage, married W.M. Inglet (eight children); Isham Clay married Florence Perkins (six children); Laura Alice, a teacher, died age 23; Homer Emmitt married Eula Christine Brown (four children); Mona E. died age four; James Hardy married Adah Simmons, (four children); Robert Oliver married first to Lula Thomas and later Mattie Anderson (two children); Rachel A., lifelong teacher, married Art Willis (four children); Paul Kruger married Hattie Howell (ten children). All the boys farmed or ranched in the Brownwood-Bangs area, except Robert Oliver, a Methodist preacher. Homer and Eula bought a stock farm at Miles, near San Angelo, and later a ranch at Eldorado. Oliver and Hardy built churches, including Rocky Creek, where several family members are buried. Martin died in 1926; Jeannette in 1928, both buried at Rocky Creek near Brownwood.

Publication: "Gentry Family in America", 1909, by Richard Gentry
Family History: "Who Am I?" by Rachel A. Willis
Fern Browder Dillard, (GGGD), 20602
Linda Diane Tunison, (GGGGD), 21662
Amy Lynne Haden, (GGGGGD), 22636

WILLIAM GEORGE born in Shenandoah, VA in 1784. William, a Methodist minister, married a Cherokee, Delilah, born 1788 in South Carolina. They were first in East Tennessee but were in Indiana by 1811. In 1834, they brought eight children to Texas in 1834 in the Burnet Colony.

Sons Stephen and William Eads and son–in–law, John Chisum, were active with Stephen Blount's company at Nacogdoches and in Nacogdoches politics.

George received a league and labor in Cherokee and Smith Counties, lived at Knoxville, and died in 1852. His children scattered. Judah married Hiram Walker, Methodist minister, and died about 1855 at Larissa. Stephen married Lucinda Anderson and died in 1865, probably at Larissa. Mary Elizabeth "Polly" married first John Van Winkle and second John Chisum. Polly and Chisum are buried on his Greer County, Texas/Oklahoma land grant.

William Eads, Methodist minister/tavern owner, married Margaret Davis, and died in Navarro County Delilah married Elijah Chisum, and both died in Limestone County. John Washington "Wash" George married Sarah Ann Anderson and moved to Navarro/Hill County. Jeremiah Jack George married Martha Jane Jolly and died in 1860 of tuberculosis in Cherokee County.

NANCY MATILDA GOODBREAD, DRT Certificate 15163-S, is probably best known for her marriage to Creed Taylor, renowned Indian fighter, Texas Ranger, veteran of Texas War for Independence and Civil War Captain. But she, too, was of sturdy pioneer stock, having lineage to those who fought in the American Revolution and a father who went to Texas in 1834 while it was still under the rule of Mexico.

Major W.A. Spencer and Caroline Hepzibeth Taylor Spencer, son-in-law and daughter of Nancy Matilda Goodbread Taylor.

The Gutrodt family origin has been traced back to the 1500s in Nordheim, Heilbronn, Wiirttemberg, West Germany. The spelling of the family was changed to Goodbread upon their arrival in America. Nancy's grandfather, great-grandfather and two uncles fought in the American Revolution.

Phillip Goodbread took a great chance when he moved his family to Texas The atmosphere was far from safe; Indians were a serious threat and Mexico had stopped all immigration in 1830. Arriving in 1834, they were considered illegal immigrants. Such spunk and spirit would be the undoing of Mexico when Texas fought for and won their independence in 1836. Two of Nancy's brothers are said to have participated in the revolution.

In 1840, Joseph, one of Nancy's brothers, was killed in Shelbyville by Charles W. Jackson, a defeated politician. Joseph's murder is said to have set off Texas' first feud, The War of the Regulators and Moderators. C.L. Sonnichsen wrote of it in his book, *Ten Texas Feuds.*

Born about 1823 in North Carolina, she was named after her mother, Nancy Webb, who died before the family moved to Texas. Nancy married Creed Taylor March 30, 1840 in Grimes County. In his memoirs Creed said, "I was struck by a case of love at first sight from which I never recovered. Six weeks later I rode away to war and was gone for three years." But Nancy evidently was in favor of Creed's ongoing efforts to keep Texas free; she certainly did her part. She took care of the home and children virtually alone and under the most dangerous of circumstances.

They had two sons, John Hays (named after the famous Texas Ranger) and Phillip Goodbread Taylor (called Doughboy). They had one daughter, Caroline Hepzibeth, named after Creed's mother. Doughboy was listed on Creed's Civil War Muster Roll as P.G. Taylor, age 16.

Neither of their sons survived the regrettable Sutton-Taylor Feud. It is ironic that Nancy was involved in two separate feuds in her lifetime ... as if life on the frontier was not hard enough. Many books have been written about the Sutton-Taylor Feud, including *The Texas Vendetta*, written by Victor Rose in 1880 and *I'll Die Before I'll Run*, by C.L. Sonnichen.

Until Nancy's death, June 15, 1865, she and Creed lived on the Ecleto Creek near what is now Stockdale. Their home was built of logs 14 inches in diameter and hand hewn by Creed. Caroline Hepzibeth spoke lovingly of her mother and said that their home was always neat, clean, and "filled with love".

There is no doubt that apron clad Nancy Matilda Goodbread Taylor sacrificed much for her family and loved ones, her community and the Republic of Texas.
Dovie Dell Tschirhart Hall

PHILLIP GOODBREAD, DRT Certificate 15164-Phillip's lineage has been traced back to 1540, Nordheim, Heilbronn, Wurttemberg, Germany. Nordheim is a small village a few miles from Struttgart, an industrial city that was virtually destroyed during World War II. However, Nordheim was left intact; thus preserving the tiny Lutheran Church and all the Gutbrodt family records of births, marriages, christenings and deaths. Gutbrodt was changed to Goodbread in America.

Phillip's grandparents, Barbara Christina and Johann Ludwig Gutbrodt, arrived in Philadelphia on Aug. 16, 1731, aboard the ship "Samuel", accompanied by their children. They settled in Pennsylvania.

Phillip's father, John Goodbread, fought in the American Revolution, as did his grandfather and two of his brothers. Phillip was born in 1784 to John Goodbread and Mary Ledbetter-Bradley. Phillip had one son, Joseph, by his first wife (name unknown). He married Nancy Webb Dec. 19, 1812 and they had six children: Minerva, Thomas, John, Phillip R., Sarah, and Nancy. Nancy must have died before July 4, 1830, for Phillip married Polly Henson on that date. They had one child, Mary Louisa.

In 1834, Phillip brought his family to the wild, raw frontier of Texas, still under the rule of Mexico. He ultimately received a First Class Headright Certificate and settled in Montgomery County.

Joseph, Phillip's oldest son, was killed by Charley Jackson in 1840. The murder, which occurred in Shelbyville, was said to have set off the War of the Regulators and Moderators; an account of the incident appears in "Ten Texas Feuds" by Dr. C.L. Sonnichen. Jackson was reflected to have been embittered over his loss of election to congress.

Phillip's daughter, Nancy, married Creed Taylor, prominent Indian fighter, veteran of Texas' War of Independence, Mexican War participant, one of Texas' youngest Texas Rangers and a Civil War Captain.

Phillip was close to 85 years of age when he died in 1869 or 1870 in Wilson County. He had buried three wives, two sons, Joseph and John, two daughters, Nancy and Minerva, and two grandsons, John Hays Taylor and Phillip Goodbread (Doughboy) Taylor; both sons of Nancy and Creed Taylor.

He endured many hardships and much sadness. Texas is deeply indebted to this hearty pioneer.
Dovie Dell Tschirhart Hall

GEORGE H. AND ELIZABETH WATSON GOODWIN-George H. Goodwin, youngest child of Henry and Sarah Goodwin, was born about 1818 after his parents left Georgia, probably in Tennessee or Alabama. George married Elizabeth N. Watson, daughter of Willis B. and Nancy Watson, about 1837 probably in Shelby County, TX where he was found on the tax list. George died after March 1886 and Elizabeth in December 1879 both are believed to be buried in the Shooks Bluff Cemetery in Cherokee County. George and Willis Watson, his father-in-law, left Texas about 1840 for a brief stay in Jackson County, FL, where five of their 12 children were born. Another was born in Louisiana probably on their way back to Texas before being enumerated in the 1850 Angelina County Census. Their children were:

(1) William A., born 1836, married Letha Ann West; (2) Martha Ann, born 1839, married James T. Thompson, Nov. 18, 1852; (3) Tabitha born Nov. 8, 1841 Florida, married first Isaac Robert Goodwin June 5, 1859, second to G.W. Adams, Aug. 5, 1866. She died Oct. 7, 1923 and is buried in the Mt. Hope Cemetery in Cherokee County; (4) Sara J. born 1844 Florida, married Ransom West; (5) Willis Henry born 1845 Florida, was a private in Company E, Randalls 28th Texas Dismounted Cavalry, Walker Division, CSA; (6) Mary Ann Goodwin, my great-grandmother, was born 1848 in Jackson County, Florida. While visiting her uncle, Andrew Wesley Goodwin, in Lee County Texas, she met and married Richard Cooper Williams, Dec. 24, 1874. "Dick" was born March 11, 1849 in Choctaw County, MS to Joseph F. Williams and Martha C. Lawrence. My grandmother, Adeline Rebecca Elizabeth Williams was born Dec. 27, 1875 in Bastrop County, TX. She told me that her mother died when she was about five years old, which would have been shortly after the 1880 census was taken at Snake Prairie in Bastrop County. It is not known where Mary Ann is buried. Richard, a violinist, married several times after her death and died himself Sept. 2, 1926 and is buried in the Jeffrey Cemetery near McMahan in Caldwell County. Adeline married Jerry Walter Calk April 30, 1896 in Kyle, Hays County, Texas. (7) Lee Anna, born 1848 Florida, married John Chandler, died in 1934 and is buried in Shooks Bluff Cemetery; (8) George C., born June 1849 in Louisiana, married Sara J. Chandler Aug. 17, 1870, died July 4, 1900 and is buried at the Shooks Bluff Cemetery; (9) Burrell G., born Nov. 22, 1850, married Catherine Rebecka Roebuck Aug. 13, 1872, died Jan. 24, 1941 in Cherokee County. He is buried at the Mt. Hope Cemetery and Catherine at Shooks Bluff; (10) Sarilda E., born 1856 Angelina County, married first Andrew Rainey and second E.C. Abshire on June 21, 1882 in Cherokee County; (11) Joseph born 1858, married Laura C. Chandler July 21, 1881, and died in 1887, in Cherokee County; (12) Thomas born 1862 and died December 1879, in Cherokee County.

This Goodwin line goes back to Thomas Goodwyn (died 1731 Surry County, VA) wife Mary, thru son William (born after 1711, died before 1770) wife Tabitha, both died in Halifax County, NC thru son George (born by 1740 Edgecombe County, NC, died 1819-1821) wife Rebecca, both died in Wilkes County, NC; thru son Henry born 1779-1780, married Sarah G., and came to Texas by 1835.
Shirley Thompson Spuhler, (GGGD)
D'Andra Holt Smith, (GGGGD)

HENRY AND SARAH GOODWIN arrived in Texas early, being enumerated in the First Census of Texas in the Teneha District. Henry was born about 1779-1780 in Bute County, NC to George and Rebecca Goodwin. Sarah was born about 1781 in South Carolina, and could possibly be a Whatley, we have no proof yet. Henry's will in Angelina County indicates that he died in June 1850 and names his wife, Sarah G. along with five sons and three daughters: (1) Shirley W., born 1799, married Elizabeth about 1820 possibly in Georgia or Hardeman County, TN; (2) Elizabeth Jane, born 1801, married Moses Gage 1819 in Tennessee, died 1859 Bastrop County buried in the Claiborne Cemetery; (3) Wilson born 1802 married Jane Beardon May 31, 1821 Lawrence County, AL. It is believed that his name is Henry Wil-

son Goodwin; (4) Susan, born 1808 married Allen Stokes Feb. 19, 1824 Lawrence County, AL; (5) Anna, born 1810 married Everitt S. Ritter May 15, 1828 Hardeman County, TN; (6) Robert born 1812 married Mary (Polly) Reynolds, died 1847 Angelina County, TX; (7) Andrew Wesley born 1815 married Mary Ann Ashworth died in Lee County and buried in the Burns-Goodwin Cemetery near Dime Box; (8) George H., born 1818 in Tennessee or Alabama, married Elizabeth N. Watson about 1837 Shelby County, TX. The first seven children were born in Wilkes County, GA.

Henry and sons Robert and Shirley received Mexican Land Grants in October 1835 for one league each in the deZavala Colony.
Shirley Thompson Spuhler, (GGGGD)
D'Andra Holt Smith, (GGGGGD)

JOHN H. GRAHAM was born about 1797 in North Carolina, and died in Robertson County, TX on Jan. 19, 1852. His wife, Margaret, was born about 1801 in Virginia. Both are buried in the Bald Prairie Cemetery in Robertson County, TX. Margaret was last found on the 1870 census of Robertson County living with her son, Charles Graham. Her age is given as 63 and his as 21.

John and Margaret Graham migrated to Texas in 1835 from Tennessee. He entered Texas with his wife and 12 others. According to stories handed down through the family a Mr. Cazey asked the Grahams to care for his son until he returned. When the father did not return the Grahams brought John Cazey to Texas with them.

John and Margaret Graham had eight children, seven girls and one son. The first five children were born in Tennessee and the last three in Texas. The children were Eliza Jane, Elizabeth Emiline, Sarah, Mary, Catherine, Martha Ann, Margaret J., and Charles A.

Eliza Jane married Rev. Thomas H. Eaton; Elizabeth married William Langford; Sarah married M.C. Henderson; Mary married Robert H. Fulbright; Catherine married Scott Cobb; Martha married James M. Brown; Margaret married Robert Cole; and Charles married Corscia S. Boatner.

On Jan. 19, 1852, John H. Graham was robbed and murdered near Wheelock, TX, when returning from a business meeting with around $250.00 in gold. He died intestate and many probate records were located in the Robertson County Court House.

John fought as a Ranger and Minuteman in the Republic of Texas. He was discharged May 9, 1836 at Harrisburg because he was not able to do camp duty. In 1837 he served in Captain Haggard's Frontier Rangers.

On Jan. 16, 1990 in the Bald Prairie Cemetery descendants of John H. and Margaret Graham honored them by dedicating Citizen and Veteran DRT grave markers.
Patsy Todd Silva, (GGGD), 14709
Charline Hereford Frank, (GGGD), 14031

DANIEL HARRIS GRAY, oldest son of Daniel and Sarah Harris Gray, was born in Berlin, (then Stephentown), July 25, 1785, and married first, Naomi Thomas, who died at Berlin, NY, Feb. 23, 1822. She was the mother of six children, four sons and two daughters. Mr. Gray married second, Phebe Godfrey, who was the mother of eight children, four sons and four daughters;

she died at Cedar Hill, Dallas County, TX, Feb. 22, 1855. Mr. Gray, as will be seen, was the father of 14 children, nine of whom were born at Berlin, two in Pike County, IL and three in Texas. He was the owner of a farm at Berlin adjacent to the old homestead, and after his father's death, in 1830, he removed to Atlas, Pike County, IL, then on the borders of the far distant west; no slight undertaking with his large family, making the long journey in the huge emigrant wagon of those days and taking his household goods with him; but it was in due time, after some stirring incidents by the way, safely accomplished. There he remained near kindred, some of whom had preceded, and others who had followed him, until the fall of 1839, when he again moved on for the new El Dorado, TX, where he arrived December 1, having crossed the Red River and the Arkansas, and braved the dangers of the wild frontier, then swarming with Indians and outlaws. There he stuck his stakes and built a house of pine logs, and set about establishing a home. The surroundings just suited his courageous, adventurous spirit.

For more than 25 years, and until his death, he remained a citizen of Texas, and participated in the stirring scenes that marked that stormy period of its history. That he was a man of great physical strength and personal prowess, is abundantly evidenced. And that he was a loyal citizen in the time that tried men's souls, that he fearlessly upheld the Flag of the Union when Secession and Rebellion would have trampled it in the dust; and when armed Traitors stalked abroad with fire and sword threatening death and destruction to all who opposed their mad schemes, Daniel H. Gray, let it forever be said to his honor, let it be recorded as the crowning glory of his life, in the midst of the storm and the tempest was true.

As evidence of Daniel H. Gray's steadfast patriotism, the following quotation from a letter written by his brother, Stephen R. Gray, of Pittsfield, IL, date of July 14, 1861, to friends at Berlin, NY is good testimony. It says: "Daniel's health is good, and his letters interesting. The old man is a true Patriot, God bless him! He says, 'I am for the Old Star Spangled Banner, come life or death!'" And again, what is still more emphatic is the following vivid portrayal by his own hand of a scene, which came near being a tragedy, in which he bravely repelled a band of Texan rebels who essayed to take his life. The letter was written to his brother Stephen, and the original is now at hand:

Cedar Hill, Dallas County, TX

Dear Brother Stephen:
June 12, 1866

Through the goodness of an all-wise God I am yet on earth. I will give you a short sketch of my life for the last four years. You had heard that I was married the third time. The lady thinking that my two sons living with would be compelled to go into the army, (Rebel) thought if she could only get rid of me, horses, cattle, all would be hers at a blow; so she raised the hue and cry that I was Abolition. All knew I voted Union. Let me say right here, my dear brother, how would my conscience have wrung with despair, to have turned against our fathers, the veterans of the Revolution! "Union!" yes, that is my motto, and will be in my dying moments. They came with a rope, and one of them put his hand on my shoulder with the threat that they had come to hang me. I turned, and strength came to me like it did to Sampson, for I exclaimed in my heart, "God help me!" In an instant I seemed

stronger than in my young days. I grabbed him by the throat, and said, "You shall die first!" He was in a vice from which he could not break away, and was struggling for life, but my strength was like iron. Three more ran to assist him. Before they could get me loose the fellow fell down; half a minute more would have done the work for him. I told them they were a set of cowards. "Hang me if you dare! My boys will be home after awhile and they will lie 'round your cabins till they get the last dog. I am an old Texas and have seen bears, panthers, wolves; I have never turned out the way yet, nor for such a set of rascals as you are!" More than 2,000 have been put to death for being Union men. I was robbed of thousands of dollars of property. Farewell, dear Stephen, and don't forget to write.

Your Brother, D.H. Gray

Mr. Gray died at Cedar Hill, Dallas County, TX, Feb. 11, 1867, less than a year from the date of the preceding letter. At the time of the desperate encounter therein recorded he must have been nearly 80 years of age. A grand old man; what metal there was in him. The descendants of his 14 children may well rise up and salute his memory.
Gerald Dean Hector Lilly, (GGGGD), 17208

RUSSELL FRANKLIN GRAY, the seventh child of Daniel Harris Gray, was born 1824 Berlin, NY. He came to Texas with his parents in 1839. He married Joicey Ferguson in 1848. They had seven children. Joicey died Jan. 19, 1866. Russell married Mary Jane Rodgers in September 1868, Falls County, TX. There were five children born of this marriage. Children of the first marriage were Deliah Ann, Robert Sealy, Wilburn Munsen, George Washington, Lizzie, Edward Moses, and Houston. Children of the second marriage were: Amanda Jane, George T., Mary Elizabeth, Laura Bell, and John Wesley.

Russell was a freightor and a Methodist Circuit Rider. He helped families coming to Texas by taking them to their destination and hauling their goods in a wagon pulled by a team of horses.

While making a haul to Temple, Russell started to mount his wagon when something spooked the horses. His foot slipped and he became tangled beneath the horses and dragged. His neck was broken and his body badly bruised. His family was notified. This is a letter from one of his sons to Edward, my great-grandfather. My grandmother told me her mother threw away the pages that were too heart rendering for her to read. The letter reads:

Mr. E.M. Gray, Llano, TX, MCH 11, 1894

Dear Brother Sister and family, it is with a sad and broken heart I try to answer your kind and welcome letter we received a few days since. We are all well except mama her health is veary bad. I hope these few lines will find you all well. I wish you all could have been here with father I know it would have been a pleasure. But when we received the telegrahm that father was hurt we were so grevied we could think of getting some one there to take care of him. We recd the telegrahm Friday and Wosh started Saturday morning Will went to Blanco after Budy the day Wosh started and Budy went Sunday.

We were intending to start home with father as soon as Wosh got here. Father got worse Tuesday night and we could not come home. Oh! It seems almost unbearable to think father could be at home he was so anxious to come home he would (end of page).

Wosh stayed several days and they sent for Will his wife was sick and he could not go. Will sent a young man in his place. Wosh arrived here with the team Wensday eve I started to Temple Thusday Feb. 14. I arrived there Thursday eve. I stayed untill dawn. Precious loving father died. Wosh came back with a load of freight he got to Temple Thursday. (End of letter)

Wosh is George Washinngton Gray, Russell's fourth child.
The Rev. Russell Franklin Gray Bible has a note written in it by his daughter Mrs. A.P. Linebarger stating that this Bible is 127 years old on Dec. 24, 1950.
Russell and Mary Jane are buried in the Llano City Cemetery. The graves are enclosed by a wrought iron fence with an engraved plate on the gate, R.F. and M.J. Gray. There are no tombstones.
Gerald Dean Hector Lilly, (GGGGD), 17208

REASON GREEN, son of Richard Green, was born Jan. 1, 1800 in Natchez, MS. He married Martha A. Rodgers in Alexandria, LA in 1822. Reason Green and his wife, Martha moved to Texas on their honeymoon. Their worldly effects were two Indian Ponies, a few quilts and other household goods were packed on one of the ponies and his wife on the other. Reason walked and led the pack, carrying his rifle on his shoulder. They reached the Lower Trinity where they located and built a camp and named the place, "Green's Ferry", which was in Liberty County, TX.

Reason Green and his wife, Martha, had five children: Stephen Green, born Oct. 27, 1828 Pt. Bolivar, TX, married twice, Jersuha Hardin and Ophelia Garrard; John J. Green, born June 27, 1832 Liberty, TX, married Martha L. Devers; Hannah Jane Green, born Jan. 11, 1833 Liberty, TX, married S.A. Hardin; Freeman (F.D.) Green, born Aug. 3, 1837 Orange County, TX, married Malina Abshier; and Reason Green Jr. born 1843 Liberty County, TX and died 1863 in Petersburg, VA, during the Civil War. Reason appears on the 1840 "Citizen of Texas" tax roll in Liberty County, TX, He also received a Bounty Certificate #3527, dated May 27, 1838, Houston, TX, showing he was entitled to 320 acres of land for service July 7 to Oct. 7, 1836 during the Texas Independence fight at the Alamo. Reason was one of the men who helped the women and children cross the Sabine during the Runaway Scrape. Reason Green died Feb. 11, 1868 and his wife, Martha died Feb. 12, 1860 and they are both buried in the Old French Cemetery, Dayton, TX.

Three of Reason Greens sons were in the Civil War; John J. Green enlisted May 8, 1861 at Liberty, TX and was a private in Co. I, 25 Regiment Texas Cavalry. F.D. Green and Reason Green Jr. both enlisted March 17, 1862 in Liberty, TX and both were Privates in Co. I, 25 Regiment Texas Cavalry. Many of Reason Greens descendants are still in Texas and take great pride in being related to the early settlers of Texas.
Rose Marie Graf Tillman, (GGGD), #21403-S

NANCY "ANN" GREER was born circa 1796 in Louisiana and married Joseph R. Dunman. With other settlers they moved to Ascosita District in Texas around 1824. Their children were; Reuben, born 1815 in Louisiana; Jane, born 1817, married Wherry B. Adams, July 21, 1841 Harris County; Reason, born 1819, married Rebecca Burns, July 20, 1841 Harris County; Mary, born 1821, married Jacob Ryan, Jan. 9, 1838 Texas; Elizabeth Josephine, born 1824, married George W. Harris, Richard B.

Morgan and Absalum Hogan, all in Harris County; Delina, born 1826 in Texas, married Peter Dyckman, Dec. 21, 1841, Harris County; Susan, born 1829, married Beckwith A. Noland and Nathaniel Williams; Joseph W., born Jan. 17, 1831, married Elizabeth West May 27, 1852; Sarah, born 1832, married Thomas J. Goodman and Louis Williams; Rebecca, born 1836; married Nathaniel Matthias Williams, Sept. 11, 1851; and Amy, born 1838, married William C. Duval, May 13, 1854.

According to the Telegraph and Texas Register of May 21, 1845, the Joseph Dunman home was one of the polling places for the "election of three delegates to be sent to the Convention to be assembled at Austin on the 4th day of July."
It is thought the Dunmans were Baptist.
Williene Smith Story, (GGGGD), 3427

JNO. (JOHN) GRIFFIN-The Griffins were originally from Scotland, then to Ireland, then migrated to America. They were one time one of the wealthiest and largest landowners in Virginia. My Griffins moved on into the Deeper South.

Jno. (John) Griffin and his wife Mary (Hays) were married in Hancock County, GA, on Sept. 20, 1813. Their daughter Precillah was born there. They lived many years in Alabama. The Texas Frontier beckoned in the early 1800s. Their children had all grown up and married and were ready to answer the Texas call—so—loaded with all their household goods, farming equipment, and slaves, Jno. and Mary (Hays)—their daughter Precillah and her husband Richard Hairston and family which consisted of three children (nine more were born in Texas from 1840-54)—Son Levi and his wife Madani Elizabeth (Runnels) and their first five children (three more were later born in Texas from 1844)—son John Jr.—son William and wife Elizabeth (Chapman) and their children all came to Texas. They all settled first in Washington County where they had land and their slaves, and played an important part in the colonization and settling of this area. Jno. is listed In the Washington County Road Commissioners Court of Roads and Revenues Minutes 1837-47 as doing work with "hands" (slaves). The landowners were required to donate work on the county roads.

They all moved on into Milam County in the late 1840s and early 1850s. We find Jno. in Milam County in 1846 and 1860, 1870. He is listed as being 73 years old in 1870. He died at Milano in Milam County.

Their children were: Levi (L) Griffin married Madani Elizabeth Runnels, William Griffin married Elizabeth Chapman, Precillah Griffin married Richard Hairston, John Griffin, Jr., Henry Griffin, Martha Griffin.

The Griffins blazed a trail across the South to Texas to find homes and finally settle in Milam County They played an important part in the colonizing and settling of this area. Their last years were lived out in the Milano-Griffin Chapel area and they are buried there in that deep Texas sand. They are gone—but part of them lives on in the genes, and chromosomes we, their descendents, have inherited. They were brave, courageous, far-seeing pioneers, and left us a great legacy—Pray, God, that we do as well. This changing world goes on—but they are at rest—dust to dust thou shall returneth—and in graves in that deep sand, they sleep on—these OLD ONES–now—WE are the OLD ONES—meeting the challenges the world of today offers.
Ethel Jewel Morgan Burch, (GGGGD of Jno. (John) Griffin), 21933-S

LEVI CHAPMAN GRIFFIN, The Griffins were originally from Scotland, then to Ireland, and then migrated to America. They were at one time one of the wealthiest and largest landowners in Virginia. My Griffins moved on into the Deeper South.

Ethel Jewell Morgan Burch and husband, Herman R. Burch

Levi Chapman Griffin was born in 1841 in Alabama. He was named after his father Levi (L) Griffin and the Chapman family the Griffins had married into. The Griffins and Chapmans all lived near each other. Levi Chapman was only three years old when they lived in Washington County in 1844. The family moved on, into Milam County in the late 40s and early 50s with all their possessions and many slaves. He grew up in the Milano area and married Mary Jane Cave, the daughter of Henry W. (Bud) Cave and Nancy (Bass) Cave. (Nancy was the daughter of Uriah Bass Jr., and Ruth (a) (Pipkin) Bass from North Carolina. Uriah was an Emissary for the Republic of Texas in 1839). Mary Jane was born in Clarke County, MS.

Levi Chapman Griffin and Mary Jane Cave were married at Milano ca. 1864/5 and lived in the area all their lives. Their children were: Martha Cizar Griffin married #1 John A. Freeman, #2 Frank Uher, Madani Elizabeth (Danie, Danna) Griffin married Sidney (S, Syd) Edmonds, Nancy Anice Griffin married Leonard Ben Winkler, Jeff James Griffin married Minnie Childress.

Levi Chapman Griffin helped his father with the managing of the vast holdings they had in the Milano area. They had "places" (plantations) at Sand Point, Sand Grove, Sandy Creek, Cedar Creek, one south of Cameron below the Little River, and one at Griffin Chapel—so named after the Griffin holdings there where his father and mother Levi (L) Griffin and Madani Elizabeth (Runnels) lived and died. The Griffins gave the land for both the white and the colored Griffin Cemeteries.

Many slave descendents still live at and maintain the Griffin Chapel African Methodist Episcopal Church at Griffin Chapel, which was organized by the Griffin Slaves when they all lived there. The church is at its third location.

Levi Chapman Griffin and his wife Mary Jane (Cave) are buried at Sand Grove Cemetery where they lived on the Griffin "place" in that area. They sleep on—those Old Ones—in marked graves. Levi Chapman Griffin played an important part in the settling and colonizing of this area.

He was an upstanding, serious, God-fearing, law abiding, hard working citizen. He was respected by his friends and neighbors. He left his mark there in that deep Texas sand, his legacy to us who follow it clear: carry on—carry on————and we, his descendents, meet that challenge, and: we carry on—carry on—.
Ethel Jewel Morgan Burch, (GGD of Levi Chapman Griffin), 21932S

LEVI (L) GRIFFIN was born in Alabama, in 1815. He was the second child born to John Griffin and Mary (Hays). The Griffins were originally from Scotland, then to Ireland, and then migrated to America. They were at one time one of the wealthiest and largest landowners in Virginia. My Griffins moved on into

the Deeper South. Levi Griffin married Madani Elizabeth Runnels in Alabama. Their first two children were born there; one of them was Levi Chapman Griffin. They had nine children. Texas offered land a'plenty, newer frontiers, and a challenge, which our Levi accepted. Our Levi arrived in Texas with much money and many slaves, with their farming equipment and household possessions. They stopped first in Washington County around Brenham. They were there in 1844. Levi (L) Griffin is listed on the Washington County Tax Roll for 1844. Much later they moved on up into Milam County in the Milano area.

Their children were: Levi Chapman Griffin married Mary Jane Cave, Drue (Drew) Griffin, James (Jim) Griffin married Catherine (Cat), Bill (William, Williamson) Griffin, John Griffin, Mary Griffin, Martha Griffin, Fannie Elizabeth Griffin, Margaret Griffin.

Levi's holdings in Milam County were extensive in the begining. He had several "places" (plantations). One was at Sand Point, one at Sand Grove, one at Sandy Creek, one at Cedar Creek, one south of Cameron, below the Little River, and one at the Griffin Chapel, so named after the Griffin's holdings, where Levi Griffin lived then.

Levi gave the land for the Griffin Chapel Cemetery (also for the colored cemetery). Descendents of the many Griffin slaves still live at Griffin Chapel and maintain the Griffin Chapel African Methodist Episcopal Church, which was organized when they all lived in that area as Griffin slaves.

Levi Griffin was designated as L. Griffin and his son Levi Chapman was called "Chap or Chapman" to distinguish him from his father.

The Griffins played an important part in the colonization and settling of this area. Levi and Madani's last years were lived out in the Griffin Chapel area. They died there and are buried the Griffin Chapel Cemetery. They rest there in that deep Texas sand.

We, their descendents, carry on in their stead—accepting the challenges of our time, as he accepted the challenges of his ....
Ethel Jewel Morgan Burch, (GGGD Levi (L) Griffin), 20014S

GEORGE GRIMES, An Unsung Hero, was not as well known as his cousin, Jesse Grimes, but did play a significant role in Texas history. George Grimes was born in North Carolina in 1781. About 1801, he married Eurydice Gardner, and they moved to Tennessee within three years. The Grimes family came to Texas between 1824 and 1827 with Stephen F. Austin and many other settlers. At this time, Texas was first being settled. He came with his wife and their children.

While Jesse Grimes was at Washington–on–the-Brazos signing the Declaration of Independence, George and two of his children, Frederick Miller Grimes and John Grimes, were gathering with General Sam Houston and others at San Jacinto. George and several other men waited at Vince's Bridge for Mexican troops. They destroyed the bridge and took care of wounded soldiers. George's other son, James, was at Goliad with Colonel Fannin and his troops waiting for Santa Anna's men.

George Grimes and his sons survived these courageous battles and went home with their families. After the battle, they lived in Nelsonville, in Austin County. Eurydice Grimes lived there with their 16 children: Abigail, Nancy A., Margaret, Susan, William C., George Washington Jr., Andrew Jackson, Jacob, John,

Eurydice Jr., Thomas Samuel, James, Catherine, Lucinda, and my great-great-grandmother, Martha Ann Grimes. Eurydice died in 1841 and was buried on the land George received as a Citizen of the Republic of Texas. George survived her until 1849, when he was buried next to her on their land.

There are many descendants of George Grimes. Some may even still live on the original land received by my ancestors. Not many people can say that their ancestors helped free the land upon which they live. The Grimes family played a significant role in Texas history, serving in combat at the Alamo, Goliad, and San Jacinto and in legislature for the Texas government, and for this, I am proud.

Sheila Killebrew
Georgia Faye Killebrew Smith #2

Bibliography:
Austin County Court House. Wills of George and Dicey Grimes

Goudreau, Barbara, L., I.H. Zimmermann, John C. Barron, Nan Polk Brady, and Emma Gene Scale. Republic of Texas Application Abstracts. p. 146.

Honor Roll of San Jacinto.

Morris, Mrs. Harry J. Citizens of the Republic of Texas. (Texas Genealogical Society)

Weed, Bob. Family History

White, Gifford. 1830 Citizens of Texas. p. 440.

White, Gifford. Character Certificates of 1830. p. 440

Whitmire, Ray. History of Calhoun Count Texas. p. 255

ISAAC GUEST was born ca. 1782, North Carolina. He married Elizabeth Frazier and had four children: Isaac, John Martin, William, and Elizabeth "Betsy". Isaac's wife Elizabeth died ca. 1818 in Cotaco (now Morgan) County, AL.

Isaac next married Mary Terry (widow Ball) ca. 1819 in Alabama. She had a son Elisha Ball who came to the Republic of Texas with his step-father, settling in Red River County. Isaac and Mary had four children: Rhoda, Mary, Orlena, and Joseph Calvin. Isaac's wife Mary died 1831 in Fayette County, TN.

On Dec. 15, 1836, Isaac and his children plus his stepson arrived in Red River County, Republic of Texas, and received a second Class Certificate, which entitled him to 1,280 acres of land in Red River and Lamar Counties. He is listed on the tax rolls and censuses from 1838 until his death in 1862.

Isaac died in June 1862, and is buried in Liberty Cemetery (formerly Guest Cemetery) near Detroit in Red River County, TX, which is located on Guest Prairie. He was a farmer, stockman, and slave owner while raising his motherless children plus two grandchildren. He is my third great-grandfather and has left a proud heritage.

Lera Kate Powell, Collin McKinney Chapter, DRT

JOSHUA HADLEY, son of Benjamin and Elizabeth King Hadley was born in North Carolina about 1794. His grandfather was Captain Thomas Hadley, patriot of the American Revolution and descendant of the Simon Hadley one line.

Joshua and his first wife, Obedience Grantham Hadley, settled in Texas in 1831. Obedience bore him five children. After Obedience died, he married a widow, Joyce Bostic Floyd, with two children. This marriage produced three sons: Joshua, William Bostic, and Anthony Drew all of whom were born in the Republic.

Joshua was a surveyor and surveyed the two leagues of land given to him as land grants on May 17, 1831 and Feb. 25, 1835. These land grants were in what is now Grimes County and Limestone County. He also purchased 15,000,000 varas of land as recorded in Washington County, TX.

He served as an officer in the Texian Army from June 30, 1836 to Sept. 30, 1836 and for this he received a bonus of 320 acres of land in Grimes County. These large amounts of land served him well, as he had a large herd of cattle. These cattle were grazed and driven as far north as Johnson County, TX.

In the Convention of 1832 he was a delegate from the District of Viesca. He was elected as the first alcalde of the newly created municipality of Washington on July 18, 1835. He was a charter member of orphan's Friend Lodge #17 organized April 8, 1842 at Fanthorpe's house in Anderson, TX.

Joshua had constructed a two-story structure which served as a house and fort to ward off Indian attacks at Hadley's Prairie.

His land grant in Limestone County was located near Parker's Fort, which was attacked by Comanches in 1836 resulting in a massacre of citizens and the capture of Cynthia Ann Parker and others. Joshua took charge of two of the Parker children (Silas and Orlena) until they could be reunited with members of the Parker family. As a result Joshua was mentioned in the Parker family probate records on file in Montgomery County.

He worked his cattle, horses, and land in close cooperation with his good friend, A.D. Kennard, who lived nearby. In 1843 he served as Justice of the Peace in Precinct 2, Montgomery County. He died at Hadley's Prairie in 1845 as a result of a fall from his horse. His name is presently inscribed on a granite marker located on the lawn of the courthouse in Anderson, Grimes County, TX. The Zuber-Hadley Chapter of the Daughters of the Republic of Texas was formed in 1910 and named for him.

In tribute to his second wife Joyce Violet Bostic Floyd, Hadley proved herself to be a survivor by marrying a third time to Samuel McGuffin, a widower with several children. One of these children was eight years old, Mary E. McGuffin, who lived with them, so with 11 children in various stages of life she managed to carry on, with a lot of trials and tribulations as all frontier women did.

Leslie D. Lightfoot Wagner, (GGGGD), 20753

JOHN C. HALE, born April 3, 1806 in Amelia County, VA. He married Barsheba Miller, born Jan. 10, 1810 on Aug. 12, 1830. Their children were: James Randolph Hale, born on March 19, 1832, died July 20, 1854 at the age of 22, having never married; Twins, Martha Jane and William Houston Hale, were born on March 30, 1834 in Missouri. William died on Sept. 11, 1843, presumably in Texas; John C. Hale, Jr. was born on Sept. 19, 1836 and died on Jan. 11, 1837, leaving Martha Jane as the only child to reach adulthood. She married Drury C. Chumley on Sept. 15, 1853 in San Augustine, TX and they had the following children: Mary Delilah, born Oct. 29, 1854; Ellen Barsheba, born April 23, 1857, married John Thomas Pickard; William A., born Feb. 1, 1861, married Nannie McCall; Drury Russell, born Sept. 27, 1867, married Frances "Frankie" Berry; Martha Jane, born May 28, 1869 married Taylor Haygood; Eugenia, born October 23, 1872; Sam Gardner, born May 26, 1875, married Bessie Golden; Joseph Charles, born Jan. 12, 1878, married Maude Warren.

John C. Hale served as a lieutenant under Sidney Sherman's

command at the Battle of San Jacinto. He became a martyr on April 21, 1836 when he was killed in the battle. He is buried in the cemetery across from the San Jacinto Monument, along with seven others who were killed that day. Their names are on the memorial obelisk there which gives a brief history of the Battle.
Shirley Ann Chumley Smith, (GGGGD), 22141

JAMES HANEY, son of Edward and Margaret (Brown) Haney, was born around 1780 in Lancaster County, PA. He married Maria Anna Ruhl Roper Fisher, a widow, on Oct. 29. 1827 in Opelousas, Parish, LA. They lived in Old River, Liberty County, TX. They had one daughter, Margaret, who was born in 1826 and married Ransom Wilburn. Margaret was her mother's eighth child.

James settled in Texas in 1824 and was a plantation owner, ferryboat operator, and cattleman. He was a first sergeant in the Mexican Militia and helped subdue the Fredonia Rebellion. James received a Headright land grant of a league and a labor of land. In his old age he lived with his daughter and her family. He died about 1854. His wife had died Jan. 1, 1845. They are buried in Stubbs Cemetery, Cove (Old River), Chambers County, TX.
Dorothy Anderson Hagen, (GGGGD), 22139S

MARY ELIZABETH "POLLY" HALL was born to John and Mary Pyle Hall in 1790 and married Samuel Washington Lindley in 1809. Her children were: Sarah, born 1810, married Thomas Steele; Barsheba born 1811, married John Sadler 1830; Mary Polly, born 1813, married William Hiram Little, 1831; Jonathan, born 1814, died at Alamo, 1836; Elizabeth, born 1815, married Samuel Collard in Texas; William, born 1817, married Mary Jane Hostetter; Martha, born 1821, married John J. Crowson and Anthony Gibson; Samuel W. Jr., born 1823 married Margaret __; Rachel, born 1827, married Benjamin Kelton and W. Hamilton O'Bannon; John, born 1829, married Elizabeth Ann Martin 1851; James born 1831, married Mary Irvine 1853; Mahala born 1833 in Texas, married Elijah Tolbert 1851; and Elijah, born 1835 Texas, married Eliza Kelton and Margaret McGill.

Polly's oldest son, Jonathan, was born Feb. 12, 1814 in Sagamon County, IL and accompanied the family to Texas. In 1835 he joined the army of Texas. He joined Captain Albert Martin's group organized to aid Travis and became one of the "Immortal Thirty-Two Men From Gonzales" who, after dark on March 1, 1835, slipped into the Alamo and died there March 6, 1836.
Williene Smith Story, (GGGGGD), 3427

AMANDA CAROLINE HARRIS was born April 10, 1810, in Georgia. She married Winford Harris ca. 1825. She and Winford were in Dallas County, AL in 1830, along with their three children, Mary Elizabeth born August 1826, Emily Caroline born April 4, 1828, and Horatio Perry Harris born April 20, 1830, near Birmingham, AL. Amanda's husband died ca. 1833 and by 1837, she and her children were in Washington County, TX where she received a head of household grant from the Republic of Texas.

Amanda remarried Dec. 4, 1843, to William J. Jackson, one of the first commissioners for the town of Brenham, TX. She moved to Aquilla, Hill County, TX where she died in November 1885 and is buried at Scott's Chapel Cemetery, Aquilla, near her son and daughter Emily Harris Gresham and other family members.

Horatio Perry (H.P.) Harris, mentioned above, married Ellouisa Raney, daughter of Clement Raney who came to Texas in 1831 and Catherine Arnold Clampitt Raney, Harris children were: Cora Angeline who married Othello M. Cato; Mary Catherine who married William Sylvester Murrell; Ella Frances; Wintford Clement who married (1) Lucy C. Ward, (2) Martha Ann Cunningham and (3) Effie Ventura Lannom; Clement Wintford who married Mary Ann Wills; William Graham who married Jennie Colvin; and Martha Potter. All children were born in Hill County. H.P. served in the 19th Texas Cavalry, Company D, during the Civil War.

Mary Elizabeth Harris married Francis Graves Clampitt Sept. 8, 1841. Their children were Helen F., Susan E. and Francis G. Clampitt. Francis Sr. died in 1848; Mary then married Willis H. Farmer in January 1849. Their children were: James, George, John, William, Robert and Mary.

Emily Caroline Harris married J.R. Gresham Sept. 27, 1847. Their children were: Horatio, William, Susan and John.
Nancy Cato Bullock, (GGGGD), 21997

MARY ANN RIDGEWAY HARRISON was born in Georgia Nov. 11, 1794. She married William Harrison and they lived in Bedford County, TN for several years. There most of their 14 children were born including Andrew Jackson, Oliver Perry, Alvarena, William Jr., Francis Marion and Mary. From Tennessee they went to Limestone County, AL, where their last child, John Ridgeway, was born in 1836. Most of the family was in Texas by 1837. They settled for a few years in what is now Houston, and Mary Ann received a land grant for 1280 acres. In 1845 they were in Bastrop County where Mary lived the rest of her life.

At least four of her sons, Andrew Jackson, Oliver Perry, William Jr. and Francis Marion were in the Indian Wars, the "Rangers", and the U.S. War with Mexico. They and their brother John R. served in the Confederate Army with William dying at the Battle of Milliken's Bend, LA. Oliver is buried in the Smithville, TX Cemetery and Francis in the Confederate Cemetery at San Antonio, TX. John is buried in the I.O.O.F. Cemetery in Colorado City, TX.

Their mother died March 7, 1875 and is buried in the Rector/Gage Cemetery just across the Bastrop County line in Fayette County. Mary Ann Ridgeway Harrison was indeed a Texas patriot.
Dorothy F. Harrison Keith, 12696

BLASSINGAME W. HARVEY, great-great-grandfather, colonist of San Augustine County, was born in Laurens County, SC. He moved to Catahoula Parish, LA and married Elizabeth Stone around 1812. They had one daughter. Harvey subsequently married Nancy (Scoggins) Bowie, widow of John Bowie, and had four children. He served in the War of 1812 as a private in the 10th Louisiana Regiment. He received a land grant in Mobile, AL for his service but sold it immediately. He moved to Texas and married Eliza Mary Ann

Blassingame W. Harvey

Prather on Sept 3, 1826. They had 10 children. Harvey was an educated man who kept a ledger from 1835 until death. He was granted a league of land in Lorenzo de Zavalla's colony on the Angelina River in 1835. The creek running through is known as Harvey's Creek. Most of the land is now covered by Sam Rayburn Reservoir. Harvey enlisted in 1837 in Captain McFarland's militia as a private. Two of Harvey's sons served in the Civil War. Eliza died July 22, 1855, and Blassingame died on July 20, 1867. Both are buried in a family cemetery, the Wood-Snell Cemetery, on the banks of Sam Rayburn Reservoir at Broaddus.
Bobbie Joyce Harvey Middleton, 16850

JAMES ALFRED HEAD, son of Richard and Mary Head was born June 25, 1797 in Georgia. He married Elizabeth Seale, daughter of Thomas and Rachel Seale on Dec. 27, 1818 in Jones County, GA. Elizabeth was born June 16, 1804 and she died about 1848. James and Elizabeth had 13 children: Rachel, Nancy Ophelia, Marah Mary, Jesse, Ephphatha, Elizabeth, Mary, Ezra Eli, Thomas Seale, Lydia, Lucinda, James Richard, and Edmond Henderson.

They lived for a time in Pike County, AL before migrating to Texas on January 21, 1835. For his service to the Nashville Company and leadership in bringing new settlers to Texas, James received land in present day Limestone County. Head family members established Ebenezer Baptist Church and the community of Headsville, also known as Heads Prairie.

On Oct. 26, 1835 James enlisted in Silas Parker's "Ranging Company," later the Texas Rangers. He served as Justice of the Peace for Navasota (now Brazos) County. In 1841 he represented Navasota County in the House of Representatives, the Sixth Congress, Republic of Texas.

James Alfred Head died on Sept. 22, 1872. In 1987, a monument in his honor was placed in Ebenezer Cemetery near Kosse, Limestone County, TX.
Leslie Gray Currey, (GGGGD) of James Alfred Head, 22058

WILLIAM HEMPHILL, son of Samuel Hemphill and Elizabeth (_?_) Hemphill, was born Sept. 29, 1779, in Mecklenburg County, NC. He married Lucretia Coleman about 1802. Lucretia was born July 1, 1783, probably in NC. William and Lucretia had nine children: Ulyssus, born 1803; Andrew Coleman, born 1805; Eloiza, born 1807, married first Seymore S. Beasley, married second Moses O. Dimon; Cornelius Murphy, born 1810, married Elizabeth Snoddy; Zeno Jackson, born 1813, married Elizabeth Rogers; Marcus Lafayette, born 1815, married Mary Rogers; William Augustus, born 1818, married first Mary Rousseau, married second Mary Jane Hill; Ellen Addison, born 1820, married first Claiborne Garrett, married second John D. Nash; Ambrose Baber, born 1824, married Martha Elizabeth Hemphill.

William Hemphill was a Senator representing Butler, Monroe, and Conecuh Counties in the Alabama State Senate before, in 1835, buying land in what is now Bastrop County, TX. Arriving in Texas in February 1836 during the "Runaway Scrape", William and his family resided temporarily in San Augustine County where sons William Augustus and Marcus Lafayette served in the militia. William Hemphill died January 9, 1837, at the Brazos River crossing of the El Camino Real (now State Highway 21) enroute to his land in Bastrop County. His grave site is unknown. Lucretia died in 1840 and is buried in the Hemphill Family Cemetery in Bastrop County.

Ambrose Baber Hemphill, listed above, married Martha Elizabeth Hemphill, daughter of Samuel Hemphill (son of William's brother, Thompson Hemphill) and Nancy Granberry in Simpson County, MS, Nov. 20, 1853. Martha Elizabeth was born April 4, 1833, in Lawrence County, MS. Their children were: (twins) Cornelius Ambrose, born Oct. 21, 1855, married first Lela Collier, married second Rosa Lee Putney; Cornelia Elizabeth, unmarried; William Thompson, born Nov. 21, 1857, married first Laura Collier, married second Mattie Taylor; Ella Amelia, born June 23, 1859, unmarried; Lola Elouisa, born March 22, 1861, married John Dennis Wright, a Baptist Minister of the Gospel; Andrew Lafayette, born July 1, 1863, died early; Martha Granberry, born and died Feb. 4, 1876.
Rosalee Morris Curtis, (GGGD), 20879

CHARLES HENSLEY was born in Maury County, TN March 9, 1811 to Harmon and Elizabeth Hensley. He came with his parents to Texas ca. 1828. He married Indiana Fitzgerald, daughter of David Fitzgerald, Feb. 22, 1839 in Washington County. Charles participated in the Mier Expedition and was a prisoner of Mexico. He is reported to have entertained his fellow prisoners with a violin made by the prisoners from a cigar box. When the prisoners were told of what has come to be called "the black bean drawing", Charles remarked "Well, boys, it will be my luck to draw a black bean, but when I am executed I'll have this old fiddle in my hand and be playing as lustily as I can 'The Yellow Rose of Texas Beats the Bell of Tennessee'". However he drew a white bean, was liberated and finally made his way back to his home near Brenham, on Mill Creek, where he had settled in 1835. He was a farmer and a concert violinist, and died at the Connor Hotel in Brenham on Oct. 29, 1856, while there to play a concert. Charles and Indiana were the parents of eight children: Alexander, Rankin, Charles Golden, William, Bradley, Eugene, Betty and James Calhoun.
Mavis Hensley Sager, (GGGD), 21192

CORNELIUS SAYLES HENLEY was born 1829 in Tennessee, probably Fayette County. He was the son of Mildred Henley and brother of Martha Ann Caroline Henley. Fayette County court minutes states that Martha Ann Caroline was the daughter of Isaac Henley, although no documented proof has been found by me, I believe that Isaac was also the father of Cornelius.

Cornelius arrived in Texas with his mother and step-father, Isaac Delaney about 1838 and settled in Sabine County. He married Caledonia Loggins in San Augustine County Aug. 23, 1849.

Cornelius served in the Confederate States Army in Company I, 26th Texas Cavalry in Debray's Regiment as blacksmith. He served as private at Galveston, TX in Walker Company. He enlisted December 1861 and served throughout the conflict.

Cornelius and Caledonia were the parents of 10 children: Isaac Lewis born 1850, Martha C. born Aug. 5, 1852, James born 1853, Samuel A.C. Henley born June 29, 1854 and married Josephine Parker, died Oct. 23, 1940 and both are buried in the Parker Cemetery. Cornelius Sayles Jr. born July 12, 1856, Robert Henley born 1860, Greenberry Henley, born June 02, 1862, John Henley, born 1865, Almer Maron, born Oct. 21, 1868, and Mildred Virginia, born June 15, 1863.

Cornelius died in Hopkins County, TX July 12, 1884. His exact burial place is unknown. Caledonia died March 22, 1920 and is buried in Chinquapin Cemetery in San Augustine County. A memorial marker has been placed by her grave for Cornelius.

Issac Lewis Henley left San Augustine County and died sometime after 1870, location unknown. Martha C. married William T. Williams on Jan. 03, 1876 and died Aug. 3, 1900. Martha is buried in the Macune Cemetery in San Augustine County, Cornelius Sayles Jr. married Mary E. Voshay, died Feb. 23, 1933 and both are buried in Chinquapin Cemetery, Robert S. is buried in Chinquapin Cemetery also. Greenberry married Sarah M. Dickerson and they are buried in the Dickerson Cemetery. Almer Maron married Sarah Dora Baker. Mildred Virginia married Joel Washington Robbins.

RICHARD HILBURN married Elizabeth Campbell on Dec. 26, 1818 in Williamson County, TN. According to Hilburn family genealogists, he was born (ca. 1798-1802) in Newberry County, SC, the son of William B. and Jane Hilburn.

Richard and Richardson Hilburn, circa 1850.

The Republic of Texas Granted Richard Headright Certificate # 64, Third Class, dated Oct. 4, 1841, when he established that he and his family had arrived in the Republic in 1839. His descendants often refer to him as the "Peace Keeper" for he chose to follow John Coffee "Jack" Hays into the Texas Rangers in 1845 rather than follow the plow. After Texas joined the Union and Captain (later Colonel) Hay's men served alongside U.S. forces in the Mexican War. Richard was appointed sergeant. His unit, Gillespies Company, Texas Mounted Rangers included fellow sergeant William A.A. ("Big Foot") Wallace. Richard subsequently joined Captain Wallace's Texian Ranging Company and recruited his son Richardson to join the force which was organized to maintain peace on the Texas Frontier. Thereafter, the two men's lives were clearly intertwined.

In the early 1850's Richard and Richardson shared property in San Antonio. After Richardson's marriage on May 10, 1851 to Maria Luisa Leal, a descendant of the Canary Islanders who helped found San Antonio in 1731, Richard married for the second time on July 31, 1854.The two men took, up land together and maintained their home place near El Camino Real where it crosses Atascoa County. Richard was laid to rest in 1867. Richardson died on Aug. 17, 1877.

Among Richard and Luisa Hilburn's children who remained in Atascosa County was Richard's namesake Richard Hilburn, born Feb. 21, 1855. He married Sarah Jane Kaufman Feb. 26, 1874.
Ethel G. Fowler Keilman, (GGGD), 22067
Patsy R. Keilman Dill Moss, (GGGGD), 20629

MARGARET DOBKINS HILL was born Jan. 6, 1842, in Smith County, TX, the fifth child of James Calhoun and Rebecca Mar Hill, their first child born in Texas. Her parents came to Texas in 1839. James built a large frame house and all the activities of the family were carried on in the big parlor. The girls were taught weaving, quilting, rug making and sewing by "Aunt Jensey" a seamstress colored slave. Also reading, writing and arithmetic until the Pleasant Hill Church school house was ready.

Dec. 5, 1865, Margaret married Daniel James Rowe. They eventually moved to Hazel Dell, Comanche County, TX, in 1870, when Hazel Dell was surveyed. It may be that Daniel Rowe helped in this as he was a surveyor. Hazel Dell was rough, tough and distinguished by the number and size of it's saloons, hotels, 10 pin alleys, and had one of the most well-populated cemeteries in Texas. There were shootings, hangings, rustlers, gamblers and general lawlessness of all kinds.

It was to this area that Margaret came with three small children. Her husband was a farmer, schoolteacher, surveyor, Justice of the Peace, and Sheriff of Comanche County.

She lived a short life, but she bore him four more children, after moving to Hazel Dell, the last of which was my grandfather. He was born Feb. 2, 1879; she died Feb. 7, 1879. The logical conclusion is that she died of infection after childbirth—a common cause of death among women who died so soon after a delivery. She was 37, and certainly played a good part in the settlement of this state.
Adella Rowe Rubenstein, (GGD)

MARY ELIZABETH HOLBROOK HILL, Robert Jefferson Holbrook and Mary Elizabeth Rutherford Holbrook traveled by wagon train from Tennessee in 1838, to Mississippi before entering Texas Jan. 2, 1841. Mary Elizabeth (my great-grandmother) was born at Boggy Creek near Daingerfield, Red River County, Republic of Texas on Nov. 10, 1844. By 1852, the family was in Mount Vernon where Robert was a merchant and cotton planter.

Mary Elizabeth Holbrook Hill

Mary Elizabeth met John Payne Hill, a widower from Virginia practicing law in Mount Pleasant. During the Civil War, Captain Hill wrote her as his company traveled from Texas to Arkansas and Missouri and the Battle of Pea Ridge. These letters are located at the Texas State Library in Austin. They married Oct. 22, 1862. John wanted to introduce his bride to his family in Virginia, which included his three children from his former marriage. The couple began a hazardous honeymoon journey in the middle of the war to meet John's family. By 1876, John died leaving Mary Elizabeth with five children: Beulah, John, Guy, Sue, Mary (my grandmother), and pregnant with Birdie. In 1893 she was appointed Postmaster of Franklin County enabling her to have an independent income. She died in 1918.
Mary Turner Brady

HENRY C. HOCKER is the son of Richard Weaver Hocker born Montgomery County, MD and Sarah Coleman. Henry was born August 1807, Ohio County, KY. He married Mary H. Mitchell Feb. 19, 1829, Ohio County, KY, the daughter of Obed Mitchell and Rhoda Sutton. They migrated to Illinois then Missouri by 1840. Henry is listed as the Justice of the Peace on May 31, 1845 in Red River County, TX. They moved to Guadelupe County, TX in 1852. Henry died between 1860 and 1870. Mary went to live with her daughter, Susan Nancy and son-in-law,

Astyanax Troy Hector in Redwood, Guadalupe County, TX near San Marcos. It is believed that she is buried in the Hector Cemetery in an unmarked grave.
Gerald Dean Hector Lilly, (GGGGGD), 17208

SARAH JANE HOCKER, born April 8, 1834, Illinois was the daughter of Henry C. Hocker and Mary H. Mitchell. Sarah married Astyanax Troy Hector Feb. 6, 1851, Guadalupe County, TX. Astyanax was born Jan. 14, 1823, Tazewell County, VA. He died Nov. 5, 1905 Hays County, TX. Sarah and Astyanax's children were: Valerus Gordon, born Dec. 1, 1851, Isabella Mathrom, born March 15, 1855, Charles Obed, born Aug. 17, 1856, Mary Elizabeth, born April 24, 1858, David Alexander, born Jan. 28, 1860, Astyanax Troy Jr., born Aug. 7, 1862, and Sallie Jane, born Nov. 24, 1864.

Sarah died four days after the birth of Sallie. Astyanax was away from home fighting in the Civil War. Valerus Gordon, her 13 year old son took care of his brothers and sisters until his father returned home. He buried his mother on the home place. Astyanax married Sarah's younger sister, Susan Nancy Hocker Oct. 24, 1865. Sarah, Susan and Astyanax are buried in the Hector Cemetery in San Marcos, TX.
Gerald Dean Hector Lilly, (GGGGGD), 17208

THOMAS ELISHA MCMATH HOGG was born in Nacogdoches County, Republic of Texas, on June 19, 1842, the eldest son of Joseph Lewis Hogg and Lucanda McMath Hogg.

Thomas Elisha McMath Hogg

He was named for his two grandfathers, Thomas Hogg (a Revolutionary War veteran buried in Texas) and Elisha McMath. He had two older sisters-Mary Frances and Julia-and later had four brothers-John, Jim, Joe Jr., and Richard. In 1861, he joined the Army of the Confederacy as a captain and fought throughout the War. On his way home through Mississippi, he met his cousin Anna Eliza Adeline McMath, who like him had been named for Elisha McMath, their mutual grandfather. They fell in love, and the next summer Tom went back to Mississippi to marry Anna and to bring her back home to Texas.

Tom Hogg was a lawyer, an editor, and an author. He wrote possibly the only epic poem to come out of the Civil War, 'The Fate of Marvin." He encouraged his daughter, Hermilla Maydee Hogg Kelso, to write poetry, a pastime she loved and practiced all her life. He died a young man at age 38, and so did not live to see his youngest surviving brother James Stephen Hogg inaugurated as the first native-born governor of Texas.
Maydee J. Scurlock

JOHN R. HOLCOMB, my great-great-grandfather, was the youngest son of Kinchen Holcomb and his first wife (unknown). He was born 1800/1810 and died April 1, 1843. He married Nancy Purnell about 1827. He came to Texas about 1838 and is listed on the 1840 Tax rolls in Red River County with 21 slaves and nine work horses.

He and Nancy had five children, all born in Maury County,

TN except the youngest, my great-grandmother Nancy. The other children were Paralee who married Dr. Alexander Bucher Nephler, Robert B. who died before 1850, Sarah Adeline also died before 1850, and John who also died young.

When John's plan fell through in Texas, he moved to Benton County, MO where he died. He had had a ferry in addition to his land, and livestock. After he died, Nancy purchased and remodeled the "Warsaw Mansion House and General Stage Office".

Nancy married her first cousin in Tennessee, and moved to Bell County, TX. After the death of her husband and children in the Flu epidemic of 1859, she married Joseph Cater, my great-grandfather.
Mrs. Jane A. Beard

BRAZILIA HOLT was born in South Carolina. Her parents were John Holt and Elizabeth Ruff Cannon. Brazilia's mother was the daughter of David Ruff and Elizabeth Gray and was born in Newberry, SC in 1792. She married William Cannon in 1806 and had six children. William died about 1815, and she married John Holt. They had four children before John died in 1837, including Brazilia who was born about 1823 in South Carolina. Shortly after John's death Elizabeth and several of her children, both Cannon and Holt, arrived in Texas. Brazilia's two Holt brothers and one sister, William, born 1820, Solomon, born 1821, and Lucinda, born 1830 are listed in several censuses and tax records of Shelby County from about 1838, including the 1850 census where they are all listed with their families along with their mother, Elizabeth, who married Louis Watkins in 1845.

Brazilia married Benjamin Franklin Adams about 1840 in Neuville, Shelby County, TX. The listing of their children is under Benjamin Franklin Adams biography in this volume. After the death of Benjamin F. between 1860-1870, Brazilia continued to live in Shelby County and raise her large family. Several of the children and grandchildren of Brazilia and Benjamin Franklin also continued to marry and raise families in Shelby County.

Brazilia died in 1906 in Shelby County, TX where she had lived all of her married life, and is buried in the Adams Cemetery on family land in Shelby County.
Patricia Anne Adams Ross
DRT Certificate number 21792S for Brazilia Holt
DRT Certificate number 21791 for Benjamin Franklin Adams

Cynthia Anne Ross Hardy
DRT Certificate number 21794S for Brazilia Holt
DRT Certificate number 21793 for Benjamin Franklin Holt

REUBEN HORNSBY, eldest son on Moses and Katherine Watts Hornsby, was born Jan. 7, 1793, near Rome, GA. He married Sarah Morrison, born July 27, 1796, on Dec. 1, 1815, near Jackson, MS.

The family sailed from Vicksburg, MS, on the steamer "Pocohontas" on Jan. 2, 1830; landed in Texas at the mouth of the Brazos River on Feb. 5, 1830. He then left his family for Stephen F. Austin's colony at San Felipe. He joined Austin and five other men in surveying the land around Austin's Upper Colony.

Reuben returned to the coast for his family and moved first to Mina (Bastrop). He and his companions continued up the Colorado basin. It is said that when Reuben saw the tract of land in a large horseshoe-shaped bend of the river he put down his gun and said, "This suits me just fine."

In July 1832, he moved his family to that tract of land, which was granted him by the Mexican State of Coahuila and Texas. Reuben, his sons and brothers, cleared land, planted the first corn raised here, and built cabins. They took part in several Indian skirmishes; in battles at Pecan Bayou and at Plum Creek; joined the Texas Rangers and the Army of Texas. Reuben served on the first jury in the present Travis County, helped survey and build the first roads, and assisted Edwin Waller in surveying the City of Austin.

To Reuben and Sarah were born 10 children: two died before the family left Mississippi: five died in Hornsby's Bend without marrying; and three (William Watts Hornsby, Josephus Hornsby, and Sarah Ann Hornsby Burditt Moore) married, established homes, and remained in Travis County.

Reuben Hornsby died Jan. 11, 1879. His wife Sarah died April 20, 1862. They are buried in the Hornsby Cemetery in Hornsby's Bend, TX.

BARNES HOLLOWAY

BARNES HOLLOWAY was born at Eatonton, GA in 1789. While serving in the Army, he was at the Battle of New Orleans.

Barnes moved to Madison County, AL where he met and married Jane Tinder, widow of Abel Tinder. The marriage was performed by Reverend Robert Donnell on March 3, 1816.

The family, including Jane's son Jesse Tinder, settled in what was to become Marion County, AL where children James M., Melissa Jane, William G., Barnes Mutitus, John Griffen and Mahala Ann Holloway were born. In 1838, the family moved to Red River County, Republic of Texas. Barnes died in 1842 in what was becoming Bowie County. Widow Jane moved to Hickory Hill, Cass County, TX in 1842 in what was becoming Bowie County. Widow Jane moved to Hickory Hill, Cass County, TX where son Jesse Tinder had bought a place for her. Jesse married Magaret Bradford at Gilmer where he died without issue.

James and William died without issue. Melissa married Wilson Wright and had several children before she died with dropsy. Barnes Mutitus married Elizabeth V. Hall. John married Lucy J. Peacock and moved to White Rock, Hunt County. Mahala, a teacher, married Francis C. Baker, whose father Job had named the Jimplecute newspaper at Jefferson, TX.
Linda McCain Stansell, 19385
Carol Brown Jasak, 20625

JOHANN CHRISTOPH HORNBURG

JOHANN CHRISTOPH HORNBURG, born 1795 in Vechelde, Germany, farmed, raised sheep. Married Marie Dorothee Christine Harms, born 1806 Kastorp, Germany, married Aug. 25, 1824. They had six children, Marie Dorothee, Marie Sophie, Christoph Heinrich, Johann Heinrich, Charles Martin, Sophie Dorothee, all born in Germany. The family left from the seaport Bremen, Germany on the ship Everhard and arrived Galveston, TX December 1845. Johann died 1871, buried in Austin or Lavaca County. After his death Dorothee moved to her

Marie Dorthee Christine Harms Hornburg

son, Charles Martin, Sandy, Blanco County, TX, their home was known as Hornburg Hill, some of the remains of home are still there, Dorothee was noted for having made cookies which she shared with people stopping for directions. She died in 1890 and buried at Sandy Cemetery. Two sons were Confederate soldiers Charles Martin survived the war, Heinrich was POW and died in Northern Prison Camp near Butler, MO. Charles Martin later was a circuit riding Baptist minister in the Texas Hill Country, still rugged and as saying goes carried Bible in one side of saddle bag and pistol in other. Three of Charles Martins sons were some of the first Ministers at First Baptist Church, Marble Falls, TX. John Bapiste Wunneburger, born 1825, Alsace Loraine, France. Married Dorothee Hornburg, born 1826 Kastorf, Germany in Victora County, TX. In 1850 moved to Peterburg County where the County Courthouse had been destroyed by fire and John and another person built the new Courthouse. The family moved to Paige, TX. John died 1909 in the home of his son Edward. Dorothee died in 1910, buried Dixon Prairie Cemetery located at Paige, TX on Hwy 21. Edward Lee Wunneburger, born 1865, died 1925, Frances Fritcher Wunneburger, born 1862 died 1939. They were married 1887 Bastrop County, TX and had eight children, five boys, one girl, two boys died at age of one and two, all buried at Dixon Prairie Cemetery. Their farm was in Bastrop County near Paige and in WWII was part of Camp Swift. Their son Wesley Henry Wunneburger, born 1897, died 1971, married Hertha Bertha Kretzschmar born 1899 died 1987, in Austin, Travis County, TX in 1925. Had one child, Aline Estelle and lived in Austin, TX. Wesley was a General Contractor and built many houses in the area and was a real craftsmen in his field. During WWII he worked on defense work. Hertha was a loving, caring Christian person and was wonderful homemaker, loved to cook and bake. I can still smell the bread and goodies from her kitchen. Both are buried at Dixon Prairie Cemetery. Aline Estelle Wunneburger Bradley born 1928 married her wartime sweetheart on June 1, 1946, and John William Bradley Jr. (S/Sgt. who served his country during WWII as in Radar, B 29s in Pacific Campaigns.) We have two children and four grandchildren with 53 wonderful years at this writing.
Aline W. Bradley, (GGGD), 16013
Linda Woods, (GGGGD), 16014
Lezlie Woods, (GGGGGD), 16015
Sarah Woods, (GGGGGD), CRT
Travis Bradley, (GGGGGS), CRT
Kelley Bradley, (GGGGGD), CRT

SARAH CREATH HOWARD

SARAH CREATH HOWARD was born Jan. 7, 1810, in Illinois. She migrated to De Witt Colony, TX in 1828 with first husband John McSherry, who was killed by Indians in 1829 after the birth of their son. Later she married John Hibbins and had another child. The family was captured in 1835 by Indians who murdered Hibbins and their infant. Sarah, escaping under cover of night came under the protection of a troop of Texas Rangers who tracked the band and rescued her young son. They were caught up in the "runaway scrape" when Texans fled the Mexican Army after the fall of the Alamo. After losing yet another husband, Sheriff Stinnett to renegades, she met and married Phillip Howard (born 1814, Kentucky) who had served in the Texas Army in 1836. They had three daughters. Sarah died in Bosque County in 1870. (Her tragedies are recorded by John Henry Brown in "Indian Wars and Pioneers of Texas").

Their daughter "Mintie" Howard (born 1842) married Stephen Decatur Greer (born 1830 Georgia) in Bosque County, TX. April 17, 1858. Stephen was the son of Nathaniel Hunt Greer and Nancy Ann Terry Roberts whose family arrived in Washington County, TX in 1837 from Alabama. (Nathaniel served as Senator in the fourth Congress

Mardell Hazel Rathmell, great-great granddaughter of Phillip and Sarah Creath Howard and Nathaniel and Nancy Greer, with her husband William Rathmell, circa 1926.

of the Republic of Texas 1838-40 and was a Colonel in Texas Militia during Mexican War). "Mintie" and Stephen Greer had five children, the eldest, Sallie, born June 26, 1860.

Sallie Greer married James Harvey Reed (born March 13, 1852 in Texas) on Dec. 30, 1883 in Eastland County, TX. Their daughter Julia Alexander Reed (born Oct. 2, 1889) married William Day Hazel (born July 1, 1882) in Eastland County on Aug. 29, 1906. They reared two daughters, Mardell and Sylvia. Mardell Hazel (born May 31, 1908, Cisco, TX) married William Rathmell (born Jan. 28, 1902) son of Coleman Co. ranchers Jacob Rathmell (born 1859 Yorkshire, England) and Ella Amanda Barnett (born 1866 Navarro County, TX) in Taylor County, TX Aug. 27, 1926. Mardell and Bill Rathmell reared 10 children and lived most of their lives in Texas. Mardell still resides in Rockwall, TX at age 91, still possessed of her forebears' pioneer spirit and faith.
Jenet Rathmell Jolly, (GGGGD), 19246
Mardell Hazel Rathmell, (GGGD), 19245

WILLIAM P. HUFF-arriving in Texas with Austin's Old Three Hundred, William and his father, George Huff made their home in present Wharton and Fort Bend Counties. William set up a business in San Felipe and sold candles, paper and other supplies to their friend and attorney, William B. Travis. Huff was in charge of provision, arms and ammunition of the volunteer army at Gonzales.

In the summer of 1837, he found bones of extinct mammals and other remains at the shoals of the Brazos. An article in the Sept. 9, 1837, "Houston Telegraph and Texas Register" gave the first information of Huff's

William Huff

discovery. In 1845, he exhibited in Galveston and New Orleans. Some of his specimens found their way to the British Museum. In 1855, the collection was sold to Dr. Charles Martin, surgeon with the U.S. Coast Survey.

In 1835, Huff married Marion Morton, daughter of William Morton. Morton was also a member of the Old Three Hundred. Huff received a league of land in 1835. He went to California in 1849 during the Gold Rush, but returned several years later to Texas. After the Civil War, he served as County clerk of Fort Bend County. He died in 1886 in Houston, TX.
Joyce Gray Clegg Robinson, (GGGD), 5821

JOHN HUGHES, (Hughs) was born about 1775-1780 in Virginia to Nathaniel Hughes. Known siblings were James, Moses, Edward and William. In the early 1800's, John and his wife Darcus were living in Abbeville, SC. In 1820 or thereabout a group of families, including several Hughes families left Abbeville, SC for Alabama. There they stayed for a number of years, but in the early part of 1835, John and Darcus Hughes and family, along with many other Hughes families immigrated to Texas. He was given a First Class Headright, along with land grants for his service in the Army of Republic of Texas. He served in Captain Colerick's Co. of Mount Vernon "Ohio" volunteers for six months and he was also a member of Captain George English's County.

Known children of John and Darcus are Tallifero (Toliver) married Rhoda Dobbins; Uriah (Rial) married (1) Williams (2) Rhoda Dobbins Hughes, (widow of Tallifero); Mary Rachel married (1) Aaron Cullins (2) James Hollingsworth; Letty Elizabeth; Sarah; and William.

It is not known when John's wife Darcus died but she was alive in December 1838 as she signed a deed in Burleson County at that time. We have nothing else on her. John Hughes died in June of 1846, his son, Uriah, was named administrator of his estate in Burleson County, TX.
Billy Lou Goforth Harper, (GGGGD), 22711

BENJAMIN FRANKLIN HUNT, son of Sion and Sarah Hunt, was born on Dec. 1, 1820 in Sumner County, TN. He married Maria Frances Donaldson, born Sept. 9, 1823 at Warren County, KY, on Aug. 26, 1845 in Warren County, KY and moved to Nacogdoches County, TX in 1845. He settled permanently in Chatfield, Navarro County, TX where he was a planter. He and Maria had nine children: Charles, born 1847, married first, Florence J. Westbrook, and second, Mary Elizabeth McFadden; Emma, born 1849, married George M. Westbrook; Dudley, born 1851; George, born 1854; Nellie, born 1857; Carrie, born 1860, married

Maria Francis Donaldson, wife of Benjamin Franklin Hunt, circa 1890.

Robert Franklin Snell; Presley, born 1863, married Lilla Belle Reece; Benjamin Franklin Jr., born 1866; and Lutie, born 1866. B.F. Hunt died Feb. 18, 1872 at Chatfield, TX. Maria died March 30, 1899 at Hill Country, TX.

Nellie Hunt, listed above, married William Butler Donaldson on Aug. 22, 1876. He was the son of William Donaldson and Minerva Hill Butler and was born on Nov 23, 1855 in Natchez, MS. They had seven children including Lutie who was born March 23, 1887 in Dallas, TX. Lutie Donaldson married Jesse Hamilton Goss, born March 6, 1879, on June 19, 1904 in Smithville, TX. They had four children including Ethel, born March 30, 1905 in Dallas, TX. Ethel Goss married Thomas Lynn Collier, born May 8, 1895 in Meridian, MS, on April 14, 1923 in Fort Worth, TX. They had two children including Shirley Anne, born August 16, 1945 in Ennis, TX. Shirley Collier married John Kenny Smith, born Jan. 28, 1944 in Mercedes, TX, on Nov. 6, 1970 in Dallas, TX. They have two daughters: Cheryl Lynn born

Nov. 25, 1972 in Dallas, TX and Laura Anne born Feb. 15, 1977 in Dallas, TX.
Shirley Anne Collier Smith, (GGGD), 21582

ARABELLA ELLIOTT HUNTER was born in 1825 in Alabama, and in early 1837 she arrived in Texas with her parents Tamar Stephens and George Elliott Hunter. She helped her mother run their hotel at the new town of Cincinnati. Her marriage to Thomas Sherman Drury produced: Amelia Leona (1843), married John Robinett; Cora Cormelia (1846), married J.0. Hightower; and Leona Tamar (1848), married Christopher Columbus Murray.

Arabella married John Stephen Smith, a widower with four children, on Sept. 10, 1851. Together they had five children. John Stephen built up quite a plantation on the Trinity River in Walker County and left Arabella well fixed at his death Nov. 15, 1859. 'Belle' (as she was called) reared her children as a single parent and was living in Huntsville in 1870 for their schooling. Hers was a strong, determined character. She died in Huntsville in 1879 and is buried at a Cincinnati Cemetery beside John Stephen.

Tamar's Stevens background included tall, agile people and they took part in military procedures. Several were law officers during peace times and quite a few died during the Civil War. The Hunters also were active, courageous patriots.
Williene Smith Story, (GGD), 3427

GEORGE ELLIOTT HUNTER was born in 1797 in Kentucky and married Dulcinia Payne Harrison. Two sons were born. George went "South with a drove of horses" which he sold and kept books in New Orleans. After marrying Tamar Stevens in 1824, George taught school.

In a wagon "pulled by four good mares", George and Tamar brought their seven children to Texas, reaching Walker County where they built a tavern in 1837.

George was five foot ten inches, weighing 155 pounds with a jolly disposition but a quick temper. He was courageous and participated with his sons in the Cherokee, Vasquez, Woll and Somerville Campaigns. He had served in the War of 1812, sustaining a shoulder wound fighting the British in Canada. His grandfather George had fought in the Battle of "Saritoga" in October 1777.

His son Samuel was a prisoner in Mexico 18 months from the Santa Fe Expedition. Samuel and brother William were killed digging gold circa 1949 in California. Son James gave distinguished service in the Confederate Army, suffering several wounds and being surrendered at Appomatox.

George was a state officer in the Masonic Order when he died, affiliated with Olive Branch Chapter of Cincinnati.
Williene Smith Story, (GGGD), 3427

MILTON IRISH was born in Union, ME, May 7, 1812. His parents were Rev. Cornelius Bailey Irish, a Quaker minister, and Polly Adams. He migrated to East Texas in 1835 and joined the Texian Army on Oct. 17, 1835 as a member of Captain John English's Company in San Augustine. He volunteered to accompany Colonel Ben Miliam's successful assault into Bexar as a member of Captain Thomas Lewellen's Co. He signed the Convention Memorial near Refugio in February 1936, before joining the San Antonio Greys in Colonel Fannin's command. This entire command was captured following the Battle of Coleto Creek and was marched out to be executed the following week at Goliad. Of approximately 400 prisoners, he was one of approximately 28 to escape. Although wounded, he walked alone back to San Augustine. For his service, he received a headright of 1/3 league of land, a Bounty Grant of 640 acres and a Donation Grant of 640 acres.

He married Emily Eaves, Nov. 26, 1845, in San Augustine. Emily was born in Perry County, AL, July 24, 1827. She was the daughter of William Burwell and Sarah Ann Eaves and migrated to San Augustine in approximately 1840. Milton and Emily had three children, Benjamin Milam, Laura Ann and Joseph Rowe. Milton served two terms (1843 and 1848) as coroner of San Augustine County.

Milton went to California in 1852 to seek gold. He died and was buried near Redwood City, CA in 1869.

Emily received a pension in 1878 as a surviving widow and a 1280-acre grant in 1881. She died Feb. 14, 1911 and is buried in New Hope Cemetery in Shelby County.

HUMPHREY JACKSON born Nov. 24, 1784 in Belfast, Ireland, arrived in New Orleans in 1808. After his first wife, Elizabeth White, died he married Sarah Merriman and fathered four children: Letitia, Hugh, John and James. Humphrey brought his family to Texas in 1823 where he joined Austin's "Old Three Hundred". He was granted a league and a labor of land on the eastern bank of the San Jacinto River. Sarah died in July 1824 and a few months later Humphrey was elected district alcalds and ex officio militia captain of the San Jacinto neighborhood. He also served as "regidor" of the Municipality of Austin during 1828.

Probably his last public service was helping to locate a road from Harrisburg to the San Jacinto River near the present site of the U.S. Highway 90 crossing. Humphrey was cutting timber when he was killed by a falling tree in January 1833. He was buried beside his wife in what is now the town of Crosby where a historical marker has been placed to designate their final resting place. Humphrey's daughter and three sons went to live with their mother's relatives in present day Chambers County where many descendants still reside.
Mary Jean Jackson Abshier, (GGGD)

ISAAC JACKSON, There were three Isaac Jacksons in Austin's Colony. One received his league of land in what is now Grimes County; one received his league of land on the waters of Jackson Creek in present day Washington County; the third and overlooked, received his league on the waters of New Years Creek in present day Washington County. His wife was Zillah (Thompson).

Isaac was involved in a log raising in late March 1831. He worked later than he should, until dark. By the time he started home, it had begun to snow and he lost his way in the storm, He survived the freezing night, but died at home the next day.

His wife was pregnant with twin girls who were born in October 1831. One of the twins, Amanda, married Pleasant Wimberley, who established Wimberley, Hays County.

Isaac's eldest son, Joseph, served in the Texas Revolution. He was with the baggage detail at Harrisburg during the battle of San Jacinto.

Zillah and six children (Elizabeth, William, Isaac Jr., Emily, Amanda and Sarah) participated in the runaway scrape. Apparently Emily died in the runaway because she does not appear in documents after that date.

Susan Slagle (Palo Duro Chapter)
Barbara Slagle (Palo Duro Chapter) 21891

SARAH ANN (WALLIS) JACKSON was born on May 20, 1825, the fifth daughter of Elisha Henry Roberts Wallis and Sarah (Sally) Barrow. When the Wallis family left Louisiana late in 1824, Mrs. Wallis was expecting a child. Thus, Sarah Ann was the first of their children born at the new home on Wallis Hill in present day Chambers County. She was married on Aug. 31, 1843 to John Jackson, son of Humphrey Jackson and his wife Sarah Merriman. The Wallis' had a total of nine children: Jonie Ann, who never married, Letitia Laura married Charles Norman Eley; Rufus Humphrey married Annie Mayes, Hugh, who lived only nine days; Judge Hugh Edward first married Ada Minter and secondly her sister, Ida Minter; Fannie Martha married Daniel P. Nelson; Lottie, who died in the 1877 smallpox epidemic; Rachel married Asa W. Robbins; and Lula married George N. Wallis.

Sarah Wallis Jackson became ill in 1868. The nature of her illness is not known, but letters indicate she had suffered with a disease for 24 years. At midnight on Aug. 7, 1869, she passed away and was buried beside her mother and father in the Wallis Family Cemetery in Wallisville.

Barbara Morgan (GGGD)

STEPHEN JACKSON, a farmer born in South Carolina July 12, 1803, entered Texas in 1831. He received a Mexican land grant of a league of land (4,428 acres) on June 10, 1835, as a member of de Zavala's colony located in the Pine Island Bayou region of old Jefferson County, now Hardin County. Jackson served in the army of the Republic of Texas from March 6, 1836 to June 6, 1836. He was awarded 320 acres of bounty land.

Stephen Jackson was married to Susan Choate (1807-1873) in 1838 by Henry Millard, chief justice of Jefferson County. Together they had six children: Ambrose, Sarah, James Andrew, Minerva, Stephen Jr., and W.J. The 1850 census listed Jackson's holdings at 800 head of cattle and seven slaves valued at $11,743.

Stephen Jackson's property contained pools of bubbling sour water springs hidden in the palmetto thicket. Jackson, on tasting the sulphurous water was heard to yell, "My God, boys, I'm pizzened!" According to old Indian tales, the water was thought to have healing medicinal properties. By 1845 a health resort was in operation around the Sour Lake Springs. At his death in 1860, Jackson held controlling interest in the spa. Sam Houston came to Sour Lake in early 1863 to bathe his battle wounds.

The oil strike of 1901 in Sour Lake ruined the mineral springs, but brought boomtown fame to the village founded on Stephen Jackson's land grant: Sour Lake, TX.

An historical marker locates the Jackson Family Cemetery in Sour Lake where he is buried along with his wife, his children and their descendants. Sour Lake is located on Texas Hwy. 105, 18 miles west of Beaumont, in the edge of the Big Thicket.

Catherine Jane Meachant, (GGD), 05579

THOMAS JEFFERSON JACKSON, an emigrant from Ireland married Louise Cottle. They had four children, two of which were mentioned in his probate record. Margaret (Jackson) Brown, George Jackson, and Lee Jackson were the known children.

Thomas J. Jackson and George Washington Cottle (Louise Cottle Jackson's brother) were killed in the Battle of the Alamo March 6, 1836.

In the book, *Alamo Defenders* by Bill Groneman relates following on Thomas J. Jackson;

"The last group to reinforce the Alamo arrived on March 1, 1836, after the siege had progressed for eight days. This was a relief force from the town of Gonzales, made up of the town's militia force (the Gonzales Ranging Company of Mounted Volunteers), plus residents of the town and surrounding area. Also individuals who were already members of the Alamo garrison but had left Bexar for various reasons made up this last group." Pg 3.

Then on page 63 the same book the following is found.
Jackson, Thomas (?-March 6, 1836)
Born: Ireland; Residence: Gonzales, TX; Rank: Private (rifleman, Gonzales Ranging company) Killed in Battle of the Alamo.

Thomas Jackson registered in DeWitt's colony on May 1, 1831.

He married Louise Cottle, sister of Alamo defender George W. Cottle and was the father of four children.

Jackson was one of the "Old Eighteen" defenders of the Gonzales cannon. He entered the Alamo as a member of the relief force from Gonzales on March 1, 1836.

WILLIAM JAMES, son of James ("Double Jimmy") James, and Elizabeth Newman, was born 1814, Virginia. He married Jane Rentfro on Feb. 28, 1835, Roane County, TN. After leaving Tennessee and spending a short residency in Missouri, they removed (circa 1844) to the Trinity River area in Texas with the group known as The Peters Colony. William and Jane had seven children: Eliza Jane (born 1838, Tennessee) who married William Daniel Hittson (rancher); Thomas B. (born 1840, Missouri) who married 1. Zorilda Ellison, 2. Nannie G.; John (born 1842 Missouri); Emily (born 1844 Missouri); William A. (born 1850 Texas) who married 1. Amanda, 2. Carrie; George Preston "Press" (born 1858 Texas) who married Annie and Rufus L. (born 1860 Texas) who married Sallie L. St. Johns.

Researched decendancy: James James, William James to son, George Preston James's, whose issue continues through son Evon P. James, grandson Preston George James to great-grandson Thomas David James, resident of Fort Worth. Eliza Jane James Hittson's issue continues through son Samuel David Hittson, grandson Earl Hittson, great-granddaughter, Barbara Hittson Skopeck, of Dana Point, CA, (and compiler of this bio), great-great-grandchildren Dorinda Marie Skopeck Malloy and Robert J. Skopeck Jr. to great-great-great-granddaughter, Madison "Madi" Pelhan Skopeck, daughter of Robert Jr. A second line continues from James James to daughter, Eliza Jane James Hittson, whose issue continues through her daughter, Lillie Leanor "Lee" Hittson Johnson, to granddaughter Eva Mae Johnson Blackburn, to great-granddaughter Billy Mae Blackburn Dickenson, to great-great-grandson Bill Scott Dickenson to great-great-great-grandsons Dalton Scott Dickenson and William Scott Dickenson. A third line begins with patriot, James James, continues through his daughter, Nancy James Wheat, whose issue continues through her daughter, Elizabeth Jane Wheat Lancaster, to grandson, John Louis Lancaster, to great-granddaughter, Trecie Faye Lancaster Wilson to great-great-grandson Joseph Lee Wilson Jr.

Thomas B. James Sr. was Sheriff of Tarrant County during Reconstruction Days. His son, Thomas B. Jr., was City Detective. He was said to have killed one of the Dalton Kin and once arrested Clyde Barrow (of "Bonnie and Clyde" fame) for chicken thievery.

George Preston "Press", and brother Rufus L., were prominent businessmen-saloon owners. At various times, they owned and operated saloons known as The Parlor Saloon, the Tennessee Saloon, the Post Office Saloon, the James Brothers Saloon, the Tennessee Liquor House Saloon and the Board of Trade Saloon (the last being located at 316 Main Street, the site of the present day Western Union office). Another brother, William Jr., was Grand Marshall of the Masons for the State of Texas. The site of the present Santa Fe Train Depot was originally the James cow pasture and the site of the Ft. Worth National Bank was originally the James Family Home.

Many of the first and second generations of the above family are buried in the cemetery at Birdsville. The patriarch of this family, James James, affectionately known as "Double Jimmy" was born in Prince William County, VA, in 1764 and was the oldest living human being in the country on the 1870 census. He died at almost 114 years of age. He was a patriot of the War of 1812. He is buried at Gooseneck Cemetery in Young County, TX.

Barbara Ann Hittson Skopeck, DRT 17582

SAMUEL A. JANUARY

SAMUEL A. JANUARY (born 1799-died ca. 1860) Consecutive records show that Pierre Janvier and his Scottish wife left the Catholics and became Protestants (Hugenots) in the late 1600s.

They were afterwards persecuted and finally forced to leave France and all their possessions. Pierre died on Ill – de – Re' in 1682. His sons, Thomas, Pierre, and Phillipe came to America.

Thomas (1664-1728) came through Philadelphia (Ship

The N. Thomas January Family, circa 1902.

Desire) and later married and settled in New Castle, DE in the early 1690's. He was naturalized in 1695. He was the first ruling elder of New Castle Presbyterian Church and lived there on The Strand.

Peter, Thomas' grandson, who migrated to Mayesville, KY, changed the spelling from Janvier to January. His family became prominent in the trade along the Ohio River. Today the large Andrew January house stands near town center, continually occupied by his descendants since 1837. Peter and his sons, Ephriam, James, John and Samuel, served Kentucky in the Revolutionary War.

Samuel A. January married his cousin, Pamelia January in 1814 and later came to Harrison County, Republic of Texas, where he served as Justice of Peace (1843-1846). He received a 640 acre land grant there. His son, George, received 320 acres. George was shot to death near Carthage in 1862.

George's wife, Elizabeth Mills, moved her family to Shelby County about 1869. Their children were: Dickson, Samuel, George, Martha, Robert, Susan and Thomas, who married Elizabeth Morris, age 14, in 1881. They lived until death on land in-

herited from her father, William Morris, in the Mt. Pleasant community. Their children were: William Burr, Samuel Elonzo, Ettie, Condy Buford (WWI Veteran-served in France), Vonnie, Troy, and Eizie.

Condy married Maud Ellington and their children were: Doyle (1920-1922), Wanda (1922), and Reba (1932).

The N.T. January Farm, Shelby County, established 1880, is listed in Family Land Heritage. 1999 owners are grandchildren, Ange January, Wanda, Don, and Mark Ramsey, Reba James and Ruby Kammerdiener.

Wanda January Ramsey, (GGGD), 17512
Reba January James, (GGGD), 17513

WILLIAM JOHNSON

WILLIAM JOHNSON, son of Harris Johnson, was born in Tennessee in 1810. Little is known of his early life, but he moved with his wife, father and stepmother to Texas in 1835. They settled in Red River County where he joined the Red River Rangers under Captain Becknell. The story handed down through the generations about my great-great-grandfather, William Johnson, is unique to Texas History. Texas history books say that after the Battle of San Jacinto the Red River Company of the Republic of Texas Army under Captain Becknell arrived there. They were too late for the battle, but were fresh so when Santa Anna was captured they chose three men from the Red River Company to guard him. The history books state that two of the men were named, but no one got the name of the third man. The Johnson family was estranged for over 100 years. Until the mid 1990's I had no information on my Johnson family history. However, the different branches of the family, when reunited, have handed down the story that William Johnson was the third man who guarded Santa Anna. Since they had no contact over the years, I think there is a good possibility that the story is true, but not provable.
Virginia E. Vitasek, 22672

ALLEN CARTER JONES

ALLEN CARTER JONES (born 1785 in North Carolina) and wife, Mary Jane "Jennie" Norris (born about 1796) are shown in the 1820 Sullivan County, IN, Census with children: Delitha (Delilah) Jones born about 1817; Keeton McLemore Jones born about 1818; and "Santiago" Jackson N. born about 1819. Other children of Mary Jane and A.C. Jones and their dates of birth were: James R. Jones (about 1821/22 in Sullivan County, IN); Charles C. Jones (about 1824 in Sullivan County, IN); Mateo (about 1824 named in Mexican Census); Theresa Jones (about 1826); Clerisa (Clarissa) (about 1828); and Allen Carter Jones. A.C. Jones and his family arrived in "Old Nacogdoches," July 1, 1826. A.C. Jones was awarded a land grant in Montgomery County.

George Washington Jones and Mary A. Simes

Mary Jane Jones died, and A.C. Jones married Maris Davis Stone July 30, 1838, in Montgomery County. She was the widow of Wm. Thornton Stone and daughter of Thomas Davis, born about 1780, and Elizabeth Bullock, born about 1783, both born in North Carolina. Maris was born in Mississippi, May 17, 1805.

The children born to her marriage to Stone with dates of their births were: "Betty" Elizabeth E. Stone (about 1827); William Martin Stone (April 27, 1829) and Mary Jane Stone (about 1833) all born in Mississippi. The children born to her marriage to Jones with dates of their births were: David Crockett Jones (about 1839), George Washington Jones (about 1840); Fannie Ann Jones (1842); and Thomas Dean Jones (about 1844). George Washington Jones served in the Civil War. David Crockett Jones and Thomas Dean Jones died in the Civil War. David Crockett Jones married Zellar Ann, and they had one child, David Hugh. Zellar Ann married C.C. Ballard after David Crockett was killed in the Civil War. Thomas Dean Jones did not marry. George Washington Jones married Mary Adeline/Adaline/Adiline Sims/Simes, and their children named in the 1880 Grimes County Census were: Elvy A.E. (age nine), William R, and George W. (age five), Sarah C.V. (age four), Fannie M. (age two); and John T. (age about one month). Maris received a land grant on behalf of her husband, Wm. Thornton Stone, in Milam County. She also owned slaves and cattle.

After the death of A.C. Jones about 1851, Maris Davis Stone Jones married John Carter August 15, 1853, in Grimes County. He was the father of Laura Ann Carter Jones, wife of Keeton McLemore Jones, Maris' stepson. He also was the father of Jiles Carter, husband of Clarissa Jones, Keeton's sister and step daughter of Maris. John Carter died in 1865, and Maris died in 1867.

Lou Shugart Ryan, (GGD of George Washington Jones and GD of Fannie Maris Jones Sullivan), DRT No. 018322

JAMES RUSSELL JONES

JAMES RUSSELL JONES, was born in 1820 in Alabama, the son of Wiley Jones and Sarah Morgan. He was in Texas by 1837 when he received a third Class Headright for 320 acres in Washington County.
James R. Jones married Margaret Wilman on Dec. 8, 1849 in Burleson County. Margaret was born in Wurtenberg, Germany in 1832. James Jones is listed as Republic of Texas Taxpayer in Brazos County in 1842. James R. Jones is listed on the Bell County Confederate Service Muster Rolls as a Private in Captain Milton

L to R: (Front) Charley, Joe Allen Jones; (Back) Cordia Alto, Eliza Ann Jones.

Damron's Company, 27th Texas Brigade in August 1861. In 1871 James R. Jones transferred 150 acres of land he received in 1854, on the waters of North Nolan Creek, in Bell County to Margaret A. Jones. Children from the U.S. Census 1850-1860 Burleson/Brazos County, 1870 Bell County and 1880 Hamilton County, TX are: Sarah, Celia, James, Allen, Wise Solomon, Narcissa, Andrew, Margaret, Wiley, Emma, George and Penny, all born in Texas. Wise Solomon Jones (1858 Texas-1885 Texas) married Mary Melinda Coward, daughter of James and Eliza Bervilia Mitchell Coward, on Dec. 24, 1877 in Bell County. Mary Melinda (1860 Alabama-1912 Texas) is buried in Falls County, TX. Widowed, Mary married a Mr. Berry. Wise Solomon and Mary Melinda Coward Jones had at least four children: Cordia Alto, Eliza Ann, Joe Allen, and Charly. Cordia Alto Jones (1879 Texas

– 1964 Texas) married J.D. Walls; Eliza Ann Jones (1880 Texas-1968 Texas) married James Daniel Welch, and Joe Allen Jones (1882 Texas – 1934 Texas) married Laura Caldonia Moring.

Bennie Lou Hook Altom, (GGGD), 20044S

JOSEPH P. JONES

JOSEPH P. JONES, son of Thomas and Elizabeth Jones was born CA 1798 in Kentucky. He married Sarah Brimberry 1819 in Illinois. Sarah was the daughter of Issac Brimberry and Mary Beethe of Bourbon County, KY. Sarah died in Milam County in Sept. 12, 1861 and is buried at Little River Baptist Church Cemetery near the village of Jones Prairie.

Joseph and Sarah had eight children. They were: James A. married Martha McKinney; Polly A. married Armstead Rogers; Juliet born 1823 in Edgar County, IL died 1873 in Milam County, TX, married Elijah White; Nancy Carolyn married Thomas Steadman; Patsy Ann, Edward Franklin; Rosetta married D.W. Campbell; Martha married L.M. Etheridge.

Joseph P. received a Mexican land Grant dated 1833, 6 1/4 labore between Little River and Cow Creek. He enlisted in the Texas Rangers Sept. 5, 1836 in Captain Barron's Company and was honorably discharged on July 3, 1837.

Joseph P. was with a surveying party in Navarro County on Oct. 28, 1838 when they were attached by Kickapoo Indians. J.P. was killed and buried at the battle site which is marked by a monument.

The Jones Prarie township takes its name from its location on the J.P. Jones land grant.

Peggy Ackers Elmore

KEETON MCLEMORE JONES

KEETON MCLEMORE JONES, colonist, Texas Army veteran, farmer, was born Jan. 9, 1818, in Sullivan County, IN, to Allen Carter Jones, born 1785 in North Carolina, and Mary Jane "Jennie" born about 1796. When Keeton was eight years old, his father, Allen C. Jones, brought the family to Texas arriving at Old Nacogdoches July 1, 1826, becoming part of the Edwards Colony.

In 1838 Keeton and his father, Allen C. Jones, received two of the earliest Headright First Class land grants issued. This land is located near Bedias Creek in Grimes County, and there they reared their families. A gin and mill were built on Allen C.'s land, and in addition to farming, Keeton and his eldest sons operated a freighting business hauling goods such as cotton, corn, pork, to and from Houston, Navasota, and Anderson. Wagons drawn by oxen were used.

Keeton Jones was a private soldier and waggoner in the Texas Army. He enlisted in March 1836 in Captain Smith's Company in Colonel Sidney Sherman's Regiment. He served in the Nacogdoches Volunteers under the command of Captain Hayden Arnold, and was at the Battle of San Jacinto.

Jones received Bounty Warrants for his service in the Texas Army, a Donation Warrant for his participation in the Battle of San Jacinto, and a Veteran Donation as a surviving Texas Army soldier of the Texas Revolution.

On Dec. 24, 1839, Keeton Jones married Laura Ann Carter, born May 15, 1822, to John and Mary Carter who had brought their family to Texas from Alabama in March 1838 settling near the Joneses. Keeton and Laura's marriage ceremony was performed by Keeton's father, Allen C. Jones, who was a Justice of the Peace at that time.

Shortly after the Civil War in late 1865, Keeton Jones moved his family from Grimes County to Bell County, TX. He settled on land he bought about nine miles northeast of Belton and west of Temple, on Pepper Creek, near the farming community of Old Howard.

When the Jones family relocated to Bell County, Keeton's family consisted of wife Laura Ann, and their 10 children, including one married daughter Margaret and her husband Joseph H. Plaster. In later years one of Keeton's granddaughters, Addie Garner of Temple, recorded the following account of their move to Bell County.

"They moved in several wagons. Two of the wagons were loaded with hewn cedar logs. These logs were to be used to build a large room on to a small one as soon as possible after their arrival at the place that was to be their future home.

"The household goods, supplies, and family members were in the other wagons, drawn by horses or by oxen four to six yoke a wagon. They rode on horse back and drove the cattle, the girls taking their turn."

Keeton's granddaughter, Addie Garner, has written that the stagecoaches which originally stopped at the home of Silas Baggett, later stopped at Jones' home near Old Howard.

Keeton Jones died April 25, 1890, and is buried with marker, in a small private cemetery on his land on Pepper Creek, near Old Howard, Bell County, TX. His wife, Laura Ann, died July 31, 1894, and is buried beside Keeton, and two of their sons who died young.

Keeton Jones and wife Laura Ann had 12 children, 10 reached maturity. All of the children were born on the Jones land on Bedias Creek in Grimes County, TX. The children were: John Carter Jones (1841-1932) a Confederate Army veteran, married Sarah Ann "Sallie" Reid, no issue; Benjamin Franklin Jones (1844-1935) a Confederate Army veteran, married Texana Georgia Dickson, four children; James A. Jones (1847-1928) married Eudora K. "Mittie" Dickson, five children; Mary Margaret Jones (1850-) married Joseph H. Plaster; eight children; Laura Ann Jones (twin, 1852-1916), married George W. Wayland, six children; Rebecca Ann "Becky" Jones (twin, 1852-1875) married James Monroe Baggett, three children; Ariadna "Addie" Jones (1854-1912) married C.B. Segur, one daughter died young; Giles McLemore Jones (1857-1857 at one month), Allen Carter "Dick" Jones (1858-1948) married Ellen Frances Chapman, three children; Charles Calvert Jones (twin, 1861-1925) married Susan Ellen "Ella" Dickson, two daughters; William M. "Will" Jones (1861-) married Lena, one daughter; Keeton David Jones (1863-1864). The above brothers, Benjamin Franklin Jones, James A. Jones, and Charles Calvert Jones, married Dickson sisters.

Betty Jane Johnson McDaniel, (GGGD) of Keeton McLemore Jones, 009414

JOHANN ERNST HEINRICH CHRISTIAN FRANZ JORDAN

JORDAN was born July 21, 1821 in Wehrstedt, Niedersachsen, Germany to Johann Heinrich Christian Jordan and Wilhelmina Grotjahn. Ernst was a linen weaver. By 19 he married Wilhelmine Uflaker. They had a daughter, Mina.

The Jordans arrived in Galveston on the "Margaretha" Nov. 25, 1845. Wilhelmine died there at Indianola from the severe weather. Ernst and little Mina traveled to New Braunfels where Mina died November 1846. Ernst moved to Fredericksburg where he helped build the First Methodist Church. In 1849 he married Lisette Bickenbach, daughter of Daniel Bickenbach and Anna

Sophia Willach. Children born were: Wilhelmina, April 1849; Peter, January 1852; Sophie, March 1854; and Heinrich, April 1856.

Ernst was granted 640 acres April 1849; became a U.S. Citizen Oct. 20, 1854; by October 1856 the Jordans finally settled their land on Willow Creek, Mason County. Children born there: Frederika, 1858; Wilhelm, 1859; Daniel, December 1860; and Ernst 1863.

Ernst Jordan farmed and ranched his land. From 1860-1870 he was a teamster. By 1890 he owned 4,000 acres and 500 head of cattle. He died Dec. 23, 1892 and Lisette died Aug. 23, 1899. Buried at the home cemetery, they were later reinterred at the Art Methodist Church Cemetery built in 1890 on land donated by Ernst Jordan.

Toni Lee Hausler Janis, 012738

ALFRED KELSO SR.

ALFRED KELSO SR., born April 21, 1808, in Lincoln County, TN. His parents were Henry Kelso and Jane Wells. Alfred married Martha Martin on July 7, 1827, and they moved to the Alabama-Mississippi border area where their first child, Alfred Kelso Jr., was born on Sept. 20, 1828. Alfred and Martha moved to Texas in 1829 and by 1835, they owned about 6000 acres on the Colorado River, near the town of Columbus.

On April 21, 1836, which was Alfred Kelso Sr.'s 28th birthday, he fought in the Battle of San Jacinto, as a corporal in Captain William J. Heard's Company F of the Army of the Republic of Texas. Alfred Sr. wrote a letter to his brother–in-law, John Henry Martin, in which Alfred gave his description of the Battle of San Jacinto. This letter was included in *The Papers of the Texas Revolution 1835-1836*. Alfred Jr. was the only one of the three children born to Alfred Sr. and Martha Martin that lived to adulthood.

Alfred Kelso Sr. was the Sheriff of Gonzales County, Republic of Texas, in 1837, 1840 and 1841. There is no record of Martha (Martin) Kelso's death. On Aug. 26, 1840, Alfred Kelso Sr. and Louisa Jane Barton were married. Louisa Jane was the daughter of Kimber W. Barton and Margaret Lockhart. Alfred Sr. died May 12, 1898, and is buried in Brite Cemetery in Atascosa County, TX.

Alfred Kelso Jr. and his wife, Catherine, bought some land in DeWitt County on Sandies Creek, and some town lots in Clinton, TX, sometime before 1850. Alfred Jr. married his second wife, Sarah Elizabeth Grier, in DeWitt County on Jan. 17, 1856, and married his third wife, Susan Ann Cunningham, in DeWitt County on March 15, 1865. Alfred Jr. and Susan (Cunningham) Kelso's first child, Robert E. Lee Kelso, was born in DeWitt County on March 10, 1869. Alfred Jr. and his family moved to Travis County where Susan died in 1870 and was buried in the Masonic Cemetery at Boggy Creek. There is no record of Alfred Jr.'s death.

Robert E. Lee Kelso married Amanda Simpson in Travis County on Dec. 19, 1891. Robert and Amanda moved to the Gonzales and Fayette Counties area near Flatonia, TX. Frank Pierce Kelso and his twin brother, Alfred Leon Kelso, were the last children born to Robert and Amanda. Frank Pierce Kelso married Helen Lounieta Ragan on Jan. 15, 1940, and they had one child, Bobbie Denise Kelso, who was born Jan. 1, 1941. Bobbie Denise Kelso married Joe Hugh Hutchins on Jan. 12, 1963, and they had one child, a son, Christopher Kyle Hutchins.

Bobbie D. (Kelso) Hutchins, (GGGD), 21650-S

MAJOR JAMES KERR was born Sept. 24, 1790 near Danville, Boyle County, KY. He was the son of James Kerr and Patience Wells Kerr. Major Kerr's grandfather, James Kerr, came from Ireland. His father, a Baptist minister, was born in Pennsylvania. In 1808 the family moved to St. Charles, MO.

Major James Kerr, for whom Kerr County, TX was named in an Act of the Sixth Texas Legislature in January 1856.

During the War of 1812, Major Kerr served as a Lieutenant with Captain Nathan Boone, a son of Daniel Boone. He also was sheriff of St. Charles County, MO, a representative to the Missouri legislature and a state senator. On July 23, 1818 Kerr was married to Angelina Caldwell.

In 1825, Major Kerr, his wife and three children moved to Texas. Kerr became the surveyor-general for Green DeWitt's colony. Soon after coming to Texas his wife and two children died. A settlement was established on Kerr Creek one mile from the present town of Gonzales. This settlement was destroyed during an Indian raid in July 1826.

Relocating to what is now Jackson County, Kerr was instrumental in initial meetings prior to the Texas Revolution, including serving as president of the Millican's Gin meeting. He married Sarah Grace Fulton, the adopted daughter of John J. Linn Jr., Sept. 24, 1833. Two of their four children grew to adulthood. One of these, Sarah, was my great-grandmother. Major James Kerr studied to become a lawyer but was actually more interested in practicing medicine. Kerr was prominent in affairs of the coastal region during the days of the Republic. He was a member of the House of Representatives during the Third Congress which met at Houston. He presented bills to prohibit dueling and to move the capital to Austin. In 1856 Kerr County was named for Major Kerr. He died Dec. 25, 1850 and was buried in a cemetery located on his farm seven miles north of present Edna.

On May 12, 1998, the Texana Chapter of the Daughters of the Republic of Texas dedicated a medallion at the grave of Major James Kerr, honoring him as a Citizen of the Republic of Texas.
Ruth Simons Ray, (GGGD), 8039

WILLIAM KINCHELOE was an early settler, always moving west from Virginia to Kentucky, where he married Nancy Taylor, on to Missouri, where he met Stephen Austin. He became one of Austin's "Old Three Hundred". He was a blacksmith, tavern keeper, surveyor, and farmer. He settled in Texas with his second wife, Mary Betts.

William organized a group of settlers, including two sons-in-law, Horacio Chriesman and Daniel Rawls, to emigrate to Texas. These 20 families embarked on their journey in flatboats, leaving in the fall of 1821. Because of winter approaching and illness among the group, the expedition was delayed until Feb. 25, 1822. In the meantime William went to New Orleans with five or six young men and chartered the schooner the *Only Son*. These young men were sent to plant a crop so that food would be available upon the immigrants' arrival. As a result of the illness, two of the Kincheloe daughters died. This delayed the group so long that they missed the sailing of *The Lively*, so William again chartered the *Only Son* and the group sailed for Texas. They landed at the mouth of the Colorado June 19, 1822, where they left the boat while the immigrants went to inspect their land. The Karankawa Indians attacked the guards and stole all the supplies. However, with a corn crop nearly ready for harvest, the settlers set about establishing their homes in the area along the Colorado. William's Spanish land grant is located in present day Wharton County.

The census of 1826 classified him as a farmer and stock raiser. In January 1827 he made a declaration of loyalty to the Mexican government and protested against the Fredonia Rebellion. He was elected police commissioner of the colony on Feb. 10, 1828.

William Kincheloe died in Wharton County in 1835. He left no will but the court established the value of his estate at $17,588.00. One of his daughters, Nancy, married (1) Andrew Castleman, who died at Velasco, and (2) James Green, who fought at San Jacinto.
Louise Green Polley, (GGGGD), 17156
Cheryl P. Walker, (GGGGGD), 18314
Jamie G. Janak, (GGGGGD), 18097
Dawn P. Garrett, (GGGGGD), 18163
Cynthia P. Worley, (GGGGGD), 18164

JOHN GLADDEN KING SR. was born on Feb. 8, 1790, in South Carolina. He married Mildred Parmelia Parchman on May 8, 1817, in Giles County, TN. Parmelia (Millie) was born March 8, 1798, in Pennsylvania. John served in the Tennessee militia during the War of 1812. They had 11 children: Nancy Gladden (1818), married first Benjamin Fuqua then William Matthews; Mary Minerva (1819, died 1880), married Robert Hall; William Philip (1820-1836): Elizabeth (1821-1822); Matilda Briggs (1823-1853), married James Foster; John Gladden Jr. (1825), married Elizabeth Tom; Zillah Parmelia (1826-1856), married Alsey Miller; Thomas D. (1829-1873), married Mary Harris; twins Eliza Ann (1832-1881), married first T.R. Rutledge then William Foster, and Ann Eliza (1832-1833); James Parchman (1835-1868) married Martha Morrison.

The Kings arrived in Texas in 1830 to settle on the Guadalupe River, near Gonzales, in DeWitt's Colony. John contributed early to the cattle industry, as indicated by the brand "JG" registered in 1831. He spoke Spanish fluently and communicated well with the Indians. In 1836 he joined the Gonzales Ranging Company of Mounted Volunteers as one of the 32 men that would go to defend the Alamo. At the last moment his oldest son William Philip, age 15, took his place, and was the youngest to die in the famous battle. The Kings and many of their descendants are buried in the King Cemetery in Gonzales County.
Almeda Doughty Hodge, (GGGD), 20896

DAVID LEVI KOKERNOT, My great-grandfather, David Levi Kokernot was born in Amsterdam, Holland, Dec. 28, 1805 and died Dec. 10, 1892 in Gonzales County, TX. His parents were Levi Moses and Elizabeth van der Beugel Kokernot.

David Levi came to New Orleans with his father in 1817. In the late 1820s he joined in the family mercantile business in New Orleans and on May 30, 1829, married Caroline Josephine Dittimar, daughter of Mrs. Julia Ann Maley, natives of Hesse Cassel, Germany.

In 1830 he was commissioned warrant officer in the United

States Revenue Cutter Service. In 1832 he moved to Anahuac, TX and participated in the Anahuac disturbances. He helped form the first Texas Navy, the three small schooners: *The Stephen F. Austin, The Water Witch,* and *The Red Rover.* He was commander of *The Red River.*

David Levi Kokernot

He joined Stephen F. Austin's small army of patriots and fought at the *Battle of Cibilo Creek,* and the *Battle of Concepcion.* Kokernot participated in what became known as "The Grass Fight". He was commissioned second lieutenant Nov. 29, 1835.

David Levi and wife had seven daughters and two sons. He moved to Gonzales County in 1853. Kokernot was a rancher and cattleman.

Ruth Kokernot Denman

HEINRICH CONRAD KOTHMANN

HEINRICH CONRAD KOTHMANN was born Jan. 31, 1798 in Wedelheine, Hanover, Germany to Hennig Heinrich Kothmann and Ilse Dorothee Marwede. While young, he played clarinet in the Hannover Municipal Band. He learned the cabinet making trade. For six years he was in the Infantry, Honorably Discharged April 25, 1824. In 1824 he married Johanne Sophie Wolters Kothmann, widow of his oldest brother, Heinrich Wilhelm. On March 1, 1831, Johanne died leaving two young children, Johann Heinrich Wilhelm and Henriette Sophie.

Ilse Katherine Pahlmann, daughter of Johann Henning Pahlmann and Ilse Dorothee Thormann, married Heinrich Conrad Kothmann on June 22, 1832. Children born in Wedelheine: Ilse Katherine, Dec. 23, 1832; Heinrich Friedrich, Feb. 10, 1835; Karl Dietrich, Feb. 14, 1837; Marie Caroline, Nov. 23, 1840; Marie Dorothee, Dec. 6, 1842.

Sailing from Bremen, the family arrived in Galveston Dec. 20, 1845. After several months they traveled to New Braunfels and by May 8, 1846 arrived and helped establish Fredericksburg. Son, William, was born Feb. 18, 1850, then Caroline on March 26, 1852. Music was furnished by Heinrich Conrad for the first wedding in Fredericksburg—namely that of Charles H. Nimitz Sr. and Miss Sophie Mueller.

In 1856 the Kothmanns moved to Upper Willow Creek (now Art), establishing their home as "Citizens and Settlers of Frontier Lands". Heinrich died Aug. 27, 1881, and Ilse Katherine on Feb. 15, 1905. Both were buried in the family cemetery at Upper Willow Creek.

Tina Hausler Baker, (012739)

JOHANN HEINRICH KRAFT

JOHANN HEINRICH KRAFT was born on June 2, 1827 in Schletzenrod, Hessen, Germany. He married Katherine Roege on Jan. 22, 1854 in Comal County, New Braunfels, TX. Katherine Roege was born Sept. 29, 1837 in Fahren, Hannover, Germany. Katherine's family came to America on the same ship as Heinrich Kraft. They left Bremen, Germany on board the *Herschel* on Sept. 23, 1844 and arrived at Galveston, TX on Dec. 8, 1844 and boarded a small schooner to the Port of Indianola. They were chosen by Prince Solms of the German Emigration Society to help build a town with total German customs and culture.

On March 21, 1845 they arrived at the springs, which are now Landa Park, New Braunfels, TX. The Kraft siblings and the Roege all became Founders of the City and Founders of the First German Protestant Church of New Braunfels, TX. Heinrich and Katherine became the parents of 12 children, of which two died in infancy. Heinrich died on Jan. 26, 1904 and Katherine died on March 15, 1917 and were buried in the cemetery on the Kraft Ranch along with their children.

Ella Kraft Seiler Brown, (GGD), 020607
Sharon Seiler Davis, (GGGD), 021324
Penny Davis Meek, (GGGGD), 021325
Julie Ann Davis, (GGGGD), 021327
Amy Marie Davis, (GGGGD), 021326

NANCY DEAN KUYKENDALL

NANCY DEAN KUYKENDALL was born Dec. 17, 1817 in Franklin County, TN. Nancy was the sixth child of John Dean (Deen) II and Marilla Farmer. Nancy married Absalom A. Kuykendall Sept. 15, 1834 in Nashville, TN.

They moved to Texas in 1837. Nancy and Absalom were granted land in the Milam District of Hamilton County in April 1837. In 1840 they moved into Fayette County occupying a place 18 miles east of La Grange, near where Absalom's brother Abner lived.

They were living in Fayette County in September 1842 when the Mexicans made a raid into Texas, capturing San Antonio. Absalom started for San Antonio to join others to repel the invaders. Nancy took their valuables to a safe hiding place and prepared to leave with other families. They were going East of the Sabine River for safety in the event the Mexican Army would march on La Grange.

Absalom reached Gonzales where he heard of the battle of Salado, and the retreat of the Mexican Army, so he returned home.

Nancy and Absalom had 10 children: Ruth Clarinda, the first born in Tennessee, July 18, 1835, married William Glenn Jett, April 22, 1852.

Nancy was a descendent of Thomas Lord de la Warr (Thomas West).

Susanna West married John Dean I in England. They had four sons. Joshua married Susanna Loveall. They had four children Jacob, Molly, Temperance and John Dean II.

Nancy was a lineal descendent of Thomas West. This family furnished the first three Governors of Colonial Virginia. The Dean (Deen) family was originally from Normandy; they participated in the invasion of England in 1066.

Nancy devoted her life to caring for her children.

Absalom was away much of the time during the struggle in the new Republic. He was appointed guard over the State Archives in moving the Capitol of Texas from Houston to Austin in 1839.

Nancy died May 2, 1853 at the age of 36. Place of burial is unknown.

Absalom died Jan. 1, 1900, and is buried in the Oakwood Cemetery on Jett Road.

Nancy's Faith, Courage and Strength are gratefully acknowledged by her descendents who merely walk in her shadow. *Dorothy Pegg Eckert (GGGD), 12964*
Bonnie Jett Miller, (GGGD), 21507
Marla Jeanne Eckert, (GGGGD), 22004
Anna Christine Eckert, (GGGGGD), 7258 C of R

THOMAS LAGOW, son of Richard and Margarey Lagow, was born in 1801 in Tennessee. He married Sara Bennett Nov. 4, 1830 in Crawford County, IL. Sara was born in Georgia in 1805. Thomas, a farmer, and Sara were charter members of the Pilgrim Baptist Church established by Daniel Parker. They traveled with 25 ox-drawn wagons to Texas Territory in 1835 settling in Grapeland, 75 miles east of Fort Parker. In May 1836 the Indians attacked the Fort where several of that party were massacred and abducted. This defeat was acknowledged to Daniel Parker Jr., Armstead Bennett and Brother Thomas Lagow June 18, 1836. Cynthia Ann, daughter of Silas and Lucy Parker, was abducted and adopted by the Comanches, was the squaw of Pete Necona and the Mother of Quannah Parker.

Thomas and Sara's six children were: Harrison, born May 13, 1833 married Margaret Samantha Matthews, William born Aug. 28, 1835, married Lucinda Murchison, John born Feb. 7, 1838 died prior to 1845, Silas born Jan. 19, 1840, first married Elizabeth Murchison and second Alice Elizabeth McReynolds; Richard born Dec. 16, 1841, married Nancy Murchison, Mary Ann born 1843 died before 1845.

Thomas Lagow, quartermaster in the Army of the Republic of Texas, received first class Headright Certificate #68 -4,428 acres and a labor of land issued Feb. 8, 1839. This land was situated on the WhiteRock Fork of the Trinity River, which became Dallas County in 1846. Though he never settled on this land, his children cleared and farmed it. Thomas received one of the largest single grants — Now the city of Dallas. He died in 1845 and Sara in 1844 with burial in Grapeland, TX.
Stella M. Lagow McClure, (GGD), 20856

JOSEPH R. LAIRD, born in Georgia in 1820. He emigrated to Texas by way of Simpson County, MS in June 1838. On Jan. 3, 1840, he received a land certificate, No. 68, for 320 acres. He received his unconditional certificate on July 5, 1841, at Jasper, TX.

Joseph married Edith (Eda) Durdin, oldest daughter of Hilliard Durdin, circa 1843. Their children included Archibald (1843-1899), married Frances F. Deason; Sarah (1844-1935), married Alcide Duclos; Hilliard Durdin (1846-1925), married Nancy Texana Frazer; Robert (1848-bef. 1860); Martha Ann (1852-1940), married Stephan Spell; Texana (1856-1949), married John E. Harris; Thomas Britton (1858-1931), married (1) Georgia Ann Slater, (2) Martha Josephine Mitchell; Nancy Jane (1861-1937), married William Jasper Rutherford; Joseph Ray (1863-1949), married Levisa Leontine Richardson.

By the time the census was taken in 1850, Joseph had settled in northern Tyler County on Russell Creek. He remained there only a short time, for by 1852 he had acquired land located in the Harmon Frazer headright on Billiams Creek. He remained at this location until 1866 or 1867. On Aug. 20, 1866, he purchased from James Barclay 77 acres located on Willow Creek in Harris County. The 1870 census shows Joseph and family living in Harris County, where they remained until 1879, when they moved to Robertson County. Joseph appears on the tax roll of that county in 1879, and the 1880 census shows that he continued to be a resident. In 1881 and 1882, Joseph appears on the tax roll of Limestone County. He must have died circa 1883 because he does not appear on the 1883 tax roll. Eda died circa 1881. Both are buried in the Tidwell Cemetery located near Thornton, Limestone County, TX.
Diane Mullins Clay, (GGGD), 014569

GEORGE WESLEY LAKEY was born around 1819 in Georgia. In 1834, as a single man, he received one third of a league of land in San Augustine County, which lay along both sides of the Ayish Bayou. He fought in the Mexican American War, the Indian War and the Civil War. He married Elizabeth Dickerson on Nov. 18, 1841 in San Augustine. He died around 1894 in Polk County.

William Wesley Lakey was born to George and Elizabeth on May 10, 1841 in San Augustine County and he married

John Mike Lakey Family (L to R): Vernon, John Mike, Nancy Georgeann, Eddrie Mae, and Audrey.

Susan Elizabeth Cahal ("itsy bitsy Grandma"), born June 11, 1859 in Meridian, MS. They were married on March 29, 1877 in San Augustine County. William Wesley Lakey also fought in the Civil War. He died April 22, 1918, and she died Jan. 17, 1955. Both are buried in Broaddus, TX. He and Susan had 10 children. They were: John Mike, born March 14, 1878, married Nancy Georgeann Beard; William Terry, born around December 1878, married Lora Runnels; Bessie, born Nov. 16, 1881, married William E. Thomas; Kate, born around January 1884, married Thomas Williams; Dorothy, born around 1887, married Riddle; Sudie, born Feb. 14, 1889; Robert Laverte, born around October 1890; Stephen A., born Jan. 6, 1895, married Idella-Lera, born around August 1897, married James Andrew Harvey; and Elma, married Jewel Langston.

John Mike Lakey, listed above, married Nancy Georgeann Beard on Nov. 30, 1901. She was born on May 10, 1875 in San Augustine County. Their children were: Audrey, born Dec. 9, 1903, died from diphtheria Jan. 6, 1909; Vernon M., born Oct. 20, 1905, married Frieda Schwabenland, then, Alice E. Powell, then, Bonnie Mae Ford Newman; Eddrie Mae, born Jan. 5, 1908, married E.D. King; Nellie Elma, born June 7, 1910, married first, Graham Hooker ("Coop"), and second, J.T. Buchanan; Velva Onita, born Jan. 19, 1913, married Edward Adrian Fitch; Bonner J., born May 15, 1915, died Nov. 30, 1916; Maureen Nancy, born Oct. 6, 1917, married William Holly Fussell Jr. ("W.H."). John Mike Lakey owned a general store in Broaddus, TX. He died Sept. 8, 1945 and his wife died June 2, 1947. Both are buried in Broaddus, TX.
Maureen Nancy Lakey, Fussell (GGD), 3684
Shari Kaye Fitch Doyle, (GGGGD), 21519

WILLIAM LAKEY, son of Francis Lakey was born about 1797, Salisbury District, Surry County, NC. He married Sarah (unknown), a native of North Carolina born around 1800, and moved to Tennessee in 1827. He emigrated to Texas thru Arkansas and Louisiana and settled in the southern part of the "Ais Creek" (Ayish Bayou). William was admitted as a colonist in the Colonization Enterprise and received a First Class Headright, June 27, 1835 in San Augustine and Sabine Counties. He and Sarah had eight children. They were as follows:

Winsey "Winnie," born around 1824, married Thomas Doyne; George W., born around 1825, married unknown, Sarah Oneal and Mary Henderson; James Troy, born around 1827, married Mary A. Curry; William Caroll, born around 1829, married Mary Elizabeth Brooks and Sarah Green Barnes; Mary Elizabeth, born around 1831; John Van Buren, born around 1835, married Martha Jane (Barnes?) and Sallie Kencil Yeager; Sam Houston, born around 1837, married Mary Miller and Charlotte (Lottie) Hickman; Noah Lafitte, born 1839, married Maggie A. Mueller.

William served in the company of Captain James Cheshire and fought in the Siege of Bexar during the Texas Revolution in 1835. He died in 1863. Sarah died between 1870-1880. They are both buried in William Lakey Cemetery in San Augustine County.

Sam Houston Lakey, listed above, married first, Mary Miller, and second, Charlotte (Lottie) Hickman April 28, 1873. She was the daughter of William Hickman born around 1819 and Catherine Hornsby born in 1830. Sam Houston and Mary's children were: Emer, who married Jackson Green Powell; Eller, who married John Clayton. Sam Houston and Lottie's children include: Grude Mack, who married Emma Beach; Margaret, who married Mr. Stovall; Elija, who married Nannie Dempsey; Elisha, who married Nannie Hightower; Sam Lee, born Oct. 12, 1880, died Feb. 6, 1960, married Emily Powell, born Oct. 13, 1890, died Sept. 19, 1960. Both are buried at Townsend Cemetery in San Augustine County.

Patsy N. Townsend Young, (GGGD), 21773

SAMUEL VALCIENT LAMOTHE

SAMUEL VALCIENT LAMOTHE, son of Polycarpe de LaMothe and Editha Wells, was born Feb. 15, 1810 in Rapides Parish, LA. Samuel married Aphia LaCroix on Dec. 7, 1837. Eight months later they left for Texas. En route, Samuel carved a cow's horn cup, engraving it, "S.V. Lamothe emigrated to Texas, 20th of August A.D. 1838", along with tools of his trade as a mason.

Their first child was born and died on Nov. 18, 1838, in Montgomery County, TX. Another son was born Sept. 19, 1840, in Austin County. Aphia died on March 2, 1842, and Samuel joined the Texian Army fighting the Vasques Campaign. Then, he married Nancy S. Stubblefield, on Nov. 19, 1842. Four of their six children survived infancy, but Nancy died on April 20, 1852. On July 25, 1852, Samuel married for a third time (his five sons were aged 2 to 11) to Matilda Miller, who died childless on Oct. 6, 1854.

Elizabeth E. McCleaster, daughter of Hiram B. McCleaster had come to Texas from Pennsylvania in 1839, at age four. Samuel and Elizabeth were married May 5, 1857, in Harris County, TX. They had two daughters: Samuel Ella, born April 19, 1858, (my great-great-grandmother) and Josephine, born in 1859.

Samuel Lamothe died on Jan. 8, 1861 and was buried in the Founders' Memorial Park Cemetery in Houston, TX.

Elizabeth Ann Garrett McCarty

ELIZABETH CAMPBELL LANE

ELIZABETH CAMPBELL LANE, born about 1798 in South Carolina and married Stephen Crawford Lane about 1816 in Marion County, SC. Stephen Crawford Lane was born about 1790 in Marion County, SC, was the son of Osborne Lane and Hepsebeth Crawford. Stephen and Elizabeth had eight or nine children. Stephen died in July of 1844 in Montgomery County, AL. Following his death, Elizabeth left Alabama with her son George W. Lane and his family, plus her own younger children to come to Texas. They settled in Fayette County. Elizabeth married M.F. Thompson in Fayette County about 1850. She died Dec. 25, 1851. Her will was probated Jan. 27, 1852 and shows her children Bryant, Benjamin, Carolina, Francis and Matilda were still with her.

Her children were Martha A. Lane 1817 – 1847, married Anthony Wayne Pouncey in 1838 in Alabama; George W. Lane 1819 – 1852, married Caroline Lloyd (widow of Wilson Hodges) 1840 in Alabama; Elizabeth Lane 1822, ?, married George W. Jackson in 1850 in Texas; Benjamin F. Lane 1829, ?, married Amanda Gibson in 1859 Gonzales County; Caroline Lane 1832, ?, married Hannian Rankin in 1852 Fayette County; Frances Lane born 1835, ?, married Marion G. Simms in 1853 in Fayette County; and Matilda born 1837, married E.B. Gill in 1860 in Fayette County, TX.

Shirley Blackmore Smith, (GGGGGD)

MILTON HAZELTON LANGFORD

MILTON HAZELTON LANGFORD, the son of Benjamin and Patsy Pace, was born Feb. 27, 1815 in Greenville County, SC. He moved west with his family through Jackson County, AL (1819); Crawford County, AR (1829); and Pope County, AR (1830). By 1837 he was in Fannin County, Republic of Texas, where he applied for a land grant and having complied with the requirements, received 640 acres. Later in 1841, the War Department of

Milton Hazelton Langford and wife, Mary Ann "Polly" Banta

the Republic of Texas issued him a promissory note for horses sold, for a total of $810.

M.H. married Mary Ann "Polly" Banta, daughter of Isaac and Elizabeth Barker, in Lamar County, TX on June 22, 1843. Records show that he cosigned the first bond recorded after the organization of Hunt County, TX. His father–in–law, Isaac Banta, was one of the county founders. During the Civil War, in 1864, after three of their children succumbed to smallpox, M.H. and Polly moved south with their family in search of a less populated area and better grazing land for their livestock. They found plenty of grass and water on the Seco, but the Indians became so troublesome they could not keep horses to tend the stock. The family finally settled in Bandera for protection and school purposes.

Altogether, they had 10 children: Martha Evelyn (Nov. 22, 1845-April 30, 1922), Benjamin Franklin (Sept. 10, 1847-Feb. 28, 1923), John D. (Aug. 8, 1849-Feb. 14, 1898), Isaac Berry (June 1, 1851-March 7, 1914), Sinai W. (July 10, 1854-July 2, 1863), Alfred W. (March 20, 1856-Aug. 15, 1863), Andrew E. (April 8, 1858-July 4, 1863), Eliza Langford (June 8, 1860-Dec. 31, 1928), Lee Wilson (Aug. 5, 1863-Oct. 1, 1926), and James Monroe (Dec. 19, 1865-Nov. 9, 1953). M.H. Langford was concerned with law and order and filled a two year term as Sheriff of Bandera County beginning in 1868 with a salary of $25.00/year.

His wife, Polly, died on June 27, 1870. She was buried in the Bandera Cemetery, one of the first to be buried there.

In 1872, M.H. married Martha Ann Rowland Cryer in Medina County, TX. The family, except for Benjamin Franklin Langford and Isaac Berry Langford who remained in Bandera, moved to a ranch on the Dry Frio, in the old Tehuacana Community in Frio

County, TX. M.H. and Martha Ann had two children: Milton Madison (Dec. 20, 1873-Dec. 13, 1943) and Mary 0. (May 17, 1876-July 13, 1935). M.H. helped organize the Tehuacana Community giving property and building to the Methodist Episcopal Church South for a church and a school. He also served as a school trustee from 1877-1884. After Martha Ann died in the Tehuacana Community on July 11, 1893, M.H. returned to Bandera. He died on Oct. 30, 1898 and is buried in the Bandera Cemetery.

Marjorie Fisher Langford, (9299S).
Lauren A. Langford Delayre, (GGGD), 22206
Elizabeth (Betsy) Grace Langford Hanzel, (GGGD), 11376

ELIZABETH CAROLINE COUCH LATHAM, born

Jan. 8, 1832 arrived in Nacogdoches, TX March 14, 1840 with her parents Chaney and Isabella Couch and her grandparents William and Elizabeth Christian.

In Nacogdoches, TX on Dec. 17, 1850, Elizabeth Caroline married John "Jack" Latham (Aug. 11, 1828, died April 1, 1891).

Their children:

John Levi, born 1852, died 1904, married Cynthia Ann Willis;

William Starling, born April 12, 1853, died Oct. 10, 1904, married Mattie Caroline Barton;

James Monroe, born 1856, died 1901, married Mary Ellen Willis;

George Washington, born 1858, died 1863, died from rattlesnake bite;

Thomas Jefferson, born 1862, died 1938, married Julia Webster;

Mary Ida, born 1864, died 1935, married W.J. Barber;

Annie Georgia, born 1867, died 1922;

Emma Alice, born 1870, died 1948, married F.B. Perry;

Albert Riley, born 1875, died 1935, married Laura Alice Haley.

The family lived in Henderson County until the early 1850's at which time they moved to San Saba County, settling on a tributary of Wallace Creek named Latham Creek for Jack Latham. About 1855 they moved and settled the Deer Creek Community in southwest San Saba County, which they helped found in 1856.

Elizabeth Caroline died Aug. 26, 1907 at Deer Creek. The Latham family still lives at Deer Creek and her home still stands as a tribute to her.

Caroline Latham Ingram, (GGGD) DRT# 11172, Supplement #12429

MARTIN BYRD LAWRENCE, son of Virginians George

and Elizabeth Byrd Lawrence, was born Nov. 23, 1794, Bertie County, NC. George lived in Tennessee then Missouri, where Jan. 12, 1823, only son married Maria Hart Davis, born 1804 Kentucky.

Martin moved to Arkansas before coming to Texas 1830, settling in Grimes County near Groce's Retreat where he established first tannery–saddlery– shoe shop in Texas, and saw mill.

Children: George Williamson, born 1823 Missouri, mar-

George Williamson Lawrence, oldest son of Martin Byrd Lawrence.

ried Sarah Howell, died 1877. Mary Ellen, born 1825 Arkansas, married Edward Boit Davis 1844, died 1905 Houston. Elizabeth Emaline, born 1827 Arkansas, married William Riley Allen 1845, died 1887. Louisa, born 1829 Arkansas, married Edward Clay Davis, died 1857. Paulina, born 1829 Arkansas, married Charles Bennett. Eliza Adeline, born 1834 Texas, married Abe Womack, died 1913. Groce, born 1836, killed 1864 Battle of Wilderness. Emily, born 1838, married William Gay,

Headstone of Martin Byrd Lawrence Died Nov 11, 1851, age 56 yrs. 11 mos. 14 days.

died 1903. Edward, 1841-1903. Ludwell, 1843-1925. Algernon, 1846-1889. Henrietta, born 1849, married S.B. Burch, died 1906.

Martin Byrd Lawrence joined Texas Army Jan. 28, 1836. In April, while Sam Houston was drilling army east of Brazos River near present-day Hempstead, and Texans were seeking safety for their families from Santa Anna reportedly advancing through area along west bank of Brazos, Martin sent 13–year-old George with note telling Houston that he would return to Army as soon as he had safe place for family. When George arrived at camp, army was preparing to move east. Houston carried George along, so April 21, 1836, George had part in Battle of San Jacinto.

Martin Byrd Lawrence died Nov. 4, 1851; Maria, Aug. 20, 1866. Buried Lawrence Cemetery near Retreat, Grimes County.

Joanne McGee Minsky, (GGGGD), 21337
Linda Vaughn Evans, (GGGGD), 21335
Jenny Ellen Evans, (GGGGD), 21336

JAMES LEE, born about 1807, presumably, in North Caro-

lina. He came to Texas in October 1831, at the age of 24 years and apparently settled in Montgomery County, TX. In the summer of 1836, he joined the Army of Texas and served two months. He was discharged due to deafness. Family story indicates that he lost his hearing while firing a cannon.

About 1837, James married Ellen Decker. According to family story, Ellen at age 7 and her sister Mary, age 9, were left behind as their father and other family members made a hasty exit by boat. The girls were left on the bank of the river crying for their mother. Mr. Decker was being pursued by the law. A family named Atkins is believed to have raised the girls.

In 1838, James received a land grant certificate for 4,605 acres of land. He also received a certificate from the Republic Of Texas as payment for service in the Montgomery County Militia. Beginning in 1840, James and Ellen gave birth to six daughters: Mary Ann, Louisa, Cathrine, Narcissa Elizabeth, Rebecca, and Josephine. The last record of James Lee appears on the 1864 Montgomery County, TX tax rolls. Ellen filed for a pension in 1876, so he died before that time. She was living in Washington County, TX, probably with a married daughter.

Frances Russell, 21492

JOHN LEE son of William and Massie West Lee was born

May 17, 1828 in Union District, SC. William died while John was a small child. Later Massie moved her family to Tennessee/ Alabama. As a youngster John joined his older brother Pertiller in Texas where he had gone in 1836. In 1837 Pertiller served in the Texas Rangers and fought Indians. As a young teen and being large for his age, John was able to serve the Rangers as a teamster. John was captured by Mexican forces while in San Antonio and was sent to Perote Prison where he was imprisoned for about 18 months.

John Lee

In 1845, prior to the Mexican War John was employed by the U.S. Army in Texas as a teamster. In 1846 John went to New Orleans and enlisted in the Quartermaster Corp under Captain Hedsal of Scott's Division and was sent to Vera Cruz.

After discharge from the military service John went to Tennessee to join his younger brother Edwin. John married twice; (1) Nancy Jane Porter of Nashville, TN on Dec. 25, 1851. They had five children—three born in Arkansas before they moved to Matagorda County, TX in 1860. Nancy Jane died 1864/65. John then married (2) Dorothy Adeline McGehee April 15, 1867. They had eight children. Dorothy Adeline died 1885. Of John's 13 children, five died prior to 1900.

Following his years as a teamster, John Lee made a living raising cattle, farming cotton, and running a ferry across the Colorado River in Matagorda County. He died Sept. 9, 1907.
Lois Lee Abshier, (GD), 16209
Laura Lee Lanigan, (GGD), 12892

JOHN LEE was a farmer from Virginia who settled near Dodd City (Fannin County, TX) in 1845. John (1797-1854) and his wife, Jane Stewart (1802-1895), a native of Tennessee, homesteaded east of Dodd City. They lived for a long period of time in Tennessee where most of their children were born. They lived in Arkansas for a short period of time where the last three children were born.

He was the first justice of the peace of Dodd City and often held court at his home east of town. Many Bonham officials visited in his home and sometimes spent several days there because of muddy roads and poor weather conditions. Family tradition tells of a visit of General Robert E. Lee to the Lee homestead in 1857. The *Bonham News* published an article on Nov. 14, 1913 reporting the death of Reese Lee, son of John Lee and brother of John Chester Lee, my ancestor, as being related to Henry "Light-Horse Harry" Lee of Virginia.

John and Jane were the parents of twelve children. Both of them are buried in the Lee Cemetery in Fannin County.
Shirley June Kruse Lightfoot, (GGGD), 20815
Leslie Dawn Lightfoot Wagner, (GGGGD), 20753

SAMUEL LEEPER, born in 1792 in what is now Kentucky. He married Sarah Bonham in Washington County, VA on Feb. 8, 1816. They had four children. The youngest, Mary Love Leeper, was my great-grandmother. After Mary was born, her mother, Sarah, died.

Samuel Leeper came to Texas in March of 1834 as stated in the Headright Certificate issued to him Jan. 20, 1838. He left his children with Sarah's parents, Hezekiah and Esther Scott Bonham, and came to Texas to fight in the Revolution and decided to stay at its close.

Samuel wrote to the Bonhams and gave them the money to have his children sent to Texas. However, the Bonhams refused to send their grandchildren to that "Indian Infested Territory." Samuel was given an honorable discharge and considerable land and stayed in Texas, but lost track of his children. Samuel's children did not know until after their Grandparents' death that he had sent for them. They discovered this when they found his letters in a trunk in the attic. Samuel married his second wife in Texas and had two children, a boy and a girl.

Samuel received two-thirds of a league and one labor of land on Jan. 20, 1838 on his Headright Certificate by the Jackson County Board. He was a member of Captain John York's Company in 1835 and on May 15, 1838 was issued Donation Certificate # 18 for 640 acres of land for participating in the Storming and Capture of Bexar, Dec. 5 through 10, 1835. He received Bounty Certificate #2955 for 320 acres of land April 18, 1838 for having served in the Army from Oct. 17 through Dec. 20, 1835. He was second Sergeant in Captain Hayden Arnold's Company at the Battle of San Jacinto. On Feb. 24, 1840, he was issued Bounty Certificate #9473 for 320 acres of land for service from March 6 to June 7, 1836.

Samuel died April 1, 1855 in Liberty County, TX. We are descended from his first wife Sarah Bonham.

Story has it that Samuel's father came to America with Lafayette to fight the British in the American Revolution. When the war was over, he stayed in America. This story has not been proven as of yet.
Mrs. Norma Webb Broach, (GGGD), 15585
Misty Janene Broach Childs, (GGGGGD), CRT# 005010, DRT# 019610
William Jason Perdue, (GGGGGS), CRT# 005011-SRT# 5551A
Larry Don Broach, (GGGGS), SRT# 5548A

JOSIAH LESTER was born March 9, 1794, in Virginia. He married Seleta Johnson on Aug. 30, 1818, in Greene County, GA. Seleta was born Jan. 1, 1799 in Georgia. Josiah and Seleta had nine children: Elias J., born 1819; Eliza, 1821; William Henry, born Nov. 7, 1823, in Louisiana; Milton, 1825; Josiah, 1829; Luther, 1831; Calvin, 1833; Travis, 1834 and Anne Elizabeth, 1839.

Josiah, Seleta and four sons came to Texas in 1829. Josiah had a large ranch in Milam County. He was a founding member of the Little River Baptist Church and donated land for the Church and cemetery. He died March 25, 1867, in Milam County. Seleta died about 1860.

William Henry Lester married Martha Anne McKinney April 24, 1849 in Milam County. She was the daughter of Roland and Rachal Sarah McKinney and was born July 4, 1832 in Mississippi. William Henry and Martha Anne had seven children: Daniel Patterson; Florence; Alice Mabel who married Benjamin Franklin Gamel; James Graves; Sarah Elizabeth; William Barrett Travis and Laura Ann. William Henry Lester died April 24, 1849 and is buried in Little River Baptist Cemetery. Martha Anne died Jan. 4, 1909 and is buried in Comanche County, TX.

MARTIN BATY LEWIS born in Clark County, IN, on Jan. 13, 1806, son of Sally (Lemasters) and Samuel S. Lewis. He married Nancy Moore, born March 1, 1817 in Ohio, the daughter of Thomas and Susan Moore. They married in Vermillion County, IN, Oct. 25, 1825. They had 11 children: John Kenny, Samuel Harper, Thomas McFarland, Sarah Ann, William McFarland,

Charlotte Harper, Stephen Austin, Malinda H. (married John Pinkney Best Jr.), Benjamin Franklin, Martin Baty, and Elizabeth LeMaster. They immigrated to Texas January 1830 and settled on Ayish Bayou (now San Augustine County), then moved to Indian Creek near Bevil (now Jasper County) in 1832.

In August 1832 Lewis was a sergeant major in the battle of Nacogdoches commanded by James Bullock, and in 1835 he was captain of East Texas volunteers in the siege of Bexar. In July 1836 he was captain of a company under General Thomas Rusk and marched to join the Army of the Republic of Texas at the Coleto, when a Mexican incursion by General Jose Urrea was feared. He resigned this command in August 1836. Lewis was county surveyor of Jasper County from 1836-1845, and was chief justice of Jasper County in 1844. In 1845 he patented title to 2,958 acres of land in Jasper County. He left Texas for the California 'gold rush' in 1849. By 1850 he was in Mariposa, CA and in 1863 he settled at Millertown, Fresno County, CA where he died before 1885.

Heather Renee Wells, (GGGGGD), 20642S

SAMUEL S. LEWIS, early Texas settler and congressman, was born to John and Sarah Lewis on July 4, 1784, in Virginia. He married Sarah LeMaster, born March 12, 1785 in Virginia, daughter of John and Sarah LeMaster. They married in Henry County, KY, on Aug. 7, 1804. They moved to Clark, Orange and Green Counties, IN, where their seven children were born: Martin Baty (married Nancy Moore), John T., Charlotte, Elizabeth, Ann, William McFarland, and Malinda.

Lewis founded Orleans, IN, and served as lieutenant with the Indiana militia in the War of 1812. In the mid-1820s the family moved to Ouachita Parish, LA, where Lewis became justice of the peace. According to his certificate of Character for Texas, by March 1832 he and his son, Martin Baty Lewis had settled their families in the Bevil municipality (now Jasper County) on Indian Creek in Texas.

Lewis served as lieutenant colonel in the battle of Nacogdoches in 1832 under Colonel Bullock, and participated in the siege of Bexar in 1835. He was a Bevil delegate to the Consultation of 1835 and represented Jasper County in the First and Second congresses of the Republic of Texas. He died during the second session of congress, on Feb. 10, 1838, at his plantation in Jasper County.

Heather Renee Wells, (GGGGGGD), 20641

JAMES W. LINAM, born July 18, 1798, Union County, SC to Thomas and Elenor (Wadlington) Linam, married Caroline D. Earle Littleton Sept. 16, 1822, Lawrence County, AL. Caroline, born Aug. 20, 1804 in South Carolina, was the daughter of Marcus and Sinah (Wadlington) Littleton. Their son, Thomas Marcus Linam, was born Aug. 6, 1828.

In 1835 the family moved from Rutherford County, TN to Texas. From Oct. 3, 1835 to Dec. 1, 1835, James W. served as private in the Jackson County Volunteers.

The Linams moved to Victoria County in 1839, where James W. received his First Class Headright certificate #125 for one league and one labor of land. That fall he was county tax assessor and then alderman on Victoria City Council.

In 1841, living in San Patricio County, James W. served as a Minute Man in the militia, later moving to Kempers Bluff in Victoria County.

Here, Thomas Marcus Linam married Mary Thomas Donaldson Nov. 3, 1853. Mary, born June 15, 1839, was the daughter of Ebenezer and Mary Donaldson. The Donaldsons arrived in the Republic of Texas in 1839, living first in Robertson County, then Victoria County.

James W. died Oct. 17, 1864; Caroline died Jan. 1, 1867.

Thomas and Mary moved to present Concho County in 1878. Thomas died there April 3, 1888 and Mary died Oct. 28, 1892.

Wanda Linam Perry, DRT #7975

MARY POLLY LINDLEY, born in Illinois in 1813 to Mary Elizabeth Polly Hall and Samuel Washington Lindley, married William Hiram Little in 1831. They traveled in an oxen-drawn covered wagon for six months (because the families bringing the Predestinarian Primitive Baptist Church would not travel on Sunday) and reached Texas in January 1835. Hiram fought in the Mohawk War in Illinois and in the Texas Revolution in 1835 and 1836. Her brother Jonathan Lindley died at the Alamo.

Her children were: Aphadelia ? (Delila)?, born May 17, 1832 in Illinois; Elizabeth, married Joseph Eubanks May, Joe Murphy and John Haislip; Jonathan, born May 26, 1836 in Texas; Katherine, born Jan. 17, 1838 Montgomery County; William M. (Dock), born Nov. 18, 1840 in Chireno, Nacogdoches County, TX; Margaret and Lavinia, twins, born 1842 in Montgomery County; Samuel, born Nov. 4, 1842; Elisa Jane, born Nov. 15, 1846; Joseph, born Feb. 29, 1848 (had son "Hi" who married a Traylor); and Mary Emily (Mollie), born Dec. 22, 1850, married Mr. Holmes. Mary Polly died in Montgomery County Jan. 28, 1893 and is buried in Willis, TX.

Williene Smith Story, (GGGGGD)

SAMUEL WASHINGTON LINDLEY, John Isaac Lindley lived in Cheshire County, England. His son James (1641) who married Alice Walsmith (1644) moved to Ireland. James' son Thomas Lindley married Ruth Hadley and moved to Chester County, PA. Thomas' son John Lindley (Sept. 13, 1742) married Sarah Pyle (April 10, 1750) and had Samuel Washington Lindley who was born in South Carolina in 1788. Samuel married Mary Elizabeth Polly Hall whose first 11 children were born in Illinois before this couple moved to settle a farm adjoining that of his brother, Joseph, in Montgomery County, TX. Their 12th child was born in Texas in 1833 and there was a 13th.

Samuel's petition (#66) for a land grant Nov. 4, 1834 is in Spanish. Recommendation for citizenship for Samuel by the Governor of Illinois is on file.

The oldest son, Jonathan, was killed in the Alamo March 6, 1836 and Samuel was administrator of his estate.

After Polly's death in 1838, Samuel married widow Eliza Tolbert in 1839 and their daughter Amanda was born in 1840. In 1845 Samuel married another widow, Mary Alyshin. Samuel died in 1859 and is buried in Danville Cemetery, Montgomery County, TX.

Williene Smith Story, (GGGGGGD), 3427

SAMUEL WASHINGTON LINDLEY and wife Mary Elizabeth (Polly) Hall and 10 children, came to Texas in early 1833, and were among the "Texas 300". So called, because they were one of the first 300 families to come to Texas under Mexican Land Grant patents and agreements. The Mexican government gave land to early colonists under Moses Austin, Stephen

F. Austin, DeWitt and others. From these colonists with early discontent with Mexican rule and treatment, plus Indian uprising, came the Texas Declaration of Independence and the Texas Revolution.

John Talbert Dick Lindley and Ida Jane Booth Lindley

His eldest son, Jonathon, a surveyor, never married, volunteered for the Texas Army in the winter of 1835; marched to San Antonio under Captain Albert Martin's Immortal 32 men from Gonzales; was killed at the Alamo, March 6, 1836.

The Lindleys came from a town in Ireland named "Danville" to America about 1713. Wherever they settled a new community in America, they named it "Danville" in

Elijah Lindley, father of John Talbert Dick Lindley.

Pennsylvania, South Carolina, Indiana, Illinois, Kentucky and Texas, birthplace of the 12th child, Elijah Lindley. Today it is a deserted ghost town located about 15 miles north of the town of Montgomery, TX.

The family of Samuel Washington Lindley, as early day colonists, became influential people in the community. This family was originally settled in the communities of what is today Montgomery, Liberty and Grimes Counties, TX. Some of the families later moved into what are now Robertson, Freestone and Limestone Counties.

Lineage of Samuel Washington Lindley (1788-1859); wife Mary Elizabeth (Polly) Hall (??-1838); 12th child Elijah Lindley (1835-1880), wife Eliza Kelton, buried Ferguson Cemetery at Oletha, TX; son John Tolbert (Dick) Lindley (1857-1920), wife Ida Jane Booth (1858-1936) both buried 20 miles south Mexia, Limestone County, TX, New Hope Cemetery (it is believed Ida is relative of John Wilkes Booth, assassin of President Abraham Lincoln: Booth family name known for founder and leadership in Salvation Army and theatre in London, England. Have not researched that lineage); sixth child, Wilmer Lindley Russell (1890-1979), husband Leonard Thomas Russell (1891-1949) both buried New Hope Cemetery; second child Dorothy Fay Russell Ford (Dec. 29, 1922), husband, Milo Westel Ford Jr. (May 26, 1918) were married Feb. 26, 1956 and live in Dayton, TX; two daughters: Gina Fay Ford Bajgier (Oct. 16, 1958) married Feb. 18, 1984 to Gary Allen Bajgier (April 4, 1959); four children: Milo Boone Bajgier (Aug. 25, 1989); Elizabeth Allene Bajgier (Aug. 15, 1992; Esther Fay Bajgier (July 19, 1995); all three born in Houston, TX.; Ruth Ann Bajgier (Aug. 31, 1998) born in Singapore. Jessica Allene Ford Mazzu (Dec. 18, 1959) married March 4, 1979 to Sam Anthony Mazzu Jr. (Oct. 24, 1957) two children; Sam Anthony Mazzu, III (April 7, 1980); Dorothy Jo Mazzu (Sept. 29, 1981); husband deceased Aug. 3, 1992; Jessica Allene Ford Mazzu remarried June 11, 1994 to John

Schaeffer Johnson (Jan. 28, 1952); his son William Schaeffer Johnson (Feb. 6, 1980).
Dorothy Fay Russell Ford, (GGGD), 13941

CHARLES LINDSEY was born in Newberry County, SC in 1778 to Thomas and Lydia King Lindsey. He was married to Mary "Polly" Bennett, daughter of Micajah Bennett. They left South Carolina with their nine children, his brother Isaac and his wife Esther for Texas in the 1820's. One daughter Amanda, was born in 1822 in Alabama enroute to Texas. Charles, his sons Micajah and Pennington, applied to the Free State of Coahuila and Texas for their land in September 1835. They received their Headright certificates in 1838.

Pennington S. Lindsey

Pennington served in the war for Texas Independence at the siege of Bexar Dec. 5-10, 1835, for which he received bounty land. After the Republic of Texas was formed, a disturbance in Shelby County occurred called the Regulator-Moderator War. The Regulators became lawless and abusive to the people they were organized to protect. Charles was a known supporter of the Moderators and deemed an enemy of the Regulators. 15 Regulators arrested Charles and two other men from nearby farms. He knew full well that they intended to hang him, and being in his late sixties, felt he didn't have many years left. He refused to take his horse or put on his shoes stating the cut-throats would get nothing from him but the cost of the rope. The Regulators held the men all day and decided to set them free after concluding the county would not tolerate the killing of three more men. Charles waited until evening to head home, avoiding the road and suspecting an ambush, he foiled two men hiding in the brush.

Sam Houston sent the St. Augustine Regiment to quell the disturbance in Shelby County and Charles provided them with a beef. Charles applied to the Republic and "late" Republic of Texas for reimbursement, but died in Shelby County, in 1849 before payment was made.
Mrs. Shirley L. Pfeiffer, (GGGGD)

HIRAM LITTLE was born in Illinois April 9, 1809 to Samuel and Sarah Nichols Little. He grew up with nine siblings in Bond, Crawford and Shelby counties, IL.

On June 5, 1831 Hiram married Mary Polly Lindley, the daughter of Samuel Washington Lindley and Mary Polly Hall, in Coles County, IL. After the birth of two children, Aphadelia and Elizabeth, the family migrated to Texas. They traveled in oxendrawn wagons bringing with them their Baptist church letters. After a journey of six months, they arrived in Montgomery County, TX, Jan. 20, 1835 where their family increased from two to 10 children as follows: Jonathan, Katherine, William, Margarette, Samuel, Eliza Jane, Joseph, and Mary Emily.

From all accounts, Hiram and Mary Polly provided a Christian home for their 10 children. *A History of Texas Baptists* by J.M. Carroll describes the Little family as being little in name only and somewhat like the seed of Abraham. This family not only boosted the membership of the Baptist church but played an important role in settling and defending the Republic of Texas. Hiram served in the Army of the Republic of Texas under the commands of Stephen F. Austin and Col. S. Sherman.

Records show that Hiram was a member of the Masonic Lodge, a farmer, and a large land owner. By 1873 he and his son, Samuel were partners in the mercantile business known as the H&S Store in the town of Willis, TX.

Hiram and Mary Polly lived to a ripe old age of 80 and 82, respectively. Hiram died Sept. 13, 1891 and Mary Polly on Jan. 28, 1893. They are buried in the Willis Cemetery.
Esther Roberts Broome, (GGD), 14837

WILLIAM HIRAM LITTLE, born 1809 in Illinois, married Mary Polly Lindley June 1831 in Coles County, IL. This couple and two daughters arrived in Texas Jan. 20, 1835 with the wagon train that brought the Pilgrim Primitive Baptist Church. His brother Samuel stopped in Anderson County and Hiram settled in Montgomery County near his in-laws.

Hiram fought under Ben Milam from November 1835 until Mexican General Cos was defeated in December. The soldiers were freed to go home for Christmas or be discharged. It is thought that Hiram and his young brother–in-law Jonathan Lindley went home together. From there, Jonathan returned to Gonzales and then to the Alamo where he died.

Hiram served the Republic of Texas Army in June 1936 in Wade's Company, second Regiment under Colonel S. Sherman, and received 320 acres bounty land and later $24.00. In May 1861 Hiram enlisted in Texas State Troops, 17th Brigade to serve the Confederacy but was discharged within a few days due to his age. This patriot, with black eyes and hair, stood six feet three inches tall and died in Willis, TX Sept. 13, 1891. His known children numbered 11.
Williene Smith Story, (GGGGD), 4327

ADDISON LITTON, native of Missouri, born 1811, was the son of Lemuel and Anne Forrester Litton of North / South Carolina. He came to Texas in 1827. In 1833 he married Mary Owen in the municipality of Mina (now Bastrop, TX). On March 23, 1835 he received title to a league of land on the Old San Antonio Road (includes mouth of Cedar Creek). He agreed to settle and cultivate the land according to existing Mexican law. (Abstract of original title in Spanish, and its translation, in the General Land Office, Austin, TX.) (Empresario Benjamin Milam's Colony.)

Addison Litton and Mary had four children: David, born 1834/5, married Eliza Jewell about 1857; Mahala, born about 1836, married Frank Yoast in 1854 and then B.F. Osborn; Francis Marion, born Sept. 6, 1839, married Sarah (Sally) Glass in 1860 and then Bettie Ann Thompson in 1874; and Mary Addison, born Dec. 13, 1843, married Charles Wolfenberger.

Addison Litton served during the Battle of San Jacinto in 1836 with Captain Gibson Kuykendall's Company at Harrisburg. He continued to be a member of the ranger service and participated in the battles of Brushy Creek and Plum Creek.

He died in 1843/1847. An Addison Litton historical marker is located about 1/4 mile east of Cedar Creek (Bastrop County), TX (Texas State Highway 21). His gravesite is 150 yards SSW from this marker (erected in 1857 by the State of Texas).

Addison Litton was my great-great-grandfather.
Betty Rose Litton Lee

MARTIN LOGGINS, son of William and Nancy Loggins, was born in Tennessee between 1781/1790. His father, William, fought in the American Revolution with Captain James Robertson and arrived in Tennessee about May 1780 being one of the first white settlers of Tennessee. Martin married Susannah Kennedy on Dec. 17, 1806 in Montgomery County, TN. This is verified by Susannah's application for Martin's War of 1812 pension in 1873. Martin served as private in the War of 1812 in Captain James Shannon's Co., Tennessee Militia.

Martin and Susannah Loggins arrived in Texas May 1839. They had eight children: Cade K., born 1808, married Nancy P. Oliphant; Samuel Martin, born 1810, married Martha Oliphant on Oct. 18, 1832 in Maury County, TN; Greenberry, born 1812; Preston J., born 1817, married R.C. Oliphant; Carter M., born 1818; Minerva born 1819; William Henry, born 1822, married Mrs. Mary Jackson Carter Gary and Harriett Sanders; Mary, born 1825, married John Bowie and John Voshay. All their children were born in Tennessee.

Martin and Susannah lived in San Augustine County, TX where Martin died Feb. 20, 1847. Susannah died between 1873 / 74 and both are buried in Chinquapin Cemetery in San Augustine County.

WADE LOVE, born in 1795 in South Carolina and served in War of 1812 from Kentucky. He married Jane Wilson Feb. 15, 1815 in South Carolina. Wade and Jane had three sons born in South Carolina: Martin A. (1817) married C. Edwards 1842 in Travis County, TX; John W. (1820); David (Oct. 31, 1821) married Mary Jane Langston March 27, 1845 in Rusk County, TX). Daughters Mary Elizabeth (1824) married Wm. Griffin 1843 in Rusk County, TX; Elinor/Ellen Jane (1828) married 1843, J.W. Darlington and son Alexander Hawkins (1832) married Adeline J. Woodall, were all born in Georgia. Son Wesley Easley (1834) married 1861 Virginia Katherine Coates in Coryell County, TX, was born in Tennessee, and son Leonard R. (1839) married 1861 Francis Powell in Coryell County, TX. was born in Travis County, TX.

Wade is in Pendleton District, SC on 1820 Census and Fayette County, GA on 1830 Census. Republic of Texas Land Grant Records reveal that third class land grant (given to settlers arriving after Oct. 1, 1837 and before Jan. 1, 1840) was made to Wade Love. Republic of Texas Poll List for 1846 lists Wade Love of Rusk County. In 1850 he is a farmer in Rusk County.

The Love family started moving into Coryell County soon after its creation in 1854. Federal Censuses of 1860 and 1870 list Wade and Jane of Coryell County. Jane Wilson Love died June 16, 1871 near Gatesville in Coryell County. She was buried in Masonic Cemetery in Gatesville. Wade married Mrs. Elizabeth Haley, widow of Mark Haley, July 25, 1872. Wade died Oct. 7, 1878 in Coryell County. He was buried beside his first wife; his widow, Elizabeth Love, died Nov. 4, 1896.

My line is through son David and wife Mary Jane Langston (May 10, 1828 in Tennessee-Aug. 31, 1859, Lampasas County, TX). They had children Wm. Wesley, Sarah Texanna, Clemmency Ann, and Cecelia Ann (my line). Mary Jane Langston Love and child are buried in old Cook Cemetery in edge of Wal-Mart parking lot in Lampasas.

David married Mary Susan Cluck in Williamson County, TX, June 7, 1860. Their children were Ally, Amanda, Fannie, Arthur and Lillian Pearl. David died Oct. 26, 1892; Mary Sept. 3, 1905.

They are buried in I.O.O.F. Cemetery in Georgetown. David Love built the store, which still bears his name on the square in Georgetown. His home at the corner of 10th and Church Street still stands.

Amelia Forrest Bogard, (GGGGD), 22318

ISAAC LOW was born July 7, 1781 in Tennessee. After marrying Elizabeth Parsons Sept. 25, 1804 and having 11 children in the next two decades, the Lows decided to move to Texas, arriving Sept. 1, 1828 after leaving Tennessee May 25, 1828. Low received a "league and labor" from, the Mexican Government in Sabine County through the Spanish Land Grant program. Isaac Low served Texas in several different capacities. During the Texas Revolution he and one of his sons operated a ferry on Low's Creek transporting Texas citizens to safety in the United States in what was known as the "Runaway Scrape." In May 1838 when Sabine Town became a port of entry, Low became one of the first municipal officers and on Jan. 30, 1840 was elected Commissioner to inspect Land Offices in Sabine County. Isaac Low died Aug. 27, 1853 and is buried in the Isaac Low Cemetery near the banks of Toledo Bend Reservoir outside Hemphill, TX.

Isaac and Elizabeth Parsons Low had 12 children. His son Joel, married Milberry Ferguson, whose son Isaac Barton Low married Patsy Ann Eubanks March 19, 1868 in Williamson County. Their daughter Patsy Ethel married George William Keel May 17, 1896, whose daughter Lola Estell married Johnny James Dean Oct. 22, 1917, who were my parents. I am the fourth of six children, having been born Oct. 24, 1927 in Luther, Howard County, TX.

Ethel Dean Cleere, (GGGGD), 15530

EDWARD GREENE LYNCH entered the Confederate Army in by the nicknames of the Second Texas Sharpshooters or the San Jacinto Guards. He served from 1861-1865 in Texas, Louisiana, Mississippi and other southern states. The Second Texas Infantry participated in more than 25 various type engagements during its career and was included among the Confederate Trans-Mississippi forces surrendered at Galveston on June 2, 1865. Records show that the unit had disbanded a short time before rather than surrender.

Edward Greene Lynch

Edward Greene Lynch, son of John R. and Siney (Choate) Lynch, was born Aug. 28, 1828, in Mississippi. His family left Mississippi and traveled to Louisiana, then on to Jasper, TX. His father was granted a third Class Head right of 640 acres on Dec. 5, 1839 in Liberty County, TX.

John R. and Siney were the parents of 13 children, which consisted of:

Edward Green, born Aug. 28, 1828, Mississippi;
Sarah, born Feb. 25, 1831, Mississippi;
William, born Nov. 08, 1833, Mississippi;
Margaret, born Nov. 08, 1835, Mississippi;
David C., born Dec. 07, 1838, Louisiana (?);
Jeffrey C., born Dec. 20, 1841, Louisiana (?);
John, born March 7, 1844, Texas;

Elizabeth, born Jan. 7, 1846, Texas;
George W., born May 8, 1848, Texas;
Nancy, born Nov. 12, 1850; Texas;
Siney, born March 22, 1853, Texas;
Louisa Jane, born July 29, 1856, Texas;
Mary Ann, born Feb. 14, 1858, Texas.

Edward married Martha Francis Choate, daughter of Jesse and Jenny Jane (Crowell) Choate, on Oct. 27, 1853 in Trinity County, TX.

Children of Edward Greene Lynch and Martha Francis (Choate) Lynch are as follows:

Amanda A., born Oct. 7, 1854;
Thomas Jefferson (Tone), born Dec. 13, 1857;
John, born 1859;
Permelia Adaline, born 1861;
Jess, born Dec. 11, 1867;
Marion, born 1868;
Janey, born March 27, 1872;
James, born (about) 1874;
William David, born April 15, 1878.

Edward, Martha and children moved to Nemo, TX in Johnson County where they lived on what was known as Lynch Mountain. Edward raised stock, farmed and was a drummer (salesman). He died on June 11, 1883. Martha and several of her children moved to Indian Territory where she died Feb. 25, 1916. They were buried in Georges Creek Cemetery, Glenrose, TX.

DRT # 016855; Wichita

BENJAMIN FRANKLIN LYON came to Texas in 1838 from Newton County, GA. He was born Feb. 15, 1815 to Martha and Jesse Lyon and he married Mary Amanda Carrington, she born July 9, 1820. They had 10 children: James (1840); Martha (1842); Mary (1844); William A. (born about 1846); Eliza (1848); Oliver Franklin (1851), Adeline (1854); Amanda (1857) and John Reason (1861). They settled in the Wesley community, south of Brenham, and all their children were born there.

Benjamin Franklin Lyon

When Burleson County came into being in 1842, and a few years later the railroad planned to lay tracks, BF purchased land in the newly formed county. Plans were to have tracks from Dallas to Galveston and the land belonging to the Lyon family had originally been known as Khrones Station. After the transfer of land to the railroad, it became known as Lyons Station and finally Lyons as it is known today. It became a thriving community with cotton gins, mercantile stores, churches, a bank, and many of them were owned and run by the children of BF and Amanda. They were lifelong members of the Methodist Church.

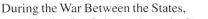
Mary Amanda Carrington Lyon

During the War Between the States, BF served in the Confederate Army in Company B, 23rd Battalion, Regiment TST. After the War they continued to live in the Wesley community, with children near and in the Lyons area. Wife Amanda died Aug. 20, 1887 and is buried in the Union Hill Cemetery in Wesley. BF spent his final years in the Lyons community with his family and when he died June 12, 1903 he was buried next to his wife.

Here are quotes from several obituaries: "He was a member of the Methodist Church for 60 years and a pioneer settler in Washington County, always active in building up the country and elevating the people who settled around him and felt a large progeny, very prominent in business and social life. Few men lived who were held in greater respect for high character and citizenship. Mr. Lyon had a large family, good management and industrious ways of doing business allowed him to pay for a good home and to supply it in that comfortable manner that made the Southerners famous. His hospitality made him always popular with all who had the good fortune of making his acquaintance."

Their youngest son John Reason Lyon (April 14, 1861) was my grandfather. He married Mary Lola McClellan in 1894 in the Lyons Methodist Church.

Aletha Look Engel, DRT# 21473-S BF Lyon; DRT# 22051-;S Amanda Lyon

WILLIAM THOMAS MALONE,

son of Marie Wallace and (?) Malone, was born about 1799 in Mississippi and died before 1870 in San Augustine County. William Thomas Malone served as a private in the Siege of Bexar under Capt. T.L.F. Parrot's Co. Artillery, in camp before Bexar, Nov. 23, 1835. Children by first wife (unk): Francis (born 1830) and William Wallace (born 1834). William Thomas married Eliza Davis (born 1812, Georgia) on Feb. 4, 1838, Ayish District now San Augustine County.

Children: John W. (born 1839), Caledonia Roelee (born 1841), Mary G. (born 1842, died 1922), Susan N. (born January 1847, died March 1907, Nacogdoches County) married Jan. 21, 1867 in Nacogdoches County to Thomas Jefferson Battle (born 1843, St. Clair County, AL, died ca. 1877, Nacogdoches County). Children: Isaac N. (September 1868, died before 1900); Eliza Jane (born 1869, died 1925); John Taylor (born Sept. 8, 1874, Nacogdoches County, died Feb. 24, 1956, Angelina County).

John Taylor married Ida Tilitha Gray (born 1889, died 1976) on Nov. 18, 1905 in Nacogdoches County. Children: Effie Mae, Ruthy Bell, Hattie Pearl, Thomas Norrel Angram, Minnie Lee (born July 16, 1917, Polk County) and John Medrial.

On June 10, 1929 Minnie Lee married Barney Erath Thornton (born June 22, 1907, Erath County, died Sept. 18, 1988, Angelina County). License recorded in Cherokee County.

Children: Ruth Mae (born Oct. 30 1932, Trinity County and died Jan. 27, 1976, Travis County); Doris Juanita (born Sept. 4 1936, Trinity County); Sara Helen (born July 26 1947, Angelina County); Joyce Kathleen (born March 13 1956, Angelina County). Doris Juanita married James William Harkness Nov. 8, 1954 in Angelina County. Children of Doris and James: David Alan (born March 7 1957) married Suzanne Byrd, and Jeff Brian (born April 19, 1960) married Shelia Ann Johnson.

Doris Harkness, (GGGD), 021848
Mary Hall Mantooth Chapter
Admitted Jan. 17, 1998

EDWARD MALLOCH,

son of John and Margaret Robertson Malloch of Perth, Scotland, born Jan 31, 1816, came to America in 1840, lived in South Carolina one year before coming to Texas. He was probably a furniture maker at that time.

Edward Malloch

He served in the Army of the Texas Republic as a private in Lewis P. Cooks Co., Mounted Gun Men, April 2, 1842 to May 9, 1842. He helped with the guns, two cannons and muskets and the five men who saved Gonzales from the second destruction from Mexican Army in 1842.

On Oct. 12, 1846 he was appointed by Gonzales County commissioners as county treasurer. He resigned this position and on the same day was appointed county assessor and collector. Later, he was elected to this position and served two more terms.

In November he was placed on a committee to superintend the funding of the completion of the courthouse. In November 1851 he was elected the 3rd Worshipful Master of Gonzales Masonic Lodge #40 AF&AM.

Married Lucy Ellen McKean Blackburn May 19, 1853 and moved to Prairie Lea, TX. Children: Margaret, Lucy Ellen, Carrie, Edward, Jean and John. He was clerk for McKean-Hardiman County. Edward died Dec. 20, 1898 and is buried in Prairie Lea Masonic Cemetery.

Margaret Morris Dempsey, (GGGD), 6857

WILLIAM LINDSAY MANN,

son of Rafe "Ralph" Mann and Eleanor Baker, was born Jan. 29, 1810, in Due West Township, Abbeville District, South Carolina. He married Matilda A. Cammack of Clarke County, Alabama, on Dec. 10, 1833. Matilda was born Aug. 1, 1816 in Clarke County, Alabama, to David Cammack and Mary George, sister to Aaron George.

According to family history, William came to Texas in 1838, where he acquired a headright of 640 acres. He settled in northern Tyler County, near the present town of Colmesneil, where he built a house on China Hill in 1854. This location served as the first post office at Billiams Creek.

William and Matilda had 13 children, three of whom died in infancy and three of whom died in the Civil War. They were: David George (born 1834, died 1862), married Sarah Angelina McCullough (McCuller); William T. (born 1836, died 1862), married Mary Jane Fortenberry; Mary Elizabeth (born 1838, died 1916, my ancestor, married Ira Ellis Sumrall; Ellen (born 1841, died 1916), married Thomas C. Cliburn; James Monroe (born 1843, died 1862); John Pinkney (born 1843, died 1915), married first, Easter McCullough (McCuller) and second, Jane Vickery; Robert Lee (born 1845, died 1931), married Mary Elizabeth Martin; Samuel Edward (born 1848, died 1925), married Minerva Ann Enloe; Christine (born July 1849); Matilda Ann (born 1850, died 1930), married A. Ferd Meadows; Thomas A. (born 1853, died 1872); Caroline (born 1855, died 1862); Margaret Jane (born 1858).

William was a participant in early Tyler County affairs. He served as a postmaster, an election judge, a road overseer, and a juryman. He signed a petition in September 1840, asking the

Congress of the Republic of Texas to divide Liberty County into two districts because of the inconvenience of traveling to Liberty, the county seat. The Menard District was formed in 1841, but was declared unconstitutional. Tyler County was created out of Liberty County in 1846. Although he did not believe in secession, William served as a second lieutenant in the Mt. Hope Home Guard during the Civil War.

William died at his home Feb. 18, 1885, and Matilda died Oct. 21, 1891. Both are buried at the Mann Cemetery near Colmesneil, TX, as are six of their children: Robert L., Samuel E., John P., Mary E., Ellen and Thomas A.

Ann Crews Laird, (GGGD), 8061

LEVI MANNING, born April 26, 1808 in Washington County, GA to Benjamin and Charity Grey Manning. Levi married Mary Patton before 1939 and they had three children, all born in Texas.

Levi was in the Texas Militia and served under Col. Bennett's command in the Summerville Campaign late in the year of 1842.

Levi died around 1849 and his widow Mary was declared dead in 1842, burial place unknown.

Charity Jane, Joseph and Elizabeth Ann, children of Levi and Mary Manning, were raised by two of Levi's brothers. May was made guardian first but died

Elizabeth Ann Manning Driver

shortly after Mary, then Reubin Manning, of Freestone County, Texas, was made guardian.

Charity Jane married George A. Sims; Joseph died in the Civil War and Elizabeth Ann "Bettie," my GG-Grandmother, married Richmond Carroll Driver in 1860. Her husband "Rich" served in the Civil War, enlisting twice. Bettie and Rich had nine children, all born in Freestone County, TX.

Richard (born 1862) married Nealey Manderville; Eliza Agnes (born 1865) married Frank Collins; Sarah Jane (born 1865, died young); Martha (born 1868) married Noah Curry; Levi Allen (born 1871) married Emma Newsom; Mary Emma (born 1874, died young); Washington B. (born 1876, died 1925); Adelaide "Addie" (born 1879) married Jack Eppes in 1898; and the ninth child Peter (born 1890, died young).

Elizabeth Ann Driver (died December 1926) and Richmond C. Driver (died January 1915) are both buried at the Driver Cemetery, Freestone County, TX.

Addie married Jack Eppes in 1898 in Freestone County, TX, they had four children. John Manning (born 1900) married Susie Madeline Gilliam; Lewis Richmond (born 1903) married Ruth Haynie; Jack Jr. (born 1913) married Atwood Massey; and Marion Joel (born 1919, died as a infant).

Jack Eppes died February 1947 and Addie Driver Eppes died December 1959 and they are buried in the Antioch Cemetery, Luna, Freestone County, TX.

John and Madeline Gilliam Eppes had three children; John Dale (born 1925) married Nelda Jean Youngblood, they had two children. Tommie Rue (born 1929) married Joe Tom Craig and they had two children. Benny Jack (born 1932) married Sharron Shippi, they had three children.

John Eppes died January 1978 and Madeline died August 1978, both are buried in the Antioch Cemetery, Freestone County, TX.

Tommie Rue Eppes Craig, 21812

SINAI MONTGOMERY DEVER PORTER MARTIN, born May 22, 1831 at Old Washington to pioneers, William Harvey Dever and Catherine Early Dever. Dr. Anson Jones ushered her into this world. Her early years were accented by the "Runaway Scrape!" Her father had been helping with the Signing Ceremonies when he was directed to take his family to safety.

Sinai Montgomery Dever Porter Martin

Sinai grew into a lovely young woman and an accomplished horsewoman. A colonel, at Lampasas, often said that "he would ride 40 miles before breakfast to see Sinai ride a horse." Sinai was very family oriented. Her brothers were William Pharis, and Nathan Early Dever. Her sisters were Nancy S., Mary M., Lydia Anne, Sarah, Francis Arabella and Alice Dever.

When Sinai married Jerome B. Porter, Mrs. Anson Jones spent some time at the home helping with the wedding preparations. Unfortunately, Mr. Porter did not survive to see his daughter Kate grow up.

Sinai married John Edward Martin, veteran of the Mexican War, and son of Charles Wingfield Martin and Maria(h) Martin at Old Washington Sept. 14, 1856. This union was blessed with John Wilbur, Edward Wilson, Annie Malinda, Emma Lewis, Leonidas, Frances and Rufus Dever Martin.

As if the formation of the Republic and the creation of the State were not challenge enough, Sinai was faced with seeing her beloved husband assuming leadership in the Army of the Confederacy. Sinai found her own role in helping the cause. When Union Soldiers came looking for wagons, Sinai graciously invited them to eat a hot chicken dinner. When ready to leave, they hitched up the wagons and as they progressed toward the road, all the wheels began to fall off. The serving of the meal had allowed time to loosen all the tapshads. The lieutenant realizing he had been nicely "whipped," formed his little army at the front gate, gave Sinai the military salute, and rode away!

The family lived in Burleson County; later moving onto 500 acres of Washington County land given to Sinai by her father. This was developed and sold in 1883. They moved to Coleman County and ran a hotel in Coleman City, before moving on to Santa Anna to raise sheep in 1888 and then to Mullin, where they donated the land for the Mullin Methodist Church. After John Edward died, Sinai made her home with daughter, Mrs. John J. Cox (Emma) in Goldthwaite and Temple where she died Aug. 1, 1910! Sinai is buried beside John Edward on one of the highest points in the Mullin Oak View Cemetery under a beautiful shade tree. The headstone reflects "CHILD OF THE REPUBLIC OF TEXAS."

Dixie Ann Harris Foster, (GGD,) 017310
Joyce Faith Martin Murray, (GGD), 011359

THOMAS MATTESON, born August 1789 in New York and Sally Matteson, born Feb. 22, 1787 in Vermont, following the trend of the times, left their home in Titusville, PA and started the long trip west in covered wagons drawn by oxen. After a journey of three months, they arrived near Nacogdoches, TX in 1839.

Following her parents, was Lydia Matteson Alderman. Lydia, born Feb. 2, 1815, in New York, and married Phelps Alderman, born July 12, 1813, in Hartford, CT. They were married in Ohio Dec. 21, 1833.

Lydia received her education in Pennsylvania in private and boarding schools. She was a constant reader of the Bible, and could quote from it fluently. She came to Texas with high aims that were sustained by devout and steadfast faith. It was her ever-growing conviction that it was a holy mission, and she was encouraged by friends back home. She found living in the wilds of Texas with four small children to take care of and to help establish a home was a difficult task.

Later Lydia announced that she desired to teach Christianity to the Negroes that were still slaves, and that did not go over well. She was bitterly criticized and threatened, and all concerned thought it best for her to go back home. She died Jan. 25, 1854 in Ohio, but her husband and children returned to Nacogdoches County shortly after her death. The names of her two youngest sons are on the Confederate muster roll in the courthouse at Nacogdoches, one of the names being Emory Phelps Alderman, born Aug. 23, 1841.
Clara Gilbert, (GGGD), 019778

JAMES N. MCADA, son of John C. and Nancy (Sansom) McAda from South Carolina was born Sept. 19, 1809 in Tennessee. He married Isabella Nancy McClure May 19, 1831 in Shelby County, TN. Four daughters were born to them in Tennessee before the family came to Texas in 1839. The youngest, an infant, died during that trip or soon after the family arrived.

James N. chose his 640 acres in Angelina County but also lived nearby on the Atovach River in San Augustine County, both in east Texas. By the time his headright was surveyed in 1852 and sold for $300, he and his family, now including three sons and two more daughters, had moved west to Bastrop County where he was a teamster hauling goods. By 1860 the family lived and raised stock in Atascosa County.

They were living in nearby Karnes County when their last child, Sarah Frances, or Fannie (born Oct. 22, 1852), married Leroy Pope Williams on Aug. 20, 1872. Fannie and L.P. Williams are my great-grandparents. In 1880 James Newton, with an amputated leg, and Isabella were living with their son James N. McAda Jr. and his family in Karnes County. Isabella died in 1883 and James in 1898. Both are buried in Shiloh Cemetery near Leming, Atascosa County, TX.
Margaret Dawn Williams Gore, (GGGD), 22016

PLEASANT MCANELLY, born Dec. 29, 1810, was one of eight boys, no girls. Some descendants place this event in Dublin, Ireland while others have claimed Tennessee. The former believe that he and three brothers came to America from Ireland and landed at Indianola. He married Anna Katrina Vogt, born in Leipzig, Germany on June 24, 1822. They would have met on the ship coming from Europe and even though she never learned to speak English, they would have courted and married on the ship.

From Indianola they all came in ox wagons to Guadalupe County, TX. Pleasant was a rancher and farmer on a ranch that he and Anna acquired in the eastern part of that county called the Smith Creek Settlement. He became a vigorous Texan soldier and also had a reputation as an Indian fighter. As an hero of the Siege of San Antonio de Bexar, he received 640 acres of Donation Land. Historical accounts report his presence at the Veramendi house with Col. Ben

Pleasant McAnelly

Milam when Milam was killed in December of 1835. According to old family letters, he was sent by horseback to Goliad to secure help for those besieged at the Alamo.

Pleasant survived the early momentous years of the Republic and eventually fathered four children. He died at the Medina County ranch of his son, Pleasant Earnest, in 1890 and is buried in the Tehuacana Cemetery south of Yancey.

WILLIAM BROWNLOW MCCLELLAN came to Texas in 1839. He was a newspaperman and joined a newly organized newspaper in Austin, *The Austin Gazette.* He was the son of John McClellan and Margaret Brownlow early educators from Washington, DC, Lexington and Abingdon, VA. William Brownlow was born May 17, 1810 in Abingdon and after his parents died, the children scattered and he came to Texas, via Alabama. The *Austin Gazette* did not continue and he moved to La-Grange to become editor of

William Bronlow McClellan and Amanda Melvina Fitzallen Moore

the *Intelligencia.* He married Amanda Melvina Fitzallen Moore of Rutersville whose parents were Edwin Lewis Moore and Elizabeth Lawson Hart Moore (see their biography in this volume). Amanda was born June 5, 1827 and died in Peoria, TX near Hillsboro, Nov. 28, 1882.

The couple had 10 children most of whom were born in LaGrange and Fayette County: William Edwin (born 1845), Carrie Amanda (born 1848), Alfred Lewis (born 1850), John Arthur (born 1852), Charlotte Vail (born 1854), James (born 1855), Joseph (born 1857), Elizabeth Brownlow (born 1861), Minnie Louise (born 1863), Sara Vail (born 1866).

In addition to his newspaper he was county tax assessor and collector. Other newspapers he was affiliated with were *The Fayette County Monument,* the *Houston Advertiser* and finally *The Austin Republican* where he died Feb. 7, 1871 and was buried in the Oakwood Cemetery.

For further information on William Brownlow McClellan, see the *Texas Handbook,* and the third edition of book by Aubrey L. McClellan (1990) *William Brownlow McClellan, Early Texas Newspaperman, His Life & His Descendants.*

Oldest son William Edwin became a Methodist minister, married Mary Lucinda Mayfield of Burton, TX; they lived in Somerville and are my great-grandparents.
Aletha Look Engel, (GGGD), William Brownlow McClellan, 20952 Amanda Melvina Fitzallen Moore, 22050-S

THOMAS MCCLURE and Elizabeth (Wilson) Rice were in the Republic of Texas by 1838, when Thomas applied for land. Thomas was born in Poultney, Rutland County, VT in 1801. In 1804, his parents, Nathan and Jemima (McClure) Rice, moved the family to Ohio. Elizabeth Wilson was born in Ireland. They were married on Sept. 28, 1824, in Salem Township, Washington County, OH, and had five children: James, Mary, Oliver and William, all born in Ohio; and Thomas, born in Texas. In 1842, the Rice family was living in DeWitt County.

When news of a Mexican force approaching the San Antonio area reached LaGrange, a group of men led by Captain Nicholas Dawson began riding that direction. Thomas and other DeWitt County men joined them. On Sept. 18, 1842, at Salado Creek, they were intercepted by 400 Mexican troops. Thirty-six of the 54 Texans were killed, including Thomas. In 1848, the Texan's remains were taken to Fayette County, where on Sept. 18, 1848, a military burial took place. The tomb is on a bluff overlooking the Colorado River at LaGrange, and is called Monument Hill.

On April 12, 1847, Elizabeth was granted an unconditional certificate for 640 acres of land. Elizabeth died in 1859, and is thought to be buried in the old Clinton Cemetery in DeWitt County.
Betty Newman Wauer, (GGGGD), 21977S

GREEN MCCOY, son of Joseph H. McCoy and Catherine Clark McCoy was 9 years of age when he came to Texas in 1828 with his parents and grandparents and other members of the McCoy clan. They settled in DeWitt's Colony around Gonzales, TX. Green's grandfather, John McCoy, and his parents obtained land grants issued by the Mexican Government.

Green McCoy was referred to as "the boy from Gonzales" described in the book, *Early Pioneers and Indian Battles in Texas*, told by Capt. George B. Earth. This episode was known as "Earth's Fight"

William Taylor McCoy, holding Texas McCoy and Mary Ann McCoy, holding William Davis Martin McCoy.

which took place Jan. 7, 1837 at Elm Creek, TX in current Milam County, TX. Earth described the event as follows: There were 13 men and boys volunteers under Capt. George B. Earth who intercepted a group of about 100 Indian raiders on the way to a nearby settlement. The men and boys drove off the Indians. During this battle, Green's maternal uncle, David Clark, was killed.

Jesse McCoy was Green McCoy's paternal uncle. Jesse was one of the 32 men volunteers from Gonzales, TX who went to aid the Alamo Defenders during the Texas Revolution. Jesse died with the other heroes March 6, 1836 defending the Alamo, contributing to the cause of Texas freedom.

Green's grandfather, John McCoy, served under Gen. Sam Houston and fought against the Mexicans in the famous battle of San Jacinto, TX on April 21, 1836. This battle was a great victory, freeing Texas from Mexican rule.

Green McCoy joined the Texas Army and served from Oct. 3, 1836 to Nov. 3, 1837. For his service he was awarded 1,280 acres granted by the Republic of Texas. Green McCoy served with the Texas Rangers in 1837 and 1838.

Green McCoy married Susan Davis on July 13, 1848. They lived in DeWitt's Colony near Gonzales, TX. They had two sons, William Taylor McCoy and Dobe Green McCoy. Green McCoy lived in Texas until his death on April 28, 1852.

William Taylor McCoy was born in Gonzales, TX on July 12, 1849. He married Mary Ann Bybee on Sept. 20, 1888 in Llano County, TX. They had three children: Texas McCoy (died at age 3). William Davis Martin McCoy and Ethel McCoy. William Taylor McCoy ranched and served as the constable in Llano County, TX.

William Davis Martin McCoy, son of William Taylor and Mary Ann McCoy, was born Dec. 13, 1891 in Babyhead, TX. Martin married Nettie Arminda Rowan on Nov. 21, 1911 in Rogers, TX. They settled in Leakey, TX where Martin McCoy served as a constable for 30 years. Martin and Nettie were married 56 years. They had five daughters, Ethel "Pat" Preece (deceased); Mary Lee Jones (deceased); La Nell Thompson (deceased); Goldie Dee McGuffin; and Lola May McKee. Martin and Nettie also raised a granddaughter, Benita Lane. Goldie McGuffin lives with her husband J.W. McGuffin in Uvalde, TX. Lola McKee lives alone in Kerrville, TX. Benita Lane lives with her husband, Sammy Joe Lane, at Pipe Creek, TX. Martin and Nettie McCoy were buried at the Leakey Cemetery.
Benita D. Lane, (GGGD), 22199

JOHN STEWART MCDONNOLD/MCDONALD, son of Reverend James and Margaret Grier McDonnold, was born in 1814 in Cumberland County, KY, raised in Overton and Wilson counties, TN.

Educated and trained as a surveyor, McDonald arrived in Nacogdoches in 1837 and was administrator of the estate of Marcus Sewell, Alamo defender.

Clintonia Bacon Samuel McDonald

J.S. McDonald

In 1842, McDonald was appointed assistant district surveyor of Nacogdoches and he re-drew boundary lines when Nacogdoches County was divided. He moved to Bexar County by 1848 as appointed surveyor after the departure of John Coffee Hays. McDonald's first duty was surveying Sulphur Springs Road between San Antonio and LaVernia, TX. He was elected district surveyor in 1849 and married Clintonia Bacon Samuel, daughter of Santa Fe trader, Giles Samuel and wife Letitia Cummins of Howard County, MO. The McDonalds had two children, Margaret Letitia and John S. Jr.

McDonald was mayor in 1851-52 and district clerk for two

non-consecutive terms. He was Worshipful Master of the Alamo Masonic Lodge. In 1856, after a surveying expedition to west Texas, McDonald was shot and killed by Mayor James M. Devine during a feud over politics and voting irregularities. An essay, *Plats, Politics, and Poetry: The Life and Death of John Stewart McDonald*, was published by the San Antonio Genealogical and Historical Society.
Frances G. Trimble

GEORGE MCENTURFF/MCINTURFF,

born in about 1789 in Tennessee to Daniel McInturff. By the 1830s, George and his wife, Sarah, were living in Arkansas with several children. Some of his children married in Arkansas, then as a family group the family moved to Missouri and on to Texas in 1841. His first land grant was in Lamar County and later he moved to Nacogdoches (Van Zandt) County and lived until his death in 1853.

According to local history he was a skilled blacksmith, mechanic and wood workman. His grandsons were some of the first horseback mail carriers in the county, much like the early pony express riders. Also, one son-in-law was the first postmaster and operated a ferry across the Sabine River. George and Sarah had nine children to live to adulthood. They were William, born about 1816, married Elizabeth Ellis; Elizabeth, born about 1818, married Allen Robinett and later Stephen Simpkins; Abraham B., born about 1820; D.R., born about 1822, married Elizabeth Friend; Emeline, born about 1824, married a Conner; Eliza Jane, born about 1826, married Calamise Beckett; George J., born about 1829, married Missouri Johnson; Sarah Miranda, born about 1835, married Isaac Anderson; and James F., born about 1838 married Mary Wills. Son James F. and grandson James L. were both killed during the War Between the States.

Elizabeth McEnturff listed above, married Allen Robinett in 1831, and came to Texas in a wagon train with her father's group in 1841. Elizabeth's last two children were born in Texas before 1845. Elizabeth and Allen's children were James L. (married Mary Angiline Jones); daughter Mary; son John; Nancy (married James Chandler); Virginia Elizabeth (married David Parks); Michael (married Mary Morris); and George. After Allen's death, Elizabeth married Stephen Simpkins and returned to Arkansas. Her son, Michael, was born, raised and buried on his grandfather's, George McEnturff, land grant.
Lois Melton Thompson, (GGGGD), 22710
Roxanne Burchfiel, (GGGGGD), 20844

JOHN W. MCHORSE

was born in Tennessee on Sept. 27, 1819. His father was said to have been born in Scotland and his mother in Tennessee. He came to Texas in 1836 at 17 years of age to participate in the Battle of San Jacinto. In 1837 John became a corporal in the North Alabama Mounted Volunteers in the Seminole War in Florida. John married Elizabeth Wil-

Texas Veterans Association Meeting, 1892. John W. McHorse is on left.

son, daughter of James W. and Delilah Wilson of Kentucky. To this union was born 10 children: Martha, Sara, Rebecca, Delilah, James, Roda, William, Isaac, John and Thomas. In 1853 John was ordained as a Baptist minister in Clark County, AR. He founded the Pleasant Hill McHorse Missionary Baptist Church in Sevier County, AR, in 1858. After the death of Elizabeth, John married Rutha Wafford of Mississippi. They had two children: Mary Ellen and Elonzo. During the Civil War John was appointed Commissioner of Relief for families of Confederate soldiers. Moving to Texas in 1864, he founded several Masonic Lodges. During the next three decades he prospered as a land trader, farmer and cattle trader. John died in Leander, TX, on Jan. 19, 1897 and was buried at the State Cemetery in Austin, TX.
Kendra McHorse Meadows, (GGGD), 018265

JOHN CLUNN MCKEAN,

son of Joseph McKean and Maria Pearson Clunn, born Feb. 20, 1797, Wheeling, VA, came to Nashville, TN, brother Joseph William McKean I, later Maria and sons Joseph and John ran a store in Columbia, Maury County, TN, 1813. He married Margaret Taylor Kearney, Williamson County, TN, Sept. 29, 1819.

Helped form Tipton County, TN, then on to form Hardiman County, TN. He helped form the Tennessee-Texas Land Co., which helped fill out the DeWitt Colony in 1830. Settled in Gonzales, where he helped lead the families to safety during the war (so called Runaway Scrape) and built rafts to get over the swollen rivers.

John Clunn McKean

After his wife died he married Nancy Ann Wilkinson. Children of first marriage: Maria, Andrew Jackson, Lucy Ellen, William Clunn; children from second marriage: Clarissa, Joseph, James, Anna B.

Was a member of the Masonic Order, also Probate Judge of Gonzales, removed to Prairie Lea, to his business, McKean Hardiman County, general store. He died July 18, 1880 and is buried in the Prairie Lea Cemetery. Marked with DRT bronze emblem.
Margaret Morris Dempsey, (GGGGD), 6857

DANIEL YOUNGER MCKINNEY,

born April 9, 1769, was a younger brother of Collin McKinney (born April 17, 1766), famous in Texas history as one of five men who wrote the Texas Declaration of Independence.

This Declaration was presented to the convention on March 1, 1836, and adopted unanimously, with amendment. Collin McKinney was also one of the signers, representing Red River County. Collin McKinney, moreover was one of the authors of the first constitution written for the State. He represented what was then Red River County in four Congresses of the Republic of Texas and in local affairs in north Texas his advice and counsel were frequently sought.

Collin and Daniel, together with their families and their aged mother, Mercy Blatchley (born 1745, died 1825) widow of Daniel McKinney (born 1730, died 1809), a Revolutionary soldier from Virginia, emigrated from Lincoln County, KY to Texas in 1824.

Wavell's Colony Roll gives dates of entry of various members of the McKinney family into Red River County.

Mercy Blatchley McKinney died July 25, 1825. Daniel Younger McKinney, her son with whom she made her home, died Aug. 29, 1825, and on Sept. 2, 1825, Margaret McClure "Peggy" McKinney, the wife of Daniel, died. The cause of death is not mentioned in letters of Collin McKinney, but deaths of malarial type fevers were common to this area. Family tradition stated that these three McKinneys were buried at Box Elder, TX, but later researchers believe that the burials took place in Hempstead County, AR.

Through his mother, Mercy Blatchley McKinney, Daniel was kin to Aaron Blatchley (born 1644, New Haven, CT, died 1699) who was one of the signers of the Fundamental Agreement of Newark, NJ, Oct. 30, 1666.

The McKinney heirs were granted lands by the congress of Texas in December 1843, in the name of their father, Daniel, who died in what was believed to be lands of Mexico in 1825.

Margaret Cannon Boyce Brown, (Mrs. Spencer)(GGGGGD), 4556
Margaret Brown Lewis, (Mrs. J. Keet III) GGGGD), 16099
Maria Stanton Boyce Brown, (GGGGD), 16100
Anne Stuart Boyce Folkes, (GGGGD), 18950

SARAH MARCELL MCKINNEY, born 1834, Matagorda County, TX, married James Madison Allen, Dec. 9, 1852, San Antonio, Bexar County. See James Madison Allen for info on children.

Sarah Marcell, age 2 yrs., and sister, Susan Elizabeth, age 6 yrs., rode horseback during the Runaway Scrape with their mother, Mary Ann Smith-McKinney (born 1813, Kentucky), often hiding her young daughters under her long skirt to protect them from the Indians. They were accompanied by Elizabeth McCoy on the trip. After the battle of San Jacinto, they returned to Matagorda.

When Sarah Marcell was 5 yrs. of age, her father, Colonist Benjamin F. McKinney (born 1800-10, Kentucky) was killed in battle Feb. 15, 1837. Location of battle, death and burial of Benjamin F. McKinney is unknown.

In October 1855, Matt and Sarah moved to Burnet County and settled on part of the B.F. McKinney league of land that Sarah had inherited from her father. They built a home on Bear Creek and lived there until 1877. The family relocated in Burnet County and in 1886 the family purchased property near Briggs on Mill Creek where they lived until 1900.

In 1900 Sarah Marcell and Matt went to Stonewall County to live with one of their children. Sarah, child and citizen of the Republic of Texas, died Nov. 12, 1900 and is buried at the Double Mountain Cemetery in Stonewall County. After Sarah died, Matt went to live with a daughter where he died in 1904.
Bonnie Allen Chambless, (GGD), 22259S

MARCUS PORTIUS MEAD, born 1808 in the Holston River Country of Tennessee. His father was Marston Mead, veteran of 1812, son of Virginia's Col. William Mead, Revolutionary War soldier. His mother was Sarah Whitehead Cobb, daughter of William and Bathsheba Whitehead Cobb whose pioneer home, "Rocky Mount," built in 1770, still stands at the confluence of Watauga and Holston Rivers.

Raised in Blount County, AL, Marcus married Nancy Moore about 1831 and had three children. Early 1837 he came to Texas, filed for land and received a 2nd Class certificate.

Left a widower, he married, about 1847 to Elizabeth Grigsby (born 1824, Kentucky), daughter of John and Hester Sharp Grigsby. They moved to Indiana, then to Crawford County, IL where Hester died in 1832. John remarried, sold out, and brought his family to Mexican Texas. His league and labor on Trinity River was granted in 1834. When the settlers rebelled, he furnished supplies to the Texan Army. His son, Crawford, fought at the Battle of San Jacinto.

Marcus and Elizabeth had four children, the youngest being Pricilla Catherine, my great-grandmother. Marcus died 1860 in Anderson County. Elizabeth died in 1866 leaving Katy's care to her married sister. Katy married James Franklin Pittman 1883, Erath County and settled in Floyd County. Both are buried in Lockney Cemetery.
Jackie Duncan Youngblood

JOHN D. MERCHANT and his brother, Edward A., took to the water at Florence, AL. They traveled down the Tennessee, Ohio and Mississippi Rivers to Natchez, MS. There they disposed of their boat and took a steamer to New Orleans and another on to Natchitoches, LA, where they hired teams and came to Texas. They crossed the Sabine River at John Lathim's Ferry and settled in what was afterward called Shelby County on March 2, 1832. Included in this journey to Texas were John D.'s wife, Sarah Pearl Walker and their four children; Edward A.'s wife, Elizabeth Little, and their three children; and Sarah's brother, Z.C. Walker.

John D. and Edward A. were sons of James Merchant (at times spelled Marchant). Their mother's name is unknown. John D. was born Aug. 24, 1800 in South Carolina. He married Sarah "Sally" Pearl Walker on March 31, 1821 in Lawrence County, TN. John D. died Dec. 9, 1876 and is buried in Pilot Point, Denton County, TX. Sarah was born Dec. 15, 1804 and died May 16, 1894. Her grave is in Abilene, Taylor County, TX.

John D. and Sarah had nine children: Edith Jane (born March 24, 1822); James S.W. (born Feb. 28, 1824); Amanda Melvina (born Oct. 16, 1826); William (born Oct. 12, 1828); Susan (born Jan. 21, 1831); Parzetta Caroline (born Dec. 15, 1833); John D. Jr. and Claiborne W. (twins) (born Aug. 31, 1836) and Richard English (born Jan. 22, 1839).

John D. was first enlisted in the service of Texas in August 1832 in a battle which occurred at Nacogdoches between the Mexicans and the Texans. Then again from Oct. 17, 1835 to Jan. 10, 1836, he served in the San Augustine Volunteer Company of the Texas Mounted Riflemen under Captain John English in the campaign of San Antonio against the Mexicans.
Jackie Merchant Roberts, (GGGD), 12501

JOHN CHRISTIAN MERTZ, born Nov. 25, 1811 in Hamburg, Germany. He was first married to Louise Heitman. To this union two children were born. Louise died while she was still a young woman. Later, Christian married Gesina Vogt, born Jan. 26, 1821 in Bremen, Germany

In 1845 the Mertz family emigrated to Texas. They settled in Austin County, raising corn, cotton, cattle and feed. Christian and his son made many trips to Galveston to sell food and buy supplies. They traveled by wagon, pulled by a yoke of oxen. They knew the route well, around hills and forests, over rivers and streams.

Christian and Gesina were the parents of eight children, all born in Texas. One of them was my great-grand-mother, Matilda Dorete Mertz. Christian Mertz was proud to be a Texan. He came to Texas while it was still a republic, and he became a United States citizen when Texas joined the union.

John Christian Mertz died Aug. 10, 1900 at the age of 88. Gesina Vogt

Headstones of Christian Mertz and Gesina Vogt

Mertz died Dec. 25, 1909 at age 75. They are buried side by side at Pilgrim's Rest Cemetery in Industry, TX.
Carleen Riemen Laurentz, 18304

CATHERINE MEYER, Catherine's parents set out for America Oct. 6, 1844, on the ship *Probus*. Their destination was Galveston, TX and from there they faced the difficult and long trek to Castroville, astro's colony. The entire Joseph Meyer/ Caroline Schofts Meyer family was aboard (except for young Catherine and Teresa [also called Josephine]). They were sent ahead with family friends, the G'sels, came over on the ship which docked in Louisiana.

Children of Nicolas Tschirhart and Catherin Meyer L to R: (Sitting) Joseph, Sebastain, Edward, Leo, twins-Henry and Nicolas, (Standing) Louis, Caroline, August, Emil, and Kate.

Nothing is known about the trip from the port of entry to Castroville and the colonies. Although those who came before them had made much progress in reference to land settlements, it must have presented reason for Catherine. Besides her probable worries about safety, entertainment and a social life in general no doubt played a major role. Her parents and other family were pleased to have her and being re-united with her loved ones must have added some peace of mind.

She was courted by a young man who was also from the area of her birthplace. Sometimes before Dec. 31, 1845, Nicolas Tschirhart asked for her hand in marriage and she accepted for they were united in marriage on that date in a ceremony performed by Castro's business manager, Louis Huth.

They wasted no time in starting a family which would include 12 children: Joseph, Sebastain, Edward, Leo, twins-Henry and Nicolas, Louis, Caroline, August, Emil, Kate and Michael who died as a small child.

There was very little for women to do beyond taking care of the family and home. Church was a blessing in many ways as families were able to practice their faith and make friends that formed another type of "family" which led to tight friendships-those who could be counted on through thick and thin.

Out of necessity, women began saving every conceivable pieces of cloth (from flour sacks and discarded clothing) to be made into quilts. Quilting bees came into being and ladies gath-

ered at each other's homes or church to quilt. Born of necessity, pioneer women soon began creating works of art, and many are in museums around the country and certainly in The Institute of Texan Culture.

Nicolas went into the freighting business and operated it until his death in 1866 of cholera. The boys ran the business until railroad shipping far surpassed freighting by way of horse/mule and wagon. They later hauled gold and silver out of Mexico.
Dovie Tschirhart Hall, 15166-S

JOHANN HEINRICH "ADOLPH" MEYER, son of Juliana Peters and Johan Georg Meyer, was born in Hanover, Germany on April 13, 1813. In 1845, at age 32, he sailed with the ship *Hercules*, arriving in Galveston and his final destination being DeWitt County and the community of what would be called Meyersville. He came to Texas with a Fisher-Miller Land Grant.

In 1847 the city of Meyersville was named for Adolph. He was the first postmaster of Meyersville. Adolph built a log home near the LaBahia Road, the stage coach changed horses and left mail at his home.

Meta Friedrichs and Johann Heinrich Adolph Meyer, founder of Meyersville, TX.

On Aug. 17, 1854 Adolph married Meta Friedrichs in San Antonio. Their children are George Edward Adolph (born March 1, 1856); Eliesa Mariane Adolphine (born Feb. 15, 1858); George Adolph Edward (born Oct. 12, 1859); Sophie Meta (born May 22, 1861); Julius William (born March 10, 1863); George Carl (born Sept. 30, 1865); Johanna (born Jan. 28, 1868); Wilhelm Heinrich Gustav "Gus" (born Aug. 12, 1870); Albert Louis (born Oct. 9, 1872); Ottilde (born Dec. 26 1874); Carl (born April 9, 1878) and Sophie (born July 16, 1881).

Their son Wilhelm Heinrich Gustav "Gus" Meyer married Levine Fromme July 10, 1907 in Victoria. Gus and Levine had two sons, Gustav Wilhelm and my father, Gordon Edward Meyer (born Nov. 17, 1908 in Yorktown).

Adolph died Oct. 14, 1899 in Meyersville and his wife Meta died Feb. 1, 1896. Both are buried at the St. Andrews Lutheran Church Cemetery in Weesatche.
Marilyn Meyer Logan, (GGD), 20621
Kay Logan Nelson, (GGGD), 21647
Karen Logan Fleeman, (GGGD), 21648

JOSEPH MEYER and his wife Catherine Schott were married on Nov. 9, 1824 in Wittleshiem, France. He is the great-great-great-grandfather of Gladys Marie Tondre Clark. Their other children: Erasmus, Michael, Josephine and Edward, sailed on the American ship *Probus* from Anvers, France on Dec. 6, 1844. They were the first of our family to come to Texas.

Their two older daughters, Catherine and Theresa, had left Europe earlier. They all came overland to Texas. Catherine and Nicholas Tschirhart got a marriage license in Bexar County, thus establishing the fact that the family was in Texas by this date. Catherine died in 1872.

Joseph was a master carpenter, 1870-1880, and lived alone in Castroville, TX. In 1881 the family drew up an official article of agreement document. It was agreed that Michael would take care of his father's keep in exchange for all his estate, the other children waiving their share.

In the *Galvesto Daily News* April 2, 1883 two deaths were reported, Joseph Meyer, 83, and Peter Fricker, 97. Two of the old colonists of their county, it seems quite singular that the two who had lived as neighbors from boyhood to such a ripe old age should die the same day.

Glades Marie Toner Clark, (GAG) 19509
Bet Marie Clark Humbly, (GAG) 20251
Debra Ann Clark Gar, (GAG) 19521

JOSEPH MEYER,

JOSEPH MEYER, born in Wittelsheim in July 1801 and died March 29, 1883. He married Catherine Schott on Nov. 19, 1824 in Wittelsheim, Alcase. Catherine was born about 1802 in Wittelsheim.

Empressario Henri Castro was recruiting Europeans to go to the new and fledgling Republic of Texas. Land was being offered to those who would come to America, specifically to help in developing and increasing the population. Joseph

Great grandsons of Joseph Meyer and Catherine Schott Meyer (L to R): Ernest, Antone and William Tschhirhart.

sought the advice of their parish priest, Father Gregory Pflanner. The Father felt the offer to be a good one and advised Joseph to make the move.

No doubt, Catherine and Joseph spent many hours discussing the advantages and disadvantages. But after many sleepless nights, the decision of a lifetime, passage was booked on the ship *Probus,* departing Oct. 6, 1844 from Anvers to destination Galveston in America. All family members made the trip except their teenage daughter, Caroline. For some unknown reason to present family descendants, she stayed behind and made the trip later with the G'sels family.

The trip over was long and not an easy one. Upon their arrival in Galveston food supplies and medicine items were scarce. Many people did not survive even long enough for transportation to Castroville. Traveling in ox drawn carts in all kinds of weather made some wish they were back in the "old country."The colonists were in for more bad news upon reaching the end of their journey. Land disputes were of the most upsetting; without land, homes of any kind could not be built. Some colonists that had received their land had no supplies to do so; people were living in mud houses that had to be rebuilt after every rain of any magnitude

Indians were a constant threat; if they didn't harm anyone, they stole horses and food. The Texas Rangers tried to help but they couldn't be everywhere at once. Colonists took turns as guards and look-outs. Crops so vital for table food as well as for livestock, were hampered by cycles of rain, drought, insects, and pilfering.

The Meyers, like many settlers, were strong and resolute to hang tough and make their lives better than those they had back in Alcase. They saw that their children were schooled, taught them be honest and that anything worth having is worth working hard for.

I'm sure a bright spot in their life was the marriage of their daughter, Catherine, to Nicolas Tschirhart which took place Dec. 31, 1845. No doubt Caroline and her name sake, Caroline, worked together with pride and joy as they made the wedding. I'll bet her mother cried at the wedding as all of us mothers do even to the present.

When Joseph presented his new baby girl to the court for proof of birth and to say who the mother was plus what they had decided to name her. Caroline had been born about 10:00 a.m. and he was over at the court with that tiny, two hour old baby. To present the baby for birth certification, he had to appear with two witness. He brought two buddies from his workplace (they were both listed as weavers and so was Joseph). He was listed on the ship list as a cultivator but almost everyone was because they knew that was the most desirable occupation when it came to settlers and pioneers for the Republic of Texas.

Joseph and Catherine were true examples of the many "little people" who courageously banded together to help the Republic get on its feet and endure until it moved into Statehood. Texas and our family are proud!
Dovie Dell Tschhirhart Hall.
Joseph Meyer, #15168-S
Catherine Schott Meyer, #15167-S

WILHELMINE MEYER arrived in Galveston in December 1845 aboard the *Auguste Meline* under the auspices of the Society for the Protection of the German immigrant in Texas. She came with her older brother, Johann Heinrich Meyer, and her younger sister, Fredericke.

In the winter and spring of 1845-46 the Texas coastal area was besieged with torrential rains making the usual route to New Braunfels from Matagorda Bay particularly difficult. The siblings finally arrived in New Braunfels but Fredericke had become ill enroute and died. She was buried in the New Braunfels Cemetery.

Wilhelmine was born May 16, 1816 and raised in

Wilhelmine Meyer

Hildesheim in the Kingdom of Hannover. She married Johann Heinrich Conrad Kappmeyer born on Nov. 11, 1816 in Eltze which is seven miles west of Hildesheim. They were married by Reverend L.C. Ervendberg, German Protestant Church, New Braunfels, TX on Oct. 18, 1846. They made their home in the New Braunfels area where Conrad became a prosperous business man.

Their children are Dorette (married Jacob Doeppenschmidt); Karoline (married Herman Roege); George; Mathilde (married Wilhelm Karbach); Theodor; August (married Olga Weilbacher). George died at 9 months of age.

Following Conrad's death, April 14, 1887, Wilhelmine made her home with her daughter Mathilde's family. She died March 24, 1899 and is buried in Comal Cemetery, New Braunfels next to Conrad in their family plot which adjoins that of her beloved brother.
Rosemarie Leissner Gregory, 20573

ROBERT M. MILBY, son of Nathaniel Milby III, was born in 1806, Sussex County, Del. Family owned "The Golden Quarter Plantation of Indian River Hundred, Del." Robert's ancestor was John Milby I who came to

America from England in 1653. Robert came to Jackson County, TX before 1834 on the ship *The Hettaby.*

He built the first blacksmith shop. In 1834 Robert bought 911 acres of Jackson County land and also land in Wharton, Lavaca and Goliad counties. Robert was present at the famous Lavaca-Navidad meeting in 1835. He served Texas Army in 1836, was commissioner 1850-65.

Mary Ann Whitson Milby

He married 14-year-old Mary Ann Whitson in the first double wedding in the county in 1842. Robert built a two-story home and a schoolhouse. His wife and seven children were tutored. Robert died in 1872 and MaryAnn in 1895. Both are buried on homeplace.

Their third child, Robert Mortimer Milby (born 1846, died 1906), married in 1864 to Annie Inez Laughter (born 1852, died 1883). Their daughter Lydia Inez Milby (born 1869, died 1914) married in 1887 to Louis A. Loudermilk (born 1851), deputy sheriff of Jackson County and died in 1900. Both are buried Enon Cemetery. Son Louis McDowell Loudermilk was a WWI soldier (born 1899, died 1970) married in 1920 to Emma Faye Willms (born 1899, died 1994), both are buried Enon Cemetery, Jackson County, TX.

Ina Lillian Loudermill Muschalek Botard, (GGGD), 22574

JAMES M. MONROE was born in Hartford, CT in 1819, and was in Texas by 1837 with a 3rd class certificate for 320 acres of land which was a single man's allotment. The land was in that part of Harrison County taken to form Old Upshur County 1/2. He married Mary Jane Baker 1846-47. She was born in Illinois in 1828. James Monroe was listed on the first school census as having a child aged 6 to 16, and listed as Methodist clergyman, storekeeper, farmer and blacksmith on the 1860 and 1870 census reports.

James and Mary Jane Monroe had eight children: Elizabeth, Henry; John, Caroline, Laura, Mary Virginia, James and

Emma. About 1871 Elizabeth married Thomas Andrew Tinsley who with his parents, Ransom and Isabella Tinsley; brother Willis and sister Margaret, had come to Texas. Thomas was given a University Grant and moved to Dexter, Cooke County to claim and survey the land. Both families moved to the new location.

In Land Book 16, page 82, Cooke County, TX, the record shows the sale of the Monroe land. Mary Jane remarried to T.P. Henry on June 3, 1880, so we can assume Mr. Monroe died in the late 1870s. Thomas and Elizabeth Tinsley had three sons: Will, Walter and Edgar.

Elizabeth died, apparently, about the same time as her father, and Thomas remarried on Aug. 14, 1879 to Mrs. Lula Atkinson Colvin, born July 3, 1858, in Columbus, GA. They had four daughters: Nora, Florence, Nan and Sallie (died in infancy). Lulu died Sept. 29, 1889 and is buried by her first husband, Sam Colvin. Thomas then married Mary Virginia Monroe Wilson, widow of Henry Wilson, and mother of Littleton Homer Wilson. Mary and Thomas had four children: Bessie Tinsley McKenzie, Seigel Andrew Tinsley, James Paul Tinsley and Margaret Mae Tinsley Harrison.

My father, James Paul Tinsley and my mother, Lignum Vita Pilcher were married Dec. 23, 1920, and were parents to two daughters. First-born, Hazel Pauline Tinsley, born Nov. 5, 1922, was married Feb. 14, 1951 to James Louis Parker. They have four children: Martha Elizabeth Parker, James Louis Parker Jr., Paul McCulloch Parker and Robinson Lee Parker.

The second child of Paul and Lignum Tinsley is Sylvia Lee Tinsley, born March 1, 1925, and married to Richard Claude Jones on May 24, 1942. They are parents to four children also: Peggy Lee Jones Howe, Claudia Jones Bennett, Lee Ann Jones McPhail and Nancy Gayle Jones Walden. R.C. Jones was born Jan. 6, 1919, and died May 23, 1981. He is buried in the Wilbarger Memorial Park in Vernon, TX. James Paul and Lignum Pilcher Tinsley are buried in The Collinsville Cemetery in Collinsville, Grayson County, TX.

Pauline Parker, (GGD), 20127
Martha Elizabeth Parker, (GGGD), 20175

JAMES NELSON MONTGOMERY, son of Robert Cicero Montgomery and Elizabeth McConnell, was born Dec. 7, 1813, Virginia. He married Catherine Batterson, DRT #83, wife of Patriot (born April 8, 1823, New York), daughter of Isaac Batterson and Amelia Nash, Dec. 8, 1840, in a double-ring ceremony with the bride's mother—this may have been the first event of its kind.

James and Catherine had 10 children: William Nelson, born Nov. 5, 1841; Janet Ann, born and died Feb. 13, 1843; Mary Emily (DRT #13, Real Daughter), born Feb. 1, 1844, married Balthaser Berleth; Ellen Amelia,

James Nelson Montgomery

born May 10, 1846, married James William Golledge Jr.; James Watson, born Oct. 1, 1848; William Owen, born Nov. 20, 1850, died April 14, 1852; Francis "Frank," born Sept. 8, 1852, died March 9, 1911; Isaac Owen, born Oct. 13, 1854, died July 16,

1856; Travis, born July 17, 1858; Katie Alpha, born March 18, 1863, married ? Hurd.

James became interested in Texas' struggle for independence and in 1836 joined the army to help in the fight. He later was a steamboat captain and assisted, with his new father-in-law, Isaac Batterson, in surveying the newly proposed town of Houston.

James died July 11, 1890 at his home in Houston. Catherine died Jan. 29, 1903 in Houston. Both are buried at Glenwood Cemetery in Houston, TX.

Ellen Amelia Montgomery, (D), 51, Real Daughter, married James William Golledge Jr.
Rose Ellen Golledge, (GD), married William Edwin Ellis
George Whitfield Ellis, (GGS), married Clara Willie Muske
Natalie Ellis, (GGGD), married Oswald Richard Stoemer
Anita Joan Stoemer, (GGOOD), 19530, married Otto Gregory Crona Jr.

JOSEPH WILLIAM MOONEYHAM, born Sept. 15, 1809, Tennessee and died Jan. 9, 1882, Texas. On July 3, 1836, in Lafayette County, MO, he married Rachel Barnes, born Feb. 18, 1818, Missouri and died Feb. 9, 1873, Texas. William, Rachel and four children moved to Texas before July 1844.

William Mooneyham was issued a Peters Colony Land Grant, Nacogdoches 3rd Class #2184. Their 640 acre grant was located in present day Farmers Branch, Dallas, TX. William engaged in farming and was involved in early Dallas civic affairs.

The Mooneyham children and known spouses were James M.; Josiah married Sarah E.; Martha A. (born 1841, died 1907) married John Sparkman, Mary Ann married John Goodson; Elizabeth Frances (born 1845, died 1908) married John Wesley Taylor; Sarah S.; Louisa married E.W. Stanley; Rachel A.; William F.; David; John Albert (born 1858, died 1933) married Cora Lee Sossaman; Jefferson L. married Eulah L. Larkin.

William, Rachel, daughters Martha A. and Elizabeth Frances and their spouses, and some grandchildren are buried in the Mooneyham-Sparkman Cemetery in Dallas. This small private cemetery is located on a portion of the original land grant.

Glenda Carrol Duncan Monroe, (GGGD), 021755
Janet Carol Monroe Mitts, (GGGGD), 021756

EDWIN LEWIS MOORE and Elizabeth Lawson Hart Moore of Rutersville are buried in a prominent spot in the old section of LaGrange Cemetery, with original headstone laying flat on the graves and new granite markets, engraved with names and dates as headstones.

La Grange Cemetery is the location of Edwin Lewis Moore's headstone(left) and Elizabeth Lawson Hart Moore's headstone (right).

Their oldest daughter, Amanda Melvina Fitzallen Moore, married William Brownlow McClellan (the newspaperman—see their biography in this volume). Their oldest son, William Edwin McClellan, my ancestor, lived in Somerville, was an early Methodist minister, and married Mary Lucinda Mayfield of Burton,

TX. They are buried side by side in the Old Round Rock Cemetery.

Aletha Look Engel, (GGGD), 21474-S, Edwin Lewis Moore 22052-S, Elizabeth Lawson Hart Moore

JOHN CANNON MOORE, born 1795/1805, died Dec. 22, 1838, and Jemima Corn Moore arrived and settled in Washington, Washington County, TX in mid to late 1836, with their four children, ages 1-7 years old. Jemima either died on the way to Texas or sometime after the family arrived. (Her grave has never been located.)

In early December 1838, John boarded the four children and a Negro lady at two different homes in the town of Washington and began moving his goods by wagon to Bastrop, TX. While John was in Bastrop, he applied for a headright of 1,280 acres. John died shortly after his arrival in Bastrop, before the move was completed. (John received his headright posthumously. His grave has never been located.)

Either someone in Bastrop knew John and knew where deceased Jemima's parents lived, or John lived long enough to tell someone that his children were in Washington, TX and should be taken back to Tennessee. Probate records show that the administrator of John's estate hired a man from Bastrop (Phillip J. Allen) to pick up John's children and the Negro lady in Washington and deliver them to Jemima's parents in Franklin County, TN. William Corn, Jemima's father, became guardian of the children. William lived only a few years after the children arrived back in Tennessee. Then, William's son, John Washington Corn, became their guardian.

John Cannon Moore's youngest daughter, Mary Ann, stated that the administrator of John's estate in Bastrop, William R. Hancock, kept young William Cannon Moore with him in Bastrop and William worked at the Hancock farm. Mary Ann said that when William, "Billie," was old enough to leave Hancock, he traveled to Tennessee to join his brother and sisters. The 1850 Tennessee census shows all four children living with Jemima Corn's family in Franklin County.

In 1851, John and Nancy Jemima's children, William Cannon Moore, born Dec. 18, 1829, died May 15, 1900; George Washington Moore, born Jan 22, 1832, died Aug. 1, 1871; and Mary Ann Moore, born Oct. 24, 1833, died 1928 returned to Bastrop. It is uncertain whether his daughter Nancy Jane, born 1833/35, died date unknown, returned to Bastrop with them for a short while or stayed in Tennessee, because in 1852 Nancy Jane married Jasper Newton Chapman in Coffee County, TN. However, by 1855/1858 Nancy Jane and Jasper Chapman lived in Cherokee County in east Texas. The other three children settled and married in Bastrop. Mary Ann eventually moved to Dripping Springs, TX with her husband George Royal Norvell. William Cannon Moore married Mississippi Susan Campbell in Bastrop County, TX on Dec. 22, 1869 and George Washington Moore married Mary Sharp Alexander in Bastrop County, TX in 1867.

Robbie Sanders, (GGGD)

JOSHUA MOORE JR., born April 9, 1783 to Joshua and Phyllis Taylor Moore. He grew to manhood in Greene County, GA, one of eight children. On March 20, 1806 he married Mary Vincent/Vinson.

The family started a westward migration in 1821, stopping in Alabama; Tennessee in 1825; arriving by Nov. 8, 1837 in Red

River County, TX, where Joshua, three sons and a son-in-law received land grants.

Joshua's will appeared for probate December 1843 in Red River County. His wife died later. No graves have been located.

Their 11 children were Rodie P., born Feb. 24, 1807, married Mary M. Hubbard; Levin Vinson, born Jan. 25, 1809, married Elizabeth Williams; Matilda, born Nov. 29, 1810, married Henry Cox; Isaac, born Dec. 22, 1812; West, born Nov. 15, 1814, died July 9, 1815; Lucinda, born Nov. 1, 1816, married Hamlin L. Williams; Arena W., born Nov. 1, 1816, married Marcus C. Suttle; Whitfield, born Sept. 2, 1820, married Mary Ann Reed; West, born March 28, 1823; Caroline Mariana, born June 22, 1826, married William Edmonson; Mary Jane, born July 25, 1827, married John Cameron.

Whitfield Moore married Mary Ann Reed Sept. 24, 1840. He died in 1894 and she in 1888. They are buried in the Woodland, Texas, Cemetery on land included in his brother Isaac's land grant and adjoining his own. Their daughter, Jeanette Moore, married Benton Gear in 1865. He was a Civil War veteran. Both are buried at Woodland.

Shirle Lamb Williams, (GGGGD), #22241

SARAH ANN HORNSBY BURDITT MOORE, born in Hornsby's Bend, TX, March 21, 1832. She was the youngest child of Reuben and Sarah Morrison Hornsby. She was the first white child born in what is now Travis County.

Sarah Ann married Jesse F. Burditt (born April 29, 1829, in Alabama), son of Jesse and Mildred Crain Burditt, in Travis County on Nov. 15, 1848. She and her husband, Jesse, had six children. Three died in childhood: Dinnah Josephine, Mackinvale and Minus Ann. They are buried in the Hornsby Cemetery. Her husband died while being held prisoner by the

Sarah Ann Hornsby Burditt Moore

Union Army during the Civil War and is buried in the family cemetery in Hornsby's Bend.

Her three other children: Polly, Ruben and Whitfield are all married. Polly and Ruben each had children of their own. After the death of her husband Jesse, Sarah Ann married Dr. T.J. Moore on May 29, 1864. She had one child by this marriage, Milton A. Moore. She died March 23, 1866, and is buried in the family cemetery in Hornsby's Bend.

JOHN GEORGE MORRISS, son of Adam and Eleanor (McWhorter) Morriss, was born Feb. 28, 1810 in Kentucky. Soon after his birth, his parents moved to Alabama. As a young man he left Alabama and rode horseback to Texas to join his brother Abner, who was living at an Indian trading post in the Red River country bordering Arkansas.

In 1832, he received a Spanish Land Grant on the head waters of the Lavaca in the DeWitt Colony, in what is now Lavaca County.

In 1835, he married Armninta Keller of Illinois. Three of their seven children lived to maturity. They were Elizabeth Jane born March 12, 1838 in Texas, married Dr. John Moore of

Halletsville, died Nov. 8, 1882; Abner McWhorter, born Oct. 21, 1839, married Ann Thompson of Halletsville in the summer of 1863, died May 15, 1924; Susan, born Feb. 18, 1841, married Airs Marian Gilmer of Halletsville, died March 14, 1884.

John George Morriss was a stock farmer and raiser and breeder of fine horses. Arminta died in 1848 and John died Nov. 28, 1897 at the ranch home of his son, Abner, in western Kerr

John George Morriss

County. He is buried in Sunset Cemetery located in Kerr County. A Citizen of The Republic of Texas marker is placed on his tombstone.

Patti Beall Morriss, (GGD), 9116
Ruth Morriss, (GGD), 9115
Janette Dixon, (GGGD), 9117
Margaret Jean Ward, (GGGGD), 1077

WILLIAM MORTON, a member of Austin's Old Three Hundred, Morton received a title to one and one-half leagues and one labor of land in present Fort Bend County. Morton, a native of Tennessee, his wife, three sons and two daughters, sailed from Mobile, AL to Texas, in 1822.

Morton was a brick mason and worked on many of the early structures in the area, including the jail and academy at San Felipe. He was granted a lot in San Felipe in February 1830, on condition that he build a brickyard on the land. He was also a farmer and stock raiser. It is reported that Morton introduced the first milk cow to the region.

The baptismal certificate of Marion Morton, daughter of William Morton, dated 1831, is signed by Father Muldoon, and Stephen F. Austin as Godfather. This document is housed at the University of Texas, Austin.

Morton Masonic Lodge No. 72, AF&AM at Richmond was named in honor of William Morton. Morton was one of 40 masons who were members of the Austin's Old 300.

Morton drowned in the flood of 1833 in the Brazos River. His body was never recovered.

Joyce Gray Clegg Robinson, (GGGGD), 5821

ANSON F. MOSS, Once upon a time in the days of the Republic, Eutaw was both a terminal and a stage depot on the Franklin-Springfield and Waco-Marlin routes, and the most important town in southern Limestone County. Today, only a Texas Historical Marker on State Highway 7, one mile east of present day Kosse, the Eutaw Cemetery and Eutaw Lodge No. 233, AF&AM serve as reminders of the site by-passed by the Houston & Texas Central Railroad in 1870. The adult children of Turner and Sally Reavis Moss left Granville County, NC and

Mary Elizabeth Moss, daughter of Anson F. and Nancy Jane McKnight Moss.

were among the first who came to settle the area just north of State Highway 7 in 1838.

Anson F. Moss met and married his first wife who died in April 1847. She was the first to be buried in what would come to be known as the Moss Cemetery. Anson established the Fire Brick and Tile Company, was a charter member of the Eutaw Masonic Lodge and became "one of the wealthiest men in the county." He owned three different farms on 2,391 acres of land and raised tobacco. He married his second wife, Nancy Jane McKnight, on Feb. 6, 1850. Together, they had two daughters and six sons.

My mother and I are direct descendants of Mary Elizabeth, the second daughter and second child born to Anson F. Moss and his second wife. In 1861, Anson went to Hempstead in Austin County and, at age 47, became Captain of the "Eutaw Blues," later known as Co. K, 12th Texas Cavalry, CSA. Anson died Sept. 14, 1888 and is buried beside his first wife in the Moss Cemetery, which now sits on private property.

Nancy Jane McKnight Moss lived until April 30, 1899 and is buried in the Stephenville West End Cemetery in Erath County, beside a number of their children. Widowed in 1876, Mary Elizabeth Moss Vinson married a widower, Benjamin Franklin Brown, on Oct. 25, 1882. They had three children—a son and a set of twin daughters. My mother and I are direct descendants of Ora Edney Brown Parton, one of the twins. Benjamin Franklin Brown died on May 20, 1904 and is buried beside his first wife in the Eutaw Cemetery. Mary Elizabeth lived another 21 years, until May 1925, and is buried in Honey Creek Cemetery, near Hico in Hamilton County, with two of her children and members of their families.

Erica Paige, 22294
Glenda Jean Parton Sandifer, 22295

AZARIAH MOSS, son of James Peterson Moss and Nancy Abernathy Moss, was born in Tennessee on May 30, 1816. He married Adeline L. Alford on Dec. 20, 1837. Following her death, he married Christiana Watson (born in Alabama July 18, 1830) on July 3, 1849. Eight children were born to Azariah and Christiana Moss (in birth order): James Fontaine Moss, Stephen Ellis Moss, Edmond L. Moss, M. Pleasant Moss, Robert L. Moss, Mary Moss (Mrs. J.W. Allen), Ida Moss (Mrs. J.B. Franklin) and Emma Moss (Mrs. Michael Huffman Thomas).

Azariah arrived in the Texas Republic on Nov. 15, 1835, and farmed in Red River County near the Arkansas line. in the early 1850s, he moved his wife and family to a plantation near Wheatland in Dallas County. He engaged in business in Dallas and was one of the founders and directors of Dallas County's first fair held near Washington Street in the 1870s. Family tradition speaks of his serving the Confederacy during the War Between The States.

He was a member of the Methodist Episcopal Church South. He predeceased his wife, dying (by his own hand) at his Wheatland home on Feb. 17, 1888. Christiana Moss died in Dallas in 1910 and is interred beside her husband in Wheatland Cemetery.

Jane Mauk Hilliard, (GGD), 21583

SAMUEL REVIS MOSS, son of Turner Moss and Sarah Revis, was born in North Carolina on May 8, 1804. He lived in North Carolina until 1825 when he made his first trip to Texas with his brothers, Anson and William, to examine land along the Old San Antonio Road near the Brazos River Crossing. He later located Antonio Manchacha who was granted 11 leagues by the Mexican Government and paid him $125 in gold for it.

Samuel settled permanently in the early 1830s. His home was south of present Hearne on Spring Creek. He married Lydia E. McKnight Hill, a widow, on June 3, 1847. (Lydia was the daughter of William McKnight and Rachel Pickens). Samuel and Lydia were the parents of 10 children: Hartwell, Sarah, Howell, Samuel Jr., William, Rachel, Ellen, Georgia, Mollie and Annie.

In the early years the Moss family farmed and operated a water mill to grind corn. In the mid-1850s, when planters came to the Brazos Valley, the mill was converted to a cotton gin.

Samuel Moss was a respected slave owner. On his land they grew cotton and corn. To get supplies for his family and slaves they had to go to Houston in a convoy of ox wagons. It was 100 miles to Houston and took a month to make the trip.

In the late 1850s, Samuel went to Houston and urged railroad builders to extend lines into central Texas. When the Houston and Texas Central Railway Company resumed construction northward after the Civil War, he donated the right-of-way through his land. In his honor the switch built south of Hearne was named as a community. One of his sons, Hartwell, was permitted to name it Sutton.

Through the late 1860s and into the 1880s the Sutton Community prospered, and Samuel built the first school near the station. He hired a teacher for the children and provided the instructor with free room and board.

Samuel Revis Moss died of measles Nov. 20, 1889. His funeral was conducted at his home in Sutton and he was buried in the family cemetery.

Connie Moss, 021998

WILLIS MURPHREY, son of Richard Murphrey of Sampson County, NC (researched and verified by Sue Abruscato of California) was born Aug. 17, 1792 in North Carolina according to a Murphrey family bible in the possession of the Eddings family. He was orphaned in the state of North Carolina, along with his brother Willie and sister Mary Jane, by May 1808, Sampson County.

He married Priscilla Dixon, daughter of David Dixon and Sylvia Boothe, in Amite County, MS on May 9, 1816. Willis served in the War of 1812 in Col. Ferdinand Claiborn's Regiment of Mississippi Milita, according to NARA 1812 enlistment records. Willis settled in De Zavala Colony prior to the Mexican Loyalty Law, approx. 1825, at least 10 years prior. He is also listed as a militiaman on the muster roll of Ayes Bowe District.

Willis and Priscilla had eight children: Virginia Narcissa, born Oct. 3, 1819 in Amite County, MS and married 1) Presnell, 2) James Murphy and 3) Sterling Eddings; Emily, born March 22, 1822 in Amite County, MS, married Fitz Green; David, born July 10, 1824 in Amite County, MS; Martha Jane, born May 5, 1827 in Sabine County, TX, married Jesse Belle Drawhorn; Jarrett Scott, born Dec. 29, 1829 in Sabine County, TX, married Temperance A. Tennison, step-daughter of William Housman, around 1856; Willis Jr., born Nov. 5, 1832, married Sarah Willingham; Elizabeth, born Aug. 5, 1836 in Sabine County, TX, married James Sloan Dewese; and Sarah Priscilla, born Oct. 7, 1840 in Sabine County, TX, married John Davis.

Willis's sister, Mary Jane Murphrey, married Theodore Dorsett who was also one of the early settlers of Texas. He was

93

listed as being in the militia of the Ayish Bayou along with Willis Murphrey in Sabine County. Early records indicate that he arrived in Sabine County as early as 1824.

Willis died Aug. 22, 1844 and Priscilla died sometime between 1858-60. Both Willis and Priscilla are buried in Sabine County, TX. Some believe they are buried in the Eddings family cemetery, others think they are buried in McMahon's Chapel Cemetery. Many of the birth and death records can be found in an old Murphrey family Bible.

JOSE ANTONIO NAVARRO, son of Don Angel Navarro and Maria Josefa Ruizy Pena, was born in San Antonio de Bexar Feb. 27, 1795. A direct descendant of prominent citizens of Spain who had emigrated direct to Texas from the Canary Islands, he inherited that dignity, culture and refinement inherent in his family and a high sense of personal honor.

He was educated in Saltillo, Mexico, New Orleans and the Universities of Spain. With his uncle, Jose Francisco Ruiz, and his brother-in-law, Juan Martin Veramendi, he was active in the political uprisings led by Augustus W. Magee, Jose Bernardo Gutierrez de Lara, and Jose Alverez de Toledo against the Spanish authorities in 1812-13 and fled to Louisiana when Toledos' forces were defeated in the Battle of the Medina River, Aug. 18, 1813. He first met Stephen F. Austin the summer of 1812, the beginning of a life-long friendship. While in exile in New Orleans, he studied law and after his return to Texas in 1816, he left to study in Spain. After the completion of his education, he returned to Texas.

He was recognized as an authority in civil law, from which much of our own jurisprudence is derived.

With the creation of the Mexican State of Coahuila and Texas in 1824, Navarro became one of the Texas representatives in the state legislature and so represented Texas interests that he was referred to as an "Americanized" Texan.

After 1824 Navarro received land grants in present Atascosa, Karnes, Guadalupe, Travis, and Bastrop counties. These grants comprised his ranch properties. At the same time, he operated a commercial house in San Antonio, practiced law, and took an active part in public affairs.

In 1825, he married Margarita de la Garza. They made their home at the ranch and at Navarro House in San Antonio. They were the parents of seven children.

While serving in the Congress of Coahuila and Texas, he assisted Stephen F. Austin in securing passage of legislation favorable to the Texas Colonists. It was he who introduced at Austin's suggestion Decree No. 70, promulgated by the governor on Jan. 13, 1829, which gave to the Texan Colonists a 12-year moratorium on debts they owed prior to coming to Texas and a most generous exemption law which formed the basis for the Homestead Law of Texas.

On March 2, 1835, he was elected deputy to the National Congress at Mexico City, but being in sympathy with the developing revolutionary sentiment in Texas, he resigned.

In February 1836, he was elected a delegate from Bexar to the Constitutional Convention which convened at Washington on the Brazos, March 1, 1836, and there signed the Texas Declaration of Independence. He served on the special committee of 21 which drafted the constitution of the Republic of Texas.

Although a Catholic, he was a member of Virtue Masonic Lodge No. 10 in Saltillo, Mexico, and on Nov. 18, 1838, the fraternal courtesies of the Grand Lodge of the Republic of Texas AF&AM were extended to him.

In 1838, he was elected to the Senate of the Republic of Texas. In 1840, President Lamar appointed him as one of three commissioners on the ill-fated Santa Fe Expedition, assigned to persuade the people of Santa Fe to annex themselves peacefully to the Republic of Texas. The expedition was captured by the Mexicans. He and his comrades were marched overland to Mexico City. The surrender of the expedition, Oct. 5, 1841, included a special provision for the protection of Navarro, but upon arrival in Mexico City, Navarro was separated from the others and placed in Acordad Prison, tried by orders of Antonio Lopez De Santa Anna, and sentenced to death. The sentence was commuted to life imprisonment. In 1844, he was transferred to a dungeon of the San Juan de Luga Prison in Vera Cruz. He escaped in a British vessel bound for Havana, Cuba, made his way to New Orleans in January 1845, and finally reached his ranch home near Geronimo in February. Family legend tells that his escape was contrived and arranged by Santa Anna, a fellow Mason.

From July 4 until Aug. 27, 1845, he was a delegate to the convention of 1845, which voted for Texas Annexation to the United States and drafted the Constitution of 1845, the only native Mexican among the delegates.

He was thrice elected to the Senate of the state of Texas, where he worthily served its people, but on account of age, declined a fourth term.

In 1861, he attended an Austin mass meeting to encourage secession. All four of his sons fought in the Confederate Army.

He died Jan. 13, 1871, and was buried beside his wife in San Fernando Cemetery No. 1 in San Antonio, TX. In 1936, the Texas Centennial Commission erected a joint monument at their graves and also placed a statue of him at Corsicana, TX. Navarro County, created in 1846, was named in his honor and its county seat, Corsicana, was named in memory of his mother's birthplace, the Island of Corsica.

The fame of this great and good man and worthy Texan will never fade. His name and record of his life will ever be an inspiration to succeeding generations.
Caroline Ross Wilkins, (GGGGD), 3446

LUDWIG HEINRICH NEEB, born in Hof, Bad Marienberg, Germany, Jan. 1, 1821. His parents were Johann Sebastian Neeb and Anne Marie Schell; his grandparents were Johann Heinrich Neeb and Anne Marie Schutz. He was baptized there Jan. 7, 1821 in the Evangelist Church.

Ludwig came to Texas soon after his father was killed in a battle near their home in Germany arriving at the port of Galveston, TX Nov. 25, 1845 aboard the ship *Washington* and settled in New Braunfels. On Feb. 10, 1850, Ludwig married Dorothea Pape, daughter of Conrad Pape and Dorothea Bodenstaedt.

Children born to Ludwig and Dorothea were Karl, Wilhelmina, Wilhehn, Bertha, Louis, Emma (died in infancy), Helena, Anna (my grandmother) and Louise.

Ludwig opened a saddle/harness shop. He was also a drayman and hauled supplies for the government. On one such trip he was attacked and scalped by Indians. Ludwig lived seven years after this attack. Information gleaned from The New Braunfelser Zeitung, March 17, 1876 states that, "Neeb, an elderly citizen, died of apoplexy; he lived in Comaltown."

During the Civil War, Ludwig served as a private in Captain F. Heidermeyer's Company of Infantry, Texas State Troops, 31st Brigade. (Company D; age 41 years).
Hilma Ann (Jacobi) Goble, (GGD), of Ludwig Heinrich Neeb, DRT 21924

ALBERT ALDRICH NELSON, son of Samuel and Cynthia Aldrich Nelson, was born May 15, 1814, in Milford, MA. He was descended from Puritan families who settled in Massachusetts in the 1600s. As a boy he went to sea as a cabin boy on ships owned by his brother-in-law. From 1833-38 he sailed on whaling vessels and during this time kept a diary of his thoughts and experiences. The diary is housed in the Stephen F. Austin University library. Tiring of this life, he made his way in 1838 to Texas to visit his brother Charles, a lawyer in Houston, and his Aldrich cousins in Crockett County.

Using skills attained at sea, he became Nacogdoches District surveyor, a position he held until late in life. He was also a city alderman in Nacogdoches and one term as mayor. He was one of the founders of Christ Episcopal Church and served faithfully as a vestryman and lay reader.

Albert married Jane Caroline Simpson, daughter of John Jordan Simpson and Jane Mercer Brooks Simpson Oct. 9, 1845, and they had seven children.

Albert Nelson served in the Cherokee War, and in the Civil War fought in the battles of Val Verde and Glorieta in New Mexico. At Glorieta he was wounded, captured by Union forces, and imprisoned at Richmond, VA. He was paroled before the end of the war and became, as a civilian, Paymaster for the Confederate Navy.

He died Sept. 24, 1892 and is buried at Oak Grove Cemetery in Nacogdoches.
Mary Louise Anderson Smith, (GGD), 22003S
Bertha Elizabeth Carmichael, (GGD), 20719

CAROLINE SIMPSON NELSON, born in Arkansas in 1825 "on the way to Texas" to John Jordan Simpson and Jane Mercer Brooks Simpson. She married Albert Aldrich Nelson Oct. 9, 1845. He was a New Englander who became the Nacogdoches District Surveyor, city alderman and mayor.

Jane and Albert had seven children: Charles Albert, born and died in 1846; John Brooks, born 1847, died 1929, married Sallie Moore; George Aldrich Nelson, born 1849, died 1899, married Emma Maria Maddux—both were physicians; Jane Amelia, born 1854; Mary Louise, born 1856, died 1876, unmarried; Frances Starr, born 1858, died 1917, unmarried; William Augustus, born 1861, died 1919, married Helen Henderson.

Jane Caroline Nelson died in 1863 in Nacogdoches and is buried at Oak Grove Cemetery.
Mary Louise Anderson Smith, (GGGD), 22002S
Bertha Elizabeth Anderson Carmichael, (GGGD), 20719

JOSEPH AUSTIN NEWMAN, son of Joseph and Rachel (Rabb) Newman, was born in Austin's Colony, TX, in 1827. Joseph's parents, his paternal grandparents, William and Mary (Smalley) Rabb; and his four Rabb uncles came to Texas as members of Stephen F. Austin's original colony, known as "The Old Three Hundred."

Joseph was 4 years old when his father died in February 1831. His mother, Rachel, and the children stayed in the Wharton County area for another 20 years, and then in the early 1850s the family began moving to the DeWitt County area.

Joseph served under Capt. Herbert (Company of Jack Hayes), 1st Regiment, Texas Mounted Rifles, in 1846, during the Mexican War. After returning to Wharton County, Joseph married Mary Rice, the daughter of Thomas McClure and Elizabeth (Wilson) Rice, on Feb. 9, 1848. They had one son, Leander Green Newman. Mary died around 1850, and in early 1852, Joseph followed his family to DeWitt County.

On July 18, 1852, Joseph and Elizabeth Dedrich Baker were married. Elizabeth, daughter of William and Vashti (White) Baker, was born in 1834, in Fayette County, AL. Joseph and Elizabeth had nine children: Joseph, Olive, James Milton (married Mary Emiline Rice), Mary, Martha, William, Elizabeth, Rachel and John, all born in DeWitt County.

Joseph died in November 1872. Elizabeth died Sept. 6, 1916, and is buried in the Post Oak Cemetery in Somerville County.
Betty Newman Wauer, (GGGD), (Pending)

JOSEPH AUSTIN NEWMAN, son of Joseph Newman and Rachel Rabb, was born in 1827 in Wharton County, TX. His parents and grandparents, William Rabb and Mary Smalley, were members of Stephen F. Austin's Old Three Hundred Families who came to Texas in 1820. Joseph Austin served with Herbert's Texas Mounted Rifles during 1846 in the Mexican War. He married Mary Rice, daughter of Thomas McClure Rice and Elizabeth Wilson on Feb. 9, 1848 in Wharton County. They had one child: Leander Green, born 1849, married Melinda Wafford.

Joseph Austin married Elizabeth Dedrick Baker, daughter of William Baker and Vashti White, on July 18, 1852 in DeWitt County, TX. They had 10 children, all born in DeWitt County: Joseph Sylvester, born 1857, married Miranda Sirmon; Olive Ann, born 1858, married Hugh Means; James Milton, born 1859, married Mary Emiline Rice, daughter of Oliver Hugh Rice and Adeline Courtney and second, Polly Elam; Thomas, born 1860; Mary Jane, born 1861, married William Wood; Martha Frances, born 1864, married William Kirkland and second, Walter Matthew; William Henry, born 1866, married Sophia Parker; Elizabeth Dedrick, born 1869, married Milton Stovall; Rachel Isabel, born 1870, married Walter Huston; John Austin, born 1871, married Julia Terry. Joseph Austin died Nov. 19, 1872 in Bexar County, TX and was buried in a San Antonio cemetery. Elizabeth died Sept. 6, 1916 in Somervell County, TX and was buried in the Post Oak Cemetery.
Patty Newman Turner, (GGD), 22509-S

JOSEPH AND RACHEL (RABB) NEWMAN were married in Warren County, OH in 1806. Joseph was born in South Carolina in 1787 and Rachel was born Jan. 17, 1790, in Fayette County, PA. Joseph, Rachel and children moved with her parents, William and Mary (Smalley) Rabb, and her brothers, from Ohio to Indiana, Illinois, Missouri and Arkansas. While in Illinois, Joseph served in the War of 1812.

In 1820, the Newman and Rabb families moved to the south side of the Red River to Jonesborough (Texas), and afterwards moved to the present-day LaGrange area, arriving there in December 1823. Joseph was a member of "The Old Three Hundred," Stephen F. Austin's original colonists. His Land Grant #59, dated July 5, 1824, consisted of League 7 on the east side of the Colorado River, north of present-day Egypt, and his labor of land located on the Brazos River, below the town of San Felipe de Austin. Joseph served as a member of the first "Ranging Company" that was formed for the protection of the Colonists.

Joseph and Rachel had 10 children: Mary, William, Louisa, Minerva, Sarah, Elizabeth, Thomas, Ali, Joseph Austin and Andrew, the last three born in Texas. Joseph died in 1831, at the age of 44, and is buried on his land near Egypt. Rachel died in 1872, living almost 83 years, and is buried in the Salt Creek Cemetery at Davy, DeWitt County, TX.

Betty Newman Wauer, (GGGGD), 21975

RACHEL RABB NEWMAN, daughter of William Rabb and Mary Smalley was born Jan. 17, 1790 in Fayette County, PA. She married Joseph Newman on June 12, 1806 in Warren County, OH. They came to Texas in 1820 with her parents and brothers, Andrew, John, Thomas and Ulysses Rabb as members of Stephen F. Austin's Old Three Hundred families.

They had 10 children: Mary "Polly," born 1808, married Preston Gilbert; William Rabb, born 1810, married Martha Shedricks; Louisa, born 1812; Minerva, born 1814, married David Silcriggs and John Ruston; Sarah Jane "Sally," born 1818, married Jesse Robinson and second, George Scull; Elizabeth, born 1820, married Joseph Tumlinson; Thomas J.R., born 1821; Ali, born 1824; Joseph Austin, born 1827, married Mary Rice and second, Elizabeth Dedrick Baker; Andrew Rabb, born 1830, married Lydia Smalley and second, Mary Lewis.

Joseph died Feb. 15, 1831 in Wharton County, TX at the age of 46 and was buried on their land at Egypt, TX. Rachel died Dec. 4, 1872 in Karnes County, TX and is buried in the Salt Creek Cemetery at Davy, TX.

Patty Newman Turner, (GGGD), 22508-S

ELINOR VANATA NORCROSS was age 43 on the 1850 Austin County Census, with children Mary, age 20; Lidia, age 16; Ann, age 14; Elizabeth, age 12; Catherine, age 8; and John age 5. Also living with the family as a laborer was a William Wells, age 20. Elenor Vanata was the wife of Allen Norcross who had returned to Indiana.

Elenor was born in New Jersey and married Allen in Indiana, possibly Wells or Adams County, in about 1835. Their oldest son, Aaron, was born in Indiana in 1836. An 1860 Austin County census shows Aaron, Albert (Allen), Eliza, with Mary, Catherine, and John. Lidia Norcross married William Wells in 1851 in Austin County. Elizabeth married William Sherrill and they settled in Burleson County.

Elinor was living with the Sherrills in 1870 according to the Burleson County census and is believed to have died between 1870-80 in Burleson County. Allen died in 1879 in Indiana. Catherine Norcross married Gilbert Thomas Humble in 1873 after his first wife Melinda Manning died. Gilbert and Catherine Norcross Humble are buried on the Humble/Schott Ranch in Medina County. John Norcross is also buried there.

Joy Hickman Putnam, (GGGGD), 22788

JAMES W. NORTHCUT was born 1820 in Virginia. Around 1841, he arrived in Shelby County, Republic of Texas. On Dec. 22, 1842, James married Catherine E. Watkins, born June 24, 1824, in Alabama. Parents and siblings are still being researched.

James and Catherine reared 11 children, only eight are known: Marion, born 1844; William, born 1846; James Barnett, born 1848,

married (1) Sarah Smith (2) Katherine Bullard (3) Mrs. Lona Eads Bishop; John Henry, born Feb. 11, 1851, married (1) ca. 1873 Martha Adaline McClure, born in July 1848, Mississippi (2) Nannie Hudson; George Washington, born 1856, married (1) Sarah J. Watkins (2) Mrs. Addie Jones McClendon (3) Mrs. Edie Kennemer; Hannah Elizabeth, born 1859, married William McClure, no children; Andrew Jackson, born 1863,

John Henry Northcut, son of James W. Northcut

married (1) Mary Herriage (2) Rebecca Thurman; and Thomas Jefferson, born 1865, never married.

During the War with Mexico, Mr. Northcut enlisted in Bell's Texas Mounted Volunteers. His unit guarded the Texas frontier from Indian attacks.

James W. was a cabinetmaker and farmer. He served as Constable of Panola County from 1855-57. By 1862, the Northcut family moved to Springville, Wood County (later renamed Emory, Rains County). In 1862-64, he served as Justice of Peace. James W. Northcut died Aug. 14, 1871, buried Emory City Cemetery. Catherine Watkins Northcut died in 1901, buried Smyrna Cemetery.

John Henry and Martha Adaline Northcut, listed above, reared seven children: Sallie, born 1875; Elizabeth, 1877; Lenora, 1880; John Woodson, 1882; William Jasper, born Nov. 30, 1883, died March 15, 1968; Susan, 1887; Calvin, 1891. Martha Adaline died May 11, 1895. In 1896, John Henry married Nannie Hudson. Their children: "Alec," Eunice, Roscoe, Ophelia, Edgar. John Henry died April 12, 1911 and is buried next to Martha Adaline in Smyrna Cemetery, Rains County.

Joe Ann McIver, (GGGD), 21926
Mary Beth Sooter, (GGGD), 21925

MALINA ODEM, my great-grandmother, was born in October 1828 in Lafayette, LA, the daughter of Dempsey Odem and Sarah Cryer Odem. She was baptized at the Cathedral of St. John the Evangelist, Lafayette, LA on Dec. 10, 1828.

When Malina was 3 years old, her mother died and she was given by her father to her eldest sister, Jamima Odem Bernan, "to raise as a good mother would." Dempsey Odem died soon after.

Malina was brought to South Texas in the late 1830s. There are family accounts that she played with turtle eggs in the Bay at Corpus Christi.

She married George B. Peerman on June 21, 1844 in Victoria, TX at the age of 15.

Ethel Peerman Jacks, granddaughter of Malina Odem Peerman, circa 1940.

When I called the Victoria County Clerk for a copy of their marriage license, I was delighted when told I could have the original hand-written license.

George and Malina were the parents of six children: George

B. Jr., Virginia, William, Missouri and twins, Frank Terry and Malina Frances. Frank Terry Peerman who married Margaret Matilda Gamble are my grandparents. Their daughter, Sarah Ethel Peerman, who married Nicholas Warren Jacks are my parents.

Frank Terry Peerman and wife, Margaret Matilda Gamble, son and daughter-in-law of Malina Odem Peerman, circa 1900.

Malina entertained her small children with stories of their papa's participation in the Texas Revolution. Aunt Carrie Holliday recalled hearing Grandma Peerman tell the story of Grandpa Peerman in the Mier Expedition.

Bettye Jacks Jensen, great granddaughter of Malina Odem Peerman.

Her husband died on Jan. 21, 1869 at their home in Alleyton, TX. Malina lived her later years near her daughter, Missouri Peerman Holliday, in Mullican, Brazos County, TX.

Malina died after 1882 and is buried next to her husband, George B. Peerman, in the Alleyton Cemetery, Colorado County, TX.

Bettye Jacks Jensen, (GGD), 10657S

ADELA BELLE ATWOOD PALM, was born in Bolivar, Hardeman County, TN Oct. 3, 1838 to William Woods Atwood and Mary Catherine Neely. Her parents brought her to Texas in January 1839 and she spent her childhood on Gilleland's Creek in Travis County near the town of Manor. She was sent back to Tennessee to stay with her grandmother, Louisa Polk Neely, to receive her schooling. When she returned she was one of the belles of Austin.

She married August B. Palm June 26, 1861. He was born in Besthult, Sweden and came to Texas in 1848 with his parents, Anders and Anna Palm, and five brothers. Mr. Palm took his bride to the home in Austin which he had purchased several years before from his cousin, S.M. Swenson. It had been the home of General and Mrs. Albert Sidney Johnston. There the Palms lived for the rest of their lives.

They had four children: Rufus Atwood, born July 24, 1864, married Edith Williams; Mary Josephine, born Sept. 29, 1866; Adela Belle, born 1869, married Henry Louis Hilgartner; and Irene Maclin, born 1872, married Lewis Sidney Morey. Adela Belle Atwood Palm died March 15, 1918 and was buried in Oakwood Cemetery, Austin, TX.

Billie Palm Bryant, (GGD), 21190S

HUGH PARSONS, son of Jesse and Elizabeth Lay Parsons was born in 1807 in Knox County, KY. Hugh married Nancy Smith on May 25, 1828, in Jackson County, MO. Hugh first appeared in Texas about 1840 near Black Jack Grove, west of Cumby, Hopkins County. He returned to get his family, and moving with him were his widow mother, the families of his brothers John and possibly James, sisters Mary Vioma Akers, Margaret Cheek, Sally Wilson, and probably Rebecca Hufft.

Since he had 540 acres in 1842, his move preceded the Mercer Colony, however, he was granted 640 acres in Hunt/Hopkins counties under that system. Hugh raised and raced fine horses. About 1853 he followed his son Robert to Granger, Williamson County. Daughter Sarah Ann Hurley remained in Hunt County. About 1858 his son Jesse was murdered over a horse race.

By 1860 Hugh's family, except daughter Oma Jane Stanton, moved to Goliad County where they lived until 1881. Daughter Susan Adams and Martha Elizabeth Holt died in Goliad County. At 74, as part of a family wagon caravan, Hugh moved with his cattle and horses to Uvalde County. They settled in the Montell area of the Nueces River canyon. In 1883 Hugh and Nancy moved into Uvalde. Hugh died after 1889 and Nancy moved to Granger to live with her daughter where she died in 1899.

ALEJO DE LA ENCARNACION PEREZ was a descendant of Canary Islander, Mateo Perez, who arrived in San Antonio in 1706. Alejo is said to be the youngest known, non-combatant during the Battle of the Alamo in 1836 and the last survivor. He left the Alamo in the arms of his mother, Maria Juana Navarro Perez.

Little is known of Alejo after he left the Alamo, but he is noted in the 1850 census of Bexar County as living with his mother, Juana, at San Jose Mission. From 1861-64, Alejo served in the Confederate Army.

After the Civil War, Alejo's contributions as a political activist were numerous. He served as a member of the Executive Council of the Young Democratic Club of Bexar County in 1868; as assistant city marshall from 1875-76 and again from 1892-93; as deputy city marshall from 1879-80; and in the police department as a police officer from 1883-90.

Alejo De La Encarnacion Perez

Alejo married Maria Antonia Rodriguez and later married Florencia Sappopa Valdez. He fathered 11 children, four with Maria and seven with Sappopa. At the time of his death, he was the last survivor of the Battle of the Alamo and is honored on the Alamo's Wall of History.

JAMES PERSINGER, born ca. 1795, in Kanawa County, WV, to John Persinger and Elizabeth Kimberline Persinger. He married (Polly) Gillespie, born ca. 1806 in Kanawa County, WV, on Feb. 14, 1822. He was a farmer, and in 1832, he moved to Perry County, IN with his wife and four children: Ursula, General Jackson, Kenneth A. and James S.

In 1836, while building the Persinger's new house, a worker insulted his wife, and to defend her honor, James and the man fought, and the worker was killed That night, the family fled Indiana with only what they could carry, seeking a sanctuary beyond the jurisdiction of the United States. With the help of friends, who were of the Masonic order, the family was secretly guided from community to community by Masonic members in each area. They were finally met by the Gillespie family, who lived in

Mexico, later to become the east Texas county of San Augustine. Having left all their possessions behind in Indiana, and to start a new life, they changed their surname from Persinger to Hardy.

They arrived at their new home in the winter of 1836, and James served with Captain Price's Kentucky Volunteers in the Texas Army from May 20 to Sept. 1, 1836. After Texas was declared independent from Mexico, he received land grants from the Republic of Texas, and moved his family to the new land in Jasper District, in what is now Newton County. The Hardy Cemetery is located on that land, and he and his wife are probably buried there, though no stones mark their graves,

A son, Joseph Lane Hardy, born Jan. 29, 1844, in Newton County, married Martha Ann Langham Oct. 23, 1866, in Newton County. He died Oct. 17, 1909, and they are buried in the Maple Grove cemetery, Minden, Rusk County, TX. They were my great-grandparents. My grandfather, Charlie Johnson Hardy, born Aug. 20, 1868, died April 30, 1966, married Emma Gertrude Pleasant, born Dec. 22, 1876, died March 3, 1961, on Nov. 20, 1897, in Nacogdoches County. Their children were twins, Blanche L. and Bernice L.; Beulah Beatrice; Luther Charles and Paul Buford. They are all buried in the Black Jack Cemetery, Nacogdoches County, TX.
Elaine Rhodes Barton, (GGGD), 21607

LEMUEL PETERS SR., son of Richard and Mary (Cass) Peters, was born on July 21, 1772 in Richmond, NH. He married Sarah Minott on March 17, 1798. In Putney, VT and lived in Richmond, NH until 1805. He and his father kept a public house and store there until the family moved to Clarksville, TN. By 1819 they had settled In Lawrence County, AL.

The Peters were educated and cultured people who provided education for all of their 10 children. They were Charles W., born around 1800, married Sarah McClellan and became a county judge In Morgan County, AL; Mahala, born around 1802, married Charles Lewis and lived in Red River County, TX; John S., born around 1804, was a physician in Alabama and Red River County, TX; Mary Cass, born May 30, 1806, married John Weaver and lived In Bowie County, TX; Martha Minott, born around 1807, married John W. Leigh and lived in Bowie County, TX; Samuel Minott, born around 1808, was a lawyer in Alabama and Red River County, TX; Thomas Minott, born Dec. 10, 1810, married Naomi S. Leetch, was a member of the Alabama House of Representatives and a Justice of the Alabama Supreme Court; Richard, born about 1815, was a lawyer who married Elizabeth Beatty and lived in Red River County, TX; Lemuel Jr., born Sept. 24, 1819, married Elizabeth M. Heatherly and was a physician in Bowie County, TX: James Joseph, born June 4, 1823, married Mary Fleming Hansell and was a lawyer in Greenville, TX.

Lemuell's wife, Sarah, died in 1833. The next year Lemuel bought land in Red River County, TX and moved his family there. It was a rough country with rich land, abundant game, and men who went about armed. Lemuel qualified for a land grant (a league and a labor of land).

In 1837 Lemuel started on a trip to visit New England. He stopped for a while in Lawrence County, AL and died. He was buried beside his wife in the Leigh Graveyard.
Dorothy Anderson Hagen, (GGGGD), 21670S

LEMUEL PETERS JR., son of Lemuel and Sarah (Minott) Peters, was born on Sept. 24, 1819 In Lawrence County, AL. He married Elizabeth M. Heatherly on Sept. 29, 1842 in Bowie County, TX. Lemuel was a physician and plantation owner. He was the first doctor in Texas with a medical degree.

Lemuel and Eliza had one son and five daughters: James Joseph, born Dec. 17, 1843, married Emma Kimbell; Sarah Margaret, born Oct. 6, 1845, married A.L. Harris; Martha Adelia Van Dyke, born July 20, 1847, married T.D. Montrose; Zrelldah "Ella" Runnels, born Feb. 10, 1850, married Nathan Kemp Anderson; Mary Wilmoth Peters, born Jan. 27, 1852, married James Harvey Anderson; Elizabeth M. Peters. born April 16, 1855.

Lemuel Jr. arrived in Red River County, Texas in December 1834 with his father and other family members. On Jan. 31, 1835, 15-year-old Lemuel wrote letters to an older brother and a younger one. He said that he was in trouble because there was no school and no books and, because his had not arrived, he could not get an education. He said that he wouldn't live there because the old settlers were a set of horse thieves. He did enjoy the hunting.

After Lemuel received his medical degree he bought land in Red River County, TX. In 1840 he signed a petition to establish Bowle County in the eastern part of the county. The petition was granted. He practiced medicine and farmed. Lemuel Jr. qualified for a land grant of 640 acres.

Dr. Lemuel Peters died June 5. 1856 in Boston, Bowie County, TX and his wife died there March 7, 1871.
Dorothy Anderson Hagen, (GGGD), 21843S

ROBERT T. PETTIT, reportedly son of Benjamin Pettit and Rebecca Larrimore, was born in Lincoln County, KY in 1783, removing to Missouri where Benjamin received a French land grant before the Louisiana Purchase. Malinda Logan, daughter of David and Nancy Thurman Logan, was born in 1802 in Lincoln County and moved to Missouri. Robert and Malinda probably married in Missouri about 1816 and lived in Madison County, before they migrated to Johnson County, AR.

In November 1835, Robert T. Pettit applied for but did not complete a Mexican land grant in Texas. In 1842, he settled in Fannin County, where he and two sons received grants. About 1847, they migrated to Gonzales County. Robert, a farmer, died in 1866; Malinda died about 1875.

Robert and Malinda produced 14 children: Elizabeth married Kuykendall; Benjamin married Mary N. Johns; Nancy married A.J. Hart; David Logan; Robert T. Jr.; Mary Ann married Isaac Huston; Martha married Leander Harrell; Malinda Dixie married Milvern Harrell; William married Mary Waddell; Artemesia married John Wilson; Sarah Jane married Montreville Harrell; Genetta married first, W.H. Clark and second, Alexander Hillary McBryde; James Logan married Sarah Frances __; George married E.A. Stone.

Mary Ann Pettit, born about 1827, and Isaac Huston, born April 16, 1819 in Edwards County, IL, received a marriage license June 28, 1844 in Fannin County.

Their children were Sarah Jane, born 1845 and died at age 12, and James Logan, born in July 1847 and died 1912. Mary Ann died soon after James's birth. Isaac married three more times and died in Kaufman County in 1871.
Diana Pearson White, (GGGGD), 20076

GEORGE WASHINGTON PETTY, the following are excerpts of the family "ancestry" letter written about George Washington Petty and his wife Marium Wood Petty:

"The last years of the 18th century found in Murphreesboro, TN, a large family of Pettys. One of the sons, John, married Delia Thrift. They in turn had a large family. Their son, George Washington, was born in 1812 and grew to young manhood there. Then in 1835 when Texas was in the throes of invasion, he and two other men mounted their horses and rode all the way to Texas. They arrived at Dr. Hoxies in Washington County and stayed there until the call to go to the front. They reached Gonzalez as it was being evacuated. George Petty participated in the Battle of Jacinto and all the other activities connected with the campaign. He met Marium Alston Wood, the daughter of John L. Wood, in the camp of "Retreat" and married her there. They bought a tract of land two miles from where Brenham was founded and lived their lives there." They reared six children, the elder being John Calvin Petty born in i838, who married Veturia Young, daughter of John Young, and reared five children in Hempstead, TX. One son, Thomas Young Petty, married Rose Willingham, who in turn had five children, one being the father of Marium Petty Roden.

JOHN BAPTISTE PEVATEAU/PEVETO,

a native of Avoyelles Parish, Louisiana, John Baptiste Pevateau was the son of Michael Pevateau and Lapolonia Broussard. On April 25, 1825, in St. Landry Parish, John married Mary Pauline Linscomb (Linchcomb), daughter of Bazil Linchcomb and D'Mary Gilcrist.

In 1838, John received a 3rd class land grant of 640 acres in Jefferson County, TX. He brought with him his wife, Mary, and three children: Dejohn, age 5; Samuel, age 3, and Michael, age 1. On the 1840 Tax Roll of Jefferson County, TX, John has 35 work horses, one cow, and the 640 acres of land.

The 1850 Federal Census of Jefferson County lists John 45, Mary 40, John 17, Samuel 15, Michael 13, Alford 11, Robert 9; Mary 6, Eliza 4, Collins 1. In 1860, Orange County has been formed and John and his family are recorded there, with Caleb age 6. In the 1870 census Samuel, age 8, is added to the family. John's occupation in each of the census years is listed as a farmer.

On the 1880 census of Orange County, John is age 75 and Mary is age 67. They are buried in the Linscomb Cemetery, Orange County.
Myra Wanda Hare Coffman, (GGGD), 021889

SAMUEL BRADFORD PIER,

born July 22, 1844 at Travis, Austin County, Republic of Texas to James Bradford Pier and his wife Lucy Merry Pier. James and Lucy had come to Texas in late 1835. James was part of the Texan Army and was at San Jacinto and Lucy took part in the Runaway Scape.

Samuel joined Co. Nichols' Regiment of the Confederate Army for six months then joined Waller's Battalion which was part of Green's Brigade. Following the War Between the States, he returned to Austin County. On Dec. 16, 1868 he married Miss Emma "Emily" Cochran daughter of Thomas Cochran and his wife Betsy Peach Walker Cochran who had also come to Texas prior to the Texas Revolution. Sam and Emily were respected and worthy citizens of the area.

Samuel Bradford Pier

Sam and Emily had seven children: Dr. Thomas J., Emma L., Anna B., Leila M., Ira O., Norris G. and Kinchen C. They also raised two nephews and a niece (children of Emily's deceased sister Mary and her husband Kinch Collins also deceased).

Emily died March 10, 1910 at Buckhorn in Austin County. Sam died March 20, 1914 as a result of an accident while stopping a runaway team of horses.
Laura Lee Lanigan, (GGD), 22564S

ANDREW MONTGOMERY PILLOW,

the third child of William Barton and Sarah Whitaker Pillow, was a farmer and wagoneer. He and his brothers Ransome Dock and Thomas Jefferson joined the Confederacy. Family tradition says that Andrew served at the Battle of Galveston and assisted in the capture of the Yankee gunboat, the *Harriet Lane*.

In 1864, he married a widow Mrs W.J. Biley (Jo) in Houston, Harris County, TX. After the war, they lived in Houston for a short time and took Andrew's younger brother, James Edwin, into their home. About 1870, Andrew and his brothers rounded up the family's cattle that had been dispensed during the Civil War and relocated in Washington County, TX. He later lived in Burleson County, TX and Lee County, TX.

According to family history, his wife was addicted to Laudinum and was eventually institutionalized. After the turn of the century, he joined his brother, Ransome Dock Pillow, in Atlanta, Cass, TX. Andrew Montgomery Pillow died Aug. 13, 1913 due to complications of a broken hip. He was buried in Huffines Community Cemetery, south of Atlanta, TX.
Frances Russell, 21492

RANSOME DOC PILLOW,

born on May 1, 1842 near Mount Vernon, Titus County, TX to William Barton Pillow and Sarah Whitaker Pillow. His father died in 1852, and his mother finally settled the family in Montgomery County, Texas on the farm of her brother, Alexander Whitaker. Ransome and his brother, Thomas, joined the Confederacy soon after the war started and brother Andrew followed. In 1863, Ransome's mother died, leaving two younger sisters and a younger brother. Two of the children lived with the Issac Coe family and the other with a Taylor family. In 1864, Ransome married Josephine Coe, daughter of Issac Coe. Josephine died a year later when their son William Joseph was born. He then married Sarah Cryer in Houston, fol-

Ransome Doc Pillow Family, circa 1898. (Back) Sarah E. "Katty," Phillip Paten, Josephine, Myrtle May and Mamie Peachey. (Front) Roy Ray, Ransome Doc and Homer Lincoln.

lowed by Mary Boudreau. Mary died with the birth of his second son, Jesse Monroe. In 1880, he married Josephine Lee, daughter of James Lee and Ellen Decker Lee. Josephine was from a Montgomery County, Texas family, and they were married in Washington County, TX. They moved to Milam County, TX where Ransome was a tenant farmer on the Holtzclaw place between Rockdale and Cameron, TX. At the turn of the century, the family moved to Cass County, TX. A total of 10 children were born, Arthur Ellis, Myrtle Mae, Mamie Peach, Phillip Paten, Sarah Ellen "Katy," William Lee, Roy Ray, Homer Lincoln,, Effie R. and Evnard Holtzclaw. Ransome died of pneumonia near the community of Cass, TX on Oct. 14, 1914 and was buried in Huffines Community Cemetery in Atlanta, TX. His wife, Josephine, died on Dec. 28, 1936 and was buried beside her husband.
Frances Russell, 21492

THOMAS JEFFERSON PILLOW, born in Texas on Feb. 23, 1844. He joined the Confederacy at Magnolia, Montgomery County, TX along with his brother, Ransome Dock Pillow. After the war, he married Mary Jane Gates, and they lived in Montgomery County, TX. Ransome's wife, Josephine Coe Pillow, died in childbirth and Thomas and Mary Jane raised the child, Jesse Monroe Pillow. Thomas died in Linestone County, TX on March 6, 1889.
Frances Russell, 21492

WILLIAM BARTON PILLOW, born in Virginia, came to Texas on Oct. 8, 1831, at the age of 25 years. He met Sarah Whitaker, age 18, and married the following year. Her family arrived in Texas in 1822 as Stephen F. Austin colonists. By 1835, they had one child, and were expecting a second, when Sarah made the trip to Falls County, TX to appear personally at the Spanish land grant office. She received over 4,000 acres in her name, located between the current towns of Marlin and Kosse, TX, in the community of Stranger. Her 18-year-old brother, Alexander Whitaker, received a Spanish grant given to a single man, and his property adjoined hers.

The William Barton Pillow family established residency in Falls County, TX and it appears that they departed with the Runaway Scrape. William Barton Pillow received a headright certificate on March 16, 1838. The family was located in Lurrisa, Cherokee County, TX in 1852, when he was killed in a mill accident at age 46. He left a 39-year-old wife with eight children. She eventually located her family in Tillis Prairie, Montgomery County, TX, near her brother Alexander Whitaker. She sent three sons to the Confederate Service and succumbed to poor health at the age of 50 in 1863. The three minor children were taken in by neighbors and relatives.
Frances Russell. 21492

PIERRE PINGENOT was born in Bretten, Haut-Rhin, France on Sept. 30, 1810. He was the son of John Remi Pingenot and Jeanne Marie Cordonnier. He served in the Army as a substitute for a young soldier of class and was awarded a Certificate of Good Conduct. The service documents were brought to America and are now in the procession of Cecilia Pingenot Forrest (GGD).

Pierre and his cousins, Phillip Pingenot and Jean Nicolas Pingenot (along with his children: Justine, Auguate and Celestin) came to Texas on the ship *Probus* as part of Henri Castro's Colonists. They arrived in Galvaston in February 1845 and made their way to San Antonio and Castroville. Pierre Pingenot and Alexis Pichot married in 1846 and soon bought a lot in Castroville where they built their home.

The home indicates Pingenot was a practical man for it is a solid and sturdy structure which originally had a thatched roof. The home was in the Pingenot family for over 60 years. The house still stands in Castroville on Paris Street. It was photographed by the Library of Congress in 1936 and in recent years has been restored.

Pingenot was a Medina County Commissioner from 1848-56. The marriage of Pierre and Alexis was blessed with nine children. On the death of Alexis, at the age of 86, it was noted that in common with all pioneers, she endured many of the hardships of a frontier country but always was of a cheerful nature.
Carol Glover Nichols, (GGGGGGD), 19510
Darlene Tondre Glover, (GGGGGD), 19512

PIERRE FRANCOIS PINGENOT was born Oct. 1, 1810 in Brentten, Haut-Rhin, France to Jean Remi Pingenot and his wife, Jeanne Marie Cordonnier. Pierre served in the French Army from 1833-40. On Oct. 6, 1844 he sailed from Anvers, France on the *Probus* and arrived in Texas in February 1845, settling in Castroville, TX.

Pierre Francois Pingenot married Alexis Pichot on Nov. 22, 1846 in Castroville. They had the following children: Celeste (1848-1901) married Emily Gast in 1882; Mary Adele (1850-1890) married August Tondre in 1870; Emelie (1853-1925); Mary Anna (1855-no record); Frank August (1858-1876); Edward (1861-1909) married Anna Carolyn Batot in 1895; Louis (1864-1928) married Regina Rudinger in 1897; infant (1868-at birth); Mary Elizabeth (1870-1952) married Jacob Bendele in 1893. They built their home in Castroville and the home was photographed by the Library of Congress and is listed in several registries of historic places.

Pierre was a farmer and also served as a Medina County Commissioner (1854-1856). He died on June 28, 1881 and his wife, Alexis, died on Nov. 2, 1912. They are buried in Saint Louis Catholic Cemetery in Castroville, TX.

There was a dedication of Grave Medallions for Pierre Francois Pingenot and Alexis Pichot Pingenot, citizens of the Republic of Texas 1836-February 1846 on Saturday, Oct. 14, 1989 at St. Louis Catholic Cemetery, Castroville, TX.
Rose Marie Graf Tillman, (GGGD), #20041-S

LUCIUS BENJAMIN POLK, born June 2, 1823, in Maury, TN, came to Texas in 1839 with his family from Tennessee. His father was Benjamin D.A. Polk, born probably in Greenbrier District of Western Virginia on Jan. 1, 1790 and died June 21, 1840. On Sept. 26, 1816, Benjamin married Margaret R. Moore, born Oct. 10, 1797, in North Carolina. By wagon they came to Texas bringing stock and some slaves. They settled in San Augustine County to farm.

Children traveling with them were the oldest, Elizabeth Ann, then James Moore, John, and Lucius. Seven other children were born: Viola Catherine, Franklin Armstad, Mary Orphelia, John Thaddeus, Margaret Jane, Robert Green, Sarah Robins.

On May 20, 1844, Lucius received a land grant in San Augustine County. He married Maggie Miller who was born Dec. 25, 1842 and died March 31, 1916. They had the following children: Benjamin F.; Matthew married Mary Border; Mollie married B.F. Sharp; Jane Margaret, born Aug. 4, 1874, married Oct. 12, 1893 to William Walter Johnson from Meredian, Mississippi, who was born Nov. 19, 1856 and died Dec. 8, 1931. Jane died June 13, 1969, age 94. Kate married Brune Wall; Edna married Randolph Nobles. Lucius B. Polk died Feb. 27, 1910.

So "real" Daughter of Republic of Texas are Mollie, Jane, Kate and Edna. They were members of Ezekiel W. Cullen Chapter, San Augustine.

Charlene Arendt Moser, (GGD), 018616

MARTIN PRICE

MARTIN PRICE was born Dec. 25, 1794 (the 1860 Lamar County, TX census shows Kentucky birth; the 1870 Lamar County, TX census shows VA birth). A veteran of the War of 1812, he married first, Elizabeth Moore Sept. 25, 1817 who was born May 6, 1799, Franklin County, TN and died Oct. 27, 1829, Monroe County, AL. Elizabeth was a daughter of James Moore, a soldier in the War of 1812.

Martin Price

Martin Price's second marriage was to Jane (maiden name unknown) on March 11, 1834. Jane was born June 8, 1815 and died Sept. 20, 1841. All birth, marriage and death dates are from the Pinckney Middleton Price family Bible which is in my possession.

Martin Price was in the Republic of Texas in 1837. Martin Price is No. 384, for 160 acres, on a list of field notes and Preemption Certificates sent to Austin by Amos Morrill Esquire on March 9, A.D. 1837 from what is now Lamar County, TX. There is a notation that Milton Ikard's field notes and certificate sent by Wm. M. Willis No. 331 were to be transferred to P.M. Price. Wm. H. Hobbs is also on this list, #386, for 160 acres. Wm. H. Hobbs was married to Martin Price's daughter, Tranquilla Simmons Price. At that time in 1837, Lamar County did not exist. Lamar County was formed from Red River County in 1840.

Dan Hembree, a great-grandson of Sidney Moore Price, wrote from his residence in Honey Grove, TX, Dec. 19, 1975, to his cousin Isabel Rountree, a granddaughter of Pinckney Middleton Price, and stated that his great-grandfather did come to Lamar County, TX in 1841 with his father Martin Price, served in the Mexican War from Lamar County with his brother P.M. Price, returned to Alabama after the Mexican War and remained there until after the Civil War.

Siblings of Martin Price were: (a) Anger Price, born ??. Enlisted with Martin Price in the War of 1812; (b) Robert Price, born ??, who located Pinckney M. "P.M." Price's land in Lamar County, TX on Sept. 1, 1838, adjacent to his own land, and was a chain-carrier for the eventual survey which was effected May 10, 1842. Some family tradition states that Robert sold out and moved to California; (c) Daniel Price was born Aug. 12, 1801, died Dec. 30, 1865, and is buried in the old Strother Cemetery three miles NW of Maxey, east of Tigertown where Martin's daughter Tranquilla Simmons Price Hobbs is also buried; (d) Alexander Price, born 1807, shown in the 1850 Jackson County, AL census, p. 176, age 43, born Virginia. His nephew, Sidney Moore Price, 24, was in that household; (e) Christiana, born 1807

(twin to Alexander). She married Alexander McCampbell. They are listed in the 1850 Jackson County, AL census with a large number of children, next door to her twin brother Alexander Price. Also in Christiana's household is Jane McCampbell, age 79 (born ca. 1770 in Virginia), presumed to be the mother of Alexander McCampbell.

Martin and Elizabeth Moore Price's five children were: Tranquilla Simmons Price, born July 25, 1818 died Jan. 30, 1864 Lamar County, TX married Wm. Henry Hobbs. She is buried in the old Strother Cemetery east of Tigertown; Pinckney Middleton "P.M. " Price born Dec. 16, 1821, Monroe County, AL, died Aug. 6, 1895 Paris, TX married first Anna Richardson on March 8, 1849 and second, Elizabeth Susan Nixon, Lamar County, TX on May 28, 1859. He is buried in the Oddfellows' Cemetery in Paris; Sidney Moore Price born Aug. 7, 1824, Monroe County, AL, died Aug. 16, 1908 Lamar County, TX, married in 1851 to Mary Jane James, and is buried in Honey Grove, TX; Irena Madison Price born Dec. 16, 1826, died March 23, 1828; and Martin Monroe Price born March 13, 1829 and died an infant.

Martin and Jane Price's children were Pleasant Henderson Price born Oct. 17, 1839, Alabama, died 1873 Lamar County; Pleasant Martin Price born Oct. 22, 1836 Alabama and died an infant.

During 1873 in Paris, TX, Martin Price's portrait was painted by the renowned artist, William Henry Huddle. This portrait is in excellent condition and is owned by the writer, Helen V. Burleson Kelso, a great-great-granddaughter of Martin Price, via his son Pinckney Middleton Price's daughter Aurora Price who married John W. Rountree, and had two children Isabel Rountree, and Eugenia Rountree who married Vivian Stanley Burleson Sept. 12, 1925 Austin, TX.

Martin Price died April 26, 1876, in Paris, and is buried in the Oddfellows' Cemetery on Price Street, Paris, TX.

Helen Burleson Kelso, (GGGD), 10273-S (DRT President General 1999-2001)

SARAH "SALLIE" BREWER PRINCE

SARAH "SALLIE" BREWER PRINCE was the fifth of 11 children born to Henry Brewer and Susannah Mitchell. She was born in Georgia on July 3, 1806. The Henry Brewer family had lived in North Carolina. Alabama, Georgia, Mississippi, and by 1832 were in Texas. The first record we find of Sarah is a marriage bond recorded in Hinds County, MS between Green Berry Brewer and Henry Brewer binding Sarah to Green Berry. On April 20, 1826, the rites of matrimony were solemnized

John Winfield and Vernettia Ann Whitaker Prince, son of George W. and Sarah Brewer Prince.

Four children were born in Mississippi: Nancy, Hannah Ann, Green Berry Jr. and Henry. By 1834 they had moved to Texas where Sarah's parents had already claimed land in Nacogdoches County. In Green Berry's application for land to the Mexican government he stated that he "emigrated to this state in the month of January 1834, being married, my family consists of six persons." When Texas later became a state this land was located in Freestone County. He and Sarah settled in Nacogdoches County near her parents between Looneyville and Nat, north of Douglass. Three more children were born to this family: George, William C. and Culwell C.

In 1839 Sarah petitioned for administration of the estate Green Berry Brewer, deceased.

In June 1841 George W. Prince, born in North Carolina ca. 1810, arrived in Nacogdoches County. On Sept, 26, 1841 he married Sarah Brewer. He was selected to serve as a Justice of Peace in December 1842. Also in 1842 their first son, Francis Marion, was born. He married Susan Jane Oswalt. Other children: Wilber Fisk (born 1843) married Cordelia Whitaker; Josephine (born 1845) married Calvin Wallace; John Winfield (born 1847) married Vernettia Ann Whitaker. (It is from John Winfield that I am descended.)

By 1855 George W. Prince was gone from the state and Sarah was left to raise her family alone. In 1880 she deeded her farm place to Wilber F. with the condition she could live there the rest of her life. However, she could not get, along with his wife. Sarah lived the last of her life with her daughter, Josephine Wallace. There she died April 12, 1885, age 79. She is buried in Redland Cemetery in Nacogdoches County.

Sarah Brewer Brewer Prince, my great-great-grandmother was a strong-willed pioneer woman who had seen Texas grow and change. She had seen Texas under Mexican rule, Independent Republic, State of the Union, Confederate State and again a part of the United States of America. Her brothers fought at San Jacinto, three of her sons were Confederate soldiers. I am proud to be listed among her descendants.
Joy Prince Coble, (GGGD), 20763

WILLIAM AND MARY (SMALLEY) RABB came to Texas in 1821. William, son of Andrew and Mary (Scott) Rabb, was born Dec. 21, 1770 in Fayette County, PA. Mary was born about 1772, also in Pennsylvania, and she and William were married around 1789. In 1803, William started westward with his wife and their children. He owned gristmills in a number of locations. In 1812, he was judge for Madison County, IL, and served in the Illinois Territory Legislature during 1814 and 1815.

In 1820, William moved his family to the south side of the Red River to Jonesborough, TX. The next year, William, Mary, and two sons, Thomas and Ulysses moved to the Colorado River, near present day LaGrange. In 1823, they were joined by daughter, Rachel, her husband, Joseph Newman, and children; sons: Andrew and wife, Margaret (Ragsdale), and John and wife, Mary (Crownover). William, his sons, Andrew, John and Thomas, and son-in-law, Joseph Newman, were all members of "The Old Three Hundred," Stephen F. Austin's Original Colonists.

Based on Austin's prior agreement with William to build a gristmill in the upper portion of the Colony, William received a total of five sitios, 13,000 acres in Fayette County and 9,000 acres in Matagorda County. His land grant, No. 58, was dated July 19, 1824. Due to Indian hostilities, the gristmill was not completed until 1831. William and Mary both died later that same year, and are buried on a hillside overlooking Rabb's Prairie in Fayette County, TX.
Betty Newman Wauer, (GGGGGD), 21976S

MARY SMALLEY RABB was born in 1773 in Fayette County, PA. Her parents are believed to be Benjamin Smalley and Rachel Cressen. Mary married William Rabb in 1789. Mary and William had five children: Rachel Rabb (born 1790) married Joseph Newman; Andrew (born 1792) married Margaret Ragsdale; John (born 1798) married Mary Crownover; Thomas (born 1801) married Serena Gilbert; and Ulysses (born 1803).

Mary and William started westward through Ohio and Illinois by 1803. They owned and operated grist mills in several locations in Illinois. In 1820 they moved to the southside of the Red River to the Jonesborough Settlement in present day Red River County, TX. They were members of Stephen F. Austin's Old Three Hundred families.

It is from the diary of her daughter-in-law, Mary Crownover Rabb, we learn much about the early life of these families and their struggles to settle in Texas. Sometime after the family arrived in Texas, the youngest son, Ulysses, died. William and Mary Smalley Rabb both died in 1831 and were buried on a hillside overlooking Rabb's Prairie in Fayette County, TX.
Patty Newman Turner, (GGGGD), 22512-S

WILLIAM RABB was born in 1770 in Fayette County, PA, to Andrew Rabb and Mary Scott. In 1803, William and his wife, Mary Smalley, started westward with their children into the Illinois Territory where they settled and built grist mills. In 1820, William moved his family to the south side of the Red River to the Jonesborough settlement in present day Red River County, TX. William, his sons and son-in-law, were members of Stephen F. Austin's Old Three Hundred Families.

William had an agreement with Stephen Austin to build a grist mill to serve the settlements in the upper portion of Austin's Colony and received a total of five sitios of land, 13,000 acres in Fayette County, TX, and 9,000 acres in Matagorda County, TX. The land grant was issued on July 19, 1824. William and Mary had five children: Rachel Rabb (born 1790) married Joseph Newman; Andrew (born 1792) married Margaret Ragsdale; John (born 1798) married Mary Crownover; Thomas (born 1801) married Serena Gilbert; and Ulysses (born 1803). William and Mary Smalley Rabb both died in 1831 and were buried on a hillside overlooking Rabb's Prairie in Fayette County, TX.
Patty Newman Turner, (GGGGD) 22510-S

JAMES RATLIFF was born in Virginia in 1780. Before emigrating to Texas on Jan. 11, 1840, he lived in Tennessee, Illinois, Arkansas and Missouri. His Texas land grant etitled him to 640 acres of land. He married Sarah Fisher about 1809 and they had eight children: Job (born Aug. 17, 1810 in Tennessee, died Sept. 18, 1898); Commack (born 1813 in Illinois) married Elizabeth Brock Jan. 22, 1835 in Missouri; James (born 1818 in Illinois) married first, Matilda Jameson and second, Charlotte Degraffenridge; Jesse Bean (born Dec. 15, 1825 in Arkansas) married Sarah Jane Farris Jan. 19, 1854. He served in the Caldwell County Texas Infantry of the Confederate States Army during the Civil War. He died May 31, 1902 and was buried in Llano County Six Mile Cemetery; Joshua (born 1829 in Arkansas, died 1852); Lavinia (born April 14, 1831, died March 6, 1896) married Henry Moses in 1845; Agnes, married Nov. 2, 1820 to William Stevens in Illinois; Matilda was born in Missouri).

In 1848, the family settled in Caldwell County. The 1850

census shows they lived in Prairie Lea. James died about 1852. His burial site is unknown.

Frances Maurine Perkins Godwin, (GGGGD), 20870-S

HERMAN LEE RAVEN

HERMAN LEE RAVEN was born Aug. 5, 1831, the first child of Ernst Raven and Johanne Friedricke Auguste Mentzel, and was baptised August 14 in the protestant parish of Gotha as Gustave Herman Leopold Raven.

Parents, Ernst and Auguste and family of four children being Herman age 6, Bertha age 4, Louise age 2 and Hugo age 6 months, lived in Gotha, Germany, then left on May 11, 1838 to come to America,

Gustave Herman Leopold Raven and Margaret Augusta Elizabeth Hamilton

and landed at Baltimore, MD Aug. 6, 1838.

In 1842, the family moved to McKean County, PA, only living there for two years, the family with an additional two small children left in route to the Republic of Texas, landing in 1844. From Galveston the family went by way of Houston to Robbins Ferry on the Trinity then to San Gabriel at the Mercer Fort and Caldwell, TX.

In the fall of 1847, the family moved to Cameron in Milam County and Herman at the age of 18 enlisted at Enchanted Rock in Capt. Sam Highsmith's Company, Bell's Regiment of Texas Mounted Volunteers on May 1, 1848 for a period of 12 months. This company of Texas Rangers was stationed opposite the little German settlement of Castell on the Llano River. The U.S. Government, Business Men of San Antonio and other places and interested citizens wanted a road established between El Paso and Chihuahua.

Capt. Highsmith's Rangers were to escort a volunteer party of about 35 men in this expedition which was known as the Chihuahua-El Paso Pioneer Expedition in 1848.

The troops were given rations for 30 days and pack mules, beginning their journey from Llano to Paint Rock Fork near the upper Nueces River to the San Carlos ranch across the Rio Grande in Mexico. The group started the return about November 1. Herman Lee was mustered out Dec. 26, 1848. He enlisted again on Nov. 5, 1850 serving under Capt. Henry L. McCullouch, where their central camp was between the Nueces and San Antonio, and this company was discharged at Fort Merrill on May 4, 1851 but reorganized the next day for another six months. New headquarters were established on the north branch of the Llano River. This Company began to recover stolen horses that a group of Indians had been robbing from the Mexicans as well as Texans. He later carried mail to Cameron, TX and was mustered out Nov. 5, 1851 at Fort Martin Scott.

He enlisted in the Ranger Company of Capt. Owen Shaw Aug. 18, 1852 on the Rio Grande and served six months. He also served in the Civil War as a Private in Co. G, Flournoy's Regiment under Capt. Fred W. Moore.

On Feb. 3, 1856, Herman L. Raven married Margaret A.E. Hamilton, born in Wilson County, TN, daughter of Samuel Hamilton and Sarah "Sally" B. Huguely, and they made their home on the farm near the Travis Williamson County line, where they had 15 children.

The children were Mary Ann (born 1856) married George Franklin Hamilton; Samuel Ernst (born 1857) married Martha Ann Wood; Bertha Sarah (born 1859) married E. Quince Thompson; Texanna Augusta (born 1864) married John Newton Thompson; Henry Hugo (born 1866) married Edith Josephine Wehrung; William Holt (born 1867) married Elnora Flint; infant (born 1869); Herman Lee (born 1871) married Lilla Fincher; Martha Eliza (born 1873) married Thomas Abel Sanders; Louisa Elizabeth (born 1875) married Ernest J. Pearson; Irene (born 1877) married Charles D. Pennington; Margaret Elizabeth (born 1879) married William Henry Spraggins; Rose Woodman (born 1882) married Robert A. Pennington.

Herman L. was a member of the M.E. Church for over a half century and died Feb. 1, 1905 and is buried beside his wife, Margaret who died July 23, 1890, in the Walnut Creek Baptist Church Cemetery in Austin.

ANSEL RED

ANSEL RED was born in 1816 in South Carolina and grew up in Georgia. He immigrated to Texas in February 1840 in response to the Republic of Texas offer for headright grants. He first received 640 acres, as a married man, in Nacogdoches District in a conditional headright grant dated Jan. 15, 1841. A second grant was issued in 1846. He purchased additional land in May 1851.

By 1850, Ansel and his first wife, Polly, had four children: Nancy, Samuel, Ansel Marion, and Osamus. Polly died in 1852 after giving birth to twin sons. William B. and William G. The beginnings of a heritage that continues today and began in the Piney Woods between the Neches and Angelina Rivers in what is now Angelina County. In the 1850 census, and those following, Ansel and his kin were identified as farmers in a land that would soon be known as "Redtown," a name that Pollok is known as today.

Ansel Marion Red and wife, Mary Luezer Alldredge Red

In 1860-62, Ansel Red served as county commissioner of Angelina County.

Ansel Red's date of death is not known. The last recorded date in his life occurred in 1879 when deeded a portion of his headright grant to his son, Ansel Marion, who owned and operated Red Ferry, a ferryboat crossing on the Neches River at Pollok for over 30 years. The 1880 census does not record Ansel's name and Anne, his second wife, is shown as the head of the family. Sixteen children were born to the household of Ansel Red. They established a legacy that was woven into the fabric of the Republic of Texas. *Submitted by Jan Cotten.*

Judith Ann Weeks Strickland (GGGGD) 21618
Jannis Colleen Allen Cotten (GGGGD) 21349

MATILDA (GAGE) REED

MATILDA (GAGE) REED was born in 1782 and was the wife of Jacob Reed of the Austin Colony. Their land grant was located south of the "Old San Antonio Road," between the Yegua

Creek and Brazos River. Matilda and Jacob were 49 years old when they arrived in Texas in May 1831, with five sons and five daughters. Matilda Reed probably died about 1864.

Matilda was a strong, compassionate frontier wife and mother. A story in the *Reminiscenes of Burleson County, TX*, tells about a Judge John Gregg, who settled on San Antonio Prairie, north of Reed's Creek. Gregg's family, who followed later, were attacked by Indians. His wife and a grown son were killed and scalped, and another son, Ellis, was wounded; the youngest son, Henry, was carried off by the savages. (Later Judge Gregg raised money to ransom Henry). Matilda Reed took Ellis and another surviving son, John, to nurse and clothe at her home.

The survivors had only the clothes they were wearing. Six spinning wheels, in the Reed neighborhood, hummed all day and late into the night making clothes for the unfortunate family.

For more on the family, refer to Jacob Reed, Vol. I. DRT, page 230.

WILSON REED, born Sept. 23, 1811 in Tennessee, was the son of Michael and Martha Reed. On his tombstone is written, "reached Texas April 6, 1831."

Wilson married Mary Ann Carter (born in Alabama about 1835). He and Mary Ann had seven children before she died in August 1857. John W. (born 1836), Geraldine 1837), Richard Carter (1840) Wiley (1843), William (1845), Annie Elizabeth (1849) and Wilson (1853).

Wilson's chief claim to fame came during his participation in what is called "The Battle of Horn Hill." The account of the battle follows as told by J.W. Baker in his book, *A History of Robertson County, TX*. "The Texans charged and the withering fire of the Indians drove them backward. The men were ordered to form a line on the open prairie but the order was misunderstood and taken as full retreat. As the Texans withdrew from the field, Indians charged from the woods, firing their guns and screaming a fierce battle cry. The Texans became disorganized and scattered through the area. Still the savages advanced, and the men were reduced to panic and forced to run for their lives. Wilson was knocked from his horse during the retreat by a tree. The Indians were close upon him coming at full speed, yelling and brandishing their tomahawks, he cried out "Lord boys, Mary Ann is a widow," but just then someone came riding by took him up and bore him off unhurt."

Wilson married a second time to Georgia Ann Bowman on April 11, 1958, and had seven children. Michael (born 1859), Lewis (1860 or 1861), Virginia (1863), Robert (1866), Justice (1869), Thomas (1872) and Franklin (1875).

Wilson died Dec. 21, 1883 and Georgia Ann July 2, 1902. They are buried in the Reed Family Plot located on a dairy farm in a grove of trees on Dilly Shaw Tap Road, northeast of Bryan, TX.

ELIZABETH WILSON RICE was born in Ireland in 1805. It is believed she emigrated to the United States with her parents about 1811 and settled in Ohio. Elizabeth married Thomas McClure Rice on Sept. 28, 1824 in Salem Township, Washington County, OH. They had five children: James (born 1828); Mary (born 1829) married Joseph Austin Newman, son of Joseph Newman and Rachel Rabb; Oliver Hugh (born 1830), married Adeline Courtney; William Wilson (born 1835) married

Nancy Ann Baker; and Thomas Richard (born 1842) married Martha Alexander.

Thomas applied for land from the Republic of Texas in 1838. On Sept. 18, 1842, Thomas Rice was killed by Mexican Troops on Salada Creek. He was serving with the Texas Army under Captain Nicholas Dawson. In 1848, the remains of the dead Texan heroes were removed from their shallow graves and taken to Fayette County, TX where on Sept. 18, 1848, a military burial took place. The tomb with the engraved names of the fallen soldiers is on a bluff overlooking the Colorado River at LaGrange and is called Monument Hill.

On April 12, 1847, Elizabeth Wilson Rice was granted an unconditional certificate for 640 acres of land in DeWitt County. On Nov. 18, 1854, she was awarded $80.75 from the state of Texas as payment for Thomas' horse and three weeks of military service to the Republic of Texas. Elizabeth never remarried. She died in 1858 and is believed to be buried in the Old Clinton Cemetery. In 1995, a historic marker honoring her was placed in the cemetery by her descendants.
Patty Newman Turner, (GGGD), 22514-S

OLIVER HUGH RICE, son of Thomas McClure and Elizabeth (Wilson) Rice, was born in Steubenville, Jefferson County, OH, in 1830. Oliver's parents brought their young family to Texas about 1838.

Oliver was 12 years old, in 1842, when his father was killed at the Battle of Salado Creek, near San Antonio. His mother raised Oliver, his sister, Mary, and three brothers, James, William and Thomas.

Adeline Prudence Courtney, daughter of Truman and Amanda (Garey) Courtney, was born 1839 in Courtland County, NY. Adeline's grandfather, Seymour Garey, was in Texas by about 1838. On March 23, 1854, Adeline Courtney and Oliver Rice were married. They had five children: Oren Adelbert, William Henry, Oliver Hugh, Amanda Elizabeth, and Mary Emiline (married James Milton Newman), all were born in DeWitt County.

Oliver died around 1861. After Oliver's death, Adeline married Abraham Bowen, and lived until 1909. Both Oliver and Adeline are buried in DeWitt County.
Betty Newman Wauer, (GGGD), pending

OLIVER HUGH RICE was born in 1830 in Steubenville, Jefferson County, OH. He emigrated to Texas with his parents, Thomas and Elizabeth Wilson, in 1838 when he was 8 years old. The family settled first in Fort Bend County, TX and then moved to Clinton, DeWitt County, TX.

In 1842 Oliver's father was killed in the Dawson Massacre at Salada Creek near San Antonio, Bexar County, TX. Oliver was only 12 years old at the time of his father's death. On March 23, 1854, Oliver married Adeline Prudence Courtney, daughter of Truman Courtney and Amanda Garey.

Adeline was born in 1839 in Cortland County, NY. After her father's death in 1851, the family emigrated to Texas from New York to join her grandfather, Seymour Garey, in DeWitt County, TX. Oliver and Adeline had five children: Oren Adelbert (born 1855) married Mary Alice Hodges; William Henry (born 1857) married Mary E. Karl; Oliver Hugh Jr., (born 1859); Amanda Elizabeth (born 1861) married James M. Wood; and Mary Emiline Rice (born 1866) married James Milton Newman, son of Joseph Austin Newman and Elizabeth Dedrick Baker.

Oliver died in 1868 and is believed to be buried in the Alexander Cemetery in DeWitt County. Adeline died in 1909 and is buried in the Alexander Cemetery.

Patty Newman Turner, (GGD), 22513-S

THOMAS MCCLURE RICE was born in Poultney, Rutland County, VT in 1801. In 1804 his parents, Nathan Rice and Jemima McClure moved the family to Ohio. Thomas married Elizabeth Wilson on Sept. 28, 1824 in Salem Township, Washington County, OH.

They had five children: James (born 1828); Mary (born 1829) married Joseph Austin Newman, son of Joseph Newman and Rachel Rabb; Oliver Hugh (born 1830) married Adeline Courtney; William Wilson (born 1835) married Nancy Ann Baker; and Thomas Richard (born 1842) married Martha Alexander.

Thomas applied for land from the Republic of Texas in 1838. On Sept. 18, 1842, Thomas was killed by Mexican Troops on Salada Creek. He was serving with the Texas Army under Captain Nicholas Dawson. In 1848, the remains of the dead Texan heroes were removed from their shallow graves and taken to Fayette County, TX where on Sept. 18, 1848, a military burial took place. The tomb with the engraved names of the fallen soldiers is on a bluff overlooking the Colorado River at LaGrange and is called Monument Hill. Elizabeth never remarried. She died in 1858 and is believed to be buried in the Old Clinton Cemetery.

Patty Newman Turner, (GGGD), 22511-S

JAMES AND MARY RICHARDSON migrated to Buna, Jasper County, TX, in 1839. They raised 12 children to maturity: Clarissa Richardson, James Marion Richardson, John Albritton Richardson, William Morris Richardson, Ann Richardson, Nancy Richardson, Stephen Richardson, Mary Elizabeth Richardson, Francis Richardson, Nathan Richardson, Durham Richardson, and Martha Jane Richardson. James and Mary were married on Oct. 11, 1828, in Simpson County, MS.

James' father, John Richardson, came to Texas also. They are buried in Antioch Cemetery near Buna, TX, in Jasper County. John was the first person to be buried in the Antioch Cemetery. His tombstone reads, "Pioneer of Texas" and "first buried in Antioch Cemetery," born March 1767 and died March 1850, age 83 years. James Richardson's tombstone gives his birthdate as July 2, 1806 and his death date as Oct. 31, 1866. Mary Morris' birth date is given as Jan. 2, 1815 and her death date as Sept. 19, 1887.

James Richardson and his father were instrumental in organizing the Antioch Primitive Baptist Church located near the cemetery. Durham Richardson (mentioned above) was a minister at the Antioch Church.

Two sons, John Albritton Richardson and William Morris Richardson, fought in the War Between the States.

Angela Farris Fannin, (GGGD), 8336

JOSHUA RICHARDSON SR., was born 1770-1780, probably in Virginia, the son of John Richardson. Mary "Polly" Cock, daughter of John Cock, was born circa 1785 in Virginia. They married Sept. 17, 1800 in Grayson County, VA. Their children were John, Jonathan, Lewis, Joshua Jr. (born March 20, 1809), Leticia, Rebecca and Thomas. Joshua Jr. married Elizabeth Harpool (born June 26, 1809 in Tennessee).

In 1845, the entire family came to Texas, forming the Richardson settlement in the Mercer Colony grant west of the Trinity River. In 1845 they moved east, building the first house in Corsicana. Joshua Sr. died there before 1850.

By 1856, the family moved in separate directions. In 1860, Lewis's family and Mary had moved to Johnson County. Joshua Jr. and family were living in Anderson County. Children of Joshua Jr. and Elizabeth were Sara Jane (born March 20, 1832 in Tennessee), William Louis, John Joshua, Rachel, Mary "Polly," Thomas, Elizabeth "Lydia" and James Preston.

James Irwin Rogers, born in Tennessee, came to East Texas in the 1840s. He and Sara Jane Richardson married Jan. 18, 1854 in Anderson County. They moved to Johnson County in 1856. Their children were John L., James J., Mary and Susan.

Nan White Morris, 15063

JAMES ANDREW JACKSON RICHEY, youngest son of Martha M. and John Richey, was born April 22, 1830, in Jefferson County, AL. His family moved to Texas before November 1839, applying for Republic of Texas land grants in Red River County.

Andrew Jackson's father died after he contracted a cold or pneumonia on this journey to Texas. Andrew Jackson Richey lived with his mother for a few years in Gilmer, TX. After his mother died about 1851, he moved to Hopkins County along with several of his siblings. As he grew older, he used the name Andrew Jackson Richey.

James Andrew Jackson Richey

Andrew met Sarah Ann Truitt, daughter of Wingate Truitt and Elizabeth J. Robinson of Dangerfield, Morris County, another Texas pioneer family who were associated with his father, John Richey. They married about 1855/56, and settled at Pine Forest, Hopkins County, where they purchased additional land from his father-in-law in 1871. They had seven children: Charles Warren, Elijah Truitt, James Albert, Nancy Ann, Andrew M., Joseph Perry and William Hervy.

Andrew was a farmer most of his life and served the confederacy as a shoemaker. He died on Jan. 29, 1911, and is buried at Omaha, TX.

Pamela Irene DeBaun, (GGGD). 14817-S

ELIHU JACKSON RIGGS was born Dec. 24, 1827 in Jackson, MS. He was the son of Lewis S. Riggs, born Oct. 1, 1797, died Feb. 6, 1860 and Edna Lassiter Riggs. Lewis S. and Edna Riggs had seven children.

Elihu Jackson Riggs married Martha Minerva Fitch (born Jan. 28, 1828 in South Carolina, died July 30, 1922). They were the parents of eight

Louis Washington Riggs and Mary Matilda Williams Riggs

children. After moving to Texas, Elihu Jackson Riggs became a Texas State Representative in Austin, TX during the late 1840s. He is listed in the Texas archives in Austin, TX. Elihu Jackson Riggs died June 29, 1912 and is buried at Pilot Grove Cemetery between Yoakum and Sweethome, TX. His wife Martha is buried there also.

One of Elihu Riggs' sons was Louis Washington Riggs (born March 27, 1855 in Hampton, AR. After moving to Texas, he married Matilda Williams (born May 26, 1853), daughter of James A. Williams and Mary Hodges Williams. Louis Washington Riggs was a Justice of the Peace and Constable in Hope and Yoakum, TX. Louis would perform weddings day and night. Louis Washington and Mary Matilda Riggs had six children. The youngest was Louis Emma Riggs, my mother, who weighed only one pound when she was born and slept in a shoe box. Her oldest sister's wedding ring would fit on her arm. Louis Emma married Vernon James Sawey in Yoakum, TX and had six children.

Louis Washington loved to play the violin for his family. Louis Washington Riggs was shot while on duty as constable and died Jan. 5, 1917. The killer was not apprehended. His wife died Nov. 19, 1909. They are both buried at Pilot Grove Cemetery.

Hazel Sawey Duncan, (GD)

JAMES W. RILEY was born in the year 1800 in the state of Kentucky. His wife, Sarah Jane (McKendree) was born in Tennessee; the place of their marriage is unknown. The 1850 census of Travis County, TX lists the family with 10 children. The three oldest children: William McKendree, Delfia and James C. were born in Greene County, IN. David, George and Richard were born in Illinois; Sarah and Mary were born in Missouri and the last two children, Phebe and John, were born in Texas.

In May 1841, during the time that Texas was a Republic, the Riley family with their 10 children arrived in Lamar County, TX where they obtained a conditional land grant for 640 acres. In 1849 the family moved to Travis County, TX were they bought land on the east side of the Colorado River, approximately four miles north of the city of Austin. In 1852 the family came to Llano County, TX and settled on Honey Creek in the area which is now known as Riley Mountain. All of this family lived on Riley Mountain; some made their permanent home there; other family members lived in the city of Llano.

Marriages: William McKenree Riley married Clementine Dancer; Delfia Riley married William Hadley; James C. Riley married Mississippi Elles Moore; David Riley married Mary Jane McClain; George Riley married Nancy Leverett; Richard Riley married Sally Barnes; Sarah Riley married F.C. Stewart; Mary Riley married James C. Leverett; Phebe Riley married Hiram Ward; John Riley married Nancy Katherine Prince.

Captain Richard Riley helped organize the Llano State Guard in 1861; William Riley also served in the State Guard as well as in the Mexican American War (1848). James, George and John enlisted under Captain James Bourland in the 31st Brigade of the Texas Frontier Army and served two stints in 1863 and 1864.

For further information on this family, see Llano County History Book.

Jo Ann Riley Cook
Dorothy Riley Creasey.

SARAH ANN STILLWELL RILEY, born Dec. 12, 1823 in Georgia, was the daughter of Elizabeth Evans and Green Lewis Stillwell. The family moved to Walker County, TX in 1839 where Green Lewis received a 620 acre headright land grant.

In the late 1840s, Sarah married John Thornton Clark, M.D. and moved to Woodville, Liberty County, TX where Dr. Clark practiced medicine until his early death in 1854. Their only child, John Thornton Clark Jr., was born July 11, 1850. Sarah returned to live with her parents in Walker County and joined them in a move to Freestone County in 1855.

Sarah Ann Stillwell, circa 1865

In 1856, Sarah married Roderick Oliver Sr. who died in 1857. Rodrick Oliver Jr. was born in 1858, after his father's death. In 1859, Sarah married Lewis Mitchell Riley who was killed in battle during the War Between the States. Their only child, a son, died in infancy. Again, Sarah returned to her people until her two sons were educated and married. Her sons married sisters: John Clark Jr. married Martha Catherine Allbritton on Oct. 2, 1881 and Roderick Oliver Jr. married Susan Elvira Albritton in 1882.

In 1888, Sarah, her two sons, their spouses and collective six children moved to Clay County, TX. Sarah died Jan. 29, 1893 and is buried in Antelope Cemetery, Clay County.

Sarah's parents gave her a Robert Nunns, Clarke & Co. piano that was built in New York in 1831, shipped to the port of New Orleans and overland to Walker County by oxen wagon. This fine instrument made all the moves with Sarah and upon her death, was handed down to the eldest son of each generation. It is presently owned by James Terrell Clark Jr.

Martha and John, listed above, had two sons born in Limestone County, TX. They were Shellie Thornton (born on Sept. 22, 1884) and William Briscoe (born Feb. 3, 1888). Shellie married Portia Fry on Dec. 25, 1904. Her parents were Jesse Fry and Jemima McCormick Fry and was born Feb. 14, 1886 in Denton County. Their children were James Terrell who married Grace Shockley; Eliza who married Edgar Shockley; John Howard who married Vera Horn; and Nina Fay who married Herman Whitsitt.

James Terrell and Grace Shockley were married Dec. 22, 1923. Charles and Georgia Anna Taylor Shockley were her parents and she was born March 7, 1907. They had six children: Billie Louise who married Jefferson Davis Williams; Bobbie Geauviene married Dr. Charles Hollingsworth; Shellie Terrell died in infancy; James Terrell Jr. married Wanda Sanderson; Iris Yvonne married Jack McCabe; and Charles married Nina Smith.

Sarah was dauntless, resolute and devoted wife and mother who exemplified all traits required in surviving the exigencies of the frontier.

Bobbie C. Hollingsworth, (GGGD), 17754

EVERETT S. RITTER was born 1810 in Alabama. He married Anna Goodwin, born 1810 in Tennessee, the daughter of Henry Goodwin in Hardeman County, TN on May 15, 1828. Everett and Anna arrived in Shelby County, TX by 1831. Later they settled in Panola County.

Everett S. served in Capt. Hooper's Company (Calvary) of

San Augustine County, TX as 2nd lieutenant during the Texas Revolution in 1836. He later served as private in the Mexican War of 1846 in Middleton T. Johnson's Company.

During the Moderator-Regulator Wars of Texas, Everett was a member of the Moderators. E. Ritter is on a list of men proscribed by Moorman (Regulator) at a meeting of the Provisional Committee of the Regulators held on July 28, 1844. This list of men was given notice to leave the county within 15 days of the meeting. Everett S. died in Texas in 1873, obviously never leaving Texas.

Everett S. and Anna raised eight children: Martha Jane (born 1832); William A. (born about 1833) married Mary Tabitha Sample, daughter of John B. Sample and Sarah Davis in 1856; Benjamin Franklin Ritter (born 1834); Elizabeth (born 1836); James Henry (born November 1842); Mary F. (born 1847); Susan Caroline (born 1848); and Everett S. (born October 1848).

Anna died before 1868 and Everett S. died in Van Zandt County, TX on Dec. 4, 1873. The exact location of their burial is unknown.

NANCY NETTIE ROBERTS

NANCY NETTIE ROBERTS was the daughter of David Roberts. David enlisted in the Texas Army under Sam Houston and was with him throughout his campaign for Texas Independence. He served in Capt. Benjamin F. Bryant's Co. and fought in the Battle of San Jacinto. He received a land grant in Anderson County for his service in the army.

David met Eliza Jane Marshall and they were married Aug. 17, 1843. The children of David and Eliza Jane were William A., John A., Luke A., Mary, Sarah Jane, Julia Hope, Ann Eliza and David Franklin (twins); and the youngest Nancy Nettie. Because of the unrest in East Texas after the Civil War, David purchased land in Johnson County, TX, near Alvarado. He was supposed to occupy this land by Jan. 1, 1871. He loaded his family and their possessions in one wagon with two yoke of oxen hitched to it. At the end of the ninth day, they were still a good day journey from their destination. David got the family up early and by hard driving of the sore-footed oxen they made it by nightfall on December 31.

Nettie grew up there, met and married John W. Carter on Jan. 31, 1883. They had three children: Lester, Vera Roney and Alma King. Nettie was a Real Daughter of the DRT. She had two daughters, Vera and Alma; three granddaughters: Mary Turner, Ruth Peek and Julia Williams; three great-granddaughters: Nettie Glidewell, Mary Ann Shawver and Sherry King; and one great-great-grand daughter, Julie Eghbal, all of which are members of the DRT.
Sherry Lynn King, #008154, (9/73)

EPHRAIM RODDY

EPHRAIM RODDY was of Irish stock. His father, John Roddy, had married Elizabeth Jameson in Cork, Ireland and they emigrated in 1785 to the Susquehanna Valley in Pennsylvania, where Ephraim Roddy was born in 1786.

Young Ephraim was an apt pupil in school, and was a boy with a love for adventure. He was delighted when in the year 1800, as a lad of 14, he was allowed to accompany his father back to Pennsylvania to finish up some business. On their journey by private conveyance, they stopped in Washington and met President Thomas Jefferson. Ephrain was charmed by the affable manner of the red-haired Virginian.

As he neared maturity Ephraim, decided to become an attorney. Ephraim graduated in law at the South Carolina State University. He served in the U.S. Army at which time he won a commission as major.

Joseph B. Roddy, son of Ephraim

In 1819, Major Roddy married Harriet Harrison Earle, youngest daughter of Col. John Earle, South Carolina planter and Revolutionary soldier. Ephraim's adventurous spirit was aroused during the westward movement and he moved his family in a covered wagon to Texas in the summer of 1831. The Roddy's moved to San Felipede, Austin where his son, Joseph Berry Roddy, was born on July 20, 1831. Major Roddy took up the practice of law and was intimately acquainted with Travis, Crockett and Bowie.

Ephraim Roddy was a delegate to the convention in 1833. Ephraim and Harriet Roddy are buried in the Liberty Hill Cemetery.
Glyn Roddy Miller, (GGD), 19808

PATTERSON ROGERS

PATTERSON ROGERS was born 1790 in Virginia, the son of James R. Rogers. He grew up in East Tennessee where he served his country in the War of 1812. He married Elizabeth Blair Long in Roane County, TN on Jan. 21, 1815. Of their 12 children, 10 lived to maturity: Anderson W., Mary, Lieuen Morgan, William Long, Bethany, Louisa Jane, Patterson Columbus, Washington Clark, Emeline Nancy and Ann Elbe.

By 1817, Patterson, Elizabeth and infant son, Anderson, had moved to Alabama, where the other children were born. They lived in Hayneville, AL until the spring of 1836 when they arrived in Texas soon after the battle of San Jacinto. Because of the unsettled state of affairs in the young Republic, Patterson moved his family to Ft. Jessup, near Many, LA. In August 1845, Patterson arrived in Corpus Christi, TX with Gen. Zachary Taylor's Army. He purchased land on Feb. 2, 1846 and moved his family from Louisiana.

On May 1, 1846, Patterson, his sons, Anderson and William, and 19 others were traveling to Fort Brown in Brownsville, TX with supplies for Gen. Taylor when they were attacked by a land of bandits. The thieves slashed the throats of all and hurled their bodies into the waters of the Arroyo Colorado near the town of Harlingen. William Long Rogers miraculously survived and lived a long life in south Texas.
Ann Bailey Fisher, (GGGGD), 20752

JOHANN HEINRICH (HENRY) RUNGE

JOHANN HEINRICH (HENRY) RUNGE was born in Bremen, Germany, April 11, 1816, the first of seven children of Johann Heinrich Runge (1784-1862) and Catherine Louise Tideman (1794-1861). Henry's siblings were: Daniel (1817-1836), George Heinrich (1819-1852), Herman Arnold Heinrich (1821-1871), Marie Louise Elizabeth (1822- 1825), Margaret Tibetha (1824-1901), and Albert Benjamin (1826-1902). The families were merchants and merchant ship owners.

During the 1830s the economic climate in Germany was burdened with restrictions which constrained commerce (exclusive rights for a territory or maintenance of artisan guilds). Merchants with little capital ventured overseas. When he was 20, he came to

Baltimore on one of the Tideman ships. He relocated to New Orleans in 1841. In 1845, he joined the German Immigration Company and relocated to Indianola and/or Indian Point. That year also, as H. Runge and Co. he opened, in a tent, the first unincorporated private bank in Texas. Through the years he was involved in numerous enterprises and partnerships i.e., a wharf to dock the ships, a supply company to provide mules, harness and drygoods, a railroad to move goods and people inland, as well as banking and shipping. He was consul to Texas from Hamburg from 1851 to 1866.

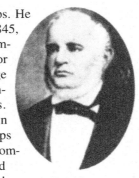

Henry Runge

During the Civil War, Federal troops took possession of the company warehouse and used it as a commissary. He moved inland and set up a cotton textile mill in New Braunfels. It was destroyed by a tornado in 1869. He returned to Indianola and then Galveston where he was managing partner of Kauffman and Runge, importers of coffee, spirits and provisions and major cotton merchants.

At age 35, in Indianola he married Julia Hornung (born April 9, 1834 in Hildesheim, Germany). Their children were: Louise (1853-1853), Johanne (1856-1933), Meta (1857-1910), Henry John (1859-1922), Louis Hermann (1861-1936), and Anna Rosa (1865-1945).

At the time of his death, *The Galveston News* stated that "In every public enterprise he was among the foremost and most liberal; in his private charities he was discriminating and generous. He had a clear perception of justice and strong sense of duty."

Henry Runge died in Galveston, TX on March 16, 1873, and is buried in Galveston Cemetery. Julia Runge died on July 27, 1895, in Hanover, Germany and is buried there.

Anita Runge Moore, (GGD)

THOMAS JEFFERSON RUSK and Mary F. Cleveland married Jan. 4, 1827 at Clarksville, GA and settled in Nacogdoches in 1834. Thomas J., a lawyer and citizen of Texas by 1835, became actively involved with the affairs of his adopted homeland and was identified with many important events of Texas from colony to statehood. His wife, Mary, daughter of Gen. Benjamin Cleveland, was equally dedicated in her role as caretaker of their home and family until she died in 1856. Thomas J., having held many offices in the governemnt of the Republic of Texas, served as the new state's senator to the U.S. Congress from 1845 until his untimely death in 1857.

Thomas David Rusk, son of Mary and T.J. Rusk, born April 3, 1841 in Nacogdoches, married Susan M. Hunter on Oct. 27, 1859. Thomas J. Rusk II, son of Thomas D. and Susan Rusk, born Dec. 3, 1860 in Nacogdoches, married Martha J. Hardegree on May 24, 1883 in Van Zandt County, TX. James Franklin Rusk, son of Thomas J. Rusk II, born Dec. 17, 1890 in Van Zandt County, TX., married Eva Victoria Evans on Dec. 7, 1913 at Bruno, Atoka County, OK. Their children are Nora Nadine Taylor, Linuel Henry Rusk, Mildred Rhea Curtis, Moahdeena Thomas, Eulilia June Clay. Mary Ruth, youngest daughter of Eva and James F. Rusk, born June 21, 1929 at Elk City, OK, married Andrew Lee Woodward on Aug. 27, 1949 at Arlington, TX. Karan Lou, daughter of Mary R. and Andrew Woodward, born Oct. 10, 1950 married

General Billy J. Boles (USAF, Ret) on July 5, 1890 at Hampton, VA. Kyle Andrew Woodward, son of Mary R. and Andrew Woodward, born Sept. 4, 1954, married Suzanne Wolgast on Aug. 9, 1980 at Buffalo, NY. Children of Suzanne and Kyle A. Woodward are Scott Andrew Woodward, born June 25, 1993 at Vista, CA., and Sarah Grace Woodward, born Nov. 20, 1995 at Vista, CA.

Mary Ruth Rusk Woodward, (GGGD), 19668

JOHN WESLEY "WES" SCALLORN, oldest son of Stephen W. Scallorn and Mary "Polly" McClure Scallorn, was born in Tennessee on Oct. 3, 1812. Stephen Scallorn born Feb. 23, 1787, Maryland, married Polly McClure in Kentucky on Feb. 14, 1811. The family moved to Alabama then to Haywood County, TN, where Stephen was a practicing physician. Polly Scallorn died March 10, 1833, soon after the birth of her 11th child. Stephen married Martha Bullock April 23, 1834 in Tennessee. They came to Texas in 1838 with all children except John Wesley who had come earlier. Stephen's brother William and his wife Allis McClure Scallorn and children came with the Stephen Scallorn family. Stephen Scallorn died Dec. 24, 1887. He is honored with a Texas Historical Marker located near Upton in Bastrop County, TX.

John Wesley "Wes" Scallorn had come to Texas in 1834 with his mother's sisters and their families. They were Elizabeth McClure and husband, Noah Karnes, and Ada McClure and husband, William A. Faires. The families settled in Fayette County. Wes fought in the Battle of San Jacinto on April 21, 1836. He married Mariam Speir in Fayette County on June 20, 1839. Their home was in Scallorn Prairie, near Plum, TX.

George W. Speir, Mariam Scallorn's father, and family, were in Texas sometime before 1835. He served in the Federal Army of Texas in December 1835, in San Antonio. He was elected a land commissioner for the county of Mina (Bastrop) and a Justice of the Peace in 1835. He died Dec. 29, 1838, and is buried in Criswell/Old Plum Grove Cemetery, West Point, TX.

Wes Scallorn was a Fayette County surveyor (elected 1840). He was a young man who stood up for what he thought was right and with the help of Speir's widow, Rebecca J. Speir, he drafted a long petition assisting and defending a landowner with an unfair title problem with his land. He was successful.

In September 1842, Wes Scallorn and younger brother, Elam, joined Nicholas Dawson and other Fayette County men. They were killed in the massacre on Sept. 18, 1842 on Salado Creek near San Antonio. They are buried in the tomb on the bluff overlooking the city of LaGrange, TX. Mariam Scallorn later remarried T.J. Scallorn, first cousin of Wes Scallorn. She had two daughters by him. Mariam died in July 1850 and is buried in Criswell/Old Plum Grove Cemetery near her father, George Speir and stepmother, Rebecca Speir.

Mariam Scallorn had only one child by her first husband, John Wesley Scallorn. He was George Wesley Scallorn, born Oct. 18, 1840. George married Missouri Ann Huff July 4, 1861 in Fayette County, TX. Missouri Ann was the youngest daughter of Henry and Elizabeth Young Huff, and granddaughter of Samuel and Jane Kerr Young. George and Missouri Ann Scallorn's children were George Franklin, Elizabeth, Alice, Wesley, Alameda Josephine (mine), Florence and Minnie. Missouri Ann died in the fall of 1875 when her daughter, Minnie was a baby. She is buried in Woods Prairie Cemetery, Fayette County, beside her parents.

George W. Scallorn, his father and grandfathers, were held in high esteem. George died in Atascosa County, TX on May 20, 1912, and is buried in Shiloh Cemetery. His grave is nicely marked, but his birth date is wrong. A Civil War veteran, his tombstone needs to be corrected and replaced with a Civil War marker.
Josephine Ella White, (GGGD), DRT #6431

STEPHEN SCALLORN,

The nation was in its infancy. George Washington had not yet been elected president and would not be for another two years. In the lush, fertile plantation country of St. Mary's County, MD, a son was born to John and Judith Scallorn. Stephen W. Scallorn was born Feb. 23, 1787, the sixth child of the pioneer family.

The family migrated from Maryland through North Carolina, Kentucky, Alabama, Tennesse and finally, Texas. Stephen W. married his first wife, Mary McClure on Feb. 14, 1811 in Kentucky. Stephen W. took up the practice of medicine which he would continue for the next 25 years. It is unknown how he acquired his medical training.

After the death of the patriarch, John Sr., the families of Peter, Stephen W. and William moved on to Fayette and Haywood counties in Tennessee. It was there Stephen's first wife, Mary McClure Scallorn, died March 10, 1833. On April 23, 1834, Stephen W. married Martha Bullock.

Two of Stephen's sons, John Wesley and Elam Scallorn, with some McClures and Faires made the trip to Texas in 1834-35. The families of William and Stephen followed shortly thereafter. Moving on foot and in covered wagons, they followed the Natchez Trace in Texas arriving in 1838. The colony included the Scallorns, Karnes and Faires. The families settled in Fayette County, TX.

Stephen Scallorn was instrumental in organizing five Primitive Baptist Churches in Texas. He died Dec. 25, 1887 at age 100 yrs. and 10 months. He is buried near Upton, TX. Stephen fathered 11 children by his first wife, Mary, and three children by his second wife, Martha. John Wesley and Elam perished during a Mexican attack on Dawson's men at Salado, TX on Sept. 18, 1842. Many Scallorn descendants reside in Texas and are leaders in their churches and communities.
Elinor F. Scallorn Clausen, (GGGD), #15625

JOHANN AUGUST SCHAPER,

son of Friederich and Justine Flagge, born Sept. 19, 1826 in Breman, Germany. He married Louisa A. Ludwig. They had seven children: August Schaper, married Ida Gohlke, died 1896 in DeWitt County; Louis Schaper, born 1856 in Texas; Lizette Schaper, born June 26, 1858, died June 11, 1944, married William Stein Jr.; William Frank Schaper, born Dec. 7, 1860, died Dec. 11, 1891, married Wilhelmina Dorotea Elizabet Muennink, born circa July 1862; Dan Schaper, born Nov. 15, 1864, married Augusta Mertz, died Jan. 25, 1949; Martha Schaper, born Sept. 5, 1873, died Dec. 24, 1892, married Henry Mertz; Henry, born June 21, 1878, died April 22, 1916. Johann served in the Methodist German Conference 1881. In 1858

Headstone of Johann August Schaper located in Elm Creek Cemetery.

he established my church, New Fountain Methodist Church, near Quihi, TX.

Texas Historical marker denotes his achievements. Johann died Oct. 8, 1912 and Louisa died Oct. 20, 1920, both are buried in the family plot with two children, Elm Creek Methodist Cemetery in Guadalupe County, Sequin, TX.

William Frank Schaper, listed above, married Mina Muennink, Nov. 6, 1880 in Medina County, daughter of Friedrich Frerichs Muennink and Antje Frieden Schoon. They had eight children: Louisa, born September 1881, married Albert Leifeste; Fred, born February 1883; Anna Catherine, born March 16, 1884, died May 1, 1959, married Albert John Weigand on Jan. 20, 1910. My paternal grandparents are buried in San Jose Cemetery, San Antonio; Lydia, born January 1887, died Aug. 27, 1970, married John Joseph Lawler, buried Sacramento, CA; Willie, born June 1888 in Texas; Malinda, born Sept. 11, 1889, died Dec. 31, 1951, married Henry F. Vordenbaum, son of Friedrich Vordenbaum and Anna Louisa Friedhoff. Second marriage to Oscar A. Schumann, son of Carl C. Schumann and Wilhelmina Orth; Hilda, born July 2, 1891, died March 1975.
Mitzie Lee Weigand Powell, (GGGD), 22474

JOHANN (JOHN) FREDERICK SCHLOBOHM,

born in Germany, emigrated to Texas in 1825 (Legend: He swam ashore in Galveston along with a cousin who had deserted the German army. The cousin later moved to Alaska then China). The Texas Revolution Muster Rolls of Captain Chenoweth's Company lists John Schlabohn (Schlaboher) (Schlabeaum) (Schlabaum) as enrolling April 27, 1835. On Dec. 8, 1835, John enlisted in the Army of the Texas Revolution under the command of Captain S.C. Hiram (Hirom). (Legend: John fought in five major battles and served the duration, 1835-45, when Texas joined the Union.) In 1838, John

John Frederick Schlobohm and Charlotte Caroline Kleibrink, circa 1850.

was granted a Headright Certificate for 1/3 league of land by the Liberty County Board.

The Muster Roll of Volunteers from the Municipal of Liberty and bound for the Army before San Antonio includes John Slayton (Slighton), private under Captain William Logan. (Legend: John fought in the battle of Bexar.) The Battle of San Jacinto includes John Slighton, Private serving under William Logan, Captain of 2nd Regiment. (Legend: John guarded Santa Anna from the time of Santa Anna's capture in the field through the first night of the capture.)

On May 10, 1836 quartered near Harrisburg, as a member of Captain Logan's Company, John Slighton received his share of the spoils taken at the battle of San Jacinto. Muster rolls of Zavalla Volunteers at Camp Johnson on Sept. 30, 1836 includes John Schlabeaum, Private.

John (Sleighburn) Schlobohm married Charlotte Caroline Kleibrink on May 2, 1850 in Harris County, TX in the home of Peter Dykerman. Caroline was born in Germany in 1824. The original home section of Schlobohm family is north of Lauder Road just a short distance west of Brookside Cemetery. John and Caroline had seven children: Mary married William Edward Morin; John Frederick married Katherine Kuehnle; Wilhelmia married Adolph Schuller; William Henry married Clara Jane Marshall; Fredericka died at age 13 and is the first person buried in Schlobohm Cemetery in Aldine, TX; Margaret Darlye married Francis Marion Dobbs; Louise Jane married James Jefferson Ferrell; Margaret Louise married Jacob Brown Autry.

The 1850 Census of Harris County lists John Staben with farmer being his occupation. John died Sept. 25, 1882; Charlotte Caroline died Jan. 18, 1886. Both are buried in the Schlobohm Family Cemetery located near the intersection of Interstate 59 and Lauder Road, Aldine, TX.

Thelma Cole Morgan, (GGD)
Frances Nicol Wiles, (GGD)
Alma Nicol Nagy, (GGD)
Cheryl Wiles Peters, (GGGD)

CATHERINE SCHOTT

CATHERINE SCHOTT was the child of Antoine Schott. She died in 1872, since we do not know when she was born, we do not know her age at death. She is the great-great-grandmother of Gladys Marie Tondre Clark. She came to the United States from Anvers, France, on the Probus Ship, according to the ship list numbers 53. She received land as a land entitlement from the state of Texas by virtue of a colonization contract. She was married to my great-great-great grandfather, Joseph Meyer.

Five of their seven children came with them. There two older daughters came over with Meyer kinfolk. They were the first of our family to come to Texas. They got off the ship in New Orleans and came the rest of the way overland to Texas. In 1845, one of their daughters, Catherine, married Nicholas Tschirhart. They got a marriage liscense in Bexar County, thus establishing that the family was in Texas by that date. The other five children's names were Erasmus, Michael, Josephine, Edward and Theresa.

Gladys Marie Tondre Clark, (GGG), 19509
Betty Marie Clark, (GGGGGG), 20251
Debra Ann Clark Goar, (GGGGGG), 19521

ANNA "AMY" W. SHACKELFORD

ANNA "AMY" W. SHACKELFORD was the oldest child of Daniel and Tabitha Nance Shackelford. Amy was born ca. 1800 in Virginia, before the emigration of the Shackelfords and others from Henry County. Her marriage to James B. Wills in Rutherford County, TN was probably in 1816.

Amy's father and her husband are listed on the Assessors List for 1821 in the Ray County, MO Courthouse (back of the first page of the first record book). Other records - plat books of Clay County, MO, show seven land acquisitions of James B. and Amy Wills.

Mary "Mollie" Emaline Wills, granddaughter, and husband George Rufuas Sanderford, July 28, 1887.

Their 640 acre land grant (Cert. #118 dated Feb. 12, 1844 (Feb. 27), was about six miles south of the Three Forks Little River (land situated on Daris Creek). It was issued by the Board of Land Commissioners in Washington County. Field notes are dated July 8, 1845; Patent is dated July 5, 1849. This is now Bell County. Narrative for James

B. Wills covers childrens names and more Texas history of the family.
Mary Lou Sanderford Smith, (GGGD), #21619-S

THOMAS P. SHAPARD

THOMAS P. SHAPARD, son of Lewis Thomas and Martha (Paine) Shapard, was born July 22, 1811 in Caswell, NC. He married Ann Hope on May 31, 1838 in Washington County, Republic of Texas. Ann, the daughter of James Hope, one of the original "Three Hundred" of Stephen F. Austin's colonists, was born Feb. 7, 1821, St. Francisville, LA. Her brothers, Adolphus, Richard, and Prosper fought in the battle of San Jacinto.

Thomas and Ann had six children: Eleanor "Ellen," born Sept. 24, 1839, married Alexander Cooke; Amanda, born Sept. 24, 1841, died October 1842; Martha, born Dec. 9, 1844, married Thomas Eanes; Annie, an educator and unmarried, born Aug. 13, 1852; Mary Catherine, born Dec. 11, 1854 married W.A. Thomson; and Richard R. Peebles, a physician, born June 13, 1858, married Mallie Lewis.

Thomas was an active attorney in the firm of Hood and Shapard in the early days of Texas. He was also a land agent and property owner and was politically active as a citizen. He served in the Republic of Texas Army in 1836. Thomas died June 3, 1859 in Hempstead, TX and Ann died Jan. 3, 1870 in Bryan, TX.
Billie Cook Bailey, (GGGGD), 22072

ELVEY ANDERSON SHEPPARD

ELVEY ANDERSON SHEPPARD, (1779-1860), daughter of Elijah Anderson, soldier of American Revolution, and Elvina Brack, born 1779 in Onslow County, NC. Elvey married William Shepperd in a double ring ceremony with her cousin, Jean Triplett and her husband, Lewis Lee of Jefferson County, GA.

William and Elvey were parents of 11 children. They were born in Georgia, some in Richmond County and others in Jefferson County.

Marker moved from Gay Cemetery to historic homestead site where John Ben Shepperd and his parents are burried.

1) Charity Shepperd, born in December 1802, died in September 1876, married Nathaniel Bonham;

2) Elizabeth Shepperd, born June 10, 1804, died Feb. 12, 1869, married Robert Brady;

3) William Shepperd Jr., born Dec. 10, 1807, married first, Mary Barnes (died between 1842 and 1848) and second, Rebecca F. Porter on May 12, 1848;

4) Lavinia Mildred Shepperd, born in 1810 in Georgia, died in 1850 in Upshur County, TX, married Mason Moseley;

5) Mary (Polly) Shepperd, born April 12, 1812 in Georgia, died March 28, 1862 in Upshur County, TX, married William Phillips;

6) Elijah Byrd Shepperd, born April 12, 1812, a twin to Mary, married first, Martha Mings and second, Frances W. Machey;

7) Elisha Eleazor Shepperd, born March 4, 1815 in Richmond County, GA, died in December 1851 in the Red Rock Community, Upshur County, TX, married Sept. 5, 1832 to Mary Ann Butler;

8) Alfred Fulton Shepperd, born Nov. 13, 1817 in Georgia,

died July 24, 1876 in Upshur County, TX, married Jan. 11, 1843 to Elverse Hardin;

9) Robert Alexander Shepperd, born Oct. 20, 1819, died Jan. 27 in Falls County, TX, married Louisa Ann Hogan;

10) Elvey Shepperd is named in probate records, but nothing else is known;

11) Allen Marin Shepperd, born 1823, died 1868, married Jane Anderson.

William Shepperd died in 1828 in Montgomery County, AL. Some report that a tree fell on him while others say he was killed by a negro.

Elvey Shepperd led her family to Texas in 1845, where with the help of sons and slaves, she built one of the first homes in Upshur County. It was a log cabin that stood for 100 years.

Elvey Shepperd died April 1860 in Upshur County, TX and is buried in the Gay Cemetery in Gladewater, TX.
Sue Marie Kennamer Triplett, (GGGGD), 019583

OTTO SICKENBERGER,

son of Wallenstine Sickenberger and wife, Catherine Felghan, migrated from Germany to America in 1837 at the age of 29. On Feb. 6, 1839, he married in West Feliciana Parish, LA to Miss Catherine Grace. Catherine was born March 15, 1807 at Castlecomer, Kilkenny County, Ireland to Joseph Grace and Mary Crenan.

Sickenberger was a cattle raiser and stockman and at once plunged into his calling. In 1841, he, with wife Catherine and daughter Mary Catherine, moved to Nacogdoches County, TX. On July 13, 1846, he was elected and served as Angelina County Coroner and from 1848-52 as Angelina County Commissioner.

Mary Catherine Sickenberger Bell, daughter of Catherine and Otto Sickenberger.

In 1857, Sickenberger moved to Cherokee County, near Rusk, TX. Having acquired considerable money in the livestock business, he was able at once to purchase considerable property and embark again into his favorite pursuit.

Otto Sickenberger and wife, Catherine, had three children: Mary Catherine Sickenberger Bell, Julia Victoria Sickenberger Jensen, and Joseph Valentine Sickenberger. He raised his family near Rusk, TX and lived there until his death in August 1860. His wife died Nov. 27, 1891. They are both buried on Highway 69 near Rusk.
DeLayne Fay Wojtkiewicz Maxwell, (GGGGD), 22015-S

JANE MERCER BROOKS SIMPSON

was born in 1800 in North Carolina to John Dimmaux Brooks and Rebecca Boyd McKaughan Brooks. Her parents' home was in Jackson County, TN, near the Cumberland River. She met John Jordan Simpson who had family near the Cumberland River in Kentucky, and they married in 1816 in North Carolina.

Jane and John Simpson had 10 children: the first four were born before the family arrived in Texas. Jane Caroline, the fourth child, was born "on the way to Texas." The other six children were born at the family plantation, Oak Forest. Mary Brooks married first, T.Y. Buford and second, Capt. W.R. Buford; Will-

iam Mercer married Letitia Buford; Jane Caroline married Albert Aldrich Nelson; Victor Jefferson married first, Harriet Arnold and second, Nannie Gilkerson; Frances Augusta married Col. Conde Raguet; Sarah Emily married Gen. J.S. Griffith; Florence Rosalie married Capt. Augustus D. Edwards; Augustus Irion married Emma Kyle.

There is a family story telling of Jane's taking the children into the forest to hide from marauding Indians. She died June 1, 1865 on a visit into Nacogdoches and is buried at Oak Grove Cemetery.
Mary Louise Anderson Smith, (GGGD). 22001-S
Bertha Elizabeth Anderson Carmichael, (GGGD), 20719

JOHN JORDAN SIMPSON

was born 1798 in Craven County, SC. He was the son of Mary and William Simpson and grandson of William and Christian Simpson, immigrants from Ulster, northern Ireland. As a child his family moved to Kentucky and then Tennessee.

John J. married Jane Mercer Brooks of Jackson County, TN in Chatham County, NC in 1816. They had 10 children: Mary Brooks, born 1817; William Mercer, born 1819; John Jr., born 1818; Jane Caroline, born 1825; Victor Jefferson, born 1829; Frances Augusta, born 1831; Sarah Emily, born 1833; Florence Rosalie, born 1835; Augustus Irion, born 1839; Isaac Jefferson, born 1841. The last six children were born at the family home, Oak Forest Plantation, east of Nacogdoches on the King's Highway.

John J. Simpson received a Headright on the west bank of the Trinity River in the Liberty District. He owned land in the Red River and Fannin Districts, Kaufman County, Van Zandt County, and five million acres in Nacogdoches County. He built the first hotel, the Planters Hotel, in Nacogdoches. The hotel also served as a home in town for his family. As devoted Methodists, John and Jane gave land known as Simpson Campground to the Methodist Church.

John J. Simpson died June 14, 1855 and is buried at Oak Forest in a small cemetery.
Mary Louise Anderson Smith, (GGGD), 22000
Bertha Elizabeth Anderson Carmichael, (GGGD), 20719

JOHN PERKINS SIMPSON

was born Oct. 17, 1806, in Sumner County, TN. He married Sina Needham on June 15, 1831 in Madison County, TN, and moved to Fannin County, TX by 1837. Sina was born Jan. 8, 1814, in Maury County, TN, and was the daughter of Lewis Wesley Needham and Amy Rosalee Tucker. John and Sina had three children: Elizabeth, born 1832, married Samuel Stinnett; Martha, born Dec. 14, 1834, married Joseph Brown; and Mary, born Dec. 21, 1837, married Pat Murphy.

John Simpson served as a lieutenant colonel of the Texas Militia in 1838. He was the first

John Perkins Simpson

sheriff elected in Fannin County and filled offices as Justice of the Peace and County Judge. He built the first mill and gin in Bonham, TX, and built the first jail at his own expense. He donated 40 acres of land on which the courthouse and principal business portion of Bonham are now. He also donated the land for Willow Wild Cemetery and Simpson Park is named for him. For over 40 years, he was a preacher for the M.E. Church South, and was one of the first members of the Masonic Constantine Lodge. In the 1860s, he wrote several articles about the early days in Fannin County. The stories were published in the Bonham newspapers.

Judge John Simpson was termed a fine specimen of manhood, and it was written in his obituary that "He rode tall in the saddle and in later years, stout in the buggy." Sina Simpson died Feb. 24, 1883, and John Simpson died Jan. 13, 1884, in Bonham, TX. Both are buried at Willow Wild Cemetery.

LuAnn Penrod Smith, (GGGGD), 22184
Allene Mitchell Penrod, (GGGD), 22213

JOSEPH ABRAHAM SKIDMORE was born May 3, 1797 in Madison County, KY to Thomas and Charity Skidmore. Abe married Celia Thompson in 1820 in Alabama. After Celia died in 1847, Abe married Celia's sister Emeline. Abe served in the West Tennessee Militia in the War of 1812. He enlisted Nov. 13, 1814 in the company of Captain Andrew Patterson. They marched to war from Bedford County, TN and were not discharged until May 1815. In 1823, Abe was the sheriff of Morgan County, AL. Abe arrived in Lamar County, TX in March 1836. He settled 12 miles south of Paris on "Skidmore's Prairie" where he had 1,280 acres. Abe died on June 15, 1861. He is buried on his farm in Biardstown, TX.

Thomas Henry Skidmore, son of Joseph A. Skidmore.

Abe's son, Thomas Henry Skidmore, was born March 19, 1923 in Morgan County, AL. From Henry's published letters and stories by or about him, we know that Henry arrived in Texas before his father. As a boy, he met Davy Crockett and when Crockett set off for Texas, Henry was to meet him at a predetermined spot. Crockett was early or Henry was late, and Crockett was ahead on the trail. Henry followed his campfires into Texas, but Crockett went on toward his destiny, while young Henry stayed in Red River with his friends. Henry became a surveyor, Presbyterian minister, school teacher, tax collector, deputy sheriff, and historian in Lamar County. He was a captain and assistant quartermaster, 9th Texas Regiment, CSA, and wrote the history of the unit. He married first, Laura Crain and second, Elizabeth J. Curlee.

Lineage: Abraham had Thomas Henry, who had William, who had Roger, who had Diane who married Anthony Kuras and had Linda Kuras and Laura Kuras, Laura had Patrick Hines and Anthony Hines.

Diane Skidmore Kuras

HARVEY SKILES, son of William and Lydia Chadwick/Chadwell Skiles, was born Dec. 8, 1807 in Jackson County, TN. He married Lettie Justus Oct. 13, 1837, Schuyler County, IL, and was in Lamar County, TX by 1841. Lettie, born 1812 in Illinois, and Harvey had four children: Mary Jane, born July 25, 1832 in Illinois, died Jan. 12, 1923 in Hill County, TX, married Jonathan Melton; James H., born 1835 in Illinois; Lydia M., born 1840 in

Iowa; William Thomas, born 1843 in Lamar County, TX, died 1881 in Navarro County, TX, married Sarah J. Smith, born 1854. Both are buried in Dresden Cemetery, Navarro County, TX. Harvey Skile's first wife, Lettie, died in 1843 in Lamar County, TX. He married second on June 15, 1844 in Lamar County, TX to Martha Parker. They had one daughter, Drucilla.

Harvey Skiles served in the Mexican War as first lieutenant under Capt. James S. Gillet, 1st Texas Mounted Volunteers. About 1853/60, he, wife Martha, her brothers, two Beaty boys, and others left Texas for the California gold fields. He died in Kern County, CA on Oct. 16, 1870.

Mary Jane Skiles, mentioned above, married on Oct. 2, 1851 in Navarro County, TX to Jonathan Melton, born 1814 in Clark County, GA, died March 16, 1874 in Navarro County, TX. Jonathan Melton paid taxes in Robertson County, TX in 1844, and he also served in the Mexican War. (His brother, Eliel Melton, died 1836 at the Alamo) Mary Jane and Jonathan's daughter, Allie D. Melton, born Sept. 12, 1857 in Navarro County, TX, married Jan. 2, 1878 to James Luther Sumner, born Sept. 29, 1855 in Missouri, died Oct. 1, 1920 in Navarro County, TX. Both are buried at Dresden Cemetery. Their son, James Henry Sumner, born Feb. 23, 1883, died Oct. 12, 1974, married Feb. 10, 1907 to Pearl Ann Stubblefield, born Jan. 19, 1890 in Warren County, TN, died Feb. 7, 1988. Both are buried in Dresden Cemetery at Navarro County, TX.

Jean Sumner Texeira, (GGGD), 16394

A.J. SMITH entered Texas in January 1837 with wife, Julia Ann Paxton, and two sons, William P. and A.J. Jr. William was 1-1/2 years and A.J. was 2 months. A.J. Sr. died several months later. His father, William D., and mother, Sally Carson, were already in Texas with children: John Carson, Daniel and Mary Moffet. Older brother, Leander and wife, Ann, were in Texas.

Leander fought at San Jacinto, and died in September 1836. A.J.'s widow married Wiley S. Thomas. The son, William P. Smith, married second in S.A. in 1875 to Robena Davis. They had Alice, Margaret, Grace, Iris, William P. Jr., Jane and John Edgar Smith.

William P. Jr. was born at Somerset on Sept. 15, 1889. He married Addie Lee Yarbrough on Nov. 11, 1920. They had two children, Billie Ruth on March 17, 1921 and Bobby Ray on Aug. 20, 1936. Billie had three marriages but no children. Her last husband was Bob Brumley. Bobby married Juanita Wolfe on June 4, 1960 and had two children. Dr. Cindy Smith Adams, born June 20, 1961 and Sandra Smith Petta, born May 3, 1964. Cindy married Steven Adams on Jan. 23, 1999 and Sandy married James Petta on Sept. 26, 1987. The Petta's had Sarah, born June 22, 1992 and Aaron, born July 16, 1995.

Since coming from Ashville, NC in 1835 to Texas, this branch of the descendants of Daniel Smith and John Carson have resided in Texas.

ANTHONY GARNETT SMITH JR. was born Jan. 25, 1809 in Oglethorpe County, GA to the Rev. Anthony Garnett Smith Sr. and Mary (Polly) Allen Smith. In 1788, the Smith family moved from Cumberland County, VA to Oglethorpe County. The Rev. Anthony G. Smith, a minister in the Methodist Episcopal Church, was ordained Deacon by Bishop Francis Asbury in 1811 and was ordained Elder by the Bishop William McKendree in 1812. In 1820, the Smiths were charter members of the Mount Pleasant

Anthony G. Smith, Jr. and Elizabeth M. Smith.

Methodist Church in Oglethorpe County. They later built a two-story home in Crawford County around 1830 which still stands.

Anthony Garnett Smith Jr. was a Georgia volunteer in the Texas Revolution. He enlisted with the Texas forces at San Felipe in 1836 after making the trip from Georgia on horseback. He later returned to his native state after being incapacitated by wounds to continue in service.

Adelaide Smith and Joshua C. Howell

On May 14, 1848, Anthony Garnett Smith Jr. and Elizabeth Murphey Smith were married in Upson County, GA. Elizabeth, the daughter of Charles Lee Smith, Sr. and Martha T. Glenn Smith, was born June 21, 1823 in Talbot County, GA. Anthony Garnett Smith and Elizabeth M. Smith had the following children: Charles A. Smith, Carey Allen Smith, Mary Elizabeth Smith, Wesley Asbury Smith, M.D., Simeon Hull Smith, M.D., Martha Johanna Smith, Garnett Daniel Smith, Emma Caroline Smith, Robert Lee Smith, Ida Virginia Smith, Eliza Eleanor Smith, Sarah Harriet Smith and Adelaide Smith. Anthony

Elizabeth Howell

Garnett Smith died on Feb. 19, 1891 and Elizabeth Murphey Smith died on Feb. 27, 1902. Both are buried in Glenwood Cemetery in Thomaston, GA.

Adelaide Smith was born July 20, 1865 in Talbot County and married Joshua Calhoun Howell on Dec. 24, 1890 in Upson County. They moved to Hill County, TX where Joshua was a schoolmaster and had a cotton farm. Joshua and Adelaide Howell had the following children: Elizabeth (Bessie) Lethella Howell,

Mamie Ross Howell, Jewell Howell, Robert Calhoun Howell and Winnie Davis Howell. The Howells were members of the First Methodist Church of West. Many family members are buried in Bell Springs Cemetery near Abbott, TX.

Elizabeth (Bessie) Howell was born Oct. 25, 1891 in Hill County and married Roy Elmer Beck on Dec. 23, 1919 in West. Elmer was employed by Wells Fargo Express Company prior to his work at the Texas Electric Railway. Bessie taught many years at North Waco Elementary School. They were members of Herring Avenue Methodist Church of Waco where Elmer served on the board of stewards and Bessie taught the Dorcas class for many years. Both are buried in Oakwood Cemetery in Waco.

Hester Beck Willis, (GGD), 12499

Roy E. Beck

ERASTUS "DEAF" SMITH was born in Dutchess County, NY, April 19, 1787 into a deeply religious family. His father's name was Chileab and his mother was named Mary. Records show his father was an enlisted man in the Fourth, or Dutchess Regiment of the Continental Line of the Revolutionary Army, which was organized June 30, 1775. Later, the family settled in Mississippi. He came to Texas in 1817 but returned. He then made a second trip to this state, never to return.

In 1825, Erastus Smith was officially engaged with Steven F. Austin's colony in introducing 400 families within designated boundaries for homesteading.

In 1828 he married Mrs. Guadalupe Ruiz Duran, a widow, whose parents were Salvador Castaneda Ruiz, of Spanish descent, and Maria Ignacia Robleau, a French lady from New Orleans and a Canary Islander descendant.

He fought with James W. Fannin and James Bowie at the Battle of Conception in October 1835 and led Colonel Frank W. Johnson's troop into San Antonio at the Battle of Bexar in December 1835.

"Deaf" Smith was chief scout for the Texas Army under General Sam Houston.

Of all his feats, the most dramatic was that of the morning of April 21, 1836, prior to the Battle of San Jacinto, when he destroyed the bridge over Vince's Bayou, cutting off the only way of retreat for the Mexican forces, thus helping the Texas Army to victory at San Jacinto, where he fought galantly on April 21, 1836.

Later in 1836, "Deaf" Smith was authorized as a Texas Ranger to command a company of rangers. On Feb. 17, 1837 from his headquarters near San Antonio, he led an expedition of rangers to Laredo to assert the Texas claim in that area. He was successful. Erastus "Deaf" Smith and his wife, Guadalupe were the parents of four children: Susan, Gertrude, Travis and Simona.

Susan married Ben Fisk. Upon her death, Ben Fisk married her sister, Simona.

Travis was unmarried and died at a young age.

Gertrude married Macario Tarin on March 24, 1847. He was a descendant of the original Canary Islanders who settled San Antonio in 1731 and created the First Civil Government in what is now San Antonio, TX. That union had five children: Guadalupe married Steven Casanova; Macario married Josefa Talamentes (2nd Brunita Garz); Camilo married Josefa Monharas; Juan Smith Tarin married Otilia Rodriguez; and Gertrude married Manuel Yndo.

Aurelia Flores Deuvall, granddaughter of Juan Smith Tarin

FRANCIS AND NANCY ANN SLAUGHTER SMITH,

Francis (born Jan. 4, 1798 in South Carolina) and Nancy Ann Slaughter Smith (born Oct. 21, 1819 in Lawrence County, MS) came to Texas on June 4, 1825 with Stephen F. Austin from Brookhaven, MS. Nancy was the daughter of Richard and Nancy Ann Terry Slaughter and granddaughter of Walter and Margaret Webb Slaughter. Granted land on May 24, 1831 by the Spanish government, they lived in Nacogdoches, moving to Louisiana in 1836 for a brief time. They returned to Texas to Burleson County (now Lee County) near Lexington, moving in 1847 to Fayette County and in 1854 to Walnut Creek in Blanco County.

Their children: Miranda, born 1821 in Mississippi, married Nathaniel Green Westfall; Sarah, born Feb. 21, 1823, in Lawrence County, MS, married Henry Rufus Smith; William died coming to Texas; Sibba M., born 1825, married William Price; Ruben, born 1826, died 1914, married Susan Wafenberger; Jane, born 1829, married Mr. Waldrup; George, born in Texas; Joel Phillip, born 1833, died 1917, married Annie E. Johnson; John H., born 1835, married Rufana Crownover; Mary married Marion Casner; Elizabeth, born 1838 in Louisiana, married Joseph Walker Moore. Killed by Indians near Bandera in 1872; Dorothy Amanda, born 1845, married Sam G. Reams Sr.

Francis died Sept. 5, 1867 and Nancy Ann died Jan. 15, 1877. Both are buried at the Walnut Creek Cemetery near Round Mountain in Blanco County. They married Oct. 21, 1819 in Lawrence County, MS.

Caroline Latham Ingram, (GGGGD), DRT 11172, Supplements 12430 and 12431

MRS. GUADALUPE RUIZ DURAN SMITH,

was born Dec. 12, 1797, the daughter of Salvador Castaneda Ruiz and Maria Ignacia Robleau.

She was a resident of the Villa de Bexar prior to the Texas Revolution. She met Erastus "Deaf" Smith, a short time after his arrival in San Antonio. They were married in 1828 in San Antonio. They had four children: Susan, Gertrude, Travis and Simona.

Aurelia Flores Deuvau, (GGD)

JOHN D. SMITH

was born in Tennessee in about 1812. He came to the Nashville Colony, TX with his parents, Sion and Sarah Smith, along with his brothers, Samuel, William and his sister Sarah. They were all on the First Census of Texas. John D. Smith married Elizabeth Nelson who had also come to Texas with her family. The Smiths settled in Robertson County on Mud Creek just below where Calvert is now. They were there as early as 1834.

John D. Smith was very active in local government. He served as a private in Captain Robertson's Ranger Company. He served as a sergeant for three months under Captain Nimrod Doyle as a volunteer ranger. He also served as an election judge from the Municipality of Robertson. Mirabeau B. Lamar appointed him the first sheriff of Robertson County on May 25, 1840 and he served in this capacity for two terms.

Sam Houston commissioned him as 1st lieutenant in the Fifth Regiment of the Second Brigade of the Militia of the Republic of Texas.

John D. Smith received 1 labor of land on Feb. 25, 1835 and 1/4 league on March 18, 1835. In 1843, John D. Smith and his wife, Elizabeth Nelson Smith, moved to a place north of Grosbeck in Limestone County where he served as postmaster. There place was known as Smith's Point. It was here that they lived with their four daughters: Emeline, Sara Ann, Elizabeth and Lydia. Emeline Smith married James Moorhead. They were my great-grandparents. James Moorhead died at an early age and Emeline married William Martin. John S. Smith died of pneumonia in 1847 at the age of 35. He had lived a full life for his early demise. As his grandson and my grandfather, John D. Moorhead, stated in a letter years later, "He served his country well."

Winona Ruth Moorhead Wilkinson, 19864

JOHN STEPHEN SMITH

was born to Mary and Eason Smith on Dec. 25, 1809, in Barnwell, SC. His siblings were Hansford; Eliza married Joseph Jones; and Mary married John G. Pearson. John Stephen married Nancy Jane Rafferty in Chicot County, AR and had Robert Eason in 1840 and twins, Quishinberry and Delila, in 1845 in Texas.

In 1850 he married Elizabeth Miliken and had John. In September 1851, he married Arabella Hunter Drury. Together they had Armilda Jemima (1852) who married Rawlings Bush; James Hansfdord (1855) married Kate Robinett and Mary White; George Hunter (1856) married Lilly Dodd; William (1857), died young; and Samuel Wallace (1858) married Gertrude Pope.

John, a planter, owned land in Polk and Walker counties. The contract for his home reveals elaborate and impressive plans. The will in his own handwriting desired that his children be "liberally educated" and "decently and gently raised but not extravagantly." He amassed an estate that required several years to settle. He was musical and was active in the Olive Branch Chapter of the Masonic Order having served as Worshipful Master at Cincinnati, TX on the Trinity River.

John Stephen died Nov. 15, 1859 and is buried near the old ghost town of Cincinnati beside Arabella.

Williene Smith Story, (GGD), 3427

MAJOR SMITH

was born March 18, 1801 in Wayne County, NC and died Dec. 28, 1880 in Lavaca County, TX. He married Sarah Teal of Natchitoches Parish in Louisiana in about 1825.

Major Smith was in Texas by 1829. In 1832 he commanded a company of volunteers at the battle of Nacogdoches. In April 1836, he enlisted as a soldier in the company of Benjamin Bryant and also served in E.M. Collins Company.

Sarah Alonzo Smith Hill

The obituary of Major Smith published in the *Methodist Newspaper* reads in part, as follows: "One more Texas veteran has gone home to rest. Major Smith was born in 1801; joined the M.E. Church with his wife, Sarah Smith, in the year 1830. She preceded him several years to the better land. He died at the residence of his daughter, Mrs.

Jane H. Morris, near Hope, Lavaca County, TX, Dec. 28, 1880, in his 80th year. He leaves six children and a number of grandchildren.

Major Smith and Sarah Teal had 10 children: Nancy, Kezia, Jane, Major J., William, Susan, Eli, Sarah Alonzo**, Elizabeth and George. Sarah Alonzo Smith was born on July 4, 1841.

Sarah A. Smith married Henry Hill on March 17, 1862. Sarah and Henry Hill had six children: Sallie (born 1869); Henrietta** (born Jan. 29, 1872); William Barrett Travis (born 1874); Richard (born 1875); Thomas (born 1878); and Mary (born about 1866).

Henry Hill died in September 1884 and Sarah Smith Hill died May 15, 1923.
Susie Elaine Brazier Toal, (GGGD), 21358

NILES F. SMITH

NILES F. SMITH was born in New York State in 1800. Around 1820 he went to St. Joseph, Berrien County, MI. He married and he and his wife had a daughter, Helen, in 1830 and in 1832 a son, Niles H. was born. Historians report that my great-grandmother died in 1833. I have been unable to learn her first name or maiden name. His second wife was named Abigail (last name unknown). She, by all accounts, was his first wife's sister. They became the parents of Elias in 1835 and Susan in in 1840. At some point, Niles F. Smith became a practicing physician. The reason he did not practice medicine full time was that there

Marker for Niles F. Smith

were not enough people on the Texas frontier at that time to justify a full time physician.

Upset over the death of his first wife, my great-grandfather left his two children with relatives and came to the Mexican province of Texas. In western Louisiana he met Sterling Clack Robertson, who was the Mexican impresario of a 25,000 square mile colony near present day Waco. Robertson sent my great-grandfather, Niles F. Smith, to Viesca, the capital city of Robertson's Colony where he was appointed as "agent to sell town lots."

On Feb. 1, 1836, Niles F. Smith served as election judge at Viesca to select delegates from Robertson's colony to attend the Convention at Washington-on-the-Brazos, where Texas independence from Mexico was declared the following March 2nd. For the next six months, according to Comptroller's Military Service Records, my great-grandfather served during the Texas Revolution in a corps of engineers and received a salary of $100 a month. During that time he became a confidant and friend of Gen. Sam Houston, Col. Philip Sublett, Col. G.W. Hockley who commanded the Texas Artillery at the Battle of San Jacinto; and Gen. Sidney Sherman, who commanded the Second Regiment of Texas Volunteers at the battle.

In 1836, Gen. Houston and Col. Sublett acquired the title to 11,000 acres of land in Sabine Pass, TX. In February 1839, Smith, Houston, Sublett and several others organized the Sabine Company at Houston. Its board of directors read much like the Texas Army's muster roll at San Jacinto. Dr. Smith bought two land certificates which contained 817 acres, the only high land at Sabine

Pass fit for a townsite. Later he joined forces with John and Neal McGaffey to found the second townsite and he continued as land agent.

By 1837, he and President Houston and the Texas government had moved to the new capitol at Houston. It is recorded that Niles F. Smith owned the building in which was housed the offices of the Texas Secretary of State. Many of my great-grandfather's papers from his Houston period are in the Texas State Archives in Austin. Houston appointed Smith the first bank examiner of the Texas Republic.

Because Sabine Pass had less than 100 persons residing there in 1840 my great-grandfather was unable to support his family by practicing only medicine and selling town lots. He became one of the town's first merchants. In 1841 he became the collector of customs for the Republic of Texas appointed by Sam Houston. To qualify for office, he had to sell his store and quit buying cargoes of cotton. Later on he reopened his store and resigned from his appointed position. There are 27 cubic feet of Sabine Pass customs house papers in the Texas State Archives and approximately six cubic feet of those papers are letters and documents written by Sam Houston and Niles F. Smith. It is so intersting to read the hand written letters that Sam Houston and Niles F. Smith wrote back and forth to each other.

Niles F. Smith and John McGaffey organized and built the first school in both Sabine Pass and Jefferson County in 1842. My great-grandfather and others erected the Methodist Church, the first church building in Sabine Pass or Jefferson County next door to where the school now stands. My great-grandfather bought the land where the Sabine Pass Cemetery is presently located and where he, his wife, son Henry and son Niles H. Smith (my grandfather) are buried. In the 1840s my great-grandparents (Niles F. and Abigail) became the parents of four more sons: Henry (who was accidently shot and killed by a playmate at age 4), Homer, Frost and Henry W. (the second child to be named Henry which was a custom of the day).

Dr. Niles F. Smith was the only physician in Sabine Pass until his death in 1856. At that time testamentary letters were issued to Abigail Smith to probate her husband's estate.

In the 1860 census, Abigail Smith was running a boarding house where eight boarders resided in addition to Abigail's four sons, her widowed daughter, Susan Shaw and two small granddaughters. Niles H. Smith and his wife, Mary Elizabeth Parr (my father's parents) had three small daughters: Kate, Helen and Susan. My father, Charles Buchannan Smith was born May 22, 1872.
Mildred Smith Barton, (GGD), 021359

SARAH ELIZABETH AND HENRY RUFUS SMITH,

Sarah Elizabeth was born Feb. 2, 1823 in Lawrence County, MS to Francis and Nancy Ann Slaughter Smith. Henry Rufus was born 1826 in Lawrence County, MS to James L. Smith and his wife nee Slaughter. He arrived in Texas by 1835. Sarah came to Texas in 1825. They married in 1848 in Texas and were living in Burleson County along with her first born child, age 5 months. They moved to Blanco County in 1857.

Henry Rufus served in three Ranger companies during the War Between the States. He first enlisted Sept. 7, 1861 in the Pedernales Home Guard, then Ranger Company G(D) on Sept. 27, 1862 and finally Company B. Mounted Frontier Regiment on Dec. 29, 1862, re-enlisting May 1, 1863. He became ill while on patrol somewhere between Bandera and Kerville and died Feb.

10, 1864. He is buried in an unknown location in Kerr County supposedly in a shallow grave in a creek bed.

Their children were James Monroe (Jingling Jim); Ruben M. (Doc), 1852-1927, married Virginia Harrington, 1859-1947, buried Post Oak; Anna Mazora, 1854-1929, married John W. Woods, 1860-1931; J.R., 1856; Victoria, 1859; Nancy Melvina, born March 15, 1861, died Oct. 24, 1917, married George Washington Bush; John Thomas, 1863-1906, buried at Post Oak Cemetery, Blanco County.

Sarah reared her children alone, braving the frontier, Indian raids, and actually tied the reins to two horses through a hole in the wall of the house to keep Indians from stealing the horses, but they cut the reins and stole them anyway! She buckled on her gun to go milk the cow, as fear of raids was so prevalent. Sarah moved her family to Mason County near Pontotoc after 1880. She died March 28, 1906 and is buried in the Pontotoc Cemetery. A memorial marker for Henry Rufus stands beside her tombstone.

Caroline Latham Ingram. (GGGD), DRT #11172, Supplement 12454

WILLIAM (BILL) SMOTHERS (SMITHERS, SMEATHERS),

"Honest Bill Smithers," as referred to by Washington Irving in *The Knickerbocker Sketchbook*, "The Early Experiences of Ralph Ringwood," was born in 1760 near the Holston River in Virginia. He was orphaned at age 12 when Indians killed his father and his mother died shortly thereafter. The Fitzpatrick family agreed to care for the children in exchange for the Smithers' farm. His uncle, Henry Chrisman (brother of William's mother), sent for him and provided for his education at a boarding school near Richmond, VA. The two younger children, James and Mary, remained with the Fitzpatrick family.

After leaving his uncle's care, he fought in The American Revolution under Colonel Isaac Shelby at King's Mountain. He received his discharge papers from Colonel Shelby, and then fought under General Nathaniel Green at Guilford Courthouse and Eutaw Springs.

He returned to the Holston River area and married Nancy Cecilia Fitzpatrick in 1782. They had four daughters: Jane, Elizabeth, Molly, and Margaret (Betsy). After Cecilia's death, Bill married Mary Winters. They had three children: John, Archibald and Mary. As he moved his families westward, he helped establish forts at Smothers Station, which would become Hartford, KY; and at Vienna, which became Calhoun, KY. In 1795, he served on the first Grand Jury of Quarter Sessions at Hartford.

In 1797-98, Bill Smothers followed a buffalo trail north to the Ohio River, and made the first permanent settlement at Yellow Banks, now Owensboro, KY. His cabin on the Ohio was used for the first court sessions and he was a member of the Grand Jury in 1803. He served as an officer in Kentucky's Cornstalk Millitia in 1803, was appointed as a land commissioner in 1808 and was acquitted of a murder charge in Owensboro in 1809. He served in the War of 1812 under General Samuel Hopkins as a captain in the Dubois Battalion of Spies. His son, John Smothers, and son-in-law, John Berry, served as privates in his company.

William Smothers first came to Texas in 1813, but was back in Kentucky in 1816. He returned to Texas before 1820. Stephen F. Austin hired Smothers as a hunter and guide for his advance party for the "Old 300." He and four others built Fort Bend, on the bank of the Brazos River, so the settlers could restock their supplies near the mid-point of their journey into Texas.

Smothers received a land grant in Austin's Colony in 1824; was a settler in DeWitt's Colony in 1826 and later retired to a cabin on the bank of the Brazos River near Columbia in what is now Brazoria County, where he died on August 13, 1837, after seeing a son and three grandsons help win the Texas War of Independence.

William Smothers is remembered on monuments and historical markers in Hartford, KY, and in Owensboro, KY, where a large riverside park is named in his honor. A stone monument recognizes Smothers, and four others, near the original site of Fort Bend in Richmond, TX; and an historical marker is located near the land he settled in Lavaca County, TX.

In both American and Texas History, Bill Smothers' contributions stand as proud examples of the courage to trail blaze the Western Frontier, military service for his country in three wars, planting the seed of settlement at future city sites, and playing a major role in the original organized effort to settle Texas.

Louise Smothers Hall, 017333

JOHN JACKSON SNIDER

was born Jan. 30, 1816 in Mercer County, KY. He married Cynthia Fanetta Ward on Nov. 21, 1841 in Hempstead County, AR.

In 1844, he and Cynthia with their two children moved to Clarksville in Red River County, Republic of Texas. He became involved in the lumber and saw mill business along with land and cattle interests. They were founding members of what is now The First Baptist Church and donated land in the area where the church was to be built.

He volunteered for duty in 1847 in the Mexican-American War, serving as an officer in the Texan Mounted Volunteers under Colonel Jack Hays and Captain Samuel W. Sims. During the same year the family moved to Van Zandt County and in 1851 they moved to Henderson County. By 1855, they had moved back to Van Zandt County. These moves were reflected on his army pension records. He applied for and received bounty land in Smith County under the Mexican-American War entitlement.

In 1856, the family moved to Johnson County, TX where John built a mercantile store in Cleburne across the street from the courthouse. There he sold goods and traded land and cattle. He was quick to give assistance to the early Texas colonists. He built a two-story 12 room house in Cleburne and as each child married and left home they were given land and financial help.

John and Cynthia were the parents of 12 children, three of which died in infancy. Cynthia died on Jan. 31, 1885 and John died April 17, 1887. They are both buried in Cleburne Cemetery in Johnson County, TX. He was buried a mason and was a charter member in the Cleburne Lodge.

Jack Charles Lightfoot, (GGGS) #6422J

ABNER BAGBY SPIER,

son of John Spier and Rachel Bagby, was born in 1808 in Georgia. He married Betsy Ann Whatley, daughter of Seaborn Jones Whatley, about 1831 in Alabama. Betsy was born in 1815 in Georgia. Abner and Betsy moved to Bastrop County, TX, in February 1835. Abner was a farmer.

Abner and Betsy had 13 children: Seaborn Jones, who married first, Sarah Meeks and second, Josephine Duncan; Nancy married John Mabry; Rebecca married Isaac Campbell; John Madison; Betsy Ann; Rachel Maberry married A.J. Glover; Mahala married first, Charles H. Glover and second, H.M. Taylor; William M.; Abner B.; Emily; Kate M. married Henry Guynes; Elizabeth married first, Michael Buckley and second, Washington Hassell.

Abner Spier received 320 acres of land for military service from July 8 to Oct. 8, 1836. The family lived in Bastrop, Panola, and Burnet counties. Abner died Dec. 6, 1874 and Betsy died July 29, 1879. Both are buried in Spier Cemetery in Bastrop County. Their graves have seals "Citizen of Republic of Texas, 1836-1846," and Abner's grave has a seal "Texas Revolutionary War Veteran 1836" and a Republic of Texas flag.

Seaborn Jones Speir, listed above, married Sarah J. Meeks on May 25, 1854 in Bastrop County. She was the daughter of Littleton Meeks and Millie White Morris and was born Feb. 8, 1837, in Mississippi. Their children were William Everett and twin brother, Waymon Holt, neither married; Laura Eller married first, James M. Hughes and second, Isaac Campbell; Nace E. married Martha Potts; Seaborn Jones Jr. married (1) Lora Jordan (2) Mary Belle Scott and (3) Ozelia Hobbs; Sarah Frances married Douglas Boggle; Tommy died young; Willard Kemper; and James Elgin married Alma Redurs.

Seaborn and Sarah and other family members are buried in Spier Cemetery in Bastrop County.

Jeannine (Hughes) Schaffer, (GGGGD), 20622
Sandra (Hudson) Bunch, (GGGGGD), 20677

THOMAS STANFORD

THOMAS STANFORD was born in South Carolina, ca. 1790. In 1830, Thomas is in Weekley County, TN, and James Bourland, a neighbor, in Weakley County, TN is later found with Thomas in Red River County, ROT, when their names appear adjacent, on a petition, requesting the formation of Lamar County, ROT.

Thomas Stanford was in Nacogdoches County in January 1835. In May 1838, Thomas Stanford was granted one league and one labor of land. He assigned his grant to David Rusk and Daniel Lacy.

Thomas Stanford and his first wife had the following children: Harrison Stanford married first, Holly Pennington and second, Mary Day; Joseph Stanford married Rebecca Kerley; Thomas Stanford (born ca. 1827) married (1) Nelly Cearly/Kerley, (2) Miranda Boyd Newman, (3) Rachel Tatum, and (4) Jane Harmon; Demitrus (Suzy) married William Driggers; Frances married William Driggers; Mary and Harriet.

Thomas, third son of Thomas, married Nelly Cearly/Kerley on April 18, 1850, Fannin County, TX. They had two sons, John Henry (born 1853) and William C., both born in Texas. John Henry married Clarinda Wylie in 1872 at Collin County, TX. They had one daughter, Rosa Etta (born 1875) in Collin County, TX. Rosa married Ralph LeSuer Corse; their children were Thelma Lee, Kenneth Stanford, Arthur St. Clair and Gilford Ralph Corse. Thelma Lee married Ewell Ray Berry; their children were LaVerne, Vernal Rose, and Betty Lee.

Thomas Stanford (b. ca. 1790, died 1859 in Carroll County, TN, and is buried in the Stanford Cemetery. Thomas Stanford (b. ca. 1827, died in Hunt County, TX in 1899). John Henry Stanford died in Indian Territory in 1907. They were all farmers.

Betty Lee Berry Craig, (GGGGD), 22160

ASA LAFITTE STARK

Asa Lafitte Stark

ASA LAFITTE STARK, born June 19, 1817 in Port Allen, LA. Parents were Daniel R. Stark and Nancy Hawley.

His first wife was Matilda Donoho, whose parents were Daniel Donoho and Nancy Larimore. There children were Julia Ann who married first William McFarland, second, William Simpson and third Phillip Dempsey; Daniel Donohoe married Julia Cassandra Daugharty; John Lawhorn married Mary Matilda Zachary; and Dennis Call married Elizabeth Bradford. (He was a Methodist minister.)

Asa and his family crossed the Sabine River into Texas around March 2, 1836, and was granted a second class Headright, (Certificate #385) by the Republic of Texas on July 5, 1838. He received 1,280 acres of land along the banks of the Sabine River, near the community of Belgrade. He and his brother, William Hawley, were in the lumber and farming business. Asa was one of the first law enforcement officers during the early days of the Republic of Texas. He became a constable in Orange, TX in 1851, and was their first tax collector.

Matilda died in 1857. He married his second wife, the same year: Hester Ann Ford. Her parents were Courtney Ann Caraway and David Ford. Their children were David Dewitt (a Methodist minister) who married Evelyn Mollie Rasco; Courtney Ann married John Bouregard Holton, M.D.; Lydia Elizabeth married Elijah Gwen Baker Ward; Asa Lafitte Jr. married Alice (he ran away from home at age 15); Prudence (died At an early age from a snake bite); William Bennett married Nancy Ellen Phifer in Kosse (Limestone, TX.) She was the oldest daughter of Calvin Hamilton Phifer, the only son of Forest Phifer, one of 12 men who founded Limestone County).

Asa moved his family to Limestone County ca. 1866, where he had farming interests. Hester died ca. 1871. He married and divorced Rebecca Ann Roberts in 1880, and died in 1881, in Pottersville (Limestone) TX. To date, the Stark Family Association does not know where either Hester or Asa are buried, but are searching.

Mildred Wilson Plummer, (GGGD), #20760

JOHN RICHARD STEPHENS JR.

JOHN RICHARD STEPHENS JR., son of John and Sarah Rodgers Stephens of Laurens, SC, was born Nov. 14, 1804. He married Mary Catherine Ware in 1825. In 1832, they moved to Benton County, AL.

In 1833, John Richard Stephens' brother, Robert F. Stephens, to escape a criminal charge, fled from South Carolina and arrived in San Augustine, TX. Robert changed his name to David Brown, taught school, and then became a very prolific surveyor in east Texas, obtaining a headright in Jefferson County and acquiring numerous other leagues. He fought in the Battle of San Jacinto as David Brown.

In 1838, John Richard Stephens and Reuben L. Stephens, two brothers of Robert aka David Brown, followed him into Texas and purchased land. My great-great-grandfather, John Richard Stephens, bought six leagues of land (one league=4,428 acres). One of his leagues is recorded in Beaumont, Jefferson County, and the other five are recorded in Woodville, Tyler County, in the "Ghost County" Menard Day Book "A."

In 1844, while John Richard Stephens and family were migrating westward to their land in Texas, both he and wife, Mary Catherine Ware, were stricken with typhoid fever. They died within a few weeks apart and were buried beside relatives in the Cherry Creek Baptist Church Cemetery in Pontotoc County, MS.

Several of their eight children continued on to Texas, one of whom was my great-grandfather, John Anderson Stephens (married Sallie Hitt Ball). His son, my grandfather, John Martin Stephens (married Lucy Catherine Bolding), migrated to Eden, Concho County where he bought his 3,000 acre ranch. He was one of the earliest pioneer settlers in Eden, and reared a large family. His son, my father, E.L. Stephens (married Olive Zola Schafer) also reared his family in Eden as did many other Stephens descendants.
Shirley Stephens Martin, DRT #19442

TAMAR STEVENS was born to Elizabeth Calk and Thomas S. Stephens in 1798 in Kentucky and married George Elliott Hunter in Eutaw, AL on March 20, 1824. From Raleigh, KY this couple came to Texas in early 1837 with Samuel and Hezekiah Lucian (his sons by a previous marrige) and their children: Arabella, Armilda, Dulcinia, William C.S. and James Thomas to build a two-story hotel of hand-sawed lumber at the newly laid out Trinity River town of Cincinnati.

Tamar, of a cherrful, happy disposition, ministered to the sick and discouraged so was well liked. She stood five feet 11 inches and weighed 155 pounds. Owning no slaves, Tamar cooked and managed the tavern while George and sons participated in Indian skirmishes and Mexican battles, ranging as far as the Colorado River on scouting expeditions.

After George was killed in a steamboat explosion March 31, 1853, Tamar perserved as a hard working pioneer until she nursed a sick traveler. Tamar became ill and was cared for by neighbors with no one suspecting Yellow Fever. Tamar, on Sept. 24, 1853, was the first to die of the epidemic that demolished Cincinnati, TX.
Williene Smith Story, (GGGD), 3427

THOMAS S. STEVENS, a veteran of the American Revolution, married Elizabeth Calk, daughter of Sarah Catlett and William Calk, June 1866 in Lincoln County, KY. Known children were Elizabeth married Edward Free in Kentucky in 1809; Joseph married Catherine Glackin in Kentucky in 1810, living in Arkansas in 1839; Parthenia married Eli Spencer and Thomas Manion in Madison County, MO; William C. married Mildred Moore, living in Carroll County, AR in 1839; Sarah married Phillip Williams in Kentucky; Fidelia married Jefferson Messick, Shelby County, TN in 1839; Drucilla married John Raines in Shelby County, TN in 1836; twins, Theny and Tamar (Tamer), married George Hunter; Thomas married Jane Kincaid; Andrew Jackson married Emily in Texas in 1838; Matson, in Texas; Mary Zelo Zosco married John Bradley and Rev. Thomas Burt Altom, settling in Walker County, TX.

Thomas' league of land in Montgomery, (now Walker) County on the Headwaters of Nelson Creek was granted in 1833 by Certificate 144 at Land Office in Austin. The younger Thomas came with Austin's old Three Hundred. Thomas, becoming blind, divided his time between the homes of Tamar Hunter at

Cincinnati, TX and son Thomas at San Jacinto. Stevens descendants have defended this country in every war.
Willidene Smith Story, (GGGGD), 3427

SAMUEL STEWART was born about 1804 in Tennessee. He moved to Limestone County, AL where he married Nancy Melinda, daughter of James and Elizabeth Gray.

Children born in Alabama were Jane who may have married Mr. Lilley, Christana Louisa who married Isaac Newton McCain and Thomas B. who died during the War Between the States.

The family arrived in Red River County in 1838, settling at Dangerfield. Samuel took part of his 640 acre headright as a town lot at Dangerfield. Nancy's brother, James N. Gray, followed, moving later to Tarrant County with wife. Treywick.

The Stewart family continued to grow after the move to the Republic with the births of William A. who died at Corinth, MS while in the Confederate Army, Samuel F. (Sam), John N. who married Terry Ann Tamir Wright, and Phoebe Caroline (Carrie) who married Alonzo Douglas Bruton and moved to Bagwell, Red River County.

In 1841, Samuel served in Captain J.D. Lilley's Special Rangers or Paschall County Minute Men. Samuel was over the ballot box for the first Titus County election at Tankersley's Old Place in 1846. Samuel died in 1850 at Dangerfield.
Linda McCain Stansell, #19385, 2242S
Dr. Melissa Stansell, #22339

FREDERICK STOCKMAN was born in Siegerland, Germany about 1746 and was the son of Johann Engelbert Stockman and Anna Marie Schmidt. He was a small child when his family migrated from Burbach in the Duchy of Nassausiegen in the fall of 1749. They arrived in Philadelphia on the ship *Fane* in October 1749.

Frederick's whereabouts for the next 30 years is not known. He appears in Mercer County, KY in 1787, and three years later in New Madrid, Spanish Missouri, where he is married to Catherine Disponet (on other census list, her name is spelled Des Bonete or De Bonete.) She was the daughter of Christopher Disponete and Mary Ann Honney. In 1790, Frederick and his family were in Natchez, MS, and in 1793, in Mobile, AL. In 1801, two sons were baptized in Mobile. In 1802, another son was baptized in New Orleans, LA.

Frederick and his family moved to Texas in March 1806. The family sailed from New Orleans to the small Spanish outpost of Atascocito on the Trinity River. The family, at this time, consisted of George, 20; Henry, 13; David, 11; John, 9; Peter, 6; and Margaret, 3. The family soon increased as baby Joseph Anthony was born while the family was temporarily staying at Atascocito.

In November 1807, Frederick and his family were listed among those stranded in the little Indian village of Orcoquistac on the Trinity River without transportation.

Soon Frederick moved his family further up the Trinity River to the Villa Trinidad de Salcedo. This community was established in September and October 1805 on the road from San Antonio to Nacogdoches by Commandant General Nemesio Salcedo as part of a plan to assure safety for commerce to the outposts. The Stockman family was among the first settlers admitted from the United States.

In Villa Trinidad de Salcedo, Frederick settled on land granted to him by the Spanish Crown some five miles below the outpost of Trinidad de Salcedo near the falls of the river. Mary Sarah Stockman was born on Jan. 7, 1811, while the Stockman's were living here. On Dec. 17, 1811, orders directing Frederick to leave Texas and never return were transmitted to Felipe de la Garza from the governor. On Jan. 12, 1812, they left for the United States and settled in Natchitoches—the Neutral Strip between Spanish Texas and Louisiana. It is still a mystery why Frederick was expelled from Texas.

Frederick and Catherine bought land located on the Rio Hondo, six miles west of Natchitoches. In 1814, they sold some of this land to their son, George. In July 1817, they sold more land to Matthew Richard for one slave named Sam and a mule. A year later, Frederick sold the slave named Sam to Renny Tottin.

In the 1820 census, Catherine Stockman and son, Henry (who was married, but with no children) were enumerated. They lived in the area west of the Rio Hondo.

The census of 1830 listed Frederick as living in Hancock County, MS. It is not known how long he lived in this area, but he returned to Texas and died in Nacogdoches. His probate is dated March 26, 1838.

The Henry Stockmans' moved back to Texas and it appears that Catherine was living with them in 1831. On the Census of 1828, she was listed as 57 years old and a widow (maybe because Frederick was in the United States). The Henry Stockman family is enumerated on the 1835 census as living in the Williams Settlement. Catherine died between 1835 and 1836. She was listed as a widow. In 1853, her heirs petitioned to the courts of the state of Texas for a league and a labor of land which was due Catherine in the days of the Republic as the head of a household. The courts awarded the land to the heirs.

Nelva Joy Stockman Bixler, (GGGGGGD), 18005
G7 Frederick Stockman,
G6 Henry Stockman,
G5 Henry Joseph Stockman,
G4 Garrison Greenwood Stockman,
G3 Durward Jeptha Stockman,
G2 John Leslie Stockman,
G1 Nelva Joy Stockman Bixler

HARDY FRANCIS STOCKMAN

was born Oct. 19, 1822 in Nacogdoches, TX. He was the second son of Henry Stockman and Dorcas Trebite. In 1840, Hardy was too young to vote, but he had obtained tentative title to 320 acres of land. Hardy married Mary Naomi Williams on March 14, 1842 in Nacogdoches. She was the eldest child of William Williams and Cinderella Bean. Mary Naomi Williams was born Jan. 1, 1827 in Texas.

Hardy F. Stockman served in Captain Jordan's company in 1838 and he served in the Mounted Rangers under Captain Alexander Jordan in 1839. He served under Major Durst in 1840 for three months, and in 1841, he served under General James Smith.

Hardy joined Company I, First Regiment, Texas Mounted Volunteers, United States Forces. He joined in June 21, 1847 in Rusk County and served until May 1, 1848. This was the time of the Mexican War. The Texas Mounted Volunteers were one of the military units to capture Mexico City.

Hardy and his family lived in Caldwell County for several years, and then they lived in Gillespie—the part of which later became Blanco County.

Hardy F. Stockman was the first elected sheriff of Blanco County, being elected on Aug. 2, 1858. He served his one year term and by 1861 Hardy and his family moved to Kerr County. Hardy F. Stockman was a candidate in the election to select delegates to the State Secession Convention. On Jan. 8, 1861, Hardy received 32 votes but his opponent received 67.

The children of Hardy F. Stockman and Mary Naomi W. Stockman were Young Hardy, born July 4, 1844; William Henry, born ca. 1846; George Green, born ca. 1848; Dorcas, born ca. 1850; Laura N., born ca. 1851; Peter Russell, born ca. 1854; Jessie Thomas, born Aug. 23, 1857; Peter Francis, born ca. 1860; and John Freeman, born ca. 1862.

Hardy Francis Stockman enlisted July 22, 1862 in Company E, First Texas Mounted Rifles.

Mary Naomi Williams Stockman died March 26, 1865. Hardy Francis Stockman died Sept. 8, 1865. Both died in Mt. Calm, TX.

Nelva Joy Stockman Bixler (GGGGD) 18005
G5 Hardy Francis Stockman, brother of Henry Joseph Stockman. Hardy F. Stockman is the GGG Uncle of N. Joy S. Bixler.
G4 Garrison Greenwood Stockman
G3 Durward Jeptha Stockman
G2 John Leslie Stockman
G1 Nelva Joy Stockman Bixler

HENRY JOSEPH STOCKMAN,

the eldest son of Henry Stockman and Dorcas Trebite, was born in Louisiana Dec. 7, 1820. The family moved to Texas before 1828 and settled in Nacogdoches County. Henry Joseph Stockman paid poll tax in 1840 in Nacogdoches County, but owned no land. He served in Captain Jordan's Company in 1838, and in Major Durst's Company in 1840. After Texas became a Republic, he applied for compensation for his service and received $121.66. In the Cherokee war of 1839, he served as an olderly sergeant in the Mounted Rangers. In 1841, he served as a scout in the Indian Wars under General James Smith.

L to R: Thelma Dillingham Mandaville and Nelva Joy Stockman Bixler.

Henry Joseph Stockman married Elizabeth Jordan Greenwood on July 5, 1842 in Nacogdoches County. She was born Sept. 13, 1822 in Illinois, the daughter of Garrison Greenwood and Elizabeth Jordan.

The children of Henry J. Stockman and Elizabeth J. Greenwood Stockman were Marion J. Stockman, born ca. 1844; Milam P. Stockman, born ca. 1846; John Henry Stockman, born ca. 1848; Lavinia Stockman, born September 1849; and Garrison Greenwood Stockman, born July 12, 1854.

In 1852, Henry J. Stockman and family lived in Lockhart, TX. Henry J. Stockman became a member of the Masonic Lodge (Lockhart Lodge #59, Lockhart, TX). He served as master mason in 1851 and as secretary in 1852. He served again as Master Mason in 1853 and 1854. Sometime in 1854, the Stockman family moved to Milam County. There, Henry J. Stockman was a member of the San Gabriel Lodge #89, Georgetown, TX—a lodge that was newly organized in Williamson County.

Henry Joseph Stockman died in 1856 of Dropsy (edema).

Family tradition is that the widow, Elizabeth G. Stockman, was asked if she would marry again. Elizabeth's answer was that she didn't know, but if she did it would be to a man that could not read. She said, "That Henry Stockman sat around with a book in his hand all the time. All he did was read!" On Feb. 9, 1857, Elizabeth married Jarvis N. Donaldson in Lampasas, TX. The ceremony was performed by her father, Garrison Greenwood. Jarvis Donaldson signed the marriage certificate with an "x."

Marion J. Stockman, eldest son of Henry and Elizabeth, enlisted in the 17th Confederate Texas Infantry at Lampasas, TX on March 15, 1852. Nothing more is known of him. Milam P. Stockman enlisted in Company D of the 17th Texas Confederate Infantry and served from April 5 until May 30, 1862, when he was discharged. He was 16 years old at the time. He then enlisted as a private in the Second Texas Calvary, United States Forces, in New Orleans, LA on Feb. 8, 1865. He was promoted to corporal March 28, 1865, and discharged Nov. 10, 1865 because this unit was dissolved by order of the War Department. Nothing more is known of Milam P. Stockman.

Lavinia Stockman married Albertus Sweet Aug. 3, 1862 in Travis County, TX.

John Henry and his friend, John N. Gracey were involved in a close scrape when they came upon a band of Indians herding stolen horses. It was April 10, 1861. The boys were 13 years old. The Indians captured Gracey, but John Stockman managed to hide in the bushes. The Indians scalped Gracey, made him run ahead of them and filled his back with arrows, killing him. John crawled through the grass and bushes eight miles to get help. However, the Indians got away. Years later, John H. Stockman married Sally Harrington.

Garrison Greenwood Stockman married Milbra Beatrice Low, daughter of Joel Low and Milbra B. Ferguson, on Aug. 4, 1872 in Lampasas, TX. Garrison Greenwood Stockman died April 1, 1899, and Milbra Low Stockman died Aug. 6, 1936.

The Stockman DRT members thank Thelma Dillingham Mandaville, a descendant of Frederick Stockman et al, for researching the Stockman lineage.

Nelva Joy Stockman Bixler (GGGGD) 18005
G5 Henry Joseph Stockman,
G4 Garrison Greenwood Stockman,
G3 Durward Jeptha Stockman,
G2 John Leslie Stockman,
G1 Nelva Joy Stockman Bixler

HENRY STOCKMAN was born 1792 in Natchez, MS. He was the son of Frederick Stockman and Catherine Disponet. At age 13 in March 1806, he came with his parents to Texas and lived at Villa Trinidad de Salcedo. When his father was expelled from Texas, he went with his family to the Neutral Strip between Texas and Louisiana.

He married Dorcas Trebite (this is the Spanish spelling of her surname-its English version is not known) ca. 1820. He had land dealings in the Neutral Strip. He returned to Texas ca. 1827. Henry was a carpenter in 1828 and 1829 while living on Pilar Street in Nacogdoches. He was executor of his brother, Joseph Anthony Stockman's estate in 1834. In 1835, Henry and his family were living on their Mexican land grant which was near Williams settlement, now Mt. Enterprise, Rusk County.

During the years prior to the Republic of Texas, Henry was an influential member of the Nacogdoches Community. He was fluent in both English and Spanish, and he served as translator for the Alcalde. He received votes for Alcalde and other elected positions.

Henry and Dorcas' children were Henry Joseph Stockman, born Dec. 7, 1820; Hardy Francis Stockman, born Oct. 19, 1822; Henrietta Stockman, born Dec. 10, 1826; Harry Satanna Stockman, born July 26, 1829; Mary Harriet Stockman, born Jan. 22, 1831; and Hiram H. Stockman, born Jan. 20, 1834.

Henry died Feb. 2, 1852 in Rusk County, TX. He drowned in Stockman Spring. He is buried in a grave on the Henry Stockman League. A large rock marks his grave.

Dorcas died Sept. 10, 1852 in Caldwell County, where she had gone to live with her sons. She made a will on Sept. 8, 1852, and died two days later.

Nelva Joy Stockman Bixler, (GGGGGD), 18005
G6 Henry Stockman,
G5 Henry Joseph Stockman,
G4 Garrison Greenwood Stockman,
G3 Durward Jeptha Stockman,
G2 John Leslie Stockman,
G1 Nelva Joy Stockman Bixler.

REINHARD (RENKE) STOELTJE and his wife, Margaret, were among the few German settlers in Texas who preceded the influx of the 1840s. Emigrating from Oldenburg, Germany, in 1833, Reinhard was 46 years old, and Margaret was 25. The ship on which they sailed ran aground and wrecked off Galveston Island where there was nothing there but the ruins of the old Mexican custom house, thousands of deer, and Indians.

After establishing a homesite on the mainland, the Texas Revolution started. The Mexican Army overtook the family while fleeing, captured Reinhard and intended to hang him. He told them that if they killed him, he would die as innocent as Jesus Christ himself. They let him go.

In 1841, Reinhard bought land and made permanent settlement in Frelsburg in Colorado County. He farmed and raised some stock. Joining Houston's Army, he fought in the battle of San Jacinto. In 1837, the Stoeltje's named their first son after their friend, General Sam Houston. Other children from this marriage were Nancy, "Mattie" (Margaret, Charles, William, Julius, Eliza, Helena and Anton.

In 1856, Reinhard moved his family to Welcome in Austin County, where he farmed until his death in 1882 at the age of 90.

Alice Lee Tetsch King, (GGGD), 20450

MARGARET STURROCK was born in Scotland near Dundee on June 12, 1814, the daughter of William and Ann Swan Sturrock. She immigrated to New York with her parents in 1830. In 1832, this family migrated again to New Orleans, eventually settling on the Red River at Natchitoches. She met Simon Wiess and married on Jan. 6, 1836.

After their marriage, Margaret and Simon settled at Nacogdoches, TX, where they remained for two years engaged in merchandising at the Old Stone Fort. Their first child, and only daughter, Pauline (later Mrs. Abel Coffin Jr.), was born in May 1837. Other children born later at Wiess Bluff, TX were Napoleon; twins, William and Mark; Valentine and Massina.

Seeing greater economic opportunity farther south, Simon in 1838, converted his merchandise inventory into bale cotton and with his family and household effects floated the first cotton-laden keelboat south to the coast. In this instance, Mrs. Weiss made the first such voyage down the Neches River for a woman.

Margaret Sturrock Wiess came to Texas during the struggle for Independence and was intimately acquainted with General Houston, Rusk, and other noted men of that day. She with her husband settled at Wiess Bluff, some miles north of Beaumont, where she lived until removed by death in May 1881.

RALPH TANDY, (born 1781, died 1836), pronounced "Raif" was born in Orange County, VA, to Henry and Ann (Mills) Tandy. His father was an American Revolution patriot who provided supplies to the Continental Army. His mother was descended from the colonial Virginia families of Clopton and Booth of England.

In 1808 Ralph married Matilda McGehee (born 1788, died ca. 1855), daughter of Edward and Frances (Lumsden) McGehee, in Louisa County, VA. In 1816 he purchased land in Christian County, KY, and resided there until 1829 when he moved his family to Greene County, AL. In 1833 he was a deacon of the Beulah Baptist Church.

Two years later Ralph and Matilda immigrated with their children: William Mills, Albert M., Mary E., Ralph A. and Christopher C., to the state of Coahuila and Texas. Their oldest daughter, Frances Ann; husband, Calvin Boales; and children had also immigrated to the province of Texas. Ralph and his family were sworn as colonists in Robertson's Colony in January 1836, the first Tandy family to come to Texas. He signed a memorial to the convention at Washington-on-the-Brazos in February 1836, which resulted in the establishment of the General Land Office of Texas in December 1836 by the First Congress of the Republic of Texas.

Ralph died in the spring of 1836 at the age of 55. His widow, Matilda, received his headright certificate for a league and labor for his heirs which was surveyed in Navarro County (present Johnson). Matilda lived in Washington County from 1837-49 when she moved to Lavaca County with her sons and their families.

Caroline Boales Bass, (GGGGD), 13302
Leona Boales Bass Marcellus, (GGGD), 14275
Avis Boales Wheeler Armstrong, (GGGD), 14298

CHARLES WILLIAM TAIT, son of Caroline Elizabeth Goode and James Asbury Tait, was born June 4, 1815, in Elbert County, GA. He moved with his family to Monroe County, AL, then to Wilcox County, AL, where the family lived in a plantation home known as Dry Fork. He took bachelor's and master's degrees at the University of Alabama in Tuscaloosa, and a medical degree from the University of Pennsylvania.

Charles William Tait

From 1837-43, he served in the USN as a surgeon. Afterwards, he returned to Dry Fork, traveling by steamboat down the Ohio and Mississippi Rivers.

After an altercation with his sister's suitor in which the suitor was fatally wounded, he made his way to Texas, arriving in September 1844.

He served in the U.S. Army in 1846 during the Mexican War, enlisting as a private, but being promoted to regimental surgeon.

In 1847, he purchased about 1000 acres on the Colorado River about 10 miles south of Columbus, TX. He named his plantation Sylvania.

Over the next several years, he greatly expanded his plantation, eventually acquiring more than 5000 acres.

There, with the labor of a steadily rising number of slaves, which at its peak reached 68, he grew cotton and corn, and raised swine cattle. He drafted a list of rules concerning the treatment of slaves that have come to be regarded as a model of benign management.

In 1848, he married Louisa Mary Williams. The couple had nine children, four of whom lived to adulthood.

He was elected to the House of Representatives of the Fifth Texas Legislature in 1853, and of the Seventh Texas Legislature in 1857.

During the Civil War, he enlisted in the Texas State Troops, achieving the rank of lieutenant colonel.

Before and after the war, he invested in railroads, though without notable success.

Tait died Nov. 2, 1878, having spent the last several years in ill health. He was buried in the family cemetery on his plantation.

He built two celebrated houses, the Sylvania Plantation home in 1847 and a large house, the Tait Townhouse, in Columbus about 10 years later.

One of his great-granddaughters, Millycent Tait Cranek, and two of his great-great-granddaughters, Jayne Easterling and Harriet McElreath, became members of the Daughters of the Republic of Texas.
Millycent Tait Cranek.

VICENTE MANUEL TARIN, a young patriot who wanted freedom for his countrymen, himself and his family. He was a corporal in Co. B, in the Second Regt. of Texas Vol. in Col. Juan N. Seguin's Ninth Co. He participated in various battles including the Battle of Conception and Battle of San Jacinto on April 21, 1836. His service record was #194. Birth and death dates unknown.

He served from November 1835 to the end of 1836. He conducted himself as a good soldier, according to a commendation he received. On Jan. 25, 1838, the Bexar County Land Board granted him a headright certificate for one-third league of land.

Tarin lived in San Antonio with his wife, Juana Leal, daughter of Joaquin Leal and Ana Maria deArocha. Both her parents were descendants of the Canary Islanders who arrived in San Antonio March 9, 1731, to establish the first civil government in what is now San Antonio, TX.
Aurelia Flores Deuvall.

JOHANN FRIEDRICH TAUSCH, born Nov. 10, 1819, in Berlin, Charlottenburg, Germany. His parents were Conrad Friedrich and Henrietta Caroline Franz Tausch. He was in the first contingent of settlers of New Braunfels, TX, under Prince Solms of Braunfels, arriving at Indianola, TX, in December 1844. Johann Friedrich Tausch is listed as #9 on the charter membership roll of Deutsch-Protestantischen Gemeinde. As a founding colonist, he received town lot #6 in April 1845 drawing. Later, he received lot #10 from Hermann Spiess, trustee for the German

Emigration Co., and granted block 85 on Comal Creek, containing 15 acres.

Johann Friedrich Tausch and Anna Kreitz were married Aug. 2, 1845. Anna Kreitz accompanied her parents to Texas in 1844. Johann Friedrich and Anna Tausch were the parents of 13 children: Max, Adolph, Emilie, Conrad, Franklin, Pauline, Mina, Karolina, Anna, Johanna, Friedrich, Julia, Karl and a child who died in infancy.

The Tausches lived on their Comal Creek property, and later purchased a ranch on Bear Creek in Comal County. This was near the community of Walhalla (later known as Sattler). After the Civil War, Johann Friedrich went to Mexico to seek better economic support for his large family. He lived for a while at Monclova, died in that area in 1869, and was buried at Muszuiz, Coahuila, Mexico. While in Mexico, he drove the Mexican government stagecoach from Mexico City to Eagle Pass, TX, carrying gold to turn over to the military at Eagle Pass for transport to Washington, D.C.

Lois Ann Tausch Sarvis is the great-granddaughter of Johann Friedrich Tausch and Anna Kreitz Tausch. #9903

CAROLINE HEPZIBETH TAYLOR

CAROLINE HEPZIBETH TAYLOR 15160-5, born Feb. 24, 1844, in Wilson County, TX; she was the only daughter of Creed Taylor and Nancy Goodbread Taylor. My mother, Delvia Nell Spencer Tschirhart, described her as loving and kind - always worrying over and trying to help others. Mother said, "She used to scare everyone to death during the night prowling around making sure they were still breathing." Like Creed, she was feisty and stubborn - all wrapped up in less than 100 pounds. She was said to have had the tiniest quilt stitch in the county.

Creed Taylor (right) and his companion John McPeters. They were "Rough Riders" of the South.

Born during perilous times in Texas, Caroline and her two older brothers, John Hays Taylor and Phillip Goodbread (nicknamed Doughboy) Taylor, took their turns in their home's Indian lookout. Creed was often away for extended periods fighting for Texas, it was primarily left up to Nancy to care for and protect herself and the children. Her own brand was recorded in Gonzalez in October 1860.

Caroline Hepzibeth Taylor's half brother, James Josiah Hays Taylor, born of Creed Taylor's second marriage to Lavinia Spencer. She was W.A. Spencer's cousin.

During the Civil War, Creed mustered and was captain of a troop of old men and young boys. On his muster roll was a boy, age 16, P.G. Taylor; he was Caroline's youngest brother. Apparently, her older brother, most often called, Hays, stayed behind to be of some assistance and protection for their mother.

When Creed first brought his Civil War acquaintance, south-

ern gentleman, W.A. Spencer, home to meet his daughter, she took her father aside and said, "That's the ugliest man I ever saw." But love crept in and W.A. Spencer stepped into place as my great-grandfather. In 1866, they were married in the family home on the Ecleto Creek. They settled in Wilson County where W.A. Spencer (most often called Will) began a political career that spanned over 50 years. He was county clerk and district clerk, serving out of the courthouse located in the boisterous town of Helena.

James Josiah "Kince" Spencer, Mineola Northcutt Spencer and their daughter, Delvia Nell Spencer.

Creed Taylor's great-great-great granddaughters, (L to R) Elfie Spencer and Delvia Nell Spencer.

Will's father, Elijah, was born Jan. 14, 1819, Henderson County, TN, and married Temperance Brown about 1840 in Henderson, TN. He died May 1854, Harrison County, TX. His brother, Carroll, was born Aug. 30, 1823, and married Frances Amanda Mann, Jan. 9, 1849. He died March 15, 1856. Also arriving in Texas early, was William S. Spencer Sr., Will's, grandfather. He was born Sept. 8, 1795, in Montgomery County, NC. He married Allafair Haltom who was born about 1800 in Montgomery County. She died about 1863 in Upshur County, TX. Elijah, Carroll and William, all three men arrived in the area and became landowners before the town of Helena was established.

The first Spencer to arrive in America was William Spencer. Born about 1736, he married Hannah Sugg, about 1840. She was the daughter of Thomas Sugg and Mary Harbard, and was born about 1745. William was one of the early pioneers in the British Colony of North Carolina. He received a warrant (#9) for 100 acres of land in Anson County. He is believed to have participated in the American Revolution under the command of Gen. Pickney. His son, Johnson, is thought to have served in the same unit.

After the death of her two brothers, Hays and Doughboy, in the regrettable Sutton-Taylor Feud and the death of her mother, Creed relocated his stock and moved to Kimble County and settled at the head of James River in Knoxville. Caroline and Will were not far behind; they settled in Junction in 1877.

Will resumed his political career; he served as district and county clerk for 10 years, sheriff for eight years and was elected county judge for several terms. Gov. Coke Stevenson said, "W.A. Spencer deserves a historical marker because he taught Texans pioneer law." He was also described as "firm, but fair." My mother described him as well educated and the perfect example of a "Southern Gentleman."

As a young man in his teens, he was in the Ranger Service along the border, protecting citizens from Indians and Mexicans.

When the War Between the States broke out, he organized a Civil War Co. of which he was elected captain. By the end of the war, he had attained the rank of major; he was referred to by the community of the time ... and by the community of today. I took Mother for a visit to Junction on a memory/research trip. Unfortunately, we went on a day the museum was closed. While visiting the courthouse to do some research the county judge at the time, overheard me inquiring about the museum's schedule, he picked up the phone, called City Hall and said, "Maj. Spencer's granddaughter is here, please open the museum and allow her to take a tour of it." It made me proud that the granddaughter he referred to, was my mother and the Maj. Spencer he referred to, was my great-grandfather.

Both Caroline and Will were prominent in the community and church. Will was a charter member of the Masonic Lodge; he was elected treasurer at the first official meeting, April 9, 1881.

They had seven children: Elfie, Minnie, William (called Willie), James Josiah (named after the elder Josiah but called Kince), Bud (named after the elder Hepzibeth's second husband, Joshua Dowlearn (called Bud most of the time) and Lennie, who died as a small child.

Retirement found Will and Caroline splitting time between the homes of their children and their own home adjacent to the courthouse, on the banks of the South Llano River. My mother always knew the sound of their hack meant lots of hugs and late night talks about old times, along with some of Grandma Spencer's "Butter Rolls," a cobbler-like dish. Mother said that Grandma Spencer almost always wore a black "head rag," the custom for a year following the death of a loved one. Unfortunately deaths occurred frequently as it did for both of her brothers, many other family members, and loved ones who did not survive the turbulent times of Reconstruction, the feared State Police and the resulting Sutton-Taylor Feud.

Caroline entered heavenly rest Oct. 14, 1920, having passed much oral family to my mother, grandmother, Mineola Northcutt and grandfather, James Josiah (Kince). She was laid to rest in the South Llano Cemetery. Will was lost without his beloved and spunky Carolina. He spent most of his time with his son, Kince and his daughter, Bessie McDonough. However, he passed away, Aug. 2, 1922, while visiting in Rock Springs.

We are indebted to the "Caroline Hepzibeth Taylors" who were inspirational apron-clad wives, mothers and community assets. Like W.A. Spencer, there were many fine lawmen of pioneer times. However, one would be hard pressed to find another who was more able to calmly guide the "rough and tumble" frontiersmen along the path of law.
Dovie Tschirhart Hall.

HEPZIBETH LUKER TAYLOR, 15162-S, History has had much to say about the men of early Texas, but little about the pioneer women, wives and mothers who possessed great stamina and courage. Without hesitation, they, gathered a few meager belongings, readied the children and bravely followed the dangerous path to the Texas wilderness. Such a woman was Hepzibeth Luker Taylor, my great-great-great-grandmother. Let me tell you about her!

Born in South Carolina about 1790, she married adventurer, Josiah Taylor Oct. 1, 1807. In 1812, Josiah went to Texas and took part in Mexico's struggle to overthrow Spain. He was wounded seven times and was gone four years before going home

to his wife and two children. Hepzibeth also struggled four years: making sure the children were fed, clothed, educated, restored them to health when they were ill and provided them with love and a well kept home. She certainly had her hands full; William Riley (born 1809) was about 3 when Josiah arrived in Texas and Hardiena (born 1812) was an infant. I wonder if Hepzibeth ever suggested that Josiah make a career change. Evidently not, for in 1824, Josiah was ready to

Delvia Spencer and Shine Spencer, great-great-great grandchildren of Hepzibeth Luker Taylor.

return to Texas; this time he took the whole family including: Joanna (born 1817), Creed (born 1820), Josiah Jr. (born 1822) Pitkin (born 1823) and Rufus (born 1824). James was born right after they arrived in Texas, and Mary Jane, a short time later.

Hepzibeth was the first person to register a cattle brand in Gonzales County; the fourth was Richard H. Chisholm who would later become famous as a cattle driver, driving cattle throughout Texas. Hepzibeth's brand was registered Feb. 1, 1829. The recording of cattle brands was covered in *"The Cattleman"* magazine, published in October 1935 in Fort Worth, TX, and I quote, "In the year 1829, one Hepsebeth Taylor registered HT as his iron." They assumed that an individual with enough strength, stamina and interest in cattle raising, simply HAD to be male. Well, there were many "manlike" duties performed by pioneer women (in addition to their regular chores), that contributed to Texas independence!

Besides her worries about Indian raids, rumors were starting to the effect that the Mexican government was feeling threatened by the number of America settlers along with the bravery and creativity and daring attributes. Right around the corner came the Texas War for Independence. Although Creed was the most adventurous, like his father, Josiah Jr. was pretty active. Five sons fought in the Battle of Salado. That was a heavy burden for a mother to bear and one can only imagine her happiness when all returned home safely.

Creed described their home as "humble but very dear; it had little finery but had everything we needed - especially love and a hard work ethic." He also said of his mother, "She taught the children to read and write - and held the family together." Josiah died in 1830 without receiving the Spanish land grant due him. Hepzibeth received the one league of land in DeWitt's Colony.

Hepzibeth married a neighbor, Patrick Dowlearn; they had one son, Joshua, who was nicknamed "Bud." Hepzibeth's granddaughter, Caroline Hepzibeth Taylor Spencer (W.A. Spencer) named one of her sons Bud in honor of Joshua "Bud."

Hepzibeth entered heavenly rest about 1840 or 1841. She is buried in the "Old Taylor" beside her beloved husband, Josiah Taylor. Both of the graves are graced by Texas historical markers, acknowledging their many contributions to the Republic of Texas.

Where would Texas be today without the women who "hung tough" no matter what came. This is submitted with great pride and sincere love and appreciation.
Dovie Dell Tschirhart Hall.

JOSIAH TAYLOR, #15161-S, born about 1781 in Virginia, Josiah first came to Texas in 1812 as a captain in the Gutierrez-Magee Expedition, a failed attempt by Anglo-Americans and Mexicans to free Mexico from Spanish rule, the forerunner of Texas independence struggle.

Josiah fought in battles at La Bahia, Alazon, Rosales and Medina. In at least two of the battles, Capt. Taylor and his company of rebel filibusters were in the center of the fray against the Royalists. In some cases the Royalists were defeated. However, in August 1813 the Filibusters encountered a new force laid in ambush inflicting catastrophic damage. Only 300 of a total force survived. Although Josiah survived, he was wounded seven times. He credited his survival to the superb horse he rode. He carried two bullet slugs in his body as he escaped to Louisiana.

James Josiah Taylor Kince, great-great grandson of the elder Josiah Taylor and his grandson Gatlon Waukeen, the son of his daughter, Delvia Nell Spencer.

When Josiah came to Texas, he left behind his wife, Hepzibeth Luker Taylor (they were married in Clarke County, GA, in 1807) and family. After recovering from his wounds, he rejoined his family in Georgia. However, Josiah still had Texas

Delvia Nell Spencer, great-great grand-daughter of Josiah Taylor with her mother, Mineola Northcutt Spencer and her husband, Ernest Hulbert Tschirhart and their daughter Dovie Nell Tschirhart.

on his mind. In 1824, he returned to Texas with his family. First documentation of the Taylor family in Texas is the Atascosita census of 1826. Besides Josiah and Hepzibeth, seven children: William, Hardiena, Joanna, Creed, Josiah Jr., Pitkin and Rufus were listed. The census of 1826 reflected an additional child, James. Their last child, Mary Ann, was born after 1826 since she was not on that year's census.

Josiah's family became DeWitt colonists. Creed quoted his father as saying, "Texans will not long stand hitched, but will rise up in arms, whip Mexico and own Texas." Indeed they did! Sadly, Josiah did not live to see the part his sons played in that endeavor for he died in 1830.

Five of his sons fought together in the Battle of Salado: William, Pitkin, Creed, Josiah Jr. and Rufus. I'm sure he looked down with pride at their bravery and brotherly unity. Creed and Josiah Jr. fought in many battles and ultimately, the Battle of San Jacinto.

Hepzibeth received a one league land grant in Green DeWitt's Colony based on Josiah's Colonization certificate from the Empresario. Josiah had applied for the grant due him as a colonist with a family. Certificate #58 was issued to him May 28, 1830, a few days after he died.

I'm proud of the legacy left by my great-great-great-grandfather, Josiah Taylor, for his spirit of adventure and his bravery that allowed me to have eighth generation grandchildren: Tyler Weston King, Travis Garret King, Creed Taylor Hall and Naomi Frances Hall. They live in "A Free TEXAS" because of Josiah Taylor and the many old Texans like him.
Dovie Dell Tschirhart Hall.

GEORGE THOMAS, born Feb. 4, 1793, in Kentucky and died June 2, 1865, in Harrison County, TX. He was the son of Richard Thomas and Mary (Dawson?) who arrived in Red River/Lamar County, TX, in 1836. (See Richard Thomas biography.) George Thomas married Sythie Richardson Jan. 4, 1816, daughter of John Richardson and Syntha Willis of Maury County, TN. She was born Feb. 9, 1798, in Georgia, and died March 5, 1864, in Harrison County, TX. George and Sythie Thomas lived in Mississippi before moving to Texas in November 1840. The Republic of Texas granted George land in Harrison, Hopkins, Delta and Wise counties. He made his home on one of these grants located eight miles northwest of Marshall, in Harrison County, TX. He was by occupation a farmer, and was always regarded as a successful man at his occupation. George and Sythie had 13 children, six sons and seven daughters.

Children of George Thomas and Sythie Richardson are: Harriett Thomas (born Dec. 23, 1816, in Mississippi) married Gideon Flint March 15, 1834. They had seven children: A.B., Josiah, Syrena, George, Rowena, George Thomas and Parthena. Gideon Flint drowned in an accident on the Sabine River. Harriett then married Benjamin "Frank" James. They had four children: Thomas Franklin, William Love, Joseph and Dudley. Benjamin "Frank" James died a month after being wounded in the Battle of Raymond, MS. Harriett never remarried.

Eliza Thomas (born March 21, 1818, in Mississippi) married Thomas Flint Dec. 24, 1837.

Josiah Thomas (born Feb. 18, 1821, in Mississippi, died Oct. 19, 1821).

John Thomas (born Jan. 21, 1823, in Mississippi) married Melissa Hill Aug. 15, 1834. They had nine children, seven girls and two boys: Judy, Sarah, Mary, Ann, Nancy, Sithy, Hattie, Dallas and Polk. They left Harrison County, TX, and moved west in about 1868 and settled in Hunt County, TX.

Mary Polly Thomas (born Nov. 27, 1824, in Mississippi) married L.H. Snowden Oct. 4, 1844.

Judah Thomas (born Aug. 7, 1826, in Mississippi, died Oct. 25, 1888, Harrison County, TX) married William Mills Richardson May 11, 1849, in Harrison County, TX. He was born Nov. 12, 1826, and died March 11, 1897, in Harrison County, TX. He was the son of the Rev. Allen Richardson and Rebecca Bailey of Maury County, TN. William Mills Richardson served in Co. H of the 7th Texas Inf., for the Confederacy in the Civil War.

Ann Thomas (born Feb. 3, 1828, in Mississippi, died Jan. 21, 1840).

James D. Thomas (born Nov. 5, 1829, in Mississippi, died Nov. 22, 1830).

William Thomas (born Oct. 19, 1831, in Mississippi, died Jan. 22, 1916, in Harrison County, TX) inherited the family home where he lived all of his life. William never married.

George Thomas (born Jan. 18, 1833, in Mississippi) died in an accident, May 1, 1862, in Memphis, Clark County, TN.

Sarah Thomas (born March 24, 1835, in Mississippi, died Oct. 22, 1842, in Texas).

Elizabeth Thomas (born Dec. 22, 1839, in Mississippi) married G.I. Goodwin May 27, 1857.

Richard Thomas (born April 8, 1844, in Harrison County, TX, died June 3, 1848, in Harrison County, TX).
Jacqueline Ann Busby Cochran, (GGGGD), #22181
Joyce Yvonne Busby Yancy, (GGGGD), #22408

JOHN DAWSON THOMAS, born 1816 in Kentucky and died in 1861 in Lamar County, TX. He came to Texas with his parents, Richard and Mary (Dawson?) Thomas in 1836. The Republic of Texas granted John D. Thomas, as a single man, a second class headright of 640 acres in Lamar County where he made his home. In 1839, he married Lavinia Johnson in Lamar County, TX. She was the daughter of John Johnson and Mary Chisum (Chisolm) who came to Lamar County, TX, in 1837. Lavinia Johnson was born in 1824 in Tennessee and died in 1863 in Lamar County, TX. John D. Thomas was the sheriff of Lamar County for one term, a merchant and a very successful plantation owner.

The children of John Dawson Thomas and Lavinia Johnson are:

Victoria O. Thomas (born 1842 in Lamar County, TX).

Richard Oldam Thomas (born Jan. 20, 1843, in Lamar County, TX, died Jan. 1, 1923, in Waco, TX) married Martha Ellis 'Mattie' Michell Jan. 17, 1872, in Waco, TX. (See Richard Oldam Thomas biography).

Mary A. Thomas was born 1844 in Lamar County, TX. She married James O. Kavinaugh May 11, 1866, in Texas.

James Thomas (born 1847 in Lamar County, TX) married Susan.

Dawson Thomas (born 1849 in Lamar County, TX).

Johnathan D. Thomas (born 1849 in Lamar County, TX).

Joseph D. Thomas (born Jan. 15, 1849, in Lamar County, TX) married Sallie Martin of Memphis, TN, the daughter of John and Eliza (Lenoir) Martin. (See Joseph D. Thomas biography.)

Martha "Mattie" Susan Thomas (born 1850 in Lamar County, TX) married Travis C. Henderson in 1866 at Lamar County, TX, shortly after the death of her mother. Travis C. Henderson served as an officer for the Confederacy in the Civil War and later became a Texas state representative for Lamar County. After the death of Martha's parents, they were appointed guardians of her sisters, Ella and Frances "Fanny," and her brothers, John J. and William.

William B.G. Thomas (born 1852 in Lamar County, TX, died before August 1871).

Frances "Fanny" E. Thomas (born 1854, died July 8, 1880, in Lamar County, TX).

Ella Thomas (born 1857 in Lamar County, TX) married Walter Lee on Dec. 18, 1878, in Red River, TX.
Jacqueline Ann Busby Cochran, (GGGGN), #22181

JOSEPH D. THOMAS, born in Lamar County, TX, Jan. 15, 1849, was the son of John Dawson Thomas and Lavinia (Johnson) Thomas. Lavinia was a native of Tennessee, the daughter of John Johnson and Mary Chisum (Chisolm), she died in Paris, Lamar County, TX, in 1863. John Dawson Thomas was a native of Kentucky, a plantation owner, merchant, the sheriff of Lamar County for one term and a member of the Christian church. John D. Thomas's parents were Richard and Mary (Dawson?) Thomas.

Joseph D. Thomas was the third of 11 children: Victoria O., Richard O., Mary A., James, Dawson, Jonathan D., Martha S. "Mattie," William B.G., Frances "Fanny" and Ella.

He received his education in the schools of Paris, TX; and

attended McKinzie College, in Red River County, TX. He opened and operated a bookstore in Paris, TX, from 1872-82, when he went into the cattle business in the West for one year. When he returned to Paris, he organized the Lyons, Thomas Hardware Co. and was a member of that firm until 1886. He then became a member of the Arctic Ice and Refrigerating Co. and treasurer of the Paris Building and Loan Association, and was city treasurer.

In 1880, he married Sallie Martin, of Memphis, TN, the daughter of John and Eliza (Lenoir) Martin, and a sister of the Honorable John Martin, president of the Farmer's and Merchants' Bank, at Paris, TX. They had at least one child, a daughter, and were both members of the Presbyterian church.
Jacqueline Ann Busby Cochran, #22181

RICHARD OLDHAM THOMAS, born Jan. 20, 1843, in Paris, Lamar County, TX, and died Jan. 1, 1923, in Clarendon, Donley County, TX. He was the son of John Dawson Thomas and Lavinia Johnson, who were some of the early pioneers of Texas. (See John Dawson Thomas biography.)

Richard O. Thomas married Martha Ellis "Mattie" Mitchell Jan. 17, 1872, in Waco, TX. She was born Nov. 26, 1852, in Champagnolle, AR, and was the daughter of John A. Mitchell and Martha Caroline Holloway. Martha died Nov. 28, 1931, in Meadow, TX.

The children of Richard Oldham and Martha "Mattie" Mitchell are: Frank Barton Thomas (born Jan. 10, 1873) married Ella Fish.

Mary Littlefield Thomas (born March 22, 1874, in Marlin, TX, died Dec. 17, 1968, in Lubbock, TX) married Marcus Leonard Malone Dec. 31, 1891, in Montague, TX.

John Dawson Thomas (born Sept. 20, 1876, in Marlin, TX) married Emma Curtis Brown Oct. 20, 1895, in Montague, TX.

Richard Oldham Thomas (born May 26, 1878, in Marlin, TX) married Mae Walling Dec. 25, 1904.

Martha "Mattie" Caroline Thomas (born April 15, 1882, in Montague, TX) married James "Jim" K. Jackson Dec. 25, 1902.

Lavinia "Viney" Thomas (born Nov. 7, 1884, in Montague, TX, died in 1974 in Dinuba, CA) married Arthur Lee Sisk Dec. 22, 1906.

William Jennings Bryan Thomas (born July 23, 1897, in Montague, TX, died Oct. 31, 1981, in San Angelo, TX) married Gracie Lee Barnes July 10, 1916, in Bowie, Montague County, TX.
Jacqueline Ann Busby Cochran, #22181

RICHARD THOMAS, born about 1773 in Virginia, died in 1842 in Lamar County, TX. He married Mary Polly (Dawson?) around 1792. She was born about 1775 and died around 1842 in Lamar County, TX. Richard and Mary Thomas lived in Kentucky and Tennessee before moving to Texas. It is believed that Richard and Mary Thomas came to Texas with Claiborne Chisum (Chisolm), George W. Wright and John Johnson. On Dec. 12, 1836, the Republic of Texas granted Richard Thomas a second class headright that contained 1,280 acres in Lamar County, TX, where they lived the rest of their lives.

Children of Richard and Mary Thomas are: George Thomas (born Feb. 4, 1793, in Kentucky, died June 2, 1865, in Harrison County, TX) married Sythie Richardson Jan. 4, 1816, daughter of John Richardson and Syntha Willis of Maury County, TN. She was born Feb. 9, 1798, in Georgia, and died March 5, 1864, in

Harrison County, TX. They had 13 children. (See George Thomas biography.)

William Thomas (born about 1797 in Kentucky, died before 1860) married Lucy Cannon Oct. 7, 1828, in Maury County, TN, daughter of John Cannon and Hannah. She was born about 1793 and died before November 1843 in Marshall, Harrison County, TX.

John Dawson Thomas (born 1816 in Kentucky, died in 1861 in Lamar County, TX) married Lavinia Johnson in 1839, daughter of John Johnson and Mary Chisum (Chisolm). She was born in 1824 in Tennessee and died in 1862, Lamar County, TX. (See John Dawson Thomas biography.)

Emily Thomas married a Williamson.

Sarah Thomas married a Nelson.

Lucy Thomas married an Allen.

Judah Thomas married a Draper.

Elizabeth Thomas also married a Draper.

Jacqueline Ann Busby Cochran, (GGGGGD), #22181
Mary Kathleen Busby Smith, (GGGGGD), #22312

JAMES THOMPSON, applied for his 320 acres in Harrisburg County, TX, Feb. 18, 1839. He was born in 1790 in Sumner County, TN, the son of Jacob Thompson. He married Nancy Denning, who was born in 1794 in North Carolina, on Oct. 24, 1811, in Sumner County, TN. He died in Polk County, TX, in 1849.

Little is known about their seven children other than the youngest, Andrew Jackson, who was born in 1825 in Sumner County, TN. He married Eleanor "Ellen" Cummin(g)s, daughter of John Henry and Elizabeth Cummings, on Sept. 5, 1850, in Walker County, TX. They had seven children also: David Denning (born Nov. 9, 1851) married Rosanah Brice; Nancy Elizabeth "Betty" (born Feb. 26, 1853) married John Newton Brice; Eliza Jane "Babe" (born 1854) married David Meek Elms; John Henry (born March 15, 1856) married Emaline Elms; Elleanor "Ella" (born May 1, 1859) married Isaac Large; Polly Melvina "Dine" (born April 27, 1861) married Hadden Elms; Andy Tracy (born July 27, 1865) married John Edward Allen. All but the youngest is buried at Leakey Floral Cemetery in Real County, TX.

Patsy Cummings McKelvy, (GGGD), #21279

ALEXANDER S. THOMSON JR., born of Scottish descent in St. Matthew's Parish, SC, Aug. 29, 1785. He was the only son of Alexander and Lucy (Fontaine) Thomson. He was reared by a pious uncle, Thomas Fontaine, in Georgia with whom he received his education and indoctrination of the Methodist church. He later moved to Georgia and in 1805 he was married to Elizabeth Maury Dowsing in Lincoln County, GA, and in 1814 they moved to Giles County, TN.

Alexander Thomson

On Aug. 30, 1830, Thomson, who was quite well educated for his time and who had mastered seven different trades, formed a partnership with his son, William Dowsing Thomson, and the Empresario Sterling Clack Robertson for the colonization of Texas and loaned Robertson $20,000 to fund the venture. This venture was known as "The Nashville Co." and appointed Thomson and Robertson as managers.

On Oct. 28, 1830, Thomson arrived in Nacogdoches with his son, W.D., and his party of 50 persons, the first group of families bound for the Nashville Colony. However, upon arrival he was informed of a new law passed April 6, 1830, barring further colonization without passports. After several days of meetings with the alcalde at Nacogdoches to plead his case to permit him to proceed without passports, he was granted permission to travel to Austin's Colony to obtain the necessary papers from Austin himself, but the rest of the families were denied entrance until his return.

After two difficult months of travel and having spent a great deal of money, he felt he had no recourse but to continue on to Robertson's Colony. At night, he returned to the colonists' camp located three miles from the garrison and decided to go around the Nacogdoches settlement by cutting a short road outside the town to connect the two existing roads. Thereafter, the road known as the "Tennesseeans Road" was called "Thomson's Pass" and was used many times by other immigrants lacking the necessary passports.

A few weeks later on November 12, Thomson and his colonists arrived "at the barracks at Mr. Williams," a site first occupied by Col. Francisco Ruiz and his Mexican soldiers and later known as the site of Fort Tenoxtitlan. The grant began at the west bank of the Navasota crossing of the old San Antonio and Nacogdoches road, west to the divided ridge between the Colorado and Brazos rivers, northwest to the Comanche trail, further to the Navasota River and south to the river's beginning. It is estimated that the colony's territory was equal to one-sixth of the entire province of Texas, some 40,000 square miles, about the size of Tennessee. It has been said that Robertson and Thomson were instrumental in bringing more families into Texas than any other Empresario, save Austin.

Thomson's second trip with colonists was made by steamboat to New Orleans, then by schooner to Harrisburg, now a part of metropolitan Houston. They arrived on April 2, 1831. After hearing that the first group he had brought to Texas in 1830 had been ordered into Austin's Colony, he went immediately to San Felipe, the capital of that Colony to gather information. While there, an order arrived requiring that he and all his families return to the U.S. Austin was in Saltillo at the time and Thomson wrote to him to intercede with the Mexican authorities to allow the colonists to settle in Austin's Colony. After much negotiating, permission was granted in late September 1831 for Austin to admit all families Robertson and Thomson had brought to Texas.

As surveyors, both Alexander Thomson and his son, William, were prominent in the affairs of the Nashville Colony. Thomson was one of 58 elected delegates to the Texas Convention of 1832 at San Felipe de Austin (Oct. 1-6, 1832), representing the Dist. of Hidalgo, which comprised all, or part of the counties of Washington, Burleson, Grimes, Milam and Lee. The delegates petitioned for the repeal of the hated Law of 1830, for tariff exemption and for independent statehood for Texas, or separation from the Mexican state of Coahuila.

Thomson hired a young Viennese immigrant, George B. Erath, to assist him and his son in surveying his own district in late fall of 1834 and chose a section of the country 25 square miles. As surveyors, no money was earned unless the land was taken by settlers, and so Thomson worked as a farmer on his own land. When the call for a general consultation for all Texas was issued for Oct. 16-17, 1835, at Columbus, Thomson was again elected as a delegate representing the municipality of Viesca. He was one of 55 settlers representing 13 municipalities.

The consultation established the first provisional government composed of a governor, lieutenant governor and an advisory council made up of one member from each municipality. Following the death of Col. Ben Milam during the Siege of Bexar, Thomson introduced the resolution on Dec. 26, 1835, changing the name of the municipality from Viesca to Milam. Thomson remained a member of the general council and was the only member of the provisional government who was still functioning in San Felipe. In fact, for one fleeting moment he was the government de facto, since all the members left to return to their homes.

Long regarded as the father of Texas Methodism, Thomson organized early congregations of family and friends on Sundays to read Wesley's sermons. In 1835 he was elected chairman of the quarterly conference of the Methodist church and was instrumental in raising $300 for the pastor's salary. This was the first effort in Texas to raise money for a Protestant minister. He helped establish the first Methodist church in Chriesman, TX, which still stands today and contains a plaque honoring his efforts.

As the father of 13 children, Thomson finally settled near Caldwell, TX, in Yellow Prairie (later renamed Chriesman), and died there June 1, 1863. Was buried along with his wife in the Thomson Cemetery in Yellow Prairie. His children were active and instrumental in the Texas Revolution and the continued settlement of Texas. One son, Jasper Newton MacDonald Thomson, was captured at Meir, and was one of 17 prisoners who drew a black bean and was executed. William D. Thomson was a second lieutenant in the Volunteer Army of Texas and served as Gen. Sam Houston's quartermaster and later served as the first county clerk and county recorder for Milam County in 1837. Later, W.D. served in the 4th Legislature for the state of Texas from Nov. 3, 1851-February 1852 representing Milam and Williamson counties. Alexander Thomson is the ancestor of many noted Texans who have served in various appointed and elected positions in state and national government including Thaddeus A. Thomson, U.S. Envoy to Colombia and signer of the Thomson-Urrutia Treaty in 1914.

The Texas Historical Survey Committee has erected two Official Texas Historical Markers honoring Alexander Thomson. The first marker erected in 1968 in Chriesman, TX, recognizes his settlement of the town known as Yellow Prairie, later changed to Chriesman. The second marker was erected in 1972 in Burleson County near Caldwell recognizing his leadership in colonizing Texas.

Helen Suzanne McCrum Marshall, (GGGGD), #19371
Kathryn Suzanne Kennedy Duncan, (GGGGGD)
Kelly Brice McCrum, (GGGGGD)

TENNESSEE "TINNIE" TIDWELL, the daughter of Absolom Tidwell. It is believed that she was part Indian and born in Tennessee.

She married Peter F. Tumlinson. They had three children: John Jackson (born 1825, Crawford County, AR), Absolom Tidwell (born Dec. 14, 1827, Crawford County AR, died Feb. 16, 1889) and William Ormond (born October 1832, Crawford County, AR, died July 1913, Leming, Atascosa County, TX). She

died in 1832, Miller County, AR, after the birth of their third child, William O.

Peter went to Texas and became a Texas Ranger. He served as a first orderly sergeant in Capt. Hooper's (later Capt. Posey's) company of cavalry. He enlisted on July 4, 1836, for a three month term.
Gerald Dean Hector Lilly, (GGGGD), #17208

NICOLAS TONDRE, (born in Bretten, Haut-Rhin, France, May 6, 1804) was the son of Pierre Francois Tondre and Elizabeth Prevot. Nicolas came to America with his wife, Marie Anna Lerch, and three children: Nicolas Francois, Celestin and Jean Baptist; and Marie, his niece.

Nicolas came to Texas on the ship *Probus* as part of Castro's Colonists. The *Probus* landed in New Orleans where the Colonists boarded another ship that landed in Port Lavaca, TX. They were met there by Henri Casto on Feb. 10, 1845. Castro arranged for ox carts to meet the ships at the dock and transport the tired colonists to Castroville.

Nicholas Harry Tondre, great grandson of Nicolas Tondre.

When they arrived in Castroville, they had to see about building some kind of home for their families. They built brush fences to keep livestock out of their gardens.

Nicolas built his home out of stone and stucco. It was a five bay front, one story with attic, garbled roof including narrowers and lower garbled extension at one end. Nicolas' home was photographed by the Library of Congress in 1936. His home still stands in Castroville on the corner of Florence and Amelia streets.

Nicolas and Marie were married 38 years and had seven children.

August, the first born in Texas, married Mary Adele Pingenot and they had nine children. My grandfather, Frank Nick, was the fifth born of August and Mary Adele.

Frank married Josephine Kempf and they had 11 children. Nicholas Harry (my father) was the seventh child of Frank and Josephine.

Nicholas married Hertha Meier and they had nine children. Nicolas was a farmer by trade.

Texas was admitted to the Union 10 months after the Tondre's set foot on Texas soil.
Darlene Tondre Glover, (GGGD), #19512
Carol Glover Nichols, (GGGGD), #19510

JAMES ALFRED TRUITT, born Oct. 23, 1795, in Buncombe County, NC, to Levi and Susannah Morgan Truitt. He married Sarah Hall, daughter of Joshua and Sarah Sellers Hall, Jan. 23, 1817, in Burke County, NC.

Truitt served as sheriff of Burke County for several years and was a lieutenant in the Cherokee War of 1838.

In 1838 the Truitt family left North Carolina for Texas, where they eventually settled in Shelby County. In 1843 Truitt was elected a justice of the peace and later that year was elected to the Eighth Congress of the Republic of Texas and in 1844 was re-elected to the Ninth Congress. He went on to represent Shelby County in six state legislatures between 1846-66.

Truitt was a moderator in the Regulator-Moderator War and represented the Moderators at a peace conference in Shelbyville in 1844. He later commanded a company of Moderators who fought beside a company of Regulators at the Battle of Monterrey in the Mexican War.

James and Sarah were the parents of 10 children: Alfred Marion, Andrew Jackson, Mary Minerva, Sarah, Levi Marion, Joshua Hall, Susan, Clarissa, Cynthia and James.

Sarah Truitt died July 3, 1848, and was buried on the Truitt family property, beginning the Truitt Cemetery. James Truitt died June 11, 1870, and was buried beside his wife, where his marker reads, in part, "A Devoted Father; Faithful to His Country."

JOHN WINGATE TRUITT, born Dec. 19, 1801, in Worchester County, MD, the son of William Truitt and Tabitha Whaley. He married Elizabeth Jane Robinson in Tennessee on his birthday in 1825. They had four children in Tennessee: William, Elijah, Sarah Ann and Edward Richard. The family moved to Alabama where two more children were born, Mattie and James L. The year after James was born the family moved to Texas and settled on a Republic of Texas land grant in Morris County near Dangerfield.

Wingate Truitt filed for his Texas land grant Nov. 13, 1839, and two more children were born, Wingate and Nancy. The family remained in Texas where Wingate died Dec. 31, 1876, and Elizabeth died Oct. 7, 1880. Both are buried in Clark Cemetery near Dangerfield in Morris County.

Sarah Ann Truitt married Andrew Jackson Richey, another Republic of Texas pioneer. About 1856 they moved to Pine Forest, Hopkins County, to live out their lives on his land grant awarded in 1857. She died Dec. 28, 1878, and is buried in Pine Forest Cemetery.

Pamela Irene DeBaun, (GGGGD), #14229

NICOLAS TSCHIRHART, born May 4, 1814, in Soppe-le-bas, Alsace, France. Lured by the unknown and the promise of land, high spirited Nicolaus answered the call of Empressario Henri Castro. Europeans were being recruited to settle and help develop Texas, a brand new, but fledgling Republic.

Single and age 30, Nicolaus became passenger #30 on the ship, *"Norvegian"* which left Anvers Oct. 19, 1844, bound for LaVaca. A sister ship, the *"Probus",* left Anvers Oct. 6, 1844, for Galveston; it carried the Meyer family who would later become Nicolas' in-laws. Some family members believe that

Ernest Hubert Tschirhart

Nicolas crossed paths with his bride-to-be en route, adding a most romantic flavor to our family saga. But the young Catherine Meyer (age 17, born Feb. 2, 1827) did not accompany her family. She and her sister, also called Josephine, were sent ahead with family friends in order for them to avoid the difficult trip from Galveston. The ship they were on docked in Louisiana.

Catherine Meyer and Nicolas did meet in Texas, fall in love

and married, Feb. 2, 1845. The ceremony was performed by Louis Huth, Castro's business manager. Their marriage license is recorded in the Bexar County Courthouse; Castroville was then a part of Bexar County.

Delvia Nell Spencer Tschirhart

Life was hard for the Castro Colonists as they faced confusion over land allotments, inadequate supplies for building even the crudest of homes, drought hindered the growth of their crops, and marauding Indians were a constant threat. Nevertheless, they began their family and had 12 children: Joseph, Sebastain, Edward, Leo, twins-Henry and Nicolas, Louis, Carolina, August, Emil and Katie (she was born a few months after Nicolas passed away). The twins, Henry and Nicolas, each lived to be 62 and died within two months of each other. Ason and Michael died as children.

Nicolas ultimately went into the freighting business. The

Anna Louise Manger Loessberg, wife of Nicolas Tschirhart and mother of Ernest Hubert Tschirhart.

work was hard and the hours were long, but nothing came easy during such turbulent times while Texas was still a virtual wilderness. All of the children were taught the value of a good work ethic. Nicolaus was described as determined, sometimes even stubborn, but caring, loving and not afraid of daily challenges.

The boys took over the freighting business until the railroad obsoleted the demand for wagon freighting. Their equipment, too large for farming, lay idle until they began hauling gold and silver out of Mexico. Edward became famous when he killed an Indian near Fort McKavitt on one of their trips. Leo was a peace officer and lost his arm in the line of duty. My daddy, Ernest Hubert Tschirhart, thought the incident occurred during a fight with an Indian. Daddy recalled that Leo had a crooked knife with three points he used to pick up bites of food. August served as Medina county commissioner for seven terms.

Nicolas' son and namesake, Nicolas John (born June 6, 1855) married Anna Louise Manger Loessberg Dec. 4, 1893. The first marriage for Nicolas John, it was the second marriage for Anna Louise from which she had one son, George. Nicolas and Anna Louise (she was most often called Louisa) had 11 children: Antone, Willie, Ernest, Della, Emil, Phillip, Clara and Henry.

My daddy, Ernest Hubert Tschirhart, described his father as a strict disciplinarian and hard worker. He was a farmer in Noonan just out of Castroville. He taught his children to tell the truth and work hard; Daddy plowed his first field when he was 6, walking behind a plow and two mules. He died Jan. 5, 1918. Daddy could, right off the top of his head, tell you the exact age his father was at the time of his death: 62 years, 6 months and 30 days. He said his father died at 3:20 p.m. The hearse that took him to the Castroville Cemetery is now on display at the Institute of Texan culture.

After Louisa lost her husband, she faced difficulty just living day to day. Her son, Willie, was kicked in the chest by a mule while he and Daddy were hauling cord wood. Daddy remembered the names of all their well and he said they were using a gentle mule, Jula, and a feisty and unpredictable Mule, Putt. Willie told Daddy, "I think I'd better walk behind Jula to hook up Putt's chain." Jula kicked him puncturing one of his lungs. Louisa was forced to sell the homestead and family farm to move the family to San Antonio in order to get the proper care Willie needed. He lived eight months. Daddy hauled his body and casket on the family wagon.

Daddy and Della were close, often getting into mischief together. Daddy fell into the creek one day trying to "ride a log." He could not swim. Della ran all the way to the house, got a rake, ran all the way to the creek and pulled him out. However, his baby sister, Clara, of course, had been showing off. But Clara, his baby sister, was his favorite.

Daddy met and married Mother, Delvia Nell Spencer, during the Great Depression. Daddy got up on their wedding at 2:00 a.m. to deliver ice by horse and buggy. Since he needed to sleep during the day, Mother cranked a hand Victrola over and over to black out noise. Daddy was never without a job during the Depression, nor did he ever stand in a soup line. He took jobs other people didn't, like working on a dairy. He often took the positions of two men at once, the whole family helped: Mineola Spencer (Mother's mother, who lived with us) helped Daddy milk 75 cows by hand, twice a day; Mother washed and sterilized milk cans and jars; my two older brothers, Gatlon and Little Ernest, helped with feeding and caring for the animals; I helped churn butter and get in the way. Daddy got paid $3.00 a week total. He also contracted to clear cedar from Texas Hill Country ranches by hand. He lived on site in a tent, coming home when he could afford the gas. Mother and her mother stayed at home in Fischer, TX, taking care of home and family.

During WWII, Daddy drove a San Antonio bus. He always worked two shifts in a row, prompting fellow drivers to refer to him as "that working son of a —." Mother and I often rode with him to keep him company; we were doing so the day the war ended ... I will never forget the pandemonium in the streets of downtown San Antonio! But what a problem it must have been to drive the bus.

I am grateful to the elder Nicolas for his willingness to accept challenge, see it through, pass the trait to his son, Nicolas, who passed it to my father and later generations.
Dovie Dell Tschirhart Hall.

WILSON VANDYKE, survivor of the Mier expedition, was born in South Carolina Dec. 25, 1817. He was the son of John and Polly VanDyke. The VanDykes came to Texas about 1837. Wilson was a stock raiser and farmer. Wilson stood 5'9" tall with a dark complexion, dark hair and blue eyes. Little has been discovered about his early life, except that his father participated in one of the Georgia land lotteries.

Wilson had arrived in Texas by October 1837 and applied for land in Bastrop County. He was also recorded as receiving a second class certificate no. 14 of 640 acres in Guadalupe County.

Wilson VanDyke

In 1842 VanDyke, along with a 43-man company from Lavaca County, joined Adam Zumwalt's company. At the Battle of Salado Creek, Zumwalt helped force Gen. Adrian Woll's Mexican army to retreat toward Mexico. Later in the same year, he joined Gen. Alexander Somervell's campaign and was assigned, as a private, to Isaac N. Mitchell's company, First Regt. of the South Western Army.

After Somervell forced the Mexican retreat, VanDyke joined the small group of Texans under Col. William S. Fischer, who wished to continue the fight. They crossed the Rio Grande into Mexico, and were captured at Mier, Tamaulipas.

On each day's march, two prisoners were shackled to one another to prevent escape. At times Wilson was shackled with Samuel Walker, who worked with Samuel Colt in developing the famed Walker Colt revolver. This revolver has been credited as the largest pistol ever made and could not be carried in a body holster; two revolvers were carried in a pair of large holsters on the pommel of the saddle. As the group was making their way to prison in Mexico, some of the 176 Texans overpowered guards and escaped. The escapees lost their way in the mountains and some died of exposure and starvation. The survivors were recaptured about a week later. Because of the escape, it was decided to execute every 10th prisoner. So 176 beans were put into an earthen jar, 17 of them were black beans. Those who drew black beans were executed. As a prisoner, Wilson participated in this Black Bean Episode, in which he drew a white bean. The family legend about his drawing a white bean came about because he had befriended a small Mexican boy that brought water to the prisoners. Wilson, being bilingual, had conversed with the boy. When it was time for Wilson to draw a bean, he was able to peek over the top of his blindfold and see the boy sitting on the prison wall. As VanDyke drew a bean, the boy shook his head, so VanDyke dropped it and took another which was white. This is a family legend and cannot be proven.

It is also believed that while Wilson was in prison, he carved a violin from sticks and pieces of wood he gathered in the prison yards. He brought the violin home with him, but no one is certain what happened to it. VanDyke was released from Perote Prison, near Mexico City, on Sept. 16, 1844. Each Texan was given a dollar at the time of his release. The former prisoners made their way to Vera Cruz. There they obtained passage aboard the schooner *"Creole"* which took them to New Orleans. They arrived in New Orleans Nov. 4, 1844.

It is not clear when Wilson returned to Texas, but he received an unconditional certificate for 640 acres of land in Gonzales County on Jan. 31, 1846. In May 1846, with the outbreak of the Mexican War, VanDyke enlisted in Capt. Benjamin McCulloch's company of Texas militia, which had become a part of Col. John Coffee "Jack" Hays's First Regt., Texas Mounted Volunteers. He was discharged Sept. 17, 1846.

On Oct. 20, 1847, Wilson married Mary Ann Power Ross in DeWitt County, TX. Three sons: John, Joseph and James Albert, were born of this union. My great-grandfather, James Albert, was born Dec. 18, 1850, in DeWitt County, TX. In the fall of 1854 Mary Ann and Wilson were granted a divorce in DeWitt County.

On Oct. 18, 1854, Wilson married Mrs. Elizabeth Montgomery in Williamson County. They were the parents of two children, Wilson and Martha Elizabeth. It is believed that they resided in San Saba County before Elizabeth's death in 1860.

Wilson's third marriage, May 18, 1860, was to Martha Jane Williams in Williamson County. This union produced nine children: Mary, Emma, George, Jasper, Louise, Alice, Alvin, Amanda and Andrew Berry.

VanDyke participated in two musters during the Civil War, which were required by law for frontier defense. His first muster was on March 18, 1864, with Capt. W.S. Gould's Co. K, First Regt., Second Bde., Texas State Troops, of Bosque and Coryell counties. On May 5, 1864, his second muster was with Capt. G. Graham's company, Second Frontier Dist., Texas State Troops, commanded by Maj. George B. Erath.

VanDyke spent the last 11 years of his life near Sparta in Bell County, where he died Aug. 3, 1881. Wilson was first buried near Sparta; his remains were later exhumed and moved to Resthaven Cemetery, Bell County, TX. A Texas historical marker was dedicated at Wilson's grave site March 24, 1985.
LeAnne VanDyke Wilden, #22516

ALBRECHT VON ROEDER, born July 31, 1811, at Marienmuster, Prussia and educated at Heidelberg and Göttingen Universities. In 1834, Albrecht, two brothers, and a sister arrived in Texas and took possession of a land tract in Central Austin County. His brother, Louis, shot a wildcat near the clear spring on the property, thus their settlement is Cat Spring.

Both joined the Texas Army, participating in the Siege of Bexar. Louis also fought at San Jacinto; Albrecht remained with a caravan in the Runaway Scrape, pulling Revolutionary Scout Deaf Smith's wife and two sets of twins across the raging Brazos River with his team of oxen.

Albrecht married Louis' widow born Caroline Ernst, daughter of the founder of Industry. In 1847, the couple moved to the Five-Mile Coleto Settlement in DeWitt County. He died June 11, 1857, near Goliad in a dispute between Texan and Mexican freight haulers, known as the Cart War. Caroline died May 12, 1902, at Lockhart.

Their son, Sigismund (born March 9, 1848), married Albertine Friske, 19-year-old immigrant from Posen, Germany. They farmed in Caldwell and Fayette counties. They died Dec. 17, 1929, and Sept. 19, 1951, at Fayetteville.

Their youngest son, Louis (born Oct. 6, 1908), married Ethel Schlenk of St. Louis, MO. They lived near Fayetteville until 1951 when they moved to Colorado County. Louis died Nov. 3, 1979, and Ethel, Aug. 3, 1993. Both are buried in Odd Fellows Cemetery in Columbus.
(GGD), #18034

JOSEPH WAGLEY, son of Abraham and Maria Henson Wagley, was born March 25, 1804, in Burke County, NC. His family moved to Illinois, then to Missouri, and finally in 1824, to Louisiana. In 1829 he married Martha Elizabeth Starks, a native of Louisiana (born 1809). She was of German descent.

By Oct. 1, 1834, Joseph was living in Red River County, TX. He lived on a hill about two miles south of Annona overlooking the Kickapoo Valley. His brother, John, settled on the next hill south. John deeded the land for the Wagley Cemetery, later named the Garland Cemetery. Joseph's home was a stagecoach inn for about 20 years on the route between Jefferson, the riverport city, and Fort Worth, TX.

Joseph and Martha had 11 children. The first three were born in Louisiana and the others were born in Red River County,

TX. They were: Starks C. (born 1830) married Frances M. Bren, died March 5, 1863, in the Civil War, buried in Columbia, TN; Thomas (born 1831); Samantha (born 1833, died 1849) was buried in the Garland Cemetery; Louisa Sabira (born Jan. 18, 1835, in Texas) married Benjamin R. Bearden in 1857, died Jan. 2, 1927, was buried in the English Cemetery in Red River County; Josiah was born in 1838, died in 1860 and was buried in the Garland Cemetery; Margaret Ann (born 1842) married Capt. William H. Wagley in 1860, died Jan. 20, 1920, buried in Hubbard, TX; Abraham Henson (born May 16, 1843) married Mattye Belle Fuller in 1870, died March 22, 1927, in Menard, TX; Martha (born Feb. 2, 1846) married Jerome William Henry Mann, June 19, 1861, died March 8, 1879, buried in the Garland Cemetery; William A. (born Oct. 7, 1848, married Georgia Ann Mauk in 1875 in McLennan County, TX, died April 6, 1913, in Altus, OK; James Wellington (born Aug. 15, 1851) married Josephine White, died Jan. 8, 1935, in Center Ridge, Conway County, AR; and Wade B. Wagley (born 1857).

Joseph's wife, Martha, died in 1857 from childbirth complications. She was buried in the Garland Cemetery. Joseph and Nancy Ann Coffee were married July 11, 1858. Nancy Ann was born in 1829 in Alabama. She and Joseph had two daughters. They were Victoria Columbia (born Nov. 1859, died 1880 in Callahan County, TX) and California (born in 1861). California died about 1872 from injuries sustained from a horse fall. Her brother had been bitten by a rattlesnake. She was scared. She got on a horse she wasn't familiar with and was on her way to get a doctor. The horse fell and she was killed.

Joseph's second wife, Nancy Ann, died in 1872 in Red River County and was buried in the Garland Cemetery.

In 1867 Joseph Wagley sold his land in Red River County and moved to Callahan County, TX, where he and a son, Abram Henson, bought 17 sections of land.

Joseph died April 6, 1878, and was buried in a pasture northeast of Putnam, TX.
Emabel Baker Fielder, (GGGD), #225158

SARAH ANN VOUCHERE WALKER, daughter of Joseph Vauchere and granddaughter of Jean Vauchere and Marguerite Lestage Vauchere, was born on her family plantation in Louisiana April 16, 1811. She married Jacob Walker, who then disposed of his land in Natchitoches, LA, in 1827. The family was in Texas by 1829 since they were recorded in Stephen F. Austin's *Book of Citizens.* The first two children were taken back to Louisiana

Brazos Cemetery marker for Sarah Ann Vouchere Walker. Pictured are Lawren Lydian Hall (GGGGG-GD) and Jessica Perry Standley (GGGG-GD).

for baptism at Natchitoches' Immaculate Conception Church in 1828 and 1830 suggesting Sarah's strong family ties and religious convictions. The family had settled in Nacogdoches in Sabine County, TX, and it was at a conference there that Sarah volunteered to take a message to Sam Houston warning the Texas Army of intended massacre by the Indians and Mexicans. Her horseback ride of 300 miles through sometimes hostile territory saved the troops.

Her husband, Jacob Walker, was the last man killed in the Battle of the Alamo. Mrs. Dickerson tells this story: "I will now describe the memorable fall of the Alamo (who witnessed it) on Feb. 23, 1836 ... Soon after he (Capt. Dickerson) left me, three unarmed gunners who abandoned their then useless guns came into the church where I was and were shot down by my side. One of them was from Nacogdoches and named Walker. He spoke to me several times during the siege about his wife and children with anxious tenderness. I saw four Mexicans toss him in the air as you would a bundle of fodder with their bayonets, and then shoot him." (*History of Texas*, M.J. Morphis, p. 174.)

One of the early acts of the Republic of Texas was to provide headright grants of land to all persons living in Texas on the day of the Declaration of Independence of Texas. The first of these were known as first class headright grants and numerous famous men of the Republic of Texas were granted this class of certificate. Jacob Walker's estate received the very first certificate issued, which is reproduced below.

Sarah moved with her family in 1850 to the land on the Brazos near what is now Waco, TX, in McLennan County. She retained and managed her properties in Nacogdoches along Big Cypress River in what is now Upshur County and Kaufman County. She had married Jim Walker, a relative of her first husband on Jan. 19, 1837; however, he had died in 1850. The 1850 census taken October 16 gives her as head of the family. According to family tradition her last child was born when she was on her way from Nacogdoches to the Brazos plantation in 1850. Altogether she lived 70 years on the Texas frontier and on her two plantations. A tiny person, only four feet, eight inches, this fair skinned, blue eyed woman had great strength of character. She remained a devout Catholic. There are published many stories of her riding ability, her hospitality on the frontier, her management of her slaves and her high standards of business conduct as found in the DRT manuscript, "Sarah Vauchere Walker's 70 Years on the Texas Frontier." Sarah Ann had nine children and family tradition was that she had a child every year of marriage. Three of her five sons predeceased her, including George A. Walker who served the Confederacy and was killed in the Battle of Bull Run. Sarah Ann Vauchere Walker died Dec. 10, 1899, and is buried with some of her children and grandchildren in the family cemetery along the banks of the Brazos river. The cemetery and some old slave quarters are all that remain of the once gracious plantation. Lawren Lydian Hall and her mother, Jessica Perry Standley, visited this plot in 1992 and are pictured in front of the Texas historical marker honoring their great-great-great-great-great-grandmother and great-great-great-great-grandmother, respectively.
Lawren Lydian Hall, (GGGGGGD), #17519

DANIEL S. WARD, born 1810 Gates County NC, son of Nathan Ward and Elizabeth Hurdle. He married Christain Brinkley May 19, 1828. Daniel was a surveyor and a blacksmith. He and Christain were parents of three children.

Nathan Owen Ward (born 1830) married Martha E. Mathews July 28, 1857, they were parents of 14 children all born in Gates County. Nathan served as second lieutenant in the "War between the States." He died 1909 in Gates County.

Daughter of Daniel and Christain was "Maranda" (born Feb. 28, 1832). She was a teacher and never married. She lived in the home of her brother, Nathan, and wife, Martha, and devoted her life to helping raise their large family. Another son was "Admiral" who died young.

Daniel S. Ward married a second time to Caroline Alzenith Keller about 1847, daughter of William W. Keller. Caroline was born June 14, 1821, Cheneyville, LA. She had a daughter, "Alzenith Elizabeth" (born 1841), by her first marriage to Richard Insall.

Daniel and Caroline were parents of three children.

Nancy Alice (born March 5, 1849) married Henry Clay Powell. They had 10 children including my father, "Albert Mathew." Henry and Nancy died November 1892, Hamilton County, TX.

William Forman Ward (born July 13, 1859) married Sarah E. Clark. They were parents of nine children. William was a minister. He died March 22, 1938, West Carroll Parish, LA.

Susan Frances "Fanny" Ward (born 1860) married Louis H. Lyles. They were parents of nine children.

I recently found an old letter written by the oldest son of Nathan Owen Ward in which he states that the middle name of Daniel S. Ward was Stallings not Sylvester as previously believed. He was named for Whitmill Stallings of Gates County, NC.

Daniel enlisted in the Army of the Republic of Texas 1836 where he remained till Texas won her independence. He received several land grants throughout Texas as well as $365.00 for service in the "Santa Fe Expedition." Daniel died Nov. 10, 1874, in Lake Charles, LA, and is probably buried in Magnolia Cemetery, Ragley, LA, along with his wife, Caroline Keller Ward.

Daniel S. Ward and Caroline were my great-grandparents.
Artie M. McDonald, (GGD), #20173

SAMUEL M. WARDEN, born in Maury County, TN, May 22, 1806. His father was James Warden (born June 2, 1775, in Kentucky, died Feb. 27, 1832, in Maury County, TN). He was buried in Rise-Warden Cemetery. Samuel's mother was Mary Ann Polly (born 1782 in Pennsylvania, died 1857).

Samuel married Louisa Harris Sept. 22, 1832. They had three children born in Tennessee before moving to Texas in 1839: Franklin Alexander (born June 30, 1833) married Mary G. Berry Oct. 6, 1853, died Dec. 3, 1904, in Llano County; Mary Ann (born 1836) married Tecumech Ross Sept. 26, 1855; Parmelia Susan (born Nov. 10, 1838, died Aug. 7, 1905). Born in Texas were: George F. (born circa 1841); Eliza Anne (born April 9, 1843, died Dec. 1, 1917); and Elizabeth E. (born Feb. 16, 1846, died Jan. 5, 1925). Samuel was a brick maker by trade. He died suddenly while working on a road from Palestine toward Rusk. His will is dated Dec. 24, 1847, and was probated on Jan. 31, 1848. He was buried in the Swanson Cemetery located near the Rusk State Railway Park. The Anderson County Historical Association has cleared and fenced the recently discovered cemetery.

Samuel's widow continued to live in Anderson County until she died April 8, 1882, and was buried in the Providence Cemetery near Slocum.
Frances Maurine Perkins Godwin, (GGGD), #22589-S

MEREDITH E. WEBB, born 1803 in North Carolina was a farmer. He married (1) Charlotta Brown before 1827 in Tennessee. Their children were: Infant, Anthony, Jefferson, Sarah, twins Celina and Levenia, Milton Blanton, Ophelia (born in Maury County, TN) and John W. (born in Texas).

Meredith married (2) Rebecca J. Snider (born April 7, 1828, Tuscaloosa, AL, died Aug. 30, 1870, Shelby County, TX) buried in the Methodist Cemetery, M.E. She was the daughter of Joel Snider and Belinda Caroline Samford. Their children were: Elizabeth, Joseph, Mary, Jane Ellen, Melissa Amanda,

Meredith E. Webb

Elijah/Elias/Elkanah, Alford, Thomas Eliciah, Matilda Jeanette and Emma Eugenia, and two unknown infants, all born in Shelby County, TX.

Meredith married (3) Ellen Tam May 7, 1871, in San Augustine County, TX. Their children were, James W. Webb and McGruder, both born in Shelby County, TX.

Meredith fathered about 23 children. He married on Jan. 10, 1878 (4) Caroline (Carroll) McDonald, mother of son-in-law, Joseph McDonald. She was born about 1833 in Louisiana, daughter of William W. Carroll and Sarah Sheridan. They had no children.

Meredith died in 1883 and is buried in an unmarked grave in the Methodist Cemetery, M.E. in Center, TX.

ELIZUR DANIEL WEBSTER, born in 1799 in The commonwealth of Massachusetts moved to Ohio with his father, Daniel Webster, in 1816. Daniel was a native of the Old Bay States. Daniel was with Andrew Jackson in The Battle of New Orleans. He died about 1824 and is buried in Massachusetts.

Elizur Daniel Webster moved to Monroe, MO, in 1824. The only way into Monroe County at that time was by foot. Elizur followed an Indian foot trail from The Mississippi River into Monroe County. By 1826 there was some travel by boat on the Salt River into Monroe County.

Elizur D. married Margaret Forman in 1825 in Monroe County, MO, where Elizur was engaged in farming. In 1825 most homes were log cabins with three legged homemade beds, these beds were attached to the walls to sturdy them up. He became a good carpenter and was skilled in all kinds of wood work. Elizur and Margaret had four children: Marcus L., William F., Marietta (died at the age of 11 years old) and Alvira. His wife, Margaret, died in 1833.

Elizur D. married Polly A. Bradley, daughter of Benjamin and Margaret Campbell Bradley, March 31, 1836, in Monroe County, MO. The family moved to Monroe County near the Salt River where he operated a grist mill and did blacksmith work along with some farming. In this wild land game for food was plentiful and the grist mill helped to improve the diet of the fron-

tier. Elizur and Polly had three children born in Missouri: Daniel Bradley, Delpha J. and Frances A.

In the early spring of 1845 Elizur and Polly and their children moved to Grayson County, TX, by covered wagon. They were the first of six families to settle four miles south of what is now Whitesboro. They were 20 miles from the nearest settlement. Elizur was a carpenter for W.S. Peters Colony and also operated a hog farm. They had 968 acres in Cooke and Grayson counties. Three children were born to Elizur and Polly in Texas: Benjamin F., George W. and Charles H. Elizur served as a commissioner in Cooke County, TX, in 1853. Elizur died Aug. 30, 1861, Polly died May 30, 1867. They are both buried in the Ben Dye Cemetery in Grayson County.
Frances W. Bynum, (GGD), #020466

SOLOMON FRANKLIN WEED, born in either Gonzales County or Hays County, Sept. 27, 1849. His great-grandfather, Benjamin Weed Sr. (born in 1792 in Louisiana), migrated with his wife, Celeste Sarah (Hanks) Weed; sister, Hannah; and brother-in-law, Benjamin Abshire, to Liberty County, TX, in 1843, where they farmed the land. Benjamin and Sarah are both buried in the Abshire Cemetery in Liberty County.

Solomon, my great-grandfather, married Eda Chaddick in about 1871. About 1890 they moved to Bandera County, where they lived the remainder of their lives. Eda died in January 1925 and is buried in Tuff. Solomon died in July 1930 and is buried in the Waresville Cemetery, Utopia.

Solomon Franklin Weed

Solomon and his three oldest sons: Asa, Jesse (my grandfather) and Benjamin, homesteaded land on Jackson Creek about 19 miles west of Bandera, near the town of Tuff. They raised a large family consisting of seven boys and seven girls.

Jesse married Evelyn Lena Bauerlein in the middle of the county road, in front of the Elam place, Jan. 18, 1895. Their eldest child, Frank, was born at Tuff; their daughter, Jeffie (my mother), was born in 1905 in Bandera County.
Loraine Darling, #22282

CHARLES HENRY WEIDENMUELLER, an early settler in the Corpus Christi area of Nueces County, TX, was born in Kassel, Germany Nov. 12, 1820, and with his wife, Margaret, emigrated to Texas landing first in Galveston in 1843 before moving to Corpus Christi Feb. 1, 1846. He and his wife are listed as passengers on the ship *Franciska*. He immediately became active as a drayman in the business life of the new settlement. This was at the time Gen. Zachary Taylor and his army were camped in the area. He filed a brand for record for

Charles Henry Weidenmueller

horses and cattle in November 1852. The brand appeared as an X over a W.

Charles Weidenmueller held many public offices during his many years of community and business activities in Nueces County. These offices included the county treasurer, judge, county assessor, mayor pro tem and alderman. He died at Corpus Christi, TX, April 7, 1886. His surviving children included three sons and a daughter by his first wife, Margaret, and one daughter by his second wife, Maria Klein. He and his two wives are buried in the old Bayview Cemetery overlooking the bay at Corpus Christi.
Rosemary H. Skaggs, (GGD), #11724

GEORGE F. WEIGHTMAN,

GEORGE F. WEIGHTMAN, born in England. At age 18 he enlisted in the U.S. Army, June 17, 1837, in New York. His obituary from New Orleans asks Montreal, New York and San Antonio papers to copy. No connection to Montreal is known other than possible port of entry.

His date of birth is March 23, 1819. He states he was from Studley in Warwickshire England. Unfortunately, to date (1999) after much expense, his parentage remains unproven. He was a chairmaker at his enlistment and his description was hazel eyes, black hair, light complexion, five foot 10 inches tall.

During his illustrious military career he served in the Florida or Seminole Wars, the Mexican War and became a captain in the Confederacy from Louisiana.

He was married three times: first to Joanna Ruggles Coates, native of Eastport, ME, Dec. 4, 1839, from whom I descend; second, Marie Antoinette Marchand, Nov. 16, 1871, no issue; third, Augusta Maria Mathilda Franck, nee Borneman.

His daughter, Gertrude, was born in Camargo, Mexico while he was in the Mexican War as a hospital steward and organized the General Hospital in Camargo and Meir. He had been with Zachary Taylor in the first occupation force of Corpus Christi.

Co. "K," 4th Arty. evacuated the town of Camargo, Mexico Aug. 12, 1848, and arrived at Fort Brown Aug. 14, 1848.

He was discharged Oct. 25, 1848, at Fort Polk, TX, by order of Maj. Gen. Zachary Taylor on his own application being unable to support his family on Army pay. After the ratification of the Treaty of Peace he felt he was no longer needed in the service of his country. He participated in the battles of Palo Alto and Resaca de la Palma.

Joanna Ruggles Coates was born circa 1823 and married at Fort Prebble, Portland Harbour, ME, while George was on a recruiting mission. She died in New Orleans, LA, Dec. 19, 1869, of smallpox and is buried in New Orleans, LA.

They had three children: Gertrude Weightman, George F. Weightman Jr. and Joseph Oglesby Weightman, who died young. Gertrude married Algernon Sidney Jordan July 3, 1867, in New Orleans.

George Weightman died Feb. 14, 1892, in St. Tammany Par-

ish, LA, and is buried in Mandeville with his third wife. George received a pension for his service in the Mexican War.

Children of Algernon Sidney Jordan and Gertrude Weightman were Julia May Jordan (born May 10, 1868) and Georgianna Jordan (born June 15, 1870), both born in New Orleans, LA. Julia May Jordan married James Samuel Willis Jr. Sept. 23, 1894, in Hammond, LA.

Children of Julia and James Samuel Willis Jr. were Edith May Willis, my mother (born Jan. 22, 1896), Mary Helen Willis (born Aug. 18, 1899) and Gertrude Irene Willis (born March 8, 1901).

Edith May Willis married, in Hammond, LA, Herbert Hillery McGehee on June 14, 1922. After 10 years daughter, Joyce May McGehee, was born Aug. 14, 1932, in Memphis, TN.

She married Robert Russell Bockemuehl June 13, 1952, in Detroit, MI, and they have one son, Kenneth Forrest Bockemuehl and two grandchildren, Brooke Nicole Bockemuehl (born Aug. 15, 1978) and Russell Forrest Bockemuehl (born Dec. 28, 1979), both in Oakland County, MI.

RICE WELLS SR.,

RICE WELLS SR., born in 1782 in Georgia married Chaney in Georgia and they moved to Smith County, TX, in 1841, where he received a fourth class land grant. He, along with several other families, pioneered the area near present-day Starville. He was considered a planter because he had improved acreage.

In 1849, he established a post office in his home in the small community, Gum Spring, which is approximately 20 miles northeast of Tyler.

He and Chaney had 10 children. They were: Albert; Felix; Mary; Telitha Sarah (born May 29, 1822, in Mississippi) married James H. McCorkle; Rice Jr. (born June 22, 1826, in Louisiana) married Rachel Jurusha Hill Feb. 5, 1852, and started a saw mill in Smith County along with his brother-in-law, James H. McCorkle; Calvin; Lucinda (born Feb. 11, 1828) married Frederick Jordan Ham; Louisa married Thomas R. Swann; and Thompson B.

Rice died Oct. 30, 1857, in Smith County, TX. After his death, Chaney went to Woods County to live with her son, Thompson. She died sometime between 1860-70.
Sharry Wells Rathburn, (GGGGD), #22376

SEABORN JONES WHATLEY,

SEABORN JONES WHATLEY, son of John Whatley and Mary Porter, was born circa 1792 in Georgia. His first wife is unknown; he married (2) Mahaly Rachel Speir. Mahaly was born circa 1803 in Georgia, the daughter of John Speir and Rachel Bagby.

Seaborn and his first wife had one known daughter, Betsey Ann Whatley (born 1815 in Georgia). Betsey Ann married Abner Bagby Speir. Abner Speir and Mahaly Speir were brother and sister.

Both families, Seaborn and Mahaly (Speir) Whatley and Abner and Betsey (Whatley) Speir, moved from Pike County, AL, to Bastrop County, TX, in February 1835; and both families are listed on Stephen F. Austin's *"Register of Families"*. Seaborn was a commissioned justice of the peace in Alabama and in Texas. In 1835 he served as a major representing the people of Mina (later Bastrop) in meetings regarding the "unsettled times." He was also a private in the First Texas Rangers (Bastrop Rangers) from June 10-Sept. 10, 1839. He received a land grant of one league and one labor.

Seaborn Whatley's family moved to Panola County where he died in 1845. His second wife, Mahaly, married (2) William Liddy in 1848 in Panola County.

Jeannine (Hughes) Shaffer, (GGGGGD), #20622
Sandra (Hudson) Bunch, (GGGGGGD), #20677

ALEXANDER WHITAKER, born in Louisiana and came to Texas in 1822. He came with his stepfather, William Fitzgibbons and mother, Nancy Whitaker Fitzgibbons; one older brother, Peter; a 12-year-old sister, Sarah; and one married brother, William and his wife, Nancy, and their two sons.

At age 18, he and sister, Sarah, who had married William Barton Pillow, appeared personally at Viesca, Falls County, TX, to apply for Spanish land grants.

Alex, as a single man, received one quarter of a league of land in Falls County, TX, adjoining the league of land granted to his sister. Alex and brother, Peter, enter the Army of Texas in 1836 from Montgomery County, TX, and Alex was wounded.

In 1838, Alex was granted a league and labor of land from the Republic of Texas.

He was married in Montgomery County, TX, in 1838 to Miss Martha Smith, and two children, Thomas and Martha, were born.

In 1842, the family lived one mile south of the town of Montgomery, TX. John Middleton, a peace officer, kept a journal about the Shelby County War. He tells of chasing the McFadgins across the country and finally found them at the house of Alex Whitaker. McNeil, sheriff of the county, was living there and at the time, was in bed with John McFadgin. A gun fight occurred and the McFadgins were taken into custody. There was no indication as to whether Alex knew his guests were running from the law.

In 1848, Alex as a 31-year-old widower with two children married the girl next door, 17-year-old Frances Arnold.

About 1856, he offered a home and farm on his place in Tillis Prarie to his widowed sister, Sarah, and her children. James Edwin, the youngest child of Sarah, saw his uncle as quite wealthy, generous and a great hunter, having many bear dogs.

Alex provided a stagecoach stop on the route between Houston and Huntsville at his home just east of the Tillis Prarie Cemetery. He became ill with "dropsy" and died in 1859 at the age of 43.

He left his 28-year-old widow; two oldest children, Thomas and Martha, by his first marriage; and four younger children: Jerome Darnell, Clarrissa, Hope Arcinda and Lord McIlhenny.

Frances Russell, #21492.

PETER WHITAKER, born in Louisiana and came to Texas in 1822. He came with his stepfather, William Fitzgibbons and mother, Nancy Whitaker Fitzgibbons; one minor brother, Alexander; one minor sister, Sarah; and one married brother, William, and his wife, Nancy.

Peter, his older brother, William, and stepfather were charged with theft of hogs in the summer of 1822. The stepfather and brother returned to the U.S. and left Peter to stand trial alone in January 1823.

John P. Coles, JP wrote a letter on Peter's behalf describing him as "having the appearance of an innocent young man and appeared much mortified." He was found guilty and had to pay a fine of $120.00, three times the value of the hog.

On Jan. 3, 1837, Peter paid his brother, Alexander, $15.00 for services rendered as a substitute in the Army of Texas. Peter was engaged in selling food to the Army.

Peter has a wife named Felicite and a daughter named Lucretia. He died Feb. 23, 1837, in Washington County, TX, and his brother, Alexander, was appointed executor of his estate and guardian of his daughter.

He received a first class headright Feb. 1, 1838, which was granted to his heirs.

Frances Russell, #21492

ELIJAH WHITE, son of Robert White and Nancy Coburn White was born Feb. 15, 1822, in Perry County, TN. He married Juliet E. Jones Dec. 31, 1843, in Walker County, TX. Juliet Jones was the daughter of Joseph P. Jones and Sarah Brimberry. She was born June 3, 1823, in Edgar County, IL. Elijah and Juliet had 11 children. They were: 1. Sarah J. (born 1844) married E.M. Moss; 2. Calvin (born 1847) married Mrs. Lou Oliver Little; 3. Joseph P. (born 1849) married Julie Osborne; 4. William P. (born 1850) married Rosa C.; 5. Leonard (born 1853) married Mrs. E.J. Bozeman King; 6. Mollie (born 1855) married A.A. Beall; 7. Augustus (born 1858, died 1861); 8. Anna (born 1857) married M.B. McKinney; 9. Martha Elizabeth "Lizzie" (born 1860) married J.W. Cargill; 10. Edward F. (born 1863); and 11. David J. (born 1868).

Elijah was a charter member of Little River Masonic Lodge #398, helped organize Little River Baptist Church and served in the Civil War, 12th Regt. Parson's Bde.

Elijah came to Texas at age 15, farmed 320 acres in Milam County. He received a land grant #155, fourth class. He died February 1886 in Milam County and is buried at Little River Baptist Church Cemetery in Milam County.

Peggy Ackers Elmore.

JOSEPH WHITE, born 1824, Anson County, NC, died 1913, Jones Prairie area, Milam County, TX. Below excerpt from "*History of Texas*" published by the Lewis Publishing Co. 1893.

"Joseph White married at the age of 17 in 1841 and undertook the battle of life with a few head of horses and cattle as his only capital. In 1844 he settled where he now lives in Jones Prairie, making a 100 acre purchase. He has reinvested some of his profits in real estate, owning now more than 720 acres and cultivating 300 acres of it. He produces a large amount of cotton

Joseph White

annually, enough to warrant his owning and operating a gin, with which he does work for the public also."

"Joseph went into the Confederate Army, entering Alfred Johnson's Spy Co. Lucky for him, he was home on furlough when the company was captured at Arkansas Post. Upon his return to the service he joined Col. Duff's regiment which operated in the Indian Nation and the Trans-Mississippi Dept."

"In 1841 Mr. White was married to Sarah "Mary Ann" Comstock of Louisiana. They were the parents of 10 children."

Joseph is buried in Seed's Cemetery at Jones Prairie, near

Old Calvert Rd. He was a Mason and a Baptist, an early member of the Little River Baptist Church.
Phyllis Jean White Poe, (GGD), #21016

MARY ANN COMSTOCK WHITE, born Dec. 25, 1825, in Louisiana, died Aug. 12, 1905, in Milam County, TX, buried in Sneed's Cemetery.

Mary Ann, aka Sarah and Polly, was the daughter of William and Elizabeth Green Comstock of Louisiana. Tradition is that Elizabeth died shortly after Mary Ann was born. Her father took her to her mother's family. An aunt that had no children reared her. Some time before 1830 her grandfather, Richard Green, moved to Texas where he acquired land in the Liberty area. She inherits her mother's share of this property in later years.

The story told by her older grandchildren is what she told them. The last time she saw her father she was 8 or 10 years old. Mary Ann remembered him as very handsome in a fine uniform with braid on the shoulders. He left a pouch with gold coins with the aunt to help with expenses until he returned. He never came back. She showed the children the pouch and the coins that were left.

Mary Ann and Joseph's children were: Henry C.; Albert; William B.; Elijah; James; Emma married Thomas Roberts; Mary married Dred Massengale; Adlee married Thomas Estes; and Sally married John Stewart.
Phyllis Jean White Poe, (GGD), #21016

NANCY COBURN WHITE, born circa 1793 in Anson County, NC, daughter of Hedley Coburn. Nancy and Robert White were parents of 12 children: Griffin Lacy (born 1810); Nancy; Hedley; Sarah; Hester; Henry A.; Elijah; Joseph; Selitha; Mary; Sanders (born 1830); and an unnamed infant.

After Robert's death Nancy continued to care for and improve her share of their land. She also cared for the four children of her deceased daughter, Selitha Brimberry. In later years she sold (or gave) her property to her youngest son, Sanders, whose land adjoined hers. Sanders descendants are still making use of the land.

One day in 1866 Nancy was riding her horse to visit a neighbor when a windstorm blew up. Both Nancy and the horse were killed by a falling tree. She was buried beside Robert in an unmarked grave surrounded by a rock fence.
Phyllis Jean White Poe, (GGGD), #21016

ROBERT WHITE, born circa. 1790, Anson County, NC, died Dec. 13, 1853, Leon County, TX, married circa 1809 to Nancy Coburn in Anson County, NC. Robert was the son of Henry and Hannah Rushing White. His siblings were Reuben (born 1787), Robert, Josiah, Nancy, Sally, David, Mary Ann, daughter name unknown, Henry Jr., Elijah, William H., Burrell W., and Albert (born 1815).

Before 1820 several White families, including Henry and Robert's moved to Perry County, TN. Phillip, Richard and Burrell Rushing show to be their neighbors in Tennessee.

In 1837 Robert joined his brother, William H., in Selby County, TX. Robert received a land grant in Montgomery County, TX, now Walker County, in 1838. The proper is now known as the Robt. White Survey. Before 1846, Robert moved his family to Leon County. He settled on a creek now named for him, White's Branch, a tributary of the Lower Keechi Creek. He remained there the rest of his life. The local newspaper noted his death: "Died on Tuesday evening 13th inst. Mr. Robert White, an old and much respected citizen of this county. He was in good health the Sunday previous to his death. His decease was pneumonia."
Phyllis Jean White Poe, (GGGD), #21016

SIMON WIESS, born in Lublin, Poland, Jan. 1, 1800. He left home to see the world and lived from Turkey to the West Indies. By the time he arrived in Texas in 1833, he could read, write, and speak, fluently seven languages.

Representing the Masonic Lodge, he visited the U.S. in 1826, coming to Texas, the Mexican government appointed him deputy collector of customs, and his friend, Sam Houston, appointed him to the same position later in the bordertown of Camp Sabine. He met, fell in love and married Margaret Sturrock, moved to Nacodoches, and opened a merchandising business using as its building the historic stone fort there. In 1838, seeing cotton as good business, he took the first load of cotton ever transported down the Neches to market in New Orleans. After selling his cotton, he left Beaumont and moved up the Neches to a place to be called Wiess Bluff.

Simon operated a flourishing merchandising business, as well as a formidable receiving and forwarding enterprise. He personally supervised the dredging of the Neches and Sabine to make way for riverboat traffic.

Cotton and shipping were not Simon's only interests. He speculated in land, cattle and horses. By 1842, Wiess Bluff was a thriving river port and trade center. He aided and abetted the Confederate cause, and losses incurred severely affected his health. He died in 1868.

VALENTINE WIESS, born July 27, 1845, at Wiess Bluff, Jasper County, TX, the son of Polish immigrant Simon Wiess and Scottish born Margaret Sturrock. Valentine served the Confederate cause in the Civil War, and returned to help his family in their merchandising at Wiess Bluff. In 1869, Valentine married Mary Elizabeth Herring. The lumber business helped gain them fortunes, and Valentine bought a store from his brother, Mark, and named it V. Wiess and Co., selling everything from insurance to hairpins. The profits helped him purchase the Reliance Lumber Co. During the 1870s Valentine and his brother, William, joined Dr. Kyle and the McFaddins in founding the Beaumont Pasture Co., which ran a herd of 10,000. McFaddin, Wiess, Kyle Trust Co. also owned a large ranch, and it was on their land that Spindletop, the greatest oil geyser in the history of the world, erupted.

Perhaps Valentine Wiess' greatest contribution to Beaumont lumbering came with the founding in 1883 of the East Texas and Louisiana Lumbermen's Association. After 1880, Valentine turned his attentions to contracting and real estate, and at his death in 1913, he was credited with being the largest taxpayer on the Beaumont tax rolls. He contracted to build Beaumont's first hotel of note. A need for banking facilities carried Valentine into private banking and the First National Bank was organized with V. Wiess as its first president.

RANSOM W. WILBURN, born Nov. 21, 1819, in Louisiana. He came to Texas with his mother and others in 1852. Dur-

ing the Texas Revolution Ransom joined the Third Co. Inf., Second Regt., Texas Volunteers under the command of Capt. Willlam M. Logan. At 16 years of age, he made the trek to relieve the men at the Alamo. During the Battle of San Jacinto, he was detailed to guard the camp at Harrisburg.

In 1840 Ransom married Margaret Haney who was born in 1826 in Saint Landry Parish, LA. Their five children were: James (born around 1843, died at Vicksburg during Civil War); Annie Elizabeth (born April 7, 1845) who married Thomas Kozlek; Robert and Susanna who died as children, Joseph Franklin.

Ransom was a stock farmer with some education. He bought land and settled with his family at Old River, Liberty County, TX. He also received a land grant.

Ransom and Margaret died of tuberculosls. He died in 1859. Margaret managed the stock farm until her death in January 1861. They are buried in a burial ground donated by Margaret to the community. It is now called the Stubbs Cemetery and is in Cove, Chambers County, TX.

Dorothy Anderson Hagen, (GGGD), #21161

JAMES A. WILLIAMS JR., born March 30, 1821, in Greenville, AL, to James A. Williams Sr. (born 1795) and Winifred Moore Williams. James Sr. built the first house in Greenville.

Winifred's parents were Louis and Fairby Moore. Louis Moore was born in 1750 and died in 1860 at age 110. His son, Lawson, lived to age 100.

James A. Williams Jr. married Mary Hodges (born Oct. 14, 1825).

Mary's parents were Charity and James Hodges who had 12 children. Charity died while they were preparing to move to Texas. They packed her body in charcoal and brought her to Texas and buried her in Burt Cemetery near Hallettsville. James Hodges was an early circuit judge.

James Jr. and Mary Williams came to Texas in 1858 with eight children including Mathilda (my Grandma who married Louis Washington Riggs). One child was born in Texas. They landed in Old Indianola and traveled to Koerth.

James, the father, joined the service at age 41. Although James hand was crippled, he helped the Navy off the Texas coast during the Civil War.

Mary Williams rode bareback helping ill people. She smoked a corncob pipe. Mary died Oct. 8, 1880, and James died Nov. 18, 1890. Both are buried at Pilot Grove.

Lucile Duncan, (GGD)

STEPHEN WILLIAMSON (born 1791/93 in South Carolina), began his westward migration at an early age. He married Sara Sweeton, daughter of Dutton, in Perry County, AL, 1822. They moved to Mississippi, Tennessee and Arkansas before arriving in Panola County, TX, in the early 1840s. The couple had 12 children; Sara died 1850. Stephen moved to Coryell County. Throughout the years he had engaged in trading with Indians and was a stock farmer. April 26, 1863, while rounding up horses, Stephen was attacked by a maudering band of Indians who killed and scalped him. He was truly a frontiersman.

Stephen and Sara's second son, John, a veteran of the Texas War for Independence, married Teressa Twomey; their oldest child was Julia Ann who married Riley Green Hampton; their youngest child was Jessie Lee who married Edward Fred

Melbern; their youngest child was Julia Ann who married Tom Marsh Robinson; and their only child was Marsha Ann who married Bryan Keith Richards.

Julia Ann Melbern Robinson, (GGGD), #13361
Marsha Ann Robinson Richards, (GGGGD) #14075

ALFRED JACKSON WILLINGHAM, son of Archibald and Eleanor Belcher Willingham, was born March 26, 1824, in Georgia. He moved to Washington County, TX, with his parents by 1839 and married there January 1855 to Martha O'Neal (born December 1834, in Arkansas), the daughter of John and Nancy Harbour O'Neal. Nancy Harbour O'Neal is the daughter of Joseph and Mary Stephens Harbour who received a land grant from Stephen F. Austin. Mary Stephens Harbour is the daughter of Pennsylvania Revolutionary War veteran Samuel and Mary Stephens.

The children of Alfred and Martha are Charles (born 1855), married Carr; Sarah (born 1859) married Dickinson; Francis Marion (born 1861) married Jones; Andrew (born 1866) married Harrison; John (born 1869) married Julia Murdock, daughter of James and Sarah York Murdock; Mary (born 1871) married Depoyster, Conner, and Harding; Annie (born 1874) married Norton, Stocking, and Eigel; Edna (born 1877) married Barrow. The children of son, John, are: Henry, Hattie, John, James Willie, Mattie and George.

Farmer and soldier, Alfred Jackson, served in the Republic of Texas, Mexican and Civil Wars. He died March 15, 1907. Martha died Jan. 12, 1919. Both are buried in the Willingham Cemetery in Washington County on the Harbour League.

Katherine Willingham Woerner, (GGD)

PETER JAMES WILLIS was born in Easton, MD, in 1815 and died 1873. He came to Houston, TX in 1836 at the age of 21 when the new Republic offered grants of land and opportunities to settlers who were willing to work. After a year he returned to Maryland to urge his three younger brothers: Richard, William Henry and Thomas, to join him in Texas where they settled on Buffalo Bayou. They worked clearing land and building houses for other settlers for room and board and $2.50 a day. They saved money to buy land and cotton, and timber for export.

Peter James (known as P.J.) and Richard moved to Montgomery County, Texas and opened a dry goods store in Washington-on-the-Brazos and later a branch store in Anderson, TX. (William Henry died of yellow fever in Texas and Thomas returned to Maryland.) In 1853 they formed a partnership with S.K. McIlhenny which later was bought out by the two brothers, Peter James and Richard. This company became known as P.J. Willis and Bros. and eventually became the largest export firm west of the Mississippi with offices in London, Paris and New York.

On the Jan. 21, 1845, Peter James Willis married Caroline Womack (born 1828, Alabama, died 1863). They had six children: William Henry (1845-1888); Peter James Jr. (1847-1912); Mary Ella (1849-1927); Tabitha Ann (1852-1864); my grandmother, Magnolia A. (1854-1933) married George Sealy in 1875; and Caroline (1856-1877).

After his wife's death he and his sons moved to Matamores to ship cotton and goods to England in exchange for cash to aid the Confederacy. He died in Missouri in 1873.

His daughter, Magnolia, married George Sealy and became one of the prominent families of Galveston in the late 19th and early 20th centuries doing business in finance, railroads and cotton.

The children of Magnolia and George Sealy were all born in Galveston: Margaret, my mother (1876-1958) married Frederick Burton in 1902; Ella (1878-1964); George (1880-1944); Caroline (1883-1968); Rebecca (1885-1979); Robert (1891-1979); and William (1893-1966). My mother had four children: Miles, Marjorie, Caroline and Jane.

Recently family letters were discovered that Peter James wrote to his older brother in Maryland around 1836 stating that Texas was thinking of creating a new capital and would be named after Stephen F. Austin.

Jane Burton Pinckard, DRT #7676, GGD

JAMES B. WILLS

JAMES B. WILLS (born circa 1798 in Tennessee) and Anna "Amy" W. Shackelford came into Texas in 1840 and they had children born in Tennessee, Missouri, and their last son born in Texas. James B. was the son of Lillie Buchanan and James Wills, born in Pennsylvania, who later lived in Montgomery County, VA, and served in the Revolutionary War and was buried in Clay County, MO.

James B. Wills' children include: Rueben (born circa 1818) married Jane Buster; Sarah J. married William McCray; Lumisa married William Connell; Tabitha L. married Alexander J. Dallas; William

James B. Wills

Riley (born Aug. 3, 1826) married Saluda Elizabeth Cross; James Wilson married Mary Ann; Daniel; David; Nancy Evaline married James L. Hogan; Almira E. married John C. Anderson; Archibald married Rebecca Pennington; and George Alexander (born October 1841, in Texas) married Sarah E. Cook.

He had two land grants (of 640 acres each) in an area west of Holland. He and other Wills were prominent in early Holland and was in the meat market business. He and son, William Riley, took stock in the company organized by Col. Robertson to build Salado College. About 1857 he signed the petition to build a Bell County Courthouse and jail.

Mary Lou Sanderford Smith, (GGGD) #21145-S

WILLIAM RILEY WILLS

WILLIAM RILEY WILLS, son of James B. Wills and Anna "Amy" Shackelford, was born Aug. 3, 1826, at Clay County, MO. He came to Texas in 1840 and was 17 years at the time of his parents' 640 acre land grant in Milam Dist. He located first in Independence, Washington County. In 1847 he enlisted to fight in the Mexican War.

William Riley sailed around the Horn to the California Gold Rush. In 1852 he returned to Texas and on March 10, 1853, married

William Riley Wills and Saluda Elizabeth Cross Wills

Saluda Elizabeth Cross, who was born in Mississippi March 9, 1837. Their children were: Lucy A. (born May 22, 1854) married William B. Ranne; Thomas (born circa 1856); Almira L. "Myra" (born circa 1858) married John L. Allman; Amy J. (born November 1860) married W. Jones Miller; James R. (born circa 1862) married Annie Sanderford; Virgil (born circa 1864); David; Mary "Mollie" Emaline (born May 27, 1870) married George Rufas Sanderford; Curtis (born circa 1872) married Lillie Jacobs; Oliver S. (born circa 1875) married Plum Garner; and John C. (born August 1877) married Ida Kaiser.

In the Civil War, he was in the Confederate Army, rounding up cattle for its troops in west Texas. In 1865 he bought 392 acres of land in Nolan Valley. He died April 27, 1902, and is buried at Pleasant Hill Cemetery in Nolanville.

Mary Lou Sanderford Smith, (GGD), #21620-S

HIRAM ABIFF WILLSON SR.

HIRAM ABIFF WILLSON SR., born Sept. 10, 1821, probably in Lincoln County, GA, was the oldest child of Dr. Stephen Pelham Willson and Mary Richardson Davis. As a child his family migrated to Arkansas, Louisiana and then in 1834 to Texas. The family settled at San Augustine, where Hiram grew to be a young man. In San Augustine, he met and married Mary Amanda Stow on Dec. 18, 1844.

Hiram Abiff Willson, Sr., and wife, Mary Amanda Stow

Mary was the granddaughter of Edley Ewing and Elizabeth Love. Mary was born circa 1828 in Tennessee. Her parents are still a mystery, although it is assumed that her mother was the daughter of Edley Ewing and died sometime before the Ewing family migrated to Texas.

The couple traveled with Dr. Willson to Tyler County, TX, prior to 1850, and settled on land near Peachtree Village. Hiram Willson was a farmer by occupation according to the census records for 1850 and 1860. The 1850 census shows that Hiram A. Willson and his wife had real estate valued at $2,800. By 1857, Hiram Willson also owned a store at St. Charles in Tyler County.

By 1860 the following members of the Hiram A. Willson family were living in the Chester area of Tyler County. Hiram A. Willson Sr., age 38; Mary A. Willson, age 28; Stephen E. Willson, age 13; Hiram A. Willson Jr. and Samuel Houston Willson, age 10; Sir John Franklin Willson, age 8; Mary Amanda Willson, age 6; Elizabeth Lou Willson, age 5; and Ida M. Willson, age 1. Another child was born to this family after 1863, Julia Ann Willson. In the 1860 census of Tyler County TX, Hiram Willson's occupation is listed as farmer with real estate valued at $3,600 and personal property valued at $9,210. Part of the personal property included slaves inherited by his wife from her grandfather, as well as slaves purchased by the Willson family.

On March 6, 1862, Hiram Willson joined thousands of other Texas by joining the Confederate Army. According to the National Archives, Hiram A. Willson enlisted as a private in Co. K, 27th Texas Cav.; also called Whitfield's Legion, First Texas Legion for a period of 12 months. The 27th Cav. was originally created as the 4th Texas Bn., Texas Cav. on Nov. 12, 1861, with four companies, A to D. It was increased to a regiment of 13 companies on April 2, 1862. The 27th Cav. served west of the Mississippi River for a brief period. It was transferred east of the Mississippi River, where it served as a dismounted unit the fall of 1862. The regiment served in the following major engagements in spring and fall of 1862 that Pvt. Willson took part in, Pearidge, Leetown and Elkhorn Tavern, AR; Iuka, MS; Cornith, MS; and the retreat to the Hatchie River, MS. Willson was captured in the fighting at Davis Bridge on Oct. 5, 1862, and paroled. After this the muster rolls indicate that Hiram Willson was a paroled prisoner. Hiram Willson did not enlist in the army until after his father, Stephen's, death in 1861. He is found in Tyler County after 1862, which is the date of Mary Richardson Davis Willson's death.

Hiram Willson acted as the agent for his brother when the family settled the estates of Dr. and Mrs. Willson. Samuel Willson had given his brother power of attorney to settle the estates. Lt. Samuel Andrew Willson was serving in the Confederate Army east of the Mississippi at this time.

After the war, Hiram Willson continued to farm in Tyler County. That he had certain influence in the community is indicated by the fact that he served in several different capacities during the years that he lived in Tyler County. In 1856, Hiram Willson was one of the trustees for Woodville College, which was established by the Texas State Legislature that year. The college met in Woodville Lodge #62. Willson was also one of the founding members of the Masonic Lodge which still holds its meetings in Chester, TX.

Hiram Willson was chosen by the citizens of Tyler County to attend the Constitutional Convention which was held in 1875. Each organized county in Texas was allowed three elected delegates to the convention, which met in Austin. The Constitutional Convention of 1875 was responsible for writing the present constitution for the state of Texas, which was adopted in 1876. The adoption of this Constitution ended Reconstruction in Texas.

Hiram Willson died in the late 1870s or early 1880s. He and his wife, Mary, are both buried at Sulpher Springs Cemetery in Tyler County, TX. The cemetery is now located on land owned by Champion International Paper Co. The children of Hiram Willson, Ida M. and Mary Amanda, are also buried at Sulpher Springs, unfortunately their grave, as well as Mary Amanda Stow Willson's grave are unmarked.

Many of the grandchildren and great-grandchildren of Hiram Abiff Willson Sr. live in Tyler County, with several still residing in Chester. The children of Hiram Willson were: Stephen Ewing Willson (born circa 1847); Hiram Abiff Willson Jr. and Samuel Houston Willson (born March 18, 1849); Sir John Franklin Willson (born Sept. 10, 1851); Mary Amanda Willson (born circa 1853), Elizabeth Lou Willson (born June 28, 1855), Ida M. Willson (born circa 1859) and Julia Ann Willson (born circa 1864). Stephen Willson married Margaret Elizabeth N. Barnes; Hiram Abiff Willson Jr. married Sidney Ann Kirby; Samuel H. Willson married Mary Ann R.J. Barnes; Frank Willson married Olive Peters; Elizabeth Willson married Joseph Hilliard Peters (Olive's brother); and Julia Willson married Levi B. Nowlin.

Carolyn JoAn Willson, (GGGGGD), #20172-S

STEPHEN PELHAM WILLSON, born in New York State Dec. 1, 1789. Sometime before 1808 he was licensed to practice medicine in Poughkeepsie, Dutchess County, NY, according to papers he filed to do the same in the Mexican state of Texas.

Dr. Willson was living in Georgia and practicing medicine in 1818. He married Miss "Polly" Mary Richardson Davis, the eldest daughter of Major Samuel Davis and Nancy Hughes in Goshen, Lincoln County, and Georgia on Jan. 31, 1819.

Stephen Pelham Willson with wife, "Polly" Mary Richardson Davis Willson and baby Hiram.

Before migrating to Texas, the Willson family moved into Arkansas probably from Georgia, since Hiram, their oldest son was born in 1821 in Georgia, and two of the daughters gave Arkansas as their birth place to at least one census taker before 1880. The family purchased land in an area on the Louisiana border in Arkansas Territory at a place called Long Prairie.

The Willson family did not stay long in this area since they were relocated to Louisiana by 1830. Claiborne Parish where the family settled is in the northern part of the state close to the Arkansas border. The 1830 census of Claiborne Parish, LA, shows the Willson family as residents of the state.

It was a turbulent time in Texas and Mexico when Dr. Stephen P. Willson arrived at San Augustine with his family in 1834. Willson's mother-in-law, Nancy Davis, and her family arrived at about the same time. Stephen Willson attempted to obtain land through Lorenzo De Zavala's impresario contract with the Mexican state of *Coahuila y Texas*. His petition, dated Sept. 26, 1834, at San Augustine, states that he was a doctor and had a family of six individuals. The document, which is in Spanish, bears his signature, but the title was never completed and no land was granted through this petition. Also on file was a character certificate, which states that Willson, was a native of New York, and had a family of six.

The family of Stephen P. Willson is on the 1835 Texas, Sabine Dist. census and his occupation is listed as physician. His wife is listed as 'May R.' instead of Mary R. Members of the Dr. Stephen Pelham Willson family according to the 1835 Mexican census were: S.P. Willson, physician, age 45; May R. Willson, age 30; Hiram, age 13; Julia, age 11; Almira, age 9; Emily, age 7; Samuel A., age 3 months. The census must have been taken in late March or April because Samuel Andrew Willson was born January 1835 in San Augustine.

The 1840 tax rolls for the Republic of Texas lists all white males over the age of 21, every owner of taxable property or their agents. There was a poll tax of $1.00 on each white male over the age of 21. The tax on slaves was assessed at $1.00 to $3.00. The 1840 tax roll list S.P. Willson of San Augustine being taxed for the ownership of two slaves, one saddle horse and one wooden clock.

By the time the Willsons moved to Tyler County, their four oldest children were married. Stephen P. Willson and his family settled on land about two miles north of Chester, called Peachtree Village.

With Stephen Willson and his wife, Mary, traveled two of their sons-in-law, Daniel Robinson Smith and Grant W. Payne; and their two daughters, Almira Smith and Julia Payne. Also the Willson's two sons, Hiram A. Willson and his wife, Mary Amanda Stow, and young Sam Willson migrated with the Willsons. Emily West and her husband, Henry, came later. Dr. Willson purchased land at Peachtree and built a home close to a family named Barnes.

Also during this time Dr. Willson operated a sanitarium at Sulpher Springs, Tyler County according to *Sketches of Tyler County History* by James E. and Josiah Wheat complied in 1986. Dr. Willson was one of five doctors in Tyler County by 1850, according to the census for that year. Dr. Willson opened a sanitarium near the location of the two springs at Sulpher Springs. This is northwest of Chester. He operated this establishment in the early 1850s.

Doctors often held more than one job during this time, and their fees although often small, could be as much as $40.00 for delivering a baby. In 1854, Willson rendered for taxation in Tyler County, 820 acres valued at $520.00. Also taxed was personal property, three slaves valued at $1,750.00. Willson also owned land in Sabine County and McLennan County. Dr. Willson also farmed and at times ran a store with the assistance of his sons-in-law.

The following information is family tradition as related by Matt Willson in his family narrative in 1955. On one occasion, Sam Barnes became very ill with what was termed, 'congestive chills.' He had already been ill twice with the same thing. The day that he became ill again was on Sunday, and there was a camp meeting near the Barnes' home that everyone had gone to. Mrs. Barnes was alone with her sick husband, and when she looked out the front of the house, she saw Dr. Willson and his wife coming. Mrs. Barnes said that she had never been so glad to see anyone in her lifetime as she was to see the Willsons. Dr. Willson stated that he thought it was better for him to come see the sick that day than go to the camp meeting. Dr. Willson then attended to Sam Barnes and the sick man began to improve before the end of the day. Mrs. Barnes said that she went out to the orchard to pray and asked the Lord if her husband was going to live, and to give her a sign. When she went back into the house, Sam pointed his finger at her and smiled, she stated that she knew he was going to live.

By September 1857, all of Dr. Willson's children were living at Peachtree Village. In 1857, Stephen Willson purchased for his daughter and son-in-law, Emily and Henry West, eight acres that joined that owned by his son, Hiram, at Peachtree. It was on this eight acres that Doctor Willson had his office until his death in 1861. There was also a store located on the acreage.

Mary Richardson Davis was born Jan. 5, 1802, in Georgia. Mary Davis Willson died in 1862. The children of Stephen Pelham and Mary Davis Willson are: Hiram Abiff Willson Sr. (born Sept. 10, 1821, in Georgia); Caroline Amanda Willson (born Dec. 2, 1823); Julia Ann Willson (born Sept. 12, 1825, in Arkansas); Lydia Almira Willson (born Feb. 22, 1827, in Arkansas); Emily Caroline L.G.A. Willson (born Feb. 7, 1830, in Louisiana); and Samuel Andrew Willson (born Jan. 9, 1835, in the Mexican state of Texas). The Stephen Willson family also included a daughter named Caroline Amanda (born 1823). She is listed in the Bible that is owned by Miss Trurlu Strickland (great-great-granddaughter of Sam Willson). Caroline died before the family migrated to Texas, since she is not mentioned in the 1835 census for the Mexican

state of Texas, Sabine Dist. Caroline was not in the 1830 census for Louisiana that the Willson family can be found on.

Hiram Abiff Willson Sr. married Mary Amanda Stow; Julia Ann Willson married Grant W. Payne; Lydia Almira Willson married Daniel Robinson Smith Sr.; and Emily Caroline Willson married Henry West. These marriages all took place in San Augustine, TX, before 1847. Samuel Andrew Willson married Susan Elizabeth Priest, daughter of Mijacah Priest and Mary Ann Hicks in Woodville, TX, on Sept. 1, 1853.
Carolyn JoAn Willson, (GGGGGGD), #19658

ABEL WILSON, according to the 1850 Tyler County Census, Abel Wilson was born in South Carolina in 1785. A census of Alabama in 1830 shows him living in Dallas County with a wife and four children, two boys and two girls.

Abel arrived in Nacogdoches, January 1839, where he received a third class grant, No. 250, for 640 acres. He settled near Billiams Creek in northern Tyler County. In 1850, the census of Tyler County shows Abel, Mary Ann, a daughter; Thomas, a son; and a Mary Williams. There is no wife listed, although Abel had married Margaret Parsons on Sept. 4, 1847.

According to a will which Abel wrote in 1851, he left 50 cents each to Robert, a son; Sarah Jane (born 1834, died 1927), my ancestor, married John Jefferson Crews; Elizabeth (born 1824, died ?) married Thomas H. Espey; Phoebe (born 1827, died 1904) married Joshua T. Saunders; and household goods, etc. to Mary Ann (born 1836, died ?) and Thomas (born 1842, died 1917).

Abel died after 1857, for he appeared in person, December 1857, in Burnet County to transfer rights to 80 acres to William Sandifer. Since he does not appear on the 1860 census, he is apparently deceased. He is buried in an unmarked grave near his home in Tyler County, TX.
Ann Crews Laird, (GGGD), #8061

FRANCIS ASBURY WILSON, born in Augusta County, VA, in 1790, to Robert and Agnes Nancy Oliver Wilson. He married Elizabeth Kountz in 1812, in Mason County, VA, now West Virginia. Francis served in the War of 1812. He was raised a Presbyterian, but converted to Methodism in 1804. In 1815, he preached his first sermon. In 1822 he was ordained a deacon and in 1824 he was ordained an elder. The family lived for a while in Ohio.

On Dec. 19, 1839, he crossed the Sabine River into the Republic of Texas. He settled in Shelbyville. He preached in the Nacogdoches circuit. In 1841 he moved to San Augustine and preached in that circuit. He was instrumental in organizing the Wesleyan Male and Female Colleges in San Augustine.

Francis and Elizabeth had 10 children, all born prior to their moving to Texas. He retired from the circuit riding in 1852. He relocated to Newton County and became a local preacher.

Elizabeth died in 1864 in Newton County. Francis died in 1867 in Calcasieu Parish, LA. They are both buried in the Belgrade Cemetery, Newton County. A Texas state historical marker was placed not far from the cemetery.
Mary Jane Pond Addison, (GGGGD), #5654

GEORGE ALEXANDER WILSON, born in Sumner County, TN, Jan. 1, 1828, to Addison and Annie Moore Wilson was reared at his birthplace in Tennessee and came to Texas in 1845. He made his home in Collin County. His parents, Addison and Annie Moore Wilson, followed him to Texas in 1849 and also made Collin County their home.

Martha Harriet Kincaid Wilson and George A. Wilson

In 1846 George Alexander went into the war against Mexico and remained until about the close. He returned to Texas to work at the carpenter's trade, farming and stock raising.

In 1855 George Alexander Wilson married Martha Harriet Kincaid. They had 14 children (one stillborn): Almarine, Annie, John Johnathan, Tollie, Elizabeth, George Milam, Lucy, Temperance, Jennie, Wallace C., Thomas Benton, Addie and Mary.

Mr. Wilson was appointed sheriff of Collin County in 1866, an office he held during the perilous times of reconstruction of Texas. Mr. Wilson became a successful farmer and stockman, as well as a surveyor, abstractor and realtor. He was a highly esteemed person, respected in his social relations and business affairs. George Alexander Wilson's life and person is best shown in this favorite family anecdote: One day a man who had come upon very hard times approached George Alexander on his farm chopping wood. The man explained to George Alexander his dire straits and asked for a loan of money. George Alexander picked up a fresh chip of wood and wrote on it to his banker to give this man a certain sum of money and signed it George Alexander Wilson. The banker gave the man the money. When the loan was repaid, the chip of wood was returned to George Alexander Wilson.

George Alexander Wilson died at McKinney, TX, March 6, 1895, and is buried in Woodlawn Cemetery in Collin County. *Mary Emily Borden, great-granddaughter.*

JAMES WILSON, born Jan. 21, 1802, in Wilkes County, GA, came to Tejas y Coahila in November 1833 with his mother-in-law, Catherine Obedience Hill (born 1785, in North Carolina, died Oct. 16, 1865, in Richards, TX), and her children and their families: Caroline and her husband, Thomas Gilmore; Linna and her husband, William Gilmore; Mary, 15; Elizabeth, 11; and the twins, Hannah and Henry, 7. Obedience's daughter, Catherine Obedience (born June 4, 1811, in Alabama, died March 3, 1896), had stayed behind in Alabama while her husband, James, came west to locate land for his family. Because they were not with him, he couldn't prove he had a family so he was granted only one headright, a third of a league, whereas Obedience and her married daughters each got a league and a labor of land (4,605 acres).

James returned to Alabama before the revolution, then came back and fought at the Battle of San Jacinto. He sold his headright. He brought his family to the Republic of Texas in 1841, and settled in Montgomery County, in the part which later became Walker County.

He and Catherine had 12 children. He died Feb. 3, 1892. He is buried in Mustang Prairie Cemetery, near Shiro, TX.

The grave of his father, Samuel Wilson, who fought in the War of 1812, has a memorial marker, placed by Jewel Wilson Powers on behalf of the U.S. Daughters of 1812.

FRANCIS WINANS, our great-great-grandfather, Francis Winans, third child of Isaac and Ruth Ayres Winans, was born the year 1790 in New Jersey.

He first married Susana Woofter, Feb. 14, 1814. They moved to Clinton County, OH, and had two children. Short time later they divorced.

Francis Winans

He married Julia Ann Whitaker Oct. 3, 1825, in Carrollton, IL. She was born in 1802 in Kentucky and was the daughter of Robert and Ann Ware Whitaker. They emigrated with Julia Ann's parents to Cedar Creek, Bastrop County, TX, in 1836.

In 1837 he served the Republic of Texas by hauling freight for the Texas soldiers stationed on the Sabine River. A certificate dated Feb. 16, 1837, shows he was paid $45.00 for hauling seven-and one-half days. He received a land grant on July 5, 1838, for 1,280 acres in Bastrop County.

During winter of 1854 and spring of 1855, he, with sons, Edward and William, drove 2,300 head of productive cattle and a number of fine-bloodied stock horses from Bastrop County to Medina County where they opened ranged in Medina, Atascosa, Frio, Uvalde, DeZavalla and Dimmit counties. From 1854-71 he resided on the Chacon Creek and engaged in stock raising under the name of F. Winans and Sons.

They were the parents of 12 children. She died in 1866, Cedar Creek, TX.

In 1871 he, with his daughter, Rosetta, and her husband, John L. Nix, pulled up roots and traveled to Spanish Honduras, Central America. While there he became sick and returned to Bastrop County, TX, where he died at the age of 85, April 27, 1876. He was buried at McDade, TX.
Helen Ione Kilborn, (GGGD), #12744
Velma Ruth Dinius, (GGGD), #12745
Dorothy Nell Denney, (GGGD), #14256

JOSEPH EDWIN WINN, son of William Winn II (born 1786) and Nancy Ann Wilkes, was born Jan. 15, 1830, in Laurens County, SC. His parents migrated from Lunenburg County, VA, to Laurens County, SC, shortly after their marriage (1806) and lived there from 1808-34. Their children were Martha (Alston) (born 1809), Thomas (born 1811), Andrew Jackson (born 1812), Eliza (Wilson) (born 1814), Frances (Humberson) (born 1817), Arminta (Sharpes) (born 1818), Hinchey (born 1821), Ridains (born 1824), William III (born 1825), Whited Wilkins (born 1827), Isaac (born 1829), Joseph Edwin (born 1830), George (born 1832) and

Elvira Anthony Winn, wife of Joseph Edwin Winn.

Welton (born 1833). William and Nancy's children migrated to Leon County, TX, in the early 1850s, possibly 1853.

Joseph married Elvira Ann Anthony Feb. 21, 1856. Elvira was the daughter of Nimrod "Rodney" Anthony (North Carolina) and Synthia Brown Anthony (Tennessee) who settled near San Augustine, TX, about 1832. The first Church of Christ in Texas was established in 1836 in their home four miles north of San Augustine. Rodney Anthony served as an elder in this church for 50 years.

Joseph and Elvira had three daughters: Nancy Porter (Ellington and Taylor) (born 1857); Sara Jane (Stevens) (born 1859); and Georgia Ann (Peace) (born 1864). Georgia Ann and Jim Peace became my great-grandparents. They lived in the Arcadia Community near Center, TX (Shelby County).

Joseph served in Gould's Bn., Co. D, 3rd Bn., Texas Cav. during the Civil War. He enlisted June 12, 1862, but little is known about Joseph after his enlistment. He died during the Civil War but his death is recorded as both 1863 and 1867. His place of burial is known. Elvira and Georgia Ann are buried in the Mt. Pleasant Cemetery near Center, TX. A Texas citizen medallion will be placed on Elvira's headstone and a Confederate marker will be placed for Joseph in a special service in October 1999 by the William Carroll Crawford Chapter of the Daughters of the Republic.

Margaret Ann Hathorn, (GGGD)

AUGUST MARTIN GERHARD "GUS" WOLFSHOHL,

born Dec. 18, 1813, Dillenburg, Nassau, Germany, was the son of Frederick and Margaret Wolfshohl. "Gus" Wolfshohl married Catherina E. Eberling July 25, 1841, in Germany. "Gus" Wolfshohl and Catherina Eberling's parents, Carl and Catherine Eberling, all signed emigration contracts in Bremen, Germany, to have land in the Republic of Texas. The families of Wolfshohl and Eberling sailed from Bremen, Germany, Sept. 25, 1845, on the ship "*Johann Dethardt*" and arrived in Galveston, TX, December 1845.

August M.G. Wolfshohl received 640 acres in the Fisher and Miller Colony in Comal County, TX. This land was located about three miles southwest from New Braunfels, TX. The family farmed and also surveyed land in the area. Wolfshohl's children were: Daniel Karl, Caroline Jacobine, Daniel Karl II, Auguste C., Margarethe, Fredrich W., Ernst, Sophie, Karoline, Ferdinand, Friedericke and Wilhelm. The Wolfshohl family were some of the early members of the German Protestant Church in New Braunfels, TX. August and Catherina died in 1892 and 1895 and are buried in the New Braunfels Cemetery. There are many Wolfshohl descendants and most live in the counties surrounding Comal County.

Gayle Pfeiffer Grantham, (GGGD), #021567

HANSEL WRIGHT, a Quaker, was born in Pittsylvania

County, VA, in 1773. A large group of Quakers left Pennsylvania in 1730, settling in Virginia. It was there that Hansel met and married Elizabeth Prichard. She was born in 1774 in North Carolina. They were the parents of Deliah, Nancy, Elizabeth Margaret, Catherine, Samuel, William Prichard, Thomas Lewis, George Hansel and Campbell Wright.

Hansel and Elizabeth lived many years in North Carolina and Tennessee before relocating to Calloway County, KY, where they received land grants.

In 1835 they came in covered wagons to Texas with their children and grandchildren.

Marker of Hansel Wright of which Wright's Cemetery is named.

Hansel, with his family, settled in Nacogdoches in 1836 receiving land grants classified as second class headright. He was given 1,280 acres listed in the General Land Office in Austin, and signed by Governor George T. Wood. Hansel also served in the Republic of Texas army in 1846.

The family remained in Nacogdoches for 10 years before settling in the New Prospect Community in Rusk County. It was there that they established their own Methodist Church known as "Wright Meeting House". The church also served as a school. The family was asked to use the Prospect Church when their church burned.

Hansel, a farmer, secured more land and donated a portion for the family cemetery near Henderson, TX, in Rusk County.

Hansel Wright died in 1856, preceded in death by Elizabeth, who died in 1853. Approximately 100 persons are buried in the Wright Cemetery. The cemetery was given a Texas historical marker by the Texas Historical Commission.

Hansel was the father of our ancestor, Thomas Lewis Wright.

Hansel was a true pioneer, who carved a future for descendants who followed. As Texans', we are honored and proud to call him our own.

Gaby Matthews Harris, (GGGGGD), #21111
Rosemary Center Cox, (GGGGGD), #19581

JOHN DAVID AND MARGARET WRIGHT, John

David arrived in south Texas circa 1822. He was born Jan. 2, 1804, in Hawkin's County, TN.

Margaret Theresa Robertson Hays was born in Louisiana circa 1789. In 1805 she married James William Hays and they settled in Opelousas, LA, where their two daughters and one son were born. In 1811 they moved to Bayou Pierre, in the neutral ground, Hays died shortly after their move. Later Margaret entered into a common law agreement with Felix Trudeau Pronounce, commander of the Post at Natchitoches. Margaret migrated to Texas with her son, Peter Hays, three years after Trudeau's death and she used the name of Madam Trudeau.

Margaret Wright

In 1822 she settled in De Leon's Colony at Guadalupe Victoria and she applied for a league of land on the west bank of the Guadalupe River, what is now the Mission Valley Road. Before title to the league of land was granted she met and married John David Wright in 1828 and they settled on the league of land.

The Wrights had two daughters, Amy Ann (born 1830) and Tennessee (born May 12, 1834). In 1833 John David secretly obtained title to the league of land, in his name only. The title is dated 1833 and is written entirely in Spanish with signatures of Martin De Leon and John David Wright.

Many marital problems stemmed from this unfair act by John. John left the Victoria area and resided Mexico, south of Eagle Pass for the next seven years. He traveled frequently to Victoria and stayed at the ranch with Margaret.

Margaret remained on the headright. She raised cattle and branded them with her own brand, E.W., which she had registered in 1838.

During the early part of the Texas Revolution she aided the survivors of the Goliad Massacre. She hid the men along the banks of the Guadalupe. She would take food in her bucket as she went to the river for water. She left the food in tree trunks and returned with water. She feared for herself and the men she was helping. There were Mexican soldiers encamped on her property. When the men gained strength and were able to travel and rejoin the Texas army she was able to steal a gun from the Mexican soldiers and give it to the Texans.

John returned to live on the ranch with Margaret and their daughters, but not for long. Margaret filed for divorce claiming habitual cruelty, fraudulent land title transfer and the murder of her son, Peter. Margaret was granted a divorce March 6, 1848.

John's headstone can be found on the league of land that once belonged to him. Margaret died in Victoria Oct. 21, 1878, and is buried in Evergreen Cemetery.

Their granddaughter, Clara Noble, was a member of DRT #570, also their great-granddaughter, Clara Margaret Fox Murphy #1049. In June 1998 their great-great-granddaughter, Tennessee Mary Ann Fox Angerstein became a member of the Daughter's of the Republic of Texas.

This is the ancestral history of Melvin Maurice Nichols (born March 19, 1925), son of Daniel and Myrtle Fox Nichols. Maurice is a deceased member of the Andrew Jackson Chapter, Houston, TX, of the Sons of the Republic of Texas. Maurice died June 17, 1997, in Commerce, TX. His ashes are reserved until a future date. *Submitted by June Foreman Nichols, wife of Maurice Nichols.*

THOMAS LEWIS WRIGHT, born in 1815, one of 10 children born to Hansel and Elizabeth Prichard Wright in Tennessee. (Rusk County History 1982) Hansel and his sons received Texas land grants when they came to Texas in 1835. Thomas L. received 640 acres located northeast of Henderson, in Rusk County. He is listed on the 1836 muster rolls of the Texas Revolution Volunteer Auxiliary Corps. The Texas Archives has a receipt in which Thomas L. provided beef for a detachment of men in 1836.

Thomas Lewis Wright married Mrs. Robert (Izetta Elizabeth) Merritt in Nacogdoches in January 1849. She was a widow, born in South Carolina, with three children: Daniel D.; Sarah Izetta (born 1843) married Capt. Alex Earp of Upshur County; and Martha Etta who married Jno. C. Bell. Thomas Lewis and Elizabeth had six children: Delila Emmalyne (born 1849) married James P. Bellamy; Mary Adalyne; Samuel Asbury (born 1856) married Mary Lucinda Sears; Nancy C.; J.W.H.; and Lewis T. Wright married Clara Stanton. Thomas is listed on the 1860 census in Rusk County as a farmer from Tennessee with property valued between $2,000.00-$6,000.00.

Samuel Asbury and Mary Lucinda "Ludie" Wright had seven children: Vie Anna (born 1875) married Herchel Hales; Etta (born 1877) married James Alvin Meecom; Alice (born 1879) married George Catron; Ella (born 1880, died young); Daniel (born 1881);

Nannie (born 1886, died young); and Lottie (born 1890) married Sidney M. Hanna.

Etta and James A. Meecom lived near Gilmer, TX, in Upshur County. They had two daughters, Nancy Lucinda "Lula" (born 1895) and Claudie Mae (born 1902). Three husbands preceded Nancy L. Meecom in death: Ed Matthews, James Earnest Center and Jess F. Snyder. Claudie married John Douglas Evans.

Nancy L. and Ed Matthews were the parents of two children, James Douglas and Marjorie Mae Matthews. Nancy L. and James Earnest Center had one child, Bobby Joe Center.

Many of the family members are buried in east Texas, near Gilmer, in Upshur County. Approximately 100 people, including Hansel and Thomas Lewis, are buried in the Wright Cemetery located northeast of Henderson in Rusk County. The Texas Historical Commission erected a marker there in May 1982 in honor of the contributions by the Wright family to the pioneer community of New Prospect.
Rosemary Center Cox, (GGGGD), #19581
Gaby Matthews Harris, (GGGGD), #21111

MICHAEL YOUNG, born in Georgia, May 10, 1801. He arrived in Texas, with his wife, Rachel, and sons, William and Anderson, to become part of Stephen F. Austin's 2nd Colony in March 1829. Michael was given a headright grant of 4,440 acres in Fort Bend County. Michael fought in the Battle of Anahuac in 1832, under the command of William Barrett Travis. In June 1836, Michael Young joined Jesse Billingsley's company of Mina Volunteers. After being honorably discharged in September 1836, Michael Young was given bounty land of 320 acres for his service to the Republic of Texas. Michael Young was still living on his league in 1838 and was a member of the first jury in Richmond in January 1838.

Michael Young, circa 1870.

In 1842 Michael was living in Bastrop County, where he was wounded by Indians who came to his plantation. Encountering Michael Young's 8-year-old son, Perry, they threw a lasso around him. Perry slipped through the loop and escaped to give the alarm. Michael Young gathered 15 neighbors and gave chase to the Indians. In the ensuing fight, which lasted some four hours, Michael Young was wounded in the breast. He recovered from his wound and lived until May 20, 1875.

Michael Young is buried in Live Oak Cemetery in Youngsport, TX.

Michael Young was the father of Perry G. Young who was the father of Michael Moore Young who was the father of Guyton Michael Young who was the father of Ruby Nell Young Matlock who was the mother of Patricia Ellen Matlock Aipperspach who is the mother of Julie Nell Aipperspach. *(Source: Recollections of Early Texas: Memoirs of John Holland Jenkins, p.272)*
Patricia Ellen Matlock Aipperspach, #22864

WILLIAM PHYSICK ZUBER, born July 6, 1820, in Twiggs County, GA, died Sept. 22, 1913, aged 93 years. He had one sister named Mary Ann Deshaza Zuber Edwards.

W.P. Zuber's parents were Abraham Zuber Jr. and Mary Ann Mann. In 1830 they moved to Dist. of Aes, San Augustine County,

TX. Abraham Zuber died at his home in Grimes County, TX, Nov. 28, 1848, aged 68 years. His wife, Mary Ann Mann Zuber, died Oct. 20, 1879, aged 86 years.

William Physick Zuber

When W.P. Zuber was 13 years old he moved with his parents from a farm they owned 25 miles north of Brazoria, TX, to Grimes County. When he was 16 years old, he enlisted as a volunteer in the Texas Army; from March 1, 1836-June 1, 1836; this was the San Jacinto Campaign.

He also served voluntarily in Co. H, 21st Regt., Texas Cav., Confederate Army from March 20, 1862, until the break-up in 1865.

In 1876 he was elected justice of the peace for Precinct 2 Grimes County until 1878.

W.P. Zuber was a prolific writer and authority on Texas history. His extensive writings are in the state archives in Austin as well as several colleges in America.

On July 17, 1851, he married Louisa Liles; he was 31 years old. She died March 15, 1904. They were the parents of two sons and one daughter. Eldest son, Daniel Carl Zuber, became a prominent merchant in Bryan, TX. He died May 26, 1902. Daniel had three daughters: Edna, Mabel and Margaret; and one son, Neill Daniel. His wife's name was Janie McDougal Zuber.

W.P. Zuber's youngest son, James Andrew Zuber, lived on his own farm near Houston Heights, Harris County, TX. J.A. Zuber had three sons and three daughters. They are John Shannon, Hamilton, W.P., Willena, Annie and Blanche Zuber.

John Shannon Zuber was born Feb. 19, 1892, and died June 26, 1950. His wife, Kathryn Naomi Gray was born 1897 and died 1988. They had three children: Shannon Reginald (born 1914, died 1978), John Kenneth (born 1917, died 1969) and Mary Grace Zuber (born Oct. 1, 1924).

Reginald married Annie Lee Janike (born 1912, died 1995). They had two boys, Shannon Reginald Zuber Jr. (born Dec. 26, 1934) and William Zuber (born 1946, died 1998).

Shannon Jr. married Silvia Schneider. They met in Germany while he was in the Air Force. They have two children, Carolyn Silvia Zuber Pitts (born Dec. 13, 1960). She is married to David Pitts and has two girls, Courtney (born 1988) and Chrystal (born 1992). Shannon and Silvia's son, John Shannon Zuber (born Sept. 14, 1963), is married to Lisa Gray Zuber (born June 6, 1965). They have a son and daughter, Gunner Zuber (born May 24, 1992) and Arden Zuber (born Aug. 8, 1993).

John Kenneth married Rollin Blakely. They had four children, three girls: Sandra, Margerie and Debra; and one son, John Kenneth Jr.

Mary Grace Zuber Horlock married Frank Prescott Horlock Jr. in 1942. Frank was born Oct. 19, 1925. They had three children, two boys and a girl.

Frank Prescott Horlock III (born Oct. 2, 1949, died July 3, 1978).

Cathryn Clark Horlock (born Dec. 11, 1953, died Oct. 11, 1997) married Casey C. Taub (born 1954). One child, daughter, Cathryn Horlock Taub (born May 17, 1983).

Christopher Shannon, Mary Grace and Frank Horlock's youngest son (born Jan. 19, 1960), married Robin Herz Horlock Sept. 26, 1998.

William Physick Zuber was my great-grandfather on my father's side of the family.
Mary Grace Horlock.

DAUGHTERS OF THE REPUBLIC OF TEXAS INDEX

Gillespie 97
Gillette 26, 27
Gilliam 83
Gilmer 92
Gilmore 140
Glackin 118
Glass 80
Glidewell 107
Glover 100, 117, 127
Goar 110
Goble 95
Godfrey 57
Godwin 50, 103, 132
Goforth 66
Gohlke 109
Golden 60
Golledge 22, 90, 91
Goodbread 55, 122
Goode 48, 121
Goodman 58
Goodson 91
Goodwin 55, 56, 106, 124
Goodwyn 36, 56
Gordon 31
Gore 84
Goss 29, 66
Gough 40
Grace 111
Gracey 120
Grady 35
Graf 58, 100
Graham 34, 56
Granberry 62
Grantham 17, 60, 141
Graves 37
Gray 35, 36, 40, 56, 57, 58, 62, 64, 82, 118, 143
Green 21, 58, 72, 93, 135
Greenwood 119
Greer 47, 58, 66
Gregg 104
Gregory 89
Gresham 61
Grey 83
Grieder 41
Grier 71
Griffin 58, 59, 80
Griffis 37
Griffith 111
Grigsby 87
Grimes 59, 60
Grisar 47
Grosvenor 28
Grotjahn 71
G'sel 88, 89
Guest 60
Gutbrodt 55
Gutrodt 55
Guynes 117

— H —

Haden 54
Hadley 60, 78, 106
Hagan 14, 19
Hagen 18, 61, 98, 136
Hague 45
Haile 17
Hainsworth 16
Hairston 58
Haisler 50
Haislip 78
Hale 16, 53, 60
Hales 142
Haley 76, 80
Hall 16, 24, 37, 55, 61, 65, 72, 78, 79, 88, 89, 116, 123, 124, 127, 129, 131
Hallock 14
Haltom 122
Ham 18, 133
Hamilton 24, 103
Hampton 30, 136
Hancock 31, 91
Haney 61, 136
Hanks 39, 132
Hanna 142
Hannan 38
Hansell 98
Hanzel 76
Harbard 122
Harbour 136
Hardegree 108
Hardie 16
Hardin 58, 111
Harding 136
Hardy 16, 39, 47, 64, 98
Hare 99
Hargraves 37
Harkness 82
Harmon 117
Harms 65
Harper 36, 50, 51, 66
Harpool 105
Harrell 23, 46, 98
Harriet 27
Harrington 116, 120
Harris 38, 56, 58, 61, 72, 74, 83, 98, 131, 141, 142
Harrison 30, 35, 61, 67, 90, 136
Hart 22, 25, 31, 46, 84, 91, 98
Harvey 61, 62, 74
Hassell 117
Hathorn 141
Hatton 47
Hausler 71, 73

Hawkins 43, 51
Hawley 117
Hay 34
Hayes 41
Haygood 46, 60
Haynie 83
Hays 19, 47, 58, 59, 85, 141
Hazel 66
Head 47, 62
Hearne 14
Heatherly 98
Heckert 40
Hector 25, 26, 33, 34, 57, 58, 64, 127
Heitman 87
Hembree 101
Hemphill 62
Henderson 31, 56, 74, 95, 125
Hendrick 16, 40
Henley 29, 47, 62, 63
Henry 90
Hensley 62
Henson 55, 130
Herndon 54
Herriage 96
Herring 135
Hibbins 65
Hickey 50
Hickman 75, 96
Hicks 19, 139
Hickson 42
Hightower 67, 75
Hilburn 28, 63
Hilgartner 97
Hill 14, 37, 49, 62, 63, 93, 115, 124, 133, 140
Hilliard 93
Hinde 14
Hines 112
Hittson 27, 68, 69
Hobbs 101, 117
Hoch 43
Hocker 25, 63, 64
Hodge 72
Hodges 54, 75, 104, 106, 136
Hogan 33, 58, 111, 137
Hogg 64
Holbrook 63
Holcomb 64
Holecomb 43
Holland 48
Holliday 53, 97
Holliman 49
Hollingsworth 66, 106
Hollis 14
Holloway 32, 65, 125

Holmes 78
Holt 16, 23, 37, 38, 56, 64, 97
Holton 117
Holtzclaw 100
Holzer 43
Honney 118
Hook 21, 70
Hooker 74
Hooper 51
Hope 110
Hopkins 24, 32
Horlock 143
Horn 106
Hornburg 65
Hornsby 54, 64, 65, 75, 92
Hornung 108
Hostetter 61
Housman 93
Houston 115
Hovey 30
Howard 40, 65, 66
Howe 90
Howell 54, 76, 113
Hoxie 99
Hubbard 92
Huddle 101
Hudson 96, 134
Hudspeth 41
Huff 66, 108
Hufft 97
Hughes 23, 66, 117, 134, 138
Huguely 103
Humberson 140
Humble 21, 96
Humbly 89
Humphrey 24
Humphries 16
Hungerford 21
Hunnicutt 22
Hunt 28, 34, 54, 66
Hunter 35, 67, 108, 114, 118
Hurd 91
Hurdle 131
Hurley 97
Huston 95, 98
Hutchins 44, 71
Huth 88, 128

— I —

Ikard 101
Ingles 39
Inglet 54
Ingram 25, 37, 41, 76, 114, 116
Insall 131

Bottom left: The Daughters of the Republic of Texas Museum.
Center: The Daughters of the Republic of Texas Library at the Alamo.
Upper right: The French Legation.

CPSIA information can be obtained
at www.ICGtesting.com
Printed in the USA
BVOW03*1623200417
481707BV00037B/403/P